W9-CMP-999

# VOTERS, ELECTIONS, AND PARTIES

## The Practice of Democratic Theory

Gerald M. Pomper

*With a New Foreword by the Author*

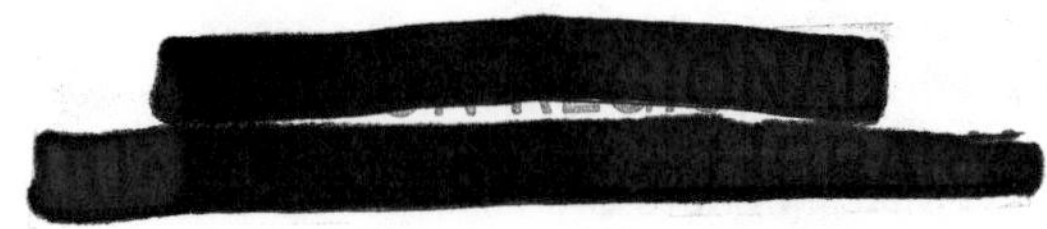

Transaction Publishers
New Brunswick (U.S.A.) and London (U.K.)

Library of Congress Catalog Number: 87-25466
ISBN: 0-88738-160-X (cloth); 1-56000-561-0 (paper)
Printed in the United States of America

Library of Congress Cataloging-in-Publication Data

Pomper, Gerald M.
Voters, elections, and parties.
Bibliography: p.
ISBN: 0-88738-160-X (cloth); 1-56000-561-0 (paper)
1. United States–Politics and government. 2. Democracy. 3. Voting–United States. 4. Elections–United States. 5. Political parties–United States. I. Title
JK274.P64 1987
324'.0873 87–25466
CIP

To Isidor H. Pomper

*We happy few, we band of brothers*

# Contents

# List of Tables and Figures

*Tables*

## *Figures*

# Foreword to the Paperback Edition

This volume argues three simple propositions: voters think about politics, elections are meaningful, political parties are critical to a viable democracy. Since this book was completed in 1987, these propositions have been further validated by major political events in many nations. Some of these are important but not surprising: most obviously the choice of a new president of the United States, and similarly normal elections in the established democracies of the West, including France, Great Britain, Canada, and Israel. In other countries we have seen significant changes in the political process, generally in the direction of greater involvement of mass electorates.

In Western democracies holding recent elections there was a common pattern of the re-election of incumbent administrations–François Mitterrand in France, Margaret Thatcher in Great Britain, Brian Mulroney in Canada, Yitzhak Shamir in Israel, and the designated successor to Ronald Reagan, George Bush, in the United States. In each of these elections the electorate faced and answered the simple question of its retrospective satisfaction with current national policies. The electorate again proved its ability to respond meaningfully.

The U.S. election of 1988 also endorsed the policies of the incumbent administration, while conveying longer-term implications.[1] Explaining the outcome begins with an important historical note. The 1988 result was the first occasion in forty years when a single political party had won control of the White House for more than two presidential terms. This outcome breaks the pattern of regular alteration of power between Democrats (in the elections of 1932-48, 1960-64, 1976) and Republicans (in 1952-56, 1968-72, and 1980-84).

---

Originally prepared for a Chinese-language edition in 1990.

The broken pattern induces inquiry into long-term, rather than transient, explanations. Commonplace analysis, however, tends to focus on short-term factors. The Republican victory in 1988, for example, has been attributed to the individual failings of the Democratic candidate, Governor Michael Dukakis, to the clever television advertisements on behalf of Vice-President Bush, or to the impact of such "issues" as mandatory saluting of the American flag, or the Massachusetts program of prisoner furloughs.[2]

Inconveniently for their proponents, these short-term explanations do not fit with much of the data on the vote. Rather than a strong candidate, Bush was the weakest Republican winner in the twentieth century. Rather than an ineffective candidate, Dukakis won more electoral votes than any Democratic loser in the past twenty years, and won a higher vote from his party's members than any Democrat since 1964, even more than the victorious Jimmy Carter. Detailed studies of voter attitudes show that Dukakis was regarded more highly than Bush as an individual, and that the electorate preferred Democratic to Republican alternatives on most current policy issues.[3]

The Bush victory cannot be explained as a victory for George Bush the individual, or for policies uniquely associated with him. Rather, Bush was the beneficiary of three closely related and longer-term trends. There has been a slow, but regular, increase in the proportion of Americans who identify themselves as ideological conservatives rather than liberals, in 1988 reaching a 33 percent-18 percent division. A parallel trend has been the gradual change in partisan loyalties, changing a onetime Democratic dominance to virtual parity in voter identifications with the two major parties. Third, and immediately relevant to the presidential election results, the electorate was generally satisfied with the results of the two Reagan administrations, even if it disagreed with some specific policies.

George Bush was the immediate beneficiary of these attitudes, but their import is of much greater significance. Events, policy failures, and individual action can change political prospects, perhaps even rapidly. In the clouded present, however, the misty view is that the United States has passed through a period of realignment. Long-awaited, often predicted, and yet never fully achieved, that realignment now seems a reality. An electorate that is conservative, balanced in its partisanship, and satisfied with the policies of the Reagan years is an electorate that is most likely to vote for Republican presidential candidates.

As in most recent Western elections, the United States in 1988 voted for continuity, providing approval of the incumbent government. These voters, however, cast more than retrospective ballots. In all of the elections, their retrospective approval also would affect, and limit, the next government. Moreover, in at least two of these elections, Canada and Israel, the voters also had to deal with vital prospective questions of the nation's future. Here too, whether rightly or wrongly, the voters proved capable of making a weighty decision, endorsing Canada's creation of a free trade zone with the United States, and choosing an assertive policy in opposition to the rebellion of Palestinian Arabs.

In other, although less conspicuous, elections, the voters specifically endorsed change. That decision was evident in Japan, for example, where the long-established control of the Liberal Democratic coalition was disrupted by an opposition victory in the selection of the upper house of the Diet. More impressive still was the victory of democratic political oppositions in Chile and Panama, where they were able to win victories despite manipulation of the balloting by authoritarian regimes.

The most striking impact of elections has come in nations of the socialist bloc, particularly the Soviet Union and Poland. In these nations, elections had been held regularly but had little effect on the course of public policy or the individual lives of the citizens. This situation has changed dramatically and quickly, but in different ways in these two nations and others. The differences provide better instruction about the political process than any academic volume.

In the Soviet Union, Mikhail Gorbachev's reformist policies included an opening of the electoral process to multiple candidacies, allowing dissent to appear publicly rather than confining it to underground newspapers, private grumbling, and individual emigration. Soviet citizens, as if born to democratic politics, campaigned, vigorously debated in local nominating caucuses, and balloted among competing politicians. Many notable but unpopular officials were defeated, a significant minority of dissidents was elected to the new Supreme Soviet, and even President Gorbachev was called to account in the new legislature for policy failures.

These changes are significant in the Soviet context, yet limited in their effects. Mr. Gorbachev's political base remains in the party Politburo and Central Committee, not in the legislature nor among the mass of voters. Certain policies remain unalterable, whatever popular wishes, when opposed by these centralized organs of power. Most clearly, the central leadership will make few concessions to rising nationalist feelings at the borders of the Soviet Union, as in the Baltic republics, or to non-Russian ethnic minorities.

The Soviet experience shows that informed voters are not sufficient for a free politics, or even an effectively freer politics. The Soviet experience shows that elections, even individually competitive elections, also are not sufficient. To empower voters and to make elections effective, there must also be empowered and effective political parties. The contrasting experience of Poland provides a definitive demonstration.

In Poland, the electoral choice in 1989 originally paralleled the new Soviet system. The slate of candidates was limited so that the Communist party and its allies would be assured a majority of seats in the lower house of the national parliament. Voters did not always have a choice of candidates in their local constituency, and disapproval could be expressed only by striking out the name of the single, usually Communist party, candidate. Opposition groups, however, had an organizational advantage absent in the Soviet Union. They could now band together openly, as the Solidarity movement was transformed from a proscribed trade union to a legitimate political party.

That single but momentous organizational change peacefully revolutionized Polish politics. In the balloting, virtually every Solidarity candidate was elected, including ninety-eight of one hundred members of the upper house of the legislature, while Communist candidates throughout the nation failed to win the required majority of the local vote, even when uncontested. Despite a pre-election agreement to continue a Communist government, the party no longer had mass legitimacy, and it was deserted by onetime allies, even by Gorbachev, the world leader of the movement. Only Solidarity could govern. In rapid order, its leaders were installed as the dominant group in the nation's cabinet, the first non-Communist government in Eastern Europe since the end of the Second World War.

Events in Poland are already affecting the rest of Eastern Europe. The reactions are expressed in different ways in different nations, and these differences again point to the importance of institutionalized political parties. Compare the regimes in Hungary and the Democratic Republic of Germany. In the latter nation, the regime remains in the Stalinist mold, and the Communist party continues to insist on a monopoly of power. Discontent obviously exists, but can be expressed only by an ultimate expression of popular repudiation, mass emigration. As of this writing, over 50,000 East Germans have abandoned their homes, families, and nation. Unable to vote in meaningful elections, they have "voted with their feet."

By contrast Hungary is attempting internal liberalization. The regime has physically removed barriers to emigration, belatedly honored leaders of the 1956 revolt, and, most importantly, legitimized political competition. The Communist party indeed has been technically abolished, changing its identity to Socialist, and is preparing for genuinely competitive elections in 1990. By legitimizing this competition, the regime has provided a means to strengthen the nation, and to avoid the problems facing Communist Germany.

These changes are not of interest here because of their possible ideological significance nor because of their implications for the course of international politics. Rather, such change is humanistically inspiring as a testament to the worth of persistence and personal conviction, exemplified by Solidarity's leaders. The change is philosophically important as empirical evidence of the moral and practical utility of nonviolent resistance. The change is politically significant for the linkage it demonstrates among the three elements of effective democratic politics: voters, elections, and parties.

In the light of recent history, we no longer need debate the political capacity of ordinary people. Even in nations with no recent history of meaningful elections, we have sewn the citizenry act craftfully, reasonably, and rationally once the ballot box was opened for honest use. Voters have shown the ability both to voice their particularistic interests and to consider their nation's general interests. The Polish electorate, illustratively, has both demanded more consumer goods and accepted the regional primary of the Soviet Union.

Voters, while capable, remain both dependent and responsible. Without appropriate political structures, mass sentiments are stillborn, like fertilized bird eggs without a brooding parent. Popular wishes for change surely existed for many years in such places as Eastern Europe. Until open competition developed among political leaders, these sentiments could only be expressed by sporadic protests and illegal acts, and elites would react only with disdain and repression.

Though dependent on appropriate structures for choice, masses do respond when choice is available. Such responsiveness is evidence in the relatively simple act of voting. Even in the settled Western democracies, influences on the vote change with the political context. Sex differences in the American vote did not exist until the 1970s, grew to a significant level in the next decade, and diminished considerably by 1988. In Britain, social class once defined politics, but now has virtually no effect.

Responsiveness is also evidence on the more general ideological level. In the United States, although a highly stable society, the explicit assertion of a conservative ideology has led to changes in mass beliefs, and changes in deeply grounded party loyalties. In Eastern Europe, despite years of indoctrination, the availability of alternatives has led to mass abandonment of state socialism. Throughout the industrial world, issues of ecology, virtually unknown before 1970, have become of major importance, spurring the development of Green parties. Even more generally, a politics of values is replacing a politics of redistribution.[4]

More than ever, competitive elections now seem to be critical means for the organization of mass politics. The spread of this vital form of political participation, however, does not mean that all elections are the same, no more than all nations are or ever will be the same. From recent experience, we might better see elections as serving different functions in different regimes, with the dominant function varying with the age of the effective regime. In new regimes–as those emerging in Eastern Europe can be considered–elections are perhaps most important as legitimization of the emerging form of government. In changing nations, albeit with long-established institutions, elections may be most significant as providing broad prospective policy direction. The nations of Latin America and East Asia, as well as Canada, are illustrative. In more settled nations, not facing major policy directions, such as the United States and the countries of Western Europe, elections are chiefly significant as retrospective judgments on the incumbent administrations.

Political parties remain critical, as argued in the following pages of this volume. Happily, there are signs of increased party vigor throughout the world. In the United States, a major decision of the Supreme Court has freed parties from burdensome state regulations, and allowed them to gain some measure of influence in the nomination of candidates.[5] The legal step is paralleled by improved finance of the national parties and by their assertion of an enlarged role in campaigning (such as sponsorship of presidential candidate debates) and finance. In Great Britain, the Social Democratic Party analyzed below (chap. 19) has fractured, but its potential role as a new opposition party has been taken over by a revived Labour party. Democratic politics remains party politics.

Change in party fortunes parallels change in the fortunes of democracy. The rise and decay of particular parties is not important in itself. The United States retains its political character as much with Republican as with Democratic party dominance, just as Great Britain can be served as well by a Labour as by a Social Democratic opposition. Truly important is that there be competitive parties, appealing to capable voters, through free elections. As recent world experience substantiates, these are the means for both individual freedom and national development.

Voters, elections, and parties promote democracy, the moral purpose of politics in all nations. Robert Michels, a fundamental theorist of modern politics, cautioned, "Democracy is a treasure which no one will ever discover by deliberate search." Yet, as he also taught us, "in continuing our search, in laboring indefatigably to discover the undiscoverable, we shall perform a work that will have fertile results."[6]

## Notes

1. A fuller discussion is available in Gerald Pomper, *The Election of 1988* (Chatham, N.J.: Chatham House, 1989), esp. chap. 5.

2. For example, see "The Inside Story of Campaign '88," *Newsweek* 112 (21 November 1988): 32-146.
3. J. Merrill Shanks and Warren Miller, "Alternative Explanations of the 1988 Election," Paper presented to the American Political Science Association (1989).
4. See the works of Ronald Inglehart, from *The Silent Revolution* (Princeton: Princeton University Press, 1977) to "The Renaissance of Political Culture," *American Political Science Review* 82 (December 1988): 203-30.
5. *Eu* v. *San Francisco County Democratic Central Committee* 109 S. Ct. 1013 (1989).
6. Robert Michels, *Political Parties* (New York: Collier Books, 1911, 1962), 368.

# Preface

This book is a hybrid of an intellectual resume and a midlife autobiography. In it, I collect, reflect on, and attempt to put into perspective the work of more than two decades of research.

The basic premise of this work is the viability of contemporary democracy, particularly in the United States. That premise has been partially an article of faith from my first awareness of American politics, when I came to know that my parents had been saved from genocidal death by this nation's open society. Later, as I worked as a scholar, this faith was reinforced by my studies, teaching, and writing.

The subject of my work, generally, is the electoral process, divided into particular topics concerning voting behavior, elections, and political parties. Modern democracy is often equated with the electoral process, so that the quality of that process becomes a measure of the quality of democracy itself. The general argument of this book is that, given proper conditions, voters are capable, elections are meaningful, and political parties are responsive. If scholars and politicians pay heed, I believe that democracy can meet the hopes and needs of the citizenry.

The volume begins with a new essay, in which I compare the empirical performance of the electoral process with the goals established in traditional political philosophy. While American democracy does not achieve all of these goals, it does contribute to significant realization of desired ends. I believe, however, that we must make significant changes in our politics if we are to maintain these contributions.

The remainder of the book consists of previous writings, including scholarly articles and papers, book chapters, and essays. They are organized into three sections—on voters, elections, and parties. Introducing each of these sections, I review the items included, putting them into context and reappraising their conclusions. Allowing for the normal human lack of objectivity, I am pleased that these works, for the most part, still seem useful and accurate. Other readers, I hope not too many, may disagree.

Beyond the substantive findings, I have tried to make two contributions to the discipline of political science, First, I have sought to combine theory with empirical methodology. For too many years, the discipline was divided between those who focused on "values" and those who were concerned with "facts." The distinction is unreal: values are facts of political life, and facts are interpreted in a framework of values. Second, I have deliberately employed diverse methodologies, as seemed appropriate to the particular subject. We can and should learn from many sources—from philosophy as much as quantitative data, from history as much as current events.

These collected essays are kept as originally published, except for minor editorial changes. After completion, an author's work belongs more to the audience than to himself. Respecting this autonomy, I have resisted the temptation to revise these works, and thereby to make them seem more insightful and less flawed than they actually were. In exposing these defects, perhaps I have also displayed their merits.

Without revision, these works occasionally show their age. Some usage now appears archaic, such as referring to blacks as Negroes, or using "he" as the neuter singular pronoun. Obviously, I intend no offense. From a contemporary viewpoint, the methodology is sometimes primitive. For example, the calculations on ethnic voting (chapter 6) were done on a manual adding machine. While I welcome the advent of large data bases and microcomputer technology, I do occasionally worry that the ability to calculate has outpaced the desire to cogitate.

This book summarizes an ongoing scholarly career. As such, it reflects the help of scores of people. Although each deserves an individual acknowledgment, I trust that they will be satisfied with this brief listing and my unwritten gratitude.

Special thanks are owed to three persons who co-authored essays included in this book. Mark Schulman and Susan Lederman were once students at Rutgers University, and Patricia Sykes was a colleague at Nuffield College, Oxford. I am proud to have been associated with them at the beginning of their promising careers.

My greatest intellectual debts are to my long-term colleagues at Rutgers University. Pleasingly, they also have become good friends. They include: Myron Aronoff, Ross Baker, Benjamin Barber, Dennis Bathory, Irving Louis Horowitz, Charles Jacob, Richard Mansbach, Richard P. McCormick, Wilson Carey McWilliams, Maureen Moakley, Alan Rosenthal, Stephen Salmore, Gordon Schochet, David Schwartz, and Roberta Sigel.

More numerous still are those who have aided my work in a variety of ways—teaching, calculating data, typing manuscripts, offering criticism, and—simply but most vitally—caring. These people I have been fortunate to know include:

Asher Arian, Edward Artinian, Paul Beck, Vernon Bogdanor, Anthony Broh, Betsy Brown, Ardath Burks, Walter Dean Burnham, James MacGregor

Burns, David Butler, Demetrious Caraley, Anthony Champagne, Leonard Champney, Julia Chase, Lorraine Cohen, John Curtice, John Davis, Michael DelliCarpini, Stanley Feingold, Milton Finegold, William Flanigan, Kathleen Frankovic, Peter Gay, Sadie Goldhawn, Laura Greyson, Bess Handaly, Shelley Hartz, Louis Hollander, Judson James, Scott Keeter, Stanley Kelley, John Kessel, Marc Landy, Kay Lawson, AnElissa Lucas, Ernest Lynton, Hyman Mandel, Joan Matthews, Emanuel and Lillian Michels, Jerome Mileur, Thomas O'Donnell, Diana Owen, Doris Paul, Clive Payne, Patrick Pierce, Rick Piltz, Henry Plotkin, Austin Ranney, Alan Reitman, Donald Robinson, Barbara Salmore, Nancy Schwartz, Sandra Schwartz, Barry Seldes, Vicki Semel, Curt Shulman, Walter Stone, James Sundquist, Efraim Torgovnik, David Truman, Ted Van Dyck, Carl Van Horn, Jennifer Verdini, John White, and Mary Wilk. I regret the death of three good persons, Donald Herzberg, John Lees, and Philip Williams.

For this book, particular thanks are due to Scott Bramson, Alex Fundock III, and Kimberly Jesuele, who directed its production for Transaction, and to Edith Saks, who once again showed her skills of organization and encouragement. Over the years, I am also thankful for financial and archival aid from the Eagleton Institute of Politics, the Institute for International Education, the Inter-University Consortium for Political and Social Research, the Nuffield Foundation, and Rutgers University's Research Council and its Center for Computer and Information Services.

Finally, I must express love, even more than thanks, for the emotional support of my family. Over the years in which these essays were written, my parents—Celia and Moe Pomper—have aged, my children—Miles, David and Marc—have grown to vibrant manhood, and my wife—Marlene Michels Pomper—has matured into an independent scholar. Amid this change, their personal comfort has been constant. Particularly important to me has been the example and encouragement of my brother, Isidor H. Pomper. I dedicate this volume to him in gratitude for a lifetime of sharing.

# Acknowledgments

The author gratefully acknowledges the following publishers and publications for permission to use previously published material:

Academy of Political Science: "The Impact of *The American Voter* on Political Science," *Political Science Quarterly* 93 (Winter 1978–79): 617–28.

American Political Science Association: "From Confusion to Clarity: Issues and American Voters, 1956–1968," *American Political Science Review* 66 (June 1972): 415–28; " 'Democracy' in British and American Political Parties," paper presented at the Annual Meetings (1982).

Chatham House: "The Presidential Election," *The Election of 1984* (1985), pp. 60–90.

Elsevier Science Publishing: "Ethnic and Group Voting in Nonpartisan Municipal Elections," *Public Opinion Quarterly* 30 (Spring 1966): 79–97.

Harper & Row: "Sex, Voting and War," *Voters' Choice* (1975), pp. 67–89, 234–36.

Institute for Scientific Information: "Citation Classic: 'From Confusion to Clarity: Issues and American Voters, 1956–1968,' " *Current Contents* 18 (July 7, 1986): 14.

Longman Inc.: "If Elected, I Promise," *Elections in America,* 2d ed. (1980), pp. 128–55, 235–38.

Praeger Publishers: "The Contribution of Political Parties to American Democracy," *Party Renewal in America* (1980), pp. 1–17.

Sage Publications: "The Decline of Partisan Politics," *The Impact of the Electoral Process: Sage Electoral Studies Yearbook* 3 (1977): 13–38.

Southern Political Science Association: "The Nomination of Hubert Humphrey for Vice-President," *Journal of Politics* 28 (August 1966): 639–59; "Classification of Presidential Elections," *Journal of Politics* 29 (August 1967): 536–66; "Toward a More Responsible Two-Party System? What, Again?" *Journal of Politics* 33 (November 1971): 916–40; "New Rules and New Games in Nominating Conventions," *Journal of Politics* 41 (November 1979): 784–805.

Transaction Inc.: "Nixon and the End of Presidential Politics, *Society* 10 (March 1973): 14–16; "Party Politics," *Society* 21 (September/October 1984): 61–67.

University of Notre Dame: "The Concept of Elections in Political Theory," *Review of Politics* 29 (October 1967): 478–91.

University Press of America: "Sex, Voting, and War," *Voters' Choice* (1983), pp. 67–89, 234–36.

University of Texas Press: "Future Southern Congressional Politics," *Southwestern Social Science Quarterly* 44 (June 1963): 14–24; " 'If Elected, I Promise': American Party Platforms," *Midwest Journal of Political Science* 11 (August 1967): 318–52; "Variability of Electoral Behavior: Longitudinal Perspectives from Causal Modeling," *American Journal of Political Science* 19, no. 1 (February 1975): 1–18.

# 1

# The Practice of Democratic Theory

Democracy's champions are numerous, yet often defensive. Their advocacy of this noble concept is frequently only halfhearted and apologetic. Aristotole, the first political scientist, found democracy the worst of the ideal forms of government, although it was acceptable as the "most tolerable" of the inevitably imperfect political works of humans.[1] Winston Churchill perhaps deserves more credit than any other individual for the survival of democracy in the contemporary world. But he could praise his inheritance as no more than "the worst form of government except all those other forms that have been tried from time to time."[2] Similarly, Reinhold Niebuhr could only give the system this indirect compliment: "Man's capacity for justice makes democracy possible, but man's inclination to injustice makes democracy necessary."[3]

This apologetic attitude reflects a disjuncture between the ageless concerns of political philosophy and the contemporary practice of democracy. Throughout recorded history, political theorists have established goals for political life. Empirical research has informed us of the realities of democratic politics in the United States and other nations. By comparing theoretical concerns to empirical reality, we may better understand the working of democracy. This essay begins a comparison that continues implicitly throughout the later chapters of this volume. We will deal here with three major topics: expectations of political theory, empirical evidence on the electoral process in the United States, and future prospects for American democracy.

### The Goals of Politics

Political theory is concerned primarily with ends, rather than means. Philosophers and statesmen seek such goals as liberty, equality, and, primarily, justice. Methods of government, such as monarchy or constitutionalism, are evaluated and proposed not for their own sake, but as ways of achieving these ends. The emphasis is clear in Plato, who constructs his entire *Republic* to attain one form of justice. It is equally clear in other philosophers; Marx, illustratively, constructs a different utopia in order to attain a different kind of justice.

Democratic theory is only a subset within theories of politics generally. It is similarly concerned with the ends of politics, rather than technique for its own sake. When they turn to methods of government, advocates of democracy frequently emphasize the role of voters, elections, and parties. They do so, however, not because of a love of the electoral process as such, but because these procedures are seen as vital contributions to the transcendent purposes of politics.

What are these purposes? Through the millennia, political theorists have considered at least five persistent goals: (1) realizing the public good through wise public policy; (2) promoting political stability; (3) protecting individuals against threats, either from other persons or from government itself; (4) fostering the development of individuals; and (5) selecting appropriate political leadership.

These purposes run through the rich tradition of political philosophy, both democratic and nondemocratic. However, the goals are not necessarily compatible. Theorists must reconcile potential conflicts among them, and even trade one off against another. A stress on stability may mean a neglect of individual development, as an emphasis on leadership may predominate over a concern for individual protection. Indeed, many of the differences among theorists can be seen as differences in priorities among these goals. Illustratively, Plato's and Marx's pursuit of justice lead them deliberately to disparage individual liberty.

More generally, liberal democratic theories can be distinguished from other philosophies by their special emphases. They particularly stress the protection of individuals from government, and fostering the development of these individuals. At the same time, democratic theories must be concerned with realizing the public good, promoting political stability, and selecting appropriate leadership. Thus, liberal democratic thought includes unique moral concerns in its consideration of politics.

Of the five goals, the most general is the first, realizing the public good through wise public policy. All philosophers are concerned with this goal and, ostensibly, so are all politicians. Rousseau illustrates the inherent difficulties in locating the public good in his formulation of the "general will":

> The general will is always right and tends to the public advantage; but it does not follow that the deliberations of the people are always equally correct. . . . There is often a great deal of difference between the will of all and the general will; the latter considers only the common interest, while the former takes private interest into account, and is no more than a sum of particular wills. . . . When in the popular assembly a law is proposed, what the people is asked is not exactly whether it approves or rejects the proposal, but whether it is in conformity with the general will, which is their will.[4]

Our second theoretical goal is promoting political stability. Stability is accomplished in part by achieving the other goals, such as good policy and individual protection, but it also can be an end in itself. Machiavelli, for example, devoted considerable attention to the means by which a ruler could maintain his power:

> One who becomes prince by favor of the population must maintain its friendship, which he will find easy, the people asking nothing but not to be oppressed. . . . Therefore a wise prince will seek means by which his subjects will always and in every possible condition of things have need of his government, and then they will always be faithful to him. . . . And yet he must not mind incurring the scandal of those vices, without which it would be difficult to save the state, for if one considers well, it will be found that some things which seem virtues would, if followed, lead to one's ruin, and some others which appear vices result in one's greater security and well-being.[5]

Political theory, especially that of liberalism, has also considered the protection of individuals. Hobbes's concern was with protection from threats created in a theoretical "state of nature." A strong, stable state could remove these dangers. Without such governmental power, humanity would live in perpetual war, "where every man is enemy to every man," and, consequently, there is

> no place for industry; . . . no culture of the earth; no navigation; . . . no commodious building; . . . no account of time; no arts; no letters; no society; and which is worst of all, continual fear, and danger of violent death; and the life of man, solitary, poor, nasty, brutish, and short."[6]

Later writers were more concerned with threats to individuals from government. Locke asserted that men had natural rights that were morally superior to the claims made by government, so that individual consent was required to justify governmental power. Jefferson, following Locke, found it "self-evident"

> that, to secure these rights, governments are instituted among men, deriving their just powers from the consent of the governed. . . .
>
> That, whenever any form of government becomes destructive of these ends, it is the right of the people to alter or to abolish it, and to institute new government, laying its foundation on such principles, and organizing its powers in such form, as to them shall seem most likely to effect their safety and happiness.[7]

Beyond protection, political theorists have sought to construct government in such a manner that it would contribute to the development of individuals. That common goal, however, has led thinkers to very different conclusions. To John Stuart Mill, full moral development of men and women required individual freedom. For Marx and Lenin, in contrast, such development required the destruction of capitalism and its replacement by a "dictatorship of the proletariat" that would eventually culminate in a voluntary society without economic distinctions:

> The state will be able to wither away completely when society has realized the rule: "From each according to his ability; to each according to his needs," i.e. when people have become accustomed to observe the fundamental rules of social life, and their labor is so productive that they voluntarily work according to their ability. . . . There will then be no need for any exact calculation by society of the quantity of products to be distributed to each of its members; each will take freely "according to his needs."[8]

Our last theoretical goal—and another route to the general good—is the selection of appropriate political leadership. Democrats' concern with leadership is reflected in their focus on elections. Plato, while himself not a democrat, posed the problem for all theorists, when he argued that wise leadership was the basic requirement for the good state:

> Unless either philosophers become kings in their countries or those who are now called kings and rulers come to be sufficiently inspired by a genuine desire for wisdom; unless, that is to say, political power and philosophy meet together, while the many natures who now go their several ways in the one or the other direction are forcibly debarred from doing so, there can be no rest from troubles, my dear Glaucon, for states, nor yet, as I believe, for all mankind.[9]

## Theory and Democratic Politics

These five goals are considered, in greater or lesser degree, by persons of widely differing views. Theories of democracy share these purposes, but they also are distinctive, in two ways. First, values. In writing about democracy, theorists illuminate the conflicts among goals that are inherent in politics. Those who favor democracy usually place a higher value on the protection and development of individuals. On the other hand, those skeptical of democracy are likely to put greater stress on pragmatic political concerns such as stability and the selection of leadership.

Second, theories of democracy must consider empirical realities, the institutions of mass participation. From the Athenian Assembly in Plato's time to our current presidential elections, democracy has always implied widespread participation among those recognized as citizens. Contemporary democracy goes even further, so that the legitimacy of government is now inseparable from universal suffrage. The justification and role of mass involvement, however, are not easily joined with the overriding value concerns of traditional political theory. Indeed, this joining is the core issue in modern analysis, both theoretical and empirical.

Part of the problem, as analyzed by Peter Natchez, is that modern democracy developed from the union of two essentially unrelated historical ancestors. The older progenitor was the liberal tradition. Electoral rights were not liberalism's central concern. Rather, the bedrock principles of individual rights and limited government were intended as means to facilitate the use of reason in the development of wise public policy. "The only way to insure that political power simultaneously served the public good and protected the rights of the individual was to organize government so that particular types of motivations ruled."

Coupling later with this progenitor was modern mass politics, in which groups gained voting rights and then used their ballots to win political and economic advantages. But "voting and elections were thrust into the constitutional design without any attempt to probe the theoretical ramifications of these changes."[10]

Because of its mixed ancestry, ambiguities run through the theory of democracy. These are sometimes expressed in phrases such as "minority rights vs. majority rule" or "liberty vs. equality," which are other ways of stating the different democratic traditions of liberal individualism and mass elections. The first tradition especially emphasizes the protection of individuals against government, which can include government directed by majorities. The second tradition emphasizes protection of particular groups and interests against each other. Stressing majority rule, it suggests the mobilization of mass publics to achieve political ends.

Similarly, the two traditions tend to define the public good in different ways, the first seeking some rational, objective wisdom, the second focusing more on particularistic needs and wants. There are differences as well in regard to the selection of leadership. The first tradition stresses the civic-mindedness of leaders, the second places greater emphasis on the representative character of leaders.

Democratic theory has the difficult task of combining these elements. It must resolve possible conflicts among basic values, while providing some role for the mass electorate, the distinctive element in modern democracy. In their efforts to deal with this task, theorists vary in two respects. First, they differ on the capability of the electorate, leading to different prescribed roles for the populace. For the sake of simplicity, we can group their views as those having relatively *lower* or relatively *higher* estimates of the ability and public-mindedness of voters.

Second, theorists differ in the emphasis they place on the different purposes of government. Again using a simple two-part classification, we can divide theorists' emphases into *moralistic* and *instrumental.*

Moralistic theorists conceptualize the state as an agency for achieving transcendent societal ideals, such as the general welfare or moral development.

The citizenry is seen as a community, sharing collective purposes. Instrumental theorists focus more on the protective aspects of the state, and its role in facilitating disparate material interests. The citizenry is seen more as an association, with government as a means of achieving mutual aid for individuals and groups. Moralists see the state more as a church, and its leaders as moral guides. Instrumentalists see the state more as a bazaar, and its leaders as ministering merchants.

If we combine these dimensions, we arrive at the fourfold classification represented in Table 1.1. Each combination results in a kind of political theory that provides differing expectations of the role of the electorate. When moralistic goals are combined with low expectations of the capability of the electorate, for example, the appropriate role for citizens is that of the *spectator*, observing the limited minority that directs the state toward its ideal goals.

When the state is regarded as instrumental in nature, an electorate of limited capability is seen not as highly involved, but as important in providing *consent* to government. A more capable electorate, but still in an instrumental state, could do more. Beyond consenting or dissenting to government, it could *respond*, autonomously and appropriately, to governmental action. Finally, when a capable electorate acts within a state devoted to moralistic ends, it can take on the larger role of *participant*.

These different roles also fit with the focus of different theories on one or another of the purposes of government, although there cannot be an exclusive focus. As we have already noted, a spectator role for the electorate is most appropriate in a theory that focuses on the goal of wise public policy. The argument would probably be made by a modern Plato, just as it is made in fact by contemporary authoritarian leaders of "guided democracies."

Similarly, we can match the values emphasized in other theories with the expected role of the electorate. Thus, when the goal of stability is given priority, the voters' role is limited to giving consent. Theorists placing greater em-

**TABLE 1.1**
**Classification of Political Theories of Democracy**

| **Purpose of Government** | **Capability of the Electorate** | |
|---|---|---|
| | **Lower** | **Higher** |
| **Moralistic** | Electorate Role: Spectator<br>Emphasis: Public Good<br>Leadership: Philosopher | Electorate Role: Participant<br>Emphasis: Moral Development<br>Leadership: Educator |
| **Instrumental** | Electorate Role: Consenter<br>Emphasis: Stability<br>Leadership: Trustee | Electorate Role: Responder<br>Emphasis: Protection<br>Leadership: Representative |

phasis on protection see the electorate as having a greater ability to respond. When individual moral development is stressed, voters are considered to be empowered participants. These relationships are also included in Table 1.1.

The final theoretical goal, the selection of appropriate leadership, constitutes the third element in the table. The nature of leadership depends on the priorities accorded to the other goals. Theorists emphasizing the search for the public good but with a low estimate of the quality of the electorate, would seek philosophers as leaders. (Walter Lippman, whom we quote below, is a modern example.) Machiavelli (or Hobbes), focusing on stability while placing limited trust in the electorate, would prefer leaders such as the *Prince*, who acts as a trustee for the state, using clever strategies to maintain power. In contrast, Locke, with greater confidence in the electorate's ability to protect its interests, would favor leaders who represent their constituents. When the state's goal is moral development and the electorate is seen as capable, Rousseau would seek leaders who are also educators.

In the realities of politics, a society attempts to pursue more than a single goal. These realities are recognized by leaders and by political theorists. Since our major interest here is in the United States, we can use James Madison, the philosopher of the United States Constitution, to illustrate the ways in which democratic political theory, especially in America, attempts to deal with the competing values of statecraft.

Madison is certainly concerned with the achievement of the public good, as well as with protecting individual liberty and group interests. He sees the particular problem of popular government, however, as instability. Democracies, he argues, "have ever been spectacles of turbulence and contention; have ever been found incompatible with personal security or the rights of property; and have in general been as short in their lives as they have been violent in their deaths."

The cause of these problems, and the threat to the goals of government, are factions, groups "whether amounting to a majority or minority of the whole, who are united and actuated by some common impulse of passion, or of interest, adverse to the rights of other citizens, or to the permanent and aggregate interests of the community."

A well-constructed government can cure these ills, Madison believes, by creating a large nation encompassing diverse interests, and by filtering the views of the populace through representatives. Although Madison has a low estimate of the capability of the electorate, which is apt to pursue narrow self-interest, he still sees a vital popular role. Through their selection of representatives, voters ensure that legislators "have an immediate dependence on, and an intimate sympathy with, the people. Frequent elections are unquestionably the only policy by which this dependence and sympathy can be effectually secured." Voting becomes the "primary control on the government," reinforced by constitutional structures such as federalism and the separation of institutions.[11]

Madison deals with all of the goals of political theory, but he does not expect democracy, in itself, to achieve all of these goals. The public good will come from the conflict of factions and the wisdom of representatives, not from the electorate. Stability and protection are the main benefits that come directly from the inclusion of the mass electorate. The appropriate leadership in this system is predominantly that of trustees, with some elements of the philosopher and the representative. Leaders reflect the wishes of the mass, but are not required to give full force to its desires. There are checks and balances between elite and mass, not only within the governmental structure.

## The Practice of Democracy

The large body of research on electoral politics has now provided us with empirical data on the practice of democracy, which we can match against the general goals of political philosophy. Where Madison saw democracies as "spectacles of turbulence and contention," we can use the data of contemporary politics to assess the degree of stability in popular attitudes. Where he argues (as Marx does later) that "the most common and durable source of factions has been the various and unequal distribution of property," we can analyze the effect of social groups on public opinion. Where he believes that representatives chosen from a large electorate will "possess the most attractive merit and the most diffusive and established characters," we can investigate the effect of candidates' personal attributes on voters' choices.[12]

In our classification, moralistic theories focus on achievement of the public good and on moral development of individuals. They differ in their estimates of the capability of the voters, viewing them either as spectators or participants. Empirical research provides some, but limited, support for the realization of these goals in democratic practice.

An early focus in voting studies was the ability of the electorate to meet the conditions of the "ideal democratic citizen." The implicit emphasis was on the theoretical goal of achieving the general good through wise public policy. Each citizen was expected to be an isolated individual, concerned with the public welfare, using his or her vote to advance that welfare. The empirical reality was found to be quite different. Rather than isolated, voters were greatly affected by their social group loyalties. Rather than concerned with contemporary issues, voters were heavily affected by traditional party loyalties and gave little attention to policy issues.

Finding the electorate unable to meet the ideal, analysts developed a different theory of democracy, in effect praising apathy and unawareness. As Berelson concluded, "if the [voting] decision were left only to the deeply concerned, well-integrated, consistently-principled ideal citizens, the political system might easily prove too rigid to adapt to changing domestic and international conditions.[13] Seeing the electorate as limited in capability, this "elitist theory of democracy" restricted it to a spectator role.[14] By *not* considering issues, by *not* being involved, the electorate would leave decisions to the few who were more informed, keeping the political system in balance.

The presumed incapacities of electorates were especially debilitating in developing long-term policies. Because governments must please their electorates with immediate benefits, critics doubted democracy's ability to devise effective means to regulate mature economics or to succeed in foreign relations. As one analyst of American foreign policy put it, "The people have imposed a veto upon the judgments of informed and responsible officials. They have compelled the governments, which usually knew what would have been wiser, or was necessary, or was more expedient, to be too late with too little, or too long with too much, too pacifist in peace and too bellicose in war, too neutralist or appeasing in negotiation or too intransigent."[15]

Democratic governments have certainly made mistakes in policy, but these errors are as much, or more, the fault of leaders as of citizens. Especially when voters are considered only spectators, they cannot be held responsible for the errors of the players on the field. Even when they become more active and leave the bleachers, voters do not take over the game entirely.

The electorate's responsibility is limited, because of the particular character of its involvement in policy decisions. Issues do have a significant impact in elections, but voters do not always focus on the general public welfare. Although many do think on a quasi-ideological or philosophical level, the proportion of such voters constitutes only a minority of the total citizenry. Moreover, there is not a single ideological dimension among the electorate, and even such common terms as "liberalism" and "conservatism" have varying meanings.

Despite these limitations, the electorate shows the capacity to fulfill a broader role than that of passive spectator. While philosophy is not always evident, a concern for the general welfare is also suggested by various data. One indicator is the development of more tolerant attitudes toward civil liberties and the civil rights of minorities. Voters' capacity is also shown by the permeability of social divisions. The electorate is not composed of fixed blocs, divided along lines of class or race or sex. Often, its attitudes go beyond matters of self-interest. For example, economic factors strongly affect elections, but voters tend to be more influenced by their view of general economic conditions than by their personal economic circumstances. These opinions reflect public more than selfish concerns.[16]

Public concerns, however, do not mean public decisions on policy. Voters tend to think selectively, rather then collectively. Most often, there are a number of issues involved in an election, each of interest to some groups, but there is not an overriding issue that is the common concern of even a majority of the electorate. An election, therefore, will rarely be a policy mandate, even when the result is a landslide victory.[17] More typically, the election involves a variety of issues, or a diffuse judgment on the overall achievements and apparent competence of competing politicians. Voting reflects an aggregation of partial interests, rather than community consideration of all aspects of the public good. Different from a simple combination of Madison's "factions," the electorate behaves more like a combination of *fr*actions, but addition of these fractions does not necessarily equal the sum of the general welfare.

It is difficult to judge the contribution of electoral democracy in regard to another theoretical goal, the moral development of individuals. Basic social institutions such as the family and religion are surely more important influences on morality than is the conduct of elections. Tocqueville insightfully argued that the customs of the United States, "the habits of the heart," encouraged both democracy and personal morality, but these customs can be changed even while elections persist.[18]

Politically, we can judge the degree of moral development in democracies only indirectly. Governments such as that of the United States have sometimes pursued immoral policies; racism, bellicosity, and poverty are not absent from democracies, nor eliminated through the electoral process. Yet, elections have provided a means to oppose these evils and a way to oust evildoers from power.

One aspect of the subject susceptible to research is voting turnout and political participation. Voting, one of the simplest acts of citizenship, would be a minimum condition, although not sufficient in itself, as an indicator of moral development. Research into the sources of and variations in voting turnout shows an electorate that only partially meets this basic expectation of a participant political system.

In the United States, only a very small percentage are involved in political associations. Even the proportion casting a ballot has generally declined in recent decades, a trend that has been deplored as reducing the degree of felt obligation, and as indicating substantial alienation. A bare majority of adult Americans voted for president in 1984, and the proportion is considerably lower for other offices.

Among those voting, moreover, much of the turnout can be explained by factors not related to individual moral development. Turnout is greater among those with more education, those who see an individual benefit from voting, and those whose voting is facilitated by external stimulation or made simpler by ease of registration. Voting occurs when there is a favorable balance of individual costs and benefits; it reflects neither moral decisions nor moral involvement.[19]

American is not a fully participant society, but its alleged apathy can be exaggerated. Voting turnout is artificially deflated by statistical factors, such as including persons ineligible to vote in the base population used for calculations. More importantly, turnout is lowered by structural difficulties faced by potential voters, particularly problems in registering to vote. Other forms of participation, such as voluntary organizations and neighborhood associations, reflect considerable, even growing, involvement of Americans.

The citizenry does not rush into politics—but it can be attracted. Citizen participation thus exemplifies the moral problems of democracy itself. A moral hope of individual development is not always fulfilled in the practices of morally imperfect men and women. This disparity requires fuller efforts to improve the political process.

## Instrumental Democracy

Instrumental theories of democracy find different roles for the electorate, depending on their assessment of the capability of the voters, and on their emphasis on the goals of stability or responsiveness.

The dominant tradition in electoral research has stressed stability in voting patterns, implying a limited role for voters as providing consent to a relatively autonomous government. This research demonstrated the importance of inherited party loyalties in voting, and found these loyalties often unrelated to issue preferences. As the leaders in these studies concluded, "The typical voter has only a modest understanding of the specific issues and may be quite ignorant of matters of public policy that more sophisticated individuals might regard as very pressing. . . . Neither do we find much evidence of the kind of structured political thinking that we might expect to characterize a well-informed electorate."

In these conditions, elections provide a means for voter consent to government, rather than control over government. Overall, "the electoral decision gives great freedom to those who must frame the policies of government. If the election returns offer little guidance on specific policies, neither do they generate pressures that restrict the scope of President and Congress in developing public policy."[20] The effect of relatively issue-less voting is to promote stability, in the party system, in public policy, and in the formal institutions of government.

Stability is evident in many aspects of electoral politics. In the United States, the two-party system has become as much of an institution as the two-house structure of Congress. Among individuals, party loyalty continues for long periods of time, becomes reinforced with the passage of political events, and is transmitted across generations. In congressional elections, the outcomes are primarily affected not only by the stable factor of partisanship, but also by another stable factor, incumbency. Nearly 95 percent of U.S. Representatives are reelected, reinforcing the elements of continuity in American politics.[21]

Other aspects of stability are evident in public opinion. Over long periods, politics tends to be concerned with a persistent overriding issue, as the issue of government responsibility for the economy has dominated since the New Deal. Change occurs in the dominant issues of a political era, and one era gives way to another, but political realignments of this sort, the evidence now indicates, do not occur suddenly, but over a number of years and elections, and depend on leaders' initiatives. In scholarly terms, "secular realignments" are more common than "critical elections."[22]

While stability is evident, voters are not inflexible, and demonstrate a capacity to respond as well as to consent. Even within the bounds of tradition, the electorate is capable of judging its particular interests, and of sensibly reacting to events and leadership. Empirical research supports those theories which see the electorate as responsive, and which focus on the goal of citizen protection.

Supporting this perspective is variability in the electorate. Voters are quite ready to change their preferences, depending on electoral circumstances, including the past performances of officeholders, the issues of the time, and the characteristics of particular candidates. In the presidential elections of 1980 and 1984, for example, less than two-thirds of the votes were consistently Democratic or Republican.[23]

Issues are not absent from elections. Indeed, they have been found to be a significant and enhanced element in voter choice. In some analyses, the effect of issue preferences on the vote is comparable in importance to candidate appeal and party preference, and independent of these factors. Separating these influences is possible statistically, but also misses their inevitable combination. The basic point is that issue preferences are themselves reasons for liking a candidate or developing loyalty to a party. The readiness of voters to change their vote and even their partisanship to match their policy views is another demonstration of the importance of issue preferences.[24]

Furthermore, there is a recognizable structure to these issue preferences among significant proportions of the electorate. Such terms as "liberalism" and "conservatism," even when vague in specific content, provide an ideological justification for over two-thirds of the electorate. More elaborate analysis shows even greater structure, so that voters' positions cohere on general principles such as social order and capitalist economics, and in substantive areas such as economic and racial policy.[25]

The involvement of voters with issues promotes the theoretical goal of protection. Even when unconcerned with issues generally, voters typically are aware of their immediate problems, clustering in discrete "issue publics."

Scholarly evidence shows that the degree of issue voting is much higher when attention is focused on what individuals consider the "most important problem" facing the country.[26] This emphasis makes it less likely that there will be a common electoral mandate, but it makes it more likely that particular voters will receive attention for their particular demands. Similarly, turnout increases when voters see an election as having a personal impact on their lives.

The effect of social group memberships on voting is another indicator of the protective aspects of elections. Voters do not make their decisions as solid blocs of blacks or women or workers, but neither are they uninfluenced by their associations. Rather, the effect of these memberships varies with the political situation. When there is an apparent threat to a group, or a potential benefit in an election, then greater group cohesiveness is evident. For example, both a racial division and a "gender gap" between the two major parties developed after issues of race and sex became major political controversies.

Party loyalty itself is not an unthinking habit or a simplistic clinging to tradition. It is better interpreted as a summation of experiences and issue preferences from the distant past, recent events, and future expectations. Voters constantly reassess political achievements and expectations. The result is a combination of stability and responsiveness: "there is an inertial element in voting behavior that cannot be ignored, but that inertial element has an experiential basis; it is *not* something learned at mommy's knee and never questioned thereafter."[27]

The electorate shows the ability to be responsive, as is consistent with the theoretical goal of protection. The reality of electoral practice depends, however, on the actions of leaders, the concern of our final theoretical goal. Elections are most obviously choices of individual leaders and, increasingly, American elections are affected by the candidates' personal attributes. To many in and out of the burgeoning industry of campaign consulting, this stress provides an opportunity for manipulation of the voters and for the "selling of the candidate" on the basis of irrelevant and contrived "images," from physical beauty to religious piety.

At various times, popular choices seem so odd that observers are tempted to repeat the lament of a disappointed politician in the play, *Fiorello*!:

> People can do what they want to,
> But I got a feeling it ain't democratic.

Doubtlessly, some knaves and fools have been democratically elected, but their kin have also risen to power in other forms of government. Examining the elements of leadership choice in electoral politics leads to a restrained optimism.

When voters assess candidates' leadership qualifications, they do so without being blinded by preconceptions. Party loyalty might reasonably be expected to color popular views of candidates, since, for example, Democratic voters and Democratic candidates share many historical experiences and issue preferences. Empirical data support this expectation, but they also show that evaluation of candidates is not just a rationalization of partisanship. In one illustrative study of a series of issues, at least a third of the respondents thought that the issue would be handled better both by a particular party and by the other party's candidate.[28]

Moreover, the criteria used to assess candidates are ones appropriate to political leadership. A considerable proportion—about 20 to 25 percent—of comments about presidential candidates deals with their issue positions. Personal comments are more frequent, but these are not statements about "personality." Rather, voters focus on "the trust factor, incorporating evaluations of basic competence, honesty, reliability and responsiveness, as well as general political orientations." In particular, voters emphasize criteria of competence, integrity, and reliability, and these factors are most closely related to their electoral decisions. At the same time, they give little weight to matters of "image" or "charisma," such as warmth, family status, religiosity, or television appearance.[29]

When voters judge candidates, they do so largely in instrumental terms. Democracy's politicians are not advanced to power to be moral guides or educators, although they sometimes do show such abilities. In keeping with the goals of stability and protection, and the electorate's roles of consent and responsiveness, voters act on the basis of past evaluations and future expectations of candidates' performance in office. Thus, a Carter presidency that brings high inflation and foreign humiliation leads to defeat, and a Reagan presidency that brings apparent economic growth and international prestige leads to support.

Voters choose, and choose on meaningful grounds, but they do so in response to leadership. In selecting public officials, voters have only a restricted choice among those who have the individual resources or the party backing to enter the electoral arena. Policy changes, even those major shifts in priorities that occur during periods of realignment, depend on the initiatives of leaders, not spontaneous demands of mass movements.[30] Voters must act on the basis of uncertain knowledge, relying on indirect information provided by politicians and the mass media. On the whole, the electorate does as well as can be expected reasonably.

This review of democratic practice leads to the conclusion that the American electorate does further the traditional goals of political philosophy, although some more than others. The goal of the public good is only partially considered, but voters do give attention to some social claims. Individual moral development is not clearly apparent, but some voters do show an involvement in the general community beyond their own interests. Stability is advanced, with elections providing a regular and peaceful means of assuring that government relies on the consent of the governed.

More evident is achievement of the goal of protection. The electoral process provides a means of defense and advancement of individual and group interests, and a means of avoiding oppression. In its ultimate task, the choice of leadership, the electorate is not always correct, but it does at least try to use the correct standards. In practice, as Tocqueville observed, American democracy justifies those who believe "that the principal object of a government is not to confer the greatest possible power and glory upon the body of the nation, but to insure the greatest enjoyment, and to avoid the most misery, to each of the individuals who comprise it."[31]

## Democratic Prospects

As is true of all human life, Americans' political grasp falls short of their reach: democratic practice does not fulfill all of the persistent goals of political philosophy. Yet, in time, a firm grasp allows renewed efforts, while a feeble hold leads to decline. Contemporary trends in the United States weaken some elements of American democracy, but other trends and a conscious program of change could bring empirical realities closer to normative ideals.

An effective democracy requires a capable electorate, a responsive leadership, and significant links between the electorate and leadership. Fulfilling these requirements has become more difficult, because of changes in both the structure of society and in the processes of politics.

One problematic trend is the decline of the private order, of those nongovernmental institutions that have provided the societal foundations of the liberal democratic state. The nation evidences a weakening of the social groups and of the established institutions that bind a people into a community. The traditional family hardly exists any longer, as evidenced by divorce rates, delayed marriages, and reduced (and often illegitimate) childbearing. Close interpersonal relationships can hardly survive in a period of farm and factory closings, geographical mobility, and declining union membership. The heterogeneity of the national community has increased, with the growth of nonwhite populations, both from differential birth rates and from substantial immigration. Without making nostalgic moral judgments on the desirability of these changes, we still must recognize that their effect is to reduce the existing basis for shared political perspectives.

The political indicator of these trends is the weakening of party identification. Parties have been one of the basic institutions of the private order, and their decline parallels the decline of the cohesion of other social groups.

As individuals feel fewer ties to family or community, they are also less likely to be attached to the party of their peers.

Today, party loyalty has less influence on the vote, and other factors, such as the characteristics and arguments of individual candidates, have more weight. If each person were able to give detailed attention to politics, such independence might be praised, but the reality is that without a grounding in the historical experience of party performance, the citizen must depend more on transient cues, which are less reliable and more subject to manipulation. Recent voting shows an uncertain electorate, unattached to candidates or parties, its views volatile during campaigns, and changeable from one contest to the next. Rather than continuing, but permeable, coalitions of interests and issue publics, the mass parties have become only temporary bands of confused individuals.

This volatility may subvert achievement of major goals of politics. At the least, it hinders the achievement of stability. More importantly, it probably confounds the ability of government to seek the public good. Without a secure electoral base, leaders may well be discouraged from taking short-term risks for long-term gains. Always uncertain of the electorate's support, their perspective is likely to be foreshortened.[32]

Reduced partisanship also complicates efforts to use the electoral process effectively for protective purposes. Party loyalty can serve as a meaningful summary of the interests and issue preferences of individuals and groups. By regularly voting Democratic, for example, a union worker can easily deal with the confusing world of politics, knowing that Democrats will usually advance his or her interests. In a volatile politics, by contrast, voters find no party or leadership consistently acceptable, and are less assured of protection.

Party loyalty can be a school of civic morality, teaching voters about the needs of others. Without continuing coalitions, groups and individuals become less likely to recognize larger problems. There are fewer commitments to causes beyond self-interest and immediate interest. By thus undermining the potential for fuller moral development, it becomes still more difficult to achieve this difficult goal of political life.

Another contemporary obstacle in effectuating democracy is the increasing complexity of issues facing the nation. In contrast to its historical good fortune, the United States now faces possibly intractable economic and foreign policy problems. Both government and citizens find it difficult to deal with a declining industrial base, the largest trade deficits and government budget deficits in world history, growing disparities between social classes, and lagging technological growth. Abroad, the U.S. has irretrievably lost the dominant world position it held after the Second World War, and finds itself unable to affect the course of events in much of the globe. The complexity of such problems undermines the electorate's ability to protect itself, much less to advance any conception of the general good.

Not only are solutions difficult to achieve, but the means of choosing solutions are less accessible to the electorate. This difficulty is not simply because the policy choices are complex. While the mass electorate cannot be expected to make sense of alternative disarmament theories or of technical economics, technical choices of this kind are not the province of the voters in any case. The difficulty, rather, is that even the choices appropriate to elections are more subject to error.

Electorates judge best when they can relate public decisions to personal experiences. As Aristotle put it, the best judge of the quality of shoes is not the cobbler, but the wearer, who knows where the shoe pinches. Ordinary citizens thus can make judgments about the performance of government. Especially in regard to economic policy, they have immediate experience of inflation, unemployment, pensions, and interest rates, and can reasonably relate that experience to political events.

However, many current controversies cannot be tested as easily by common experience. If social investment in health, education, and technology is neglected, the nation's human and physical resources will be quietly eroded before the public can notice and demand remedial action. If contrasting life styles proliferate without examination, the bases for a common moral life can disappear without immediate notice or regret. Most definitively, if a disarmament policy fails, leading to nuclear war, there will be no opportunity to remove incompetent strategists from office.

Error also is more likely because of limitations inherent in the means voters now have for acquiring information. In a smaller community, people can judge potential leaders on the basis of direct communication and a history of personal contacts. Today, almost no voters personally know a candidate for any significant office. Instead, they must rely on indirect and artificial information, most obviously that of the mass media. Indicative of this change is that we now speak of television interviews or debates as "face-to-face" interactions, when they obviously are only electronic messages, artfully designed by the politician and suspiciously received by the voter.

In large nations with mass electorates, democracy inevitably requires indirect communication. More novel is the decline of intermediate agents who could offer their own appraisals of candidates in place of direct communication. Local political parties were the most important of these agents. If a voter could not know a candidate personally, he still could judge the trustworthiness of his local party leader. In regard to presidents, voters certainly could not know the personal qualities of potential candidates. However, party delegates to a national convention would have more direct knowledge, and could impose a rough kind of "peer review."

These substitutes, too, are no longer available. Parties in the United States are no longer meaningful organizations in most local areas. There is evidence of renewed party strength in some functions, but it is the strength of mass marketeers, not that of intimate retailers. Even nominations show less party control, so that presidential choice is not screened by knowledgeable party activists, but depends largely on individualist campaigns conducted through the mass media. That same pattern is evident on lower levels of office, so that many candidates will meet voters for no other reason than to gain a spot on the evening news, before they retreat to their office to review the next television commercial or analyze the latest anonymous poll.

Institutional changes also complicate the voters' task. As the nonelected bureaucracy necessarily takes on more of the complex tasks of modern life, voters are less able to control officials. When presidents reach the White House through personal campaigns, they are less subject to the checks and balances of party and Congress, and these restraints are particularly ineffective in regard to the decisive, yet often secret, issues of foreign policy. Even among legislative officials, the growth of personal campaigning and the advantages of incumbency make it simpler for individual representatives to win election. Yet, when the legislature becomes less coherent, it also becomes more difficult for the electorate to enforce collective responsibility for public policy.

Current trends in the United States may limit the contributions of democratic practice to the goals of politics. There is less stability, less of a common life directed toward the public good and individual development, more difficulty in understanding issues to provide protection, and more obstacles in making wise choices of leaders. However, there are countervailing trends as well, and there are deliberate policies that could enhance the contributions to effective politics of the electoral process.

Social stability is needed for political stability, and both could be promoted by deliberate public policies. While many platitudes are uttered on behalf of families, for example, a meaningful profamily policy is not evident. Such a policy would move away from the irreconcilable issue of abortion, and instead focus on means to sustain families as coherent units, whatever the number of children. It would include revisions in welfare and tax laws and provisions for child care and parental leaves, affordable housing, and expanded economic opportunities. Similarly, a program to sustain communities would recognize that plant closings and farm bankruptcies are more than private transactions, but have an effect on the closely woven social fibers that bind men and women to joint efforts.

Political change can also be directed, so as to increase the capacity of the electorate to perform its functions well. Information is complex, but it can make voting choices clearer when presented simply. Increased television coverage of government is an obvious step. The popularity of televised broadcasts of the House and Senate shows that the citizenry does appreciate televised politics, even when the material is relatively dull. Televised debates also can make a contribution. Despite their staged character, they do provide some opportunity for voters to judge their would-be leaders in direct confrontation, and thereby to gain some measure of their relative worth.

Probably the most important changes will come through revitalization of the political parties. By summarizing issues and confronting candidates, parties provide the critical means to link the electorate to government, promoting the responsiveness that is the major element of democratic practice. Already, some signs of party revitalization are evident—in the electorate, the party organizations, and formal governmental institutions. More can be accomplished through deliberate action.

Among voters, party revival is suggested by higher levels of identification. More people are becoming willing to call themselves Republicans or Democrats, rather than neuter Independents. Moreover, there is a greater ideological coherence within party ranks, the Republicans being increasingly identified as conservative, the Democrats tending to acquire the liberal label.

This shuffling of voters between the two major parties does not necessarily imply the onset of a grand party realignment, leading to the dominance of one party or another. Still, there no longer can be any doubt that there has been a considerable change in the composition of the parties. Their social coalitions are quite different from those that were solidified in the era of Franklin Roosevelt, and their altered policy emphases parallel these shifts. Voters now see a Republican party that is oriented toward individual economic enterprise and reassertion of tradition, and a Democratic party oriented toward social equity and adaptation to change. These alignments facilitate voter responsiveness in the interest of protection.[33]

The parties are also becoming more nationalized and more centralized. As competition between the parties has become more widespread throughout the nation, politicians have come to realize that they may share a common fate at the polls, that they cannot fully escape the responsibility for a party record, and that their self-interest requires a degree of cooperation. As a result, national and state party organizations have become major sources of campaign advice, funding, and even direction. On the legislative level, the recognition of these common interests has strengthened party leadership bodies in Congress. Further evidence of the new significance of the legislative parties comes in rollcall voting, where intraparty cohesion and interparty distinctions are at the highest levels of recent decades.[34]

The importance of political parties is also gaining public recognition. In a series of decisions since 1975, the U.S. Supreme Court has upheld the autonomy of the parties, giving them substantially more freedom to regulate their own affairs.[35] A presidential commission and the semi-official Advisory Commission on Intergovernmental Relations have endorsed their vital role. Most recently, a prestigious private Commission on National Elections made news by its argument that reform ''should begin by seeking to strengthen the role of the political parties,'' and by such suggestions as the sponsorship of presidential debates by the national parties, rather than the "impartial" League of Women Voters.[36]

Full reform will have to go much further. It will require overcoming traditions of hostility to parties, a hostility that itself has often been identified with the cause of reform. Freedom from partisanship has long been honored, as evidenced by the pride of independent voters, the respect paid to maverick legislators, the spread of local nonpartisan election systems, and the reverential annual readings of George Washington's Farewell Address. The consistent direction of reform has been to limit the role of parties—in nominations, campaign finance, municipal government, the civil service, and even in congressional roll calls and the conduct of the presidency.

Effective party renewal will need to be still more bold than the limited suggestions of the National Commission on Elections. Such actions might include: providing government subsidies to the parties for their regular operations; channeling campaign contributions to parties rather than to individual candidates; requiring free television time for periodic party broadcasts; registering voters automatically through government bureaucracies such as motor vehicle agencies; and replacing presidential primaries with increased use of party bodies such as caucuses and state committees.

Beyond presidential elections, other party-building proposals are needed: party endorsement of candidates in primaries; formal dues-paying memberships in the parties, with formal state and local charters; and national party conferences in nonpresidential years. Each of the possible actions listed here are in effect in some state or some other democracy. Though all are themselves debatable, they do have the virtue of being consistently directed toward an extensive strengthening of the party organizations.

This reconstruction of the political parties is the means to enhance democratic practice to better fulfill the eternal goals of politics. In pursuing this program, true reformers might recall the Constitutional Convention of 1787, our most successful innovation in government, particularly Washington's opening challenge: "If to please the people, we offer what we ourselves disapprove, how can we afterwards defend our work? Let us raise a standard to which the wise and the honest can repair."

## Notes

1. Aristotle, *Politics*, 4.2.1289, trans. Benjamin Jowett (New York: Modern Library, 1943), p. 171.
2. Winston Churchill, House of Commons, November 11, 1947.
3. Reinhold Niebuhr, *The Children of Light and the Children of Darkness* (New York: Scribner's, 1944), p. xi.
4. Jean Jacques Rousseau, *The Social Contract*, Everyman ed. (New York: Dutton, 1950), pp. 26, 106.
5. Niccolo Machiavelli, *The Prince*, chaps. 9, 15 (New York: Modern Library, 1940), pp. 37, 39, 57.

6. Thomas Hobbes, *Leviathan*, Everyman ed. (New York: Dutton, 1950), p. 104.
7. Thomas Jefferson, *Declaration of Independence*.
8. V. I. Lenin, *State and Revolution* (New York: International Publishers, 1932), p. 79f.
9. Plato, *The Republic*, 5.473, trans. Francis Cornford (New York: Oxford University Press, 1950), p. 178f.
10. Peter Natchez, *Images of Voting/Visions of Democracy* (New York: Basic Books, 1985), pp. 34–35.
11. James Madison, *The Federalist*, Nos. 10, 52, 51 (New York: Modern Library, 1941), pp. 58, 54, 343, 337.
12. Madison, *The Federalist*, No. 10, pp. 56–60.
13. Bernard Berelson et al., *Voting* (Chicago: University of Chicago Press, 1954), p. 316.
14. Jack Walker, "A Critique of the Elitist Theory of Democracy," *American Political Science Review* 60 (June 1966): 285–95; Peter Bachrach, *The Theory of Democratic Elitism* (Boston: Little Brown, 1967).
15. Walter Lippman, *The Public Philosophy* (New York: New American Library, 1955), p. 23f.
16. Relevant literature includes Herbert McClosky and Alida Brill, *Dimensions of Tolerance* (New York: Russell Sage, 1983); John Sullivan et al., *Political Tolerance and American Democracy* (Chicago: University of Chicago Press, 1982); D. Roderick Kiewiet, *Macroeconomics and Microeconomics* (Chicago: University of Chicago Press, 1983).
17. Stanley Kelley, Jr., *Interpreting Elections* (Princeton: Princeton University Press, 1983).
18. Alexis de Tocqueville, *Democracy in America*, ed. Phillips Bradley (New York: Vintage, 1954), vol. 1, chap. 17. Robert Bellah et al. find a marked and threatening change in these customs, in *Habits of the Heart* (Berkeley: University of California Press, 1985).
19. Ray Wolfinger and Steven Rosenstone, *Who Votes?* (New Haven: Yale University Press, 1980); Benjamin Ginsberg, *The Consequences of Consent* (Reading, Mass.: Addison-Wesley, 1982).
20. Angus Campbell et al., *The American Voter* (New York: Wiley, 1960), pp. 542, 544. See my extensive comments in chap. 7 below.
21. Barbara Hinckley, *Congressional Elections* (Washington: Congressional Quarterly Press, 1981), chap. 3.
22. Jerome Clubb et al., *Partisan Realignment* (Los Angeles: Sage Publications, 1980), chap. 8.
23. *National Journal* 16 (November 10, 1984): 2131.
24. The literature is now voluminous. Among the important works are David Repass, "Issue Salience and Party Choice," *American Political Science Review* 65 (June 1971): 389–400; Charles H. Franklin and John E. Jackson, "The Dynamics of Party Identification," *American Political Science Review* 77 (December 1983): 957–73; Norman Nie et al., *The Changing American Voter* (Cambridge: Harvard University Press, 1976); Morris Fiorina, *Retrospective Voting in American National Elections* (New Haven: Yale University Press, 1981).
25. See Teresa Levitin and Warren Miller, "Ideological Interpretations of Presidential Elections," *American Political Science Review* 73 (September 1979): 751–71; Pamela Johnston Conover and Stanley Feldman, "The Origins and Meaning of Liberal/Conservative Self-Identifications," *American Journal of Political Science* 25 (November 1981): 617–45; Mark Peffley and Jon Hurwitz, "A Hierarchical Model of Attitude Constraint," *American Journal of Political Science* 29 (November 1985): 871–90.

26. Philip Converse, "The Nature of Belief Systems in Mass Publics," in David Apter, ed., *Ideology and Discontent* (New York: The Free Press, 1964), chap. 6; George Rabinowitz et al., "Salience as a Factor in the Impact of Issues on Candidate Evaluation," *Journal of Politics* 44 (February 1982): 41–63.
27. Fiorina, *Retrospective Voting*, p. 102. See also Charles Franklin, "Issue Preferences, Socialization and the Evolution of Party Identification," *American Journal of Political Science* 28 (August 1984): 459–78.
28. Samuel Popkin et al., "What Have You Done for Me Lately? Toward an Investment Theory of Voting," *American Political Science Review* 70 (September 1976): 793.
29. Jeffrey Smith, *American Presidential Elections: Trust and the Rational Voter* (New York: Praeger, 1980), p. 181; Arthur Miller et al., "Schematic Assessments of Presidential Candidates," *American Political Science Review* 80 (June 1986): 521–40.
30. The point is made again in regard to current realignment by Edward Carmines and James Stimson, "On the Structure and Sequence of Issue Evolution," *American Political Science Review* 80 (September 1986): 901–20.
31. Tocqueville, vol. 1, chap. 14, p. 262.
32. This consequence is suggested in a different context by Anthony Downs, in *An Economic Theory of Democracy* (New York: Harper, 1957), pp. 52–69.
33. Recent analyses of changing voting coalitions include James Sundquist, "Whither the American Party System?—Revisited," *Political Science Quarterly* 98 (Winter 1983–84): 573–93; Harold Stanley et al., "Partisanship and Group Support Over Time," *American Political Science Review* 80 (September 1986): 969–76; and items in n. 7, introduction to Part 2.
34. Joseph Schlesinger, "The New American Political Party," *American Political Science Review* 79 (December 1985): 1152–69; Xandra Kayden and Eddie Mahe, *The Party Goes On* (New York: Basic Books, 1985); Cornelius Cotter et al., *Party Organizations in American Politics* (New York: Praeger, 1984).
35. *Tashjian* v. *Republican Party of Connecticut*, No. 85–766 (1986); *Democratic Party* v. *Wisconsin*, 450 U.S. 107 (1981); *Cousins* v. *Wigoda*, 419 U.S. 477 (1975).
36. *Electing the President: A Program for Reform* (Washington: Georgetown University Center for Strategic and International Studies, 1986). In discussing this report, I draw on my review essay, "Political Reform in America," excerpted with permission from *Political Corruption* (1987).

# PART I
# Voters

# *Part I: Voters*

Voters think about politics.

These few words summarize the theme of this first section. My theme appears self-evident, perhaps simplistic, but it requires demonstration and elaboration. The traditional literature of political science and sociology often has been unkind to the electorate, which has been the object of a variety of slings and arrows. Voters have been depicted as essentially unthinking registers of depoliticized demographic characteristics such as their ethnic group or sex, or as unchanging carriers of inherited political loyalties, or as the passive subjects of campaign manipulation.

The critiques are diverse, but they share a characteristic point of view. Voters are seen as essentially isolated from one another. To be sure, they do share group characteristics such as ethnic identification or gender, they do identify with a Democratic or Republican symbol, and they do receive messages from candidates and propagandists. In these interpretations, however, voters only interact as blacks or whites, women or men, as traditional party identifiers, or as the detached audience for distant performers. The electorate is seen as not actively involved, but as dependent on simple cues, whether sociological or psychological, and as responding only to external stimuli.

From this viewpoint, voters are not truly citizens, participants in a truly political dialogue. Their conversation reflects only their personal experience and immediate self-interest, not considerations of the public good. Short-run reactions to "the nature of the times" predominate over longer-term evaluations of governmental performance and policies. Candidates are judged as personalities, not as potential leaders of the nation. Electoral decision becomes another consumer decision, scarcely different from the choice between Burger King and McDonald's.

My own position in the essays in this section is different. I see voters as responsive, as *potential* participants. Realizing this potentiality depends on political conditions, not on the voters themselves. The mass public is capable of involvement and reasonable judgment, I argue, but only in the proper environment, as established by structural conditions and the actions of political leaders.

I do not see most voters as capable of understanding theories of Keynesian or supply-side economics, or the deadly logic of nuclear deterrence. But, I argue, such detailed knowledge is not only impossible, but unnecessary. Voters do draw politically relevant data from their own experience of unemployment and inflation, and they do respond in sensible ways to foreign policy alternatives presented by political candidates.

The ordinary men and women of the United States or any other democracy cannot be expected to devote a large part of their limited time and energy to researching the arcane lore of government. However, when their choices are comprehensible and their preferences can be effected, they do justify the faith of democratic theory. V. O. Key, as so often is the case, perhaps stated this thesis best. As I quote him at the end of two of these essays: "In the large the electorate behaves about as rationally and responsibly as we should expect, given the clarity of the alternatives presented to it and the character of the information available to it."[1]

The first essay specifies the general argument. Examining voting surveys shows that voters sharply changed their views of the major political parties between 1956 and 1968.[2] Over this period, voters' party loyalty became more congruent with their issue preferences, differences between Democrats and Republicans became more evident, and Democrats came to be recognized as the more liberal party.

While these empirical data are themselves significant, their theoretical explanation is more important. Demographic changes such as the entrance of new voters or the nation's higher educational level could not explain these shifts. Rather, politics was the cause of these changed voter perceptions. As parties and politicians emphasized their ideological differences, the voters responded. The American mass public was shown to be capable of true citizenship, if their leaders provided the opportunity.

The major conclusions of this work have held up. Indeed, even while party attachments have become weaker, there is little change in the perception of party differences.[3] Although less central to the argument, the predictions implied in the article were less accurate. I suggested that the election of 1964 was a critical election, reconstituting the parties and possibly initiating a new period of Democratic party dominance. There is certainly no Democratic dominance evident, when the party has lost all but one of the last five presidential elections. Rather than a time of realignment of the party system, most observers see this intervening period as one of extended party dealignment. My limited prediction was faulty, because I did not foresee the effect of racial attitudes in eroding support for the Democrats.[4]

The original article drew considerable notice, and helped to redirect attention to voters as rational participants in politics. Eventually, the article became acknowledged as a "classic," because of its frequent inclusion in the *Social Science Citation Index*. The second item in this section is a personal retrospective on the article, with some musings on possible reasons for its scholarly use.

The next essay, "Variability in Electoral Behavior," is a more elegant development of the major thesis. Following the lead of Mark Schulman, we use the sophisticated techniques of causal path analysis to explain three presidential elections—those of 1956, 1964, and 1972.[5] Traditional party loyalties are found to be predominant in the first contest, while the impact of issue preferences grows in the later years. Again, the cause is found in the changing political environment, not in the demographic factors. The electorate does not suffer from "inherent limitations," as some have claimed. Instead, it is only bounded by the choices presented.

A different potential limit is biology. In particular, sex sometimes has been seen as defining not only our biological character, but our political lives. "Sex, Voting, and War" focuses on two aspects of women in politics: voting participation and attitudes toward the use of force. It correctly predicted that women's traditionally lower turnout would disappear with the entrance of younger, better educated women into the electorate.

The most interesting finding in this essay is women's persistent endorsement of more pacific solutions to social problems, from international conflict to domestic crime. Although later investigations substantiate the association of gender and attitudes toward force,[6] I still cannot fully explain this relationship. Its significance, however, again demonstrates the relevance of the political environment. The attitudinal difference between women and men seems to be longstanding, but it only became electorally relevant in 1972, when the nation focused on issues involving the use of force, particularly the Vietnam War. Women's more peaceful attitudes were then transformed from admirable sentiments to partisan effects. Using these data, I was able to locate the beginnings of the "gender gap," the greater likelihood of women than men to support Democrats, in 1972, earlier then most analysts.

Voter response is also affected by the structure of elections. The next essay examines the effect of the formal ballot on electoral behavior, particularly the influence of ethnicity. Two elections in the city of Newark are compared, one nonpartisan in form, the other with political party labels on the ballot. In the former case, ethnic loyalties predominate, submerging any effect of policy attitudes. In the second election, blacks, Italian-Americans, and Jews unite to support a party team across ethnic lines. Voters can be parochial, but can also respond to broader appeals.

This section ends with a critical analysis of the most important published work on electoral behavior, *The American Voter*,[7] written by four scholars then at the University of Michigan. The essay disputes a long list of propositions drawn from this work, and suggests some serious flaws. Originally prepared for oral presentation at a scholarly conference, my written work now seems to me to have a harsh, even strident, tone that is inappropriate and undeserved. I regret that tone, even while I stand by the substantive comments. Although the Michigan authors hardly need my commendation, their monument to scholarship deserves full recognition of its multiple merits.

The study of voting behavior essentially is the study of individuals. Politics, however, is more than individual psychology or a collection of individual choices. The collective importance of voting is its impact through elections, which in turn are shaped by the political parties. The following sections will deal with these subjects.

## Notes

1. V. O. Key, Jr., *The Responsible Electorate* (Cambridge: Harvard University Press, 1966), p. 7.
2. The data analysis was expanded to include the election of 1972 in *Voters' Choice* (New York: Harper & Row, 1975), chap. 8.
3. Martin Wattenberg, *The Decline of American Political Parties* (Cambridge: Harvard University Press, 1984), pp. 52–60.
4. Edward G. Carmines and James A. Stimson, "Issue Evolution, Population Replacement, and Normal Partisan Change," *American Political Science Review* 75 (March 1981): 107–18.
5. The same techniques have been replicated to analyze the elections of 1960, 1968, and 1976 by Frederick Hartwig et al., "Research Update," *American Journal of Political Science* 24 (August 1980):553–58. Causal path analysis is widely applied now, for example in a leading analysis of the 1980 and 1984 presidential elections: J. Merrill Shanks and Warren E. Miller, "Policy Direction and Performance Evaluation" (paper presented to the American Political Science Association, 1985).
6. Kathleen Frankovic, "Sex and Politics—New Alignments, Old Issues," *PS* 15 (Summer 1982):439–48.
7. Angus Campbell, Philip Converse, Warren Miller, and Donald Stokes, *The American Voter* (New York: Wiley, 1960).

# 2

# From Confusion to Clarity: Issues and American Voters

Students of politics, from Plato to Marcuse, have frequently sneered at the inability of the "masses" to discern political reality. Whether citizens are misled by the shadows on the wall of the cave or by the shadows of the television tube, they are deemed to be fundamentally unequipped consciously to control political elites and rationally to direct public policy.

In contemporary times, such conclusions have been unintentionally strengthened by selected and often distorted findings of empirical voting research. In broad terms, political scientists have found voters to have limited interest in politics, to be strongly attached to their traditional parties and social groups, and to lack ideological coherence in their views of political issues.[1] Of particular concern here is the electorate's perception of issues, of coherent ideologies, and of the links between issue preferences and partisan preferences. Much voting research has indicated that these perceptions are cloudy. Large proportions of voters have "no opinion" or "don't know" their opinion on specific policy issues.[2] Only 12 percent of the citizenry has been found to hold an ideological view of the parties.[3] The links between issue preferences and party choice are weak. Party identification was found in *The American Voter* to have little relation to general ideology,[4] and McClosky, dealing with the same period, found "that substantial differences of opinion exist among the electorate on only five of the 24 issues" he examined.[5] The Michigan volume indicated that there was little belief among the electorate that the parties differed on particular issues, and little agreement on the direction of whatever differences were perceived.[6] Although the findings were carefully qualified, their general thrust justified the conclusion: "The electoral decision gives great freedom to those who must frame the policies of government. If the election returns offer little guidance on specific policies, neither do they generate pressures that restrict the scope of President and Congress in developing public policy."[7]

Reaction to these conclusions has varied. Some publicists or would-be "hidden persuaders" have selectively drawn from the voting studies to compose a picture of an irrational voter, easily manipulated by possessors of this arcane knowledge. Thus, a widely quoted book on "the New Politics" is taken seriously when it warns, "These new managers . . . can play upon the voters like virtuosos. They can push a pedal here, strike a chord there, and presumably, they can get precisely the response they seek."[8] To Bernard Berelson, the voting findings offered the occasion to develop a new theory of democracy, in which stability depended on the limited involvement of the population.[9]

V. O. Key saw the danger that the findings of voting research could be misused to convert popular democracy into a system of elitist manipulation, in which, "fed a steady diet of buncombe, the people may come to expect and to respond with highest predictability to buncombe."[10] In his last work, he sought to revive the notion that issue and voting preferences are closely related. While he did demonstrate a certain consistency in the electorate's choices, he could not prove a causal connection. Key's work, along with Arthur Goldberg's,[11] however, did bring a renewed emphasis on the analysis of policy preferences to electoral studies.

In the past few years, this renewed emphasis has been evident in a number of independent reappraisals of *The American Voter*'s finding of ideological unawareness among the electorate. One set of authors argues that mass ideological awareness has always been present to a greater degree than found by Campbell, Converse, Miller, and Stokes, but that appropriate methods have not been employed to observe this awareness. Thus, focusing on local concerns, Luttbeg found considerable "constraint" or coherence, in mass attitudes.[12] Similarly, using a series of prepared statements, Brown found no difference in ideological awareness between political articulates a nd inarticulates.[13] Most notable is the work of Lane, who was able to discern a developed ideology among New Haven workers through lengthy interviews.[14] These strands suggest that previous studies demonstated not the absence of ideology, but the absence of the ability to articulate hidden ideology.[15]

Another criticism is that the findings of *The American Voter* are time-bound. They may show a low degree of ideology among voters in 1956, but only because the 1956 election did not stimulate ideological feelings. Replicating the Michigan study for the contrasting 1964 election, in which ideology was emphasized, Field and Anderson found a substantial increase in ideological awareness. In the Goldwater-Johnson context, a third of the respondents are classified as ideological, more than double the proportion of 1956 voters, and nearly three times the proportion of the total sample in the earlier study.[16]

The recent work of Pierce combines these two revisions. Using three measures of ideological awareness derived from Survey Research Center materials, instead of only one, Pierce also tested the change in awareness over time. A greater proportion of the sample was classified as ideological under the three-pronged analysis, and the proportion was found to have increased considerably from 1956 through 1960 to 1964.[17] These recent findings suggest an increased awareness of politics among American voters. The analysis below provides further evidence to support this conclusion.

## Changing Perceptions of Parties and Policies

The research presented here does not deal with general ideology, but with voter opinions and perceptions on the six precise policy questions which have been asked consistently of the national Survey Research Center sample in each quadrennial study since 1956. I will analyze the relationship between issue preferences and three partisan variables: party identification, the awareness of differences between the parties on these six issues, and the consensus among the electorate on the positions of the parties on these issues. In each of the three instances, we will find an increase in voter consciousness during the 1956–1968 period.

The six policy issues are: federal aid to education, government provision of medical care, government guarantee of full employment, federal enforcement of fair employment and fair housing, federal enforcement of school integration, and foreign aid. Although the questions are not worded identically in the four surveys, they are sufficiently close to be highly comparable. Moreover, we are not concerned with the trend of opinion itself, but rather with comparisons of the structure of opinion in each of the election years, so that identical wording is not critical.[18]

In Table 2.1, positions on these issues are presented along a five-point scale of party identification. The statistic reported is the percentage taking the "liberal" position (i.e., in favor of federal government action). For 1956, the data clearly support the contention of *The American Voter* that issue preferences were essentially unrelated to party identification. A linear relationship between the two variables existed only on the issue of medical care. The situation changed substantially, however, over the next twelve years. By 1968, a linear relationship existed essentially on all issues but foreign aid. The change was not gradual, but became suddenly apparent in the election of 1964. When John Kennedy was elected President, the relationship of opinion and party identification was hardly different from that of the Eisenhower period. By 1964, however, linear relationships were evident on four of the six issues, and they began to appear on the other two as well.

The same pattern is evident in the increasing spread between the extremes. Strong Democrats and Strong Republicans were already distinct on the issue of medical care in 1956, but the difference almost doubled in 1964 and remained considerably widened in 1968. The same pattern is evident on the other issues as well. Party differences became quite high by 1964 and then

**TABLE 2.1**
**Party Identification and Policy Position, 1956, 1960, 1964, and 1968**
**(In Percentages Supporting "Liberal" Position)**

| Party Identification | Aid to Education | | | | Medical Care | | | | Job Guarantee | | | |
|---|---|---|---|---|---|---|---|---|---|---|---|---|
| | '56 | '60 | '64 | '68 | '56 | '60 | '64 | '68 | '56 | '60 | '64 | '68 |
| Strong Democrat | 80.0 | 66.8 | 51.0 | 53.6 | 74.2 | 74.5 | 78.2 | 81.3 | 75.6 | 71.2 | 52.6 | 53.1 |
| Weak Democrat | 78.1 | 59.0 | 44.1 | 38.3 | 67.3 | 60.2 | 65.2 | 72.1 | 64.0 | 62.4 | 38.4 | 39.7 |
| Independent | 71.0 | 53.2 | 39.3 | 32.9 | 55.8 | 56.7 | 57.2 | 55.3 | 55.0 | 56.6 | 31.0 | 27.0 |
| Weak Republican | 68.7 | 39.1 | 21.5 | 22.5 | 51.4 | 47.5 | 43.5 | 39.3 | 59.5 | 43.9 | 25.9 | 24.9 |
| Strong Republican | 67.7 | 44.5 | 15.5 | 12.0 | 45.9 | 54.2 | 23.6 | 42.7 | 51.5 | 52.7 | 16.1 | 25.4 |
| Gamma | .15 | .20 | .34 | .36 | .24 | .18 | .45 | .41 | .19 | .16 | .31 | .25 |
| Party Identification | Fair Employment | | | | School Integration | | | | Foreign Aid | | | |
| | '56 | '60 | '64 | '68 | '56 | '60 | '64 | '68 | '56 | '60 | '64 | '68 |
| Strong Democrat | 73.3 | 63.0 | 56.3 | 61.9 | 38.7 | 39.8 | 53.7 | 58.9 | 49.5 | 51.4 | 64.7 | 51.3 |
| Weak Democrat | 71.3 | 63.1 | 42.9 | 43.5 | 44.4 | 37.5 | 43.2 | 44.6 | 55.4 | 48.8 | 59.2 | 45.8 |
| Independent | 66.6 | 65.4 | 50.3 | 37.7 | 48.8 | 47.1 | 49.0 | 37.3 | 49.9 | 53.2 | 57.5 | 42.7 |
| Weak Republican | 70.8 | 62.7 | 36.3 | 37.8 | 49.3 | 43.0 | 50.5 | 37.4 | 48.2 | 54.0 | 56.6 | 47.0 |
| Strong Republican | 66.8 | 65.9 | 20.6 | 31.3 | 38.8 | 41.5 | 34.8 | 31.5 | 51.4 | 61.5 | 49.7 | 41.8 |
| Gamma | .04 | −.02 | .22 | .24 | .04 | −.01 | .08 | .43 | .01 | −.03 | .08 | .04 |

decreased slightly (on job guarantees, fair employment, and foreign aid) or increased slightly (on aid to education and school integration) four years later.

The increased policy distinctiveness of partisans is summarized by the increases in the ordinal correlation (*gamma*) included in the last row of Table 2.1. Policy and party preferences became far more congruent in 1964, and the correlation was very similar in 1968. The only major exception is the issue of school integration. For the first three elections in this period, no meaningful correlation existed between party identification and support of federal action on the issue (*gammas* = .04, −.01, .08). But by 1968, there was a considerable relationship, and the *gamma* statistic (.43) is higher than in any other instance. On five of the six issues—all but foreign aid—party identification meant something by 1968 other than a traditional reaffirmation: it was now related to the policy preferences of the voter.

A second change is evident in the awareness of party differences on these six policy questions. In 1956, the Survey Research Center found little awareness of differences. It subjected its respondents to a series of questions on each policy question. It eliminated those who had no interest in, or opinion on, an issue, as well as those who, holding an opinion on the issue, could not decide if "the government is going too far, doing less than it should, or what?" This latter question typically eliminated more respondents than the query on the issue itself. Those who were left after the multiple screening were then asked whether there was a difference between the parties. This remaining sample was presumably a relatively knowledgeable group, but in 1956 even *they* found rather little distinction between the parties on most issues.[19] In later surveys, the question on the government's program was eliminated. Therefore, the remaining sample asked to differentiate the parties was larger, and presumably less informed. Nevertheless, they perceived more of a difference between the parties.

This changing awareness is seen in Table 2.2. Over time, the parties have come to be seen as more different on questions of federal government power. Again, the issue of foreign aid is exceptional. The critical effect of the 1964 election is evident once more, as the proportions seeing party differences changed most dramatically in the Goldwater-Johnson contest. In 1968, there was a regression downward toward lessened perceptions of party splits, although it was not a full regression. Only on the distinct issue of foreign aid was the perception of party difference in 1968 at or below the level of the Eisenhower period. For the other issues, during the decade of the 1960s, a significant and apparently enduring political lesson was learned about the existence of party differences. The lesson was particularly well learned by the stronger partisans. On virtually all issues and in all elections, the strong partisans were more likely to see party differences than were weak partisans, who in turn were more likely to see differences than independents. These results clearly accord with the concept and significance of party identification.

A more important finding is involved in the third change, relating to the ideological identity of the parties. In 1956, even among the sample remaining after various filterings, there was relatively little consensus on the position of the parties. The greatest consensus existed on another question dealing with ownership of electric power and housing. On this item, three-fourths of those who saw a party difference also agreed that the Republicans were more favorable to private ownership of these industries.[20] The identification of the parties' ideological positions was lower on the six issues we are considering. (The item on power and housing was not used in later surveys, so it cannot be analyzed here.)

By 1968, as seen in Table 2.3, each of the two parties seemed to have a much clearer identity. The proportion seeing the Democrats as the more liberal or activist party had risen on every question, even on foreign aid. It is particularly significant that in almost all cases the perceptions of the parties showed a consensus greater than that which existed on the exceptional issue of ownership of industry in the Eisenhower period. By 1968, in other words, to judge by six important items, the majority of the electorate had become more aware of party differences and had come to agree that the Democratic party was the liberal party.[21]

The change in perceptions of the parties' positions is not affected by controls for party identification. In all partisan groups, the Democrats were in-

## TABLE 2.2
## Perceptions of Parties on Policy Issues, by Party Identification

| Group | Existence of Party Differences | | | | | | | | | | | |
|---|---|---|---|---|---|---|---|---|---|---|---|---|
| | Aid to Education | | | | Medical Care | | | | Job Guarantee | | | |
| | '56 | '60 | '64 | '68 | '56 | '60 | '64 | '68 | '56 | '60 | '64 | '68 |
| | *(Percentages of Those with Opinions Perceiving Party Differences)* | | | | | | | | | | | |
| Strong Democrat | 58.1 | 62.8 | 73.8 | 75.7 | 63.2 | 68.6 | 86.4 | 85.8 | 73.0 | 74.5 | 80.3 | 78.1 |
| Weak Democrat | 44.2 | 53.2 | 60.9 | 53.0 | 48.9 | 59.0 | 77.2 | 71.2 | 54.2 | 66.3 | 69.3 | 65.4 |
| Independent | 43.4 | 52.3 | 53.5 | 48.0 | 41.2 | 45.3 | 77.4 | 62.3 | 36.4 | 57.6 | 55.2 | 54.2 |
| Weak Republican | 48.0 | 41.8 | 58.9 | 53.3 | 50.0 | 68.6 | 75.3 | 65.8 | 50.3 | 50.5 | 61.3 | 64.1 |
| Strong Republican | 59.0 | 63.0 | 78.4 | 73.3 | 64.9 | 66.7 | 87.7 | 75.9 | 63.7 | 42.5 | 76.7 | 79.1 |
| Total Sample | 52 | 55 | 66 | 59 | 54 | 58 | 82 | 71 | 55 | 64 | 70 | 63 |

| Group | Fair Employment | | | | School Integration | | | | Foreign Aid | | | |
|---|---|---|---|---|---|---|---|---|---|---|---|---|
| | '56 | '60 | '64 | '68 | '56 | '60 | '64 | '68 | '56 | '60 | '64 | '68 |
| | *(Percentages of Those with Opinions Perceiving Party Differences)* | | | | | | | | | | | |
| Strong Democrat | 50.0 | 52.5 | 77.5 | 78.5 | 55.6 | 50.6 | 70.0 | 75.9 | 46.5 | 44.7 | 61.5 | 64.7 |
| Weak Democrat | 46.9 | 38.7 | 70.1 | 64.9 | 55.6 | 34.9 | 63.7 | 62.5 | 40.4 | 37.5 | 52.7 | 43.8 |
| Independent | 38.5 | 38.7 | 58.8 | 55.0 | 42.3 | 30.8 | 59.0 | 51.1 | 33.6 | 32.7 | 50.8 | 39.3 |
| Weak Republican | 46.0 | 44.3 | 53.2 | 47.7 | 50.0 | 36.4 | 52.1 | 53.1 | 50.0 | 32.0 | 50.3 | 42.8 |
| Strong Republican | 52.3 | 50.0 | 75.0 | 60.5 | 57.5 | 39.2 | 66.2 | 60.5 | 63.9 | 47.4 | 61.8 | 48.0 |
| Total Sample | 47 | 44 | 69 | 62 | 51 | 36 | 64 | 60 | 49 | 39 | 56 | 46 |

## TABLE 2.3
## Consensus on Positions of Parties on Policy Issues, by Party Identification

| Group | Consensus on Party Positions | | | | | | | | | | | |
|---|---|---|---|---|---|---|---|---|---|---|---|---|
| | Aid to Education | | | | Medical Care | | | | Job Guarantee | | | |
| | '56 | '60 | '64 | '68 | '56 | '60 | '64 | '68 | '56 | '60 | '64 | '68 |
| | *(Percentage of Those Perceiving Difference Selecting Democrats as Liberal)* | | | | | | | | | | | |
| Strong Democrat | 90.5 | 95.2 | 96.5 | 94.1 | 93.9 | 95.8 | 98.2 | 98.8 | 85.5 | 98.8 | 98.8 | 97.0 |
| Weak Democrat | 86.5 | 90.5 | 93.6 | 82.6 | 84.6 | 90.4 | 95.8 | 88.7 | 71.8 | 93.3 | 93.9 | 88.5 |
| Independent | 66.3 | 74.6 | 83.8 | 64.3 | 76.4 | 87.7 | 93.5 | 82.7 | 61.9 | 82.3 | 89.3 | 71.4 |
| Weak Republican | 37.2 | 60.9 | 55.8 | 58.7 | 64.3 | 52.2 | 77.6 | 85.0 | 60.0 | 67.3 | 72.5 | 69.4 |
| Strong Republican | 31.6 | 47.9 | 55.0 | 41.2 | 57.8 | 51.3 | 79.8 | 63.6 | 47.0 | 32.3 | 63.8 | 53.9 |
| Total Sample | 67 | 76 | 81 | 73 | 77 | 81 | 92 | 87 | 69 | 80 | 88 | 80 |

| Group | Fair Employment | | | | School Integration | | | | Foreign Aid | | | |
|---|---|---|---|---|---|---|---|---|---|---|---|---|
| | '56 | '60 | '64 | '68 | '56 | '60 | '64 | '68 | '56 | '60 | '64 | '68 |
| | *(Percentage of Those Perceiving Difference Selecting Democrats as Liberal)* | | | | | | | | | | | |
| Strong Democrat | 64.6 | 83.5 | 96.9 | 97.3 | 39.1 | 34.7 | 96.2 | 95.3 | 57.1 | 80.9 | 98.1 | 93.0 |
| Weak Democrat | 63.6 | 65.5 | 93.9 | 88.3 | 51.5 | 42.5 | 90.3 | 87.1 | 53.0 | 60.2 | 94.2 | 89.2 |
| Independent | 49.4 | 53.4 | 89.5 | 75.6 | 45.8 | 46.4 | 91.8 | 83.4 | 54.5 | 46.8 | 88.1 | 83.1 |
| Weak Republican | 23.6 | 18.3 | 81.0 | 70.2 | 45.1 | 49.3 | 83.9 | 75.4 | 46.2 | 13.0 | 67.8 | 81.5 |
| Strong Republican | 6.0 | 17.2 | 67.6 | 56.4 | 59.4 | 48.5 | 71.3 | 69.5 | 29.3 | 21.4 | 70.8 | 61.6 |
| Total Sample | 48 | 52 | 89 | 83 | 48 | 44 | 89 | 86 | 43 | 49 | 88 | 85 |

creasingly recognized as the liberal party on each of the six issues. Democrats were most likely to make this judgment, but by 1964 a majority even of Strong Republicans recognized the liberal credentials of the opposition. In 1956, by contrast, the Strong Republicans conceded this "honor" to the Democrats on only two issues.

The acceptance of the liberalism of the Democrats is most evident in the 1964 survey, conducted during the contest of Goldwater and Johnson. It was not solely related to that election, however, for important changes in perceptions of party position on the economic issues of aid to education, medical care, and job guarantees can be located as early as the 1960 campaign. The identification of the Democratic party as the liberal faction largely persisted through the 1968 election as well, although there was some lessening of perceived party positions, most notably on the issue of federal aid to education.

The most striking change occurred on racial issues. In 1956, there was no consensus on the parties' stands on the issues of school integration and fair employment. Differences between the parties were less likely to be seen, and Republicans were as likely as Democrats to be perceived as favoring federal action on civil rights. A startling reversal occurred in 1964: all partisan groups recognized the existence of a difference on this issue, and all were convinced that the Democrats stood more for government programs on behalf of blacks. Even Strong Republicans conceded the point they argued in the Eisenhower years. The identification of the Democrats with civil rights was slightly attenuated in 1968, but it still was a clearer perception than existed on any other issue.

## Sources of Change

What accounts for these shifts? The increasing correspondence of party identification with policy preferences is probably related to the new perceptions of the parties as holding relatively distinctive and identifiable positions on these issues. Generational change is one possible explanation of these new perceptions. Younger, more ideologically attuned voters may have replaced older and less sensitive electors. To test this possibility, age is controlled in Table 2.4. Respondents in the age groupings used in the 1956 survey are compared to cohorts four, eight, and twelve years older in 1960, 1964, and 1968, respectively. If generational replacement is the main reason for the changed perceptions, the greatest differences would be seen between the upper-right and lower-left segments of each set of percentages. If political aging is not an explanation, changes would be most evident among cohort groups.[22]

The data show that both conclusions are valid to some extent but that generational turnover is not an adequate explanation in itself. In virtually all comparisons, the new generation (below age 23 in 1964 or below age 27 in

## TABLE 2.4
## Perceptions of Parties on Policy Issues, by Age

Existence of Party Differences

| Group | | Aid to Education | | | | Medical Care | | | |
|---|---|---|---|---|---|---|---|---|---|
| Age in '56 | Age in '68 | '56 | '60 | '64 | '68 | '56 | '60 | '64 | '68 |
| | | *(Percentages of Those with Opinions Perceiving Party Differences)* | | | | | | | |
| ——— | Under 27 | — | — | 60.0 | 52.2 | — | — | 84.7 | 64.6 |
| Under 25 | 27–36 | 49.1 | 67.2 | 58.4 | 56.7 | 57.8 | 74.0 | 83.9 | 68.7 |
| 25–34 | 37–46 | 49.1 | 45.7 | 65.3 | 59.8 | 49.0 | 51.4 | 82.5 | 77.8 |
| 35–44 | 47–56 | 45.2 | 53.1 | 72.7 | 62.9 | 50.2 | 66.1 | 81.0 | 68.6 |
| 45–54 | 57–66 | 53.3 | 58.0 | 65.9 | 59.6 | 54.0 | 52.0 | 76.6 | 71.4 |
| 55–64 | Over 66 | 52.2 | 58.8 | 55.2 | 56.5 | 59.0 | 58.0 | 78.1 | 74.9 |
| 65 and over | ——— | 54.0 | 59.3 | — | — | 53.5 | 52.6 | — | — |

| Group | | Job Guarantee | | | | Fair Employment | | | |
|---|---|---|---|---|---|---|---|---|---|
| Age in '56 | Age in '68 | '56 | '60 | '64 | '68 | '56 | '60 | '64 | '68 |
| | | *(Percentages of Those with Opinions Perceiving Party Differences)* | | | | | | | |
| ——— | Under 27 | — | — | 65.8 | 65.8 | — | — | 78.1 | 60.5 |
| Under 25 | 27–36 | 46.6 | 68.7 | 66.0 | 61.5 | 50.7 | 57.3 | 69.9 | 64.3 |
| 25–34 | 37–46 | 55.3 | 66.3 | 73.0 | 70.8 | 51.5 | 37.8 | 68.1 | 63.3 |
| 35–44 | 47–56 | 49.5 | 66.0 | 68.2 | 74.6 | 44.1 | 39.0 | 66.3 | 65.0 |
| 45–54 | 57–66 | 58.0 | 62.3 | 71.8 | 62.2 | 50.2 | 48.5 | 66.8 | 54.0 |
| 55–64 | Over 66 | 63.9 | 59.0 | 66.2 | 70.3 | 39.1 | 42.6 | 65.6 | 58.2 |
| 65 and over | ——— | 58.8 | 54.5 | — | — | 52.7 | 46.7 | — | — |

| Group | | School Integration | | | | Foreign Aid | | | |
|---|---|---|---|---|---|---|---|---|---|
| Age in '56 | Age in '68 | '56 | '60 | '64 | '68 | '56 | '60 | '64 | '68 |
| | | *(Percentages of Those with Opinions Perceiving Party Differences)* | | | | | | | |
| ——— | Under 27 | — | — | 75.6 | 56.2 | — | — | 54.5 | 42.2 |
| Under 25 | 27–36 | 58.2 | 41.1 | 67.1 | 59.6 | 42.5 | 42.3 | 55.1 | 39.2 |
| 25–34 | 37–46 | 52.7 | 38.4 | 61.6 | 65.4 | 48.8 | 38.9 | 60.6 | 49.3 |
| 35–44 | 47–56 | 50.2 | 46.6 | 64.9 | 57.7 | 40.4 | 37.4 | 55.0 | 47.5 |
| 45–54 | 57–66 | 49.3 | 40.6 | 61.9 | 61.3 | 44.5 | 37.8 | 55.6 | 47.2 |
| 55–64 | Over 66 | 53.1 | 28.5 | 54.7 | 56.9 | 44.9 | 33.0 | 54.8 | 50.6 |
| 65 and over | ——— | 50.0 | 34.4 | — | — | 47.2 | 46.6 | — | — |

TABLE 2.4 (*Continued*)

| Group | | Consensus on Party Positions: Aid to Education | | | | Medical Care | | | |
|---|---|---|---|---|---|---|---|---|---|
| Age in '56 | Age in '68 | '56 | '60 | '64 | '68 | '56 | '60 | '64 | '68 |
| | | *(Percentages of Those Perceiving Differences Selecting Democrats as Liberal)* | | | | | | | |
| ——— | Under 27 | — | — | 89.9 | 65.6 | — | — | 96.7 | 86.0 |
| Under 25 | 27–36 | 51.8 | 77.9 | 86.2 | 72.3 | 73.8 | 82.4 | 92.2 | 88.6 |
| 25–34 | 37–46 | 66.0 | 73.5 | 84.8 | 79.4 | 78.9 | 89.4 | 94.1 | 91.5 |
| 35–44 | 47–56 | 75.8 | 74.6 | 77.4 | 67.0 | 81.6 | 80.0 | 87.5 | 87.6 |
| 45–54 | 57–66 | 69.7 | 90.2 | 86.5 | 73.1 | 80.2 | 82.7 | 95.5 | 83.3 |
| 55–64 | Over 66 | 67.1 | 72.6 | 74.0 | 73.1 | 72.0 | 71.3 | 90.6 | 80.8 |
| 65 and over | ——— | 51.8 | 60.8 | — | — | 64.5 | 75.9 | — | — |

| Group | | Job Guarantee | | | | Fair Employment | | | |
|---|---|---|---|---|---|---|---|---|---|
| Age in '56 | Age in '68 | '56 | '60 | '64 | '68 | '56 | '60 | '64 | '68 |
| | | *(Percentages of Those Perceiving Differences Selecting Democrats as Liberal)* | | | | | | | |
| ——— | Under 27 | — | — | 92.0 | 79.0 | — | — | 93.6 | 83.7 |
| Under 25 | 27–36 | 76.0 | 82.6 | 92.7 | 78.3 | 54.7 | 55.4 | 93.0 | 83.0 |
| 25–34 | 37–46 | 65.0 | 82.4 | 88.5 | 85.9 | 43.6 | 52.5 | 88.3 | 83.5 |
| 35–44 | 47–56 | 72.2 | 81.6 | 85.4 | 66.7 | 42.7 | 45.3 | 85.8 | 84.7 |
| 45–54 | 57–66 | 65.8 | 85.2 | 89.0 | 83.9 | 53.0 | 63.1 | 91.5 | 82.0 |
| 55–64 | Over 66 | 62.5 | 72.1 | 90.8 | 74.5 | 48.0 | 42.0 | 89.3 | 75.6 |
| 65 and over | ——— | 71.4 | 64.9 | — | — | 47.7 | 56.2 | — | — |

| Group | | School Integration | | | | Foreign Aid | | | |
|---|---|---|---|---|---|---|---|---|---|
| Age in '56 | Age in '68 | '56 | '60 | '64 | '68 | '56 | '60 | '64 | '68 |
| | | *(Percentages of Those Perceiving Differences Selecting Democrats as Liberal)* | | | | | | | |
| ——— | Under 27 | — | — | 91.2 | 85.5 | — | — | 87.5 | 85.2 |
| Under 25 | 27–36 | 50.0 | 34.9 | 92.6 | 84.5 | 34.8 | 50.0 | 90.6 | 85.8 |
| 25–34 | 37–46 | 42.6 | 44.6 | 92.0 | 90.0 | 60.1 | 44.0 | 88.1 | 87.7 |
| 35–44 | 47–56 | 46.8 | 40.0 | 85.8 | 85.3 | 40.6 | 46.0 | 86.5 | 85.9 |
| 45–54 | 57–66 | 51.0 | 50.0 | 90.0 | 84.6 | 48.1 | 60.1 | 88.0 | 83.2 |
| 55–64 | Over 66 | 57.2 | 35.2 | 86.9 | 79.6 | 47.3 | 50.0 | 83.7 | 80.5 |
| 65 and over | ——— | 49.0 | 52.3 | — | — | 38.6 | 46.0 | — | — |

1968) was more aware of party differences and more perceptive of Democratic liberalism than those it replaced (those 65 or older in 1956, or 69 or older in 1960, who were too depleted by 1964 and 1968 to be included). These differences are not as large, however, as are the changes of matched cohorts. Some political learning occurred in all age groups. Thus, in 1956 and 1960, most age groups did not see a party difference on racial issues, and all of them tended to identify the Republicans as more liberal. Particularly in 1964 and even in 1968, all age groups came to perceive a party difference, and there was intergenerational agreement on the Democratic party's greater support of fair employment and school integration.

The data give some indication of greater growth in awareness among older, rather than younger voters. The cohort aged 25–34 in 1956 (37 to 46 in 1968) appears to have become particularly aware of Democratic liberalism in 1964 and to have held to its new perceptions in 1968. Speculating on the source of this change, we could note that this group came of age politically just after the realignment of the New Deal. Hence this group may not have been immediately affected by the political events of that period but may have been particularly susceptible to the effect of similar issues in 1964.

Degree of educational achievement might be an alternative explanation. The average level of schooling has increased considerably in the United States in this twelve-year period. Greater perception might result from the intellectual upgrading of the population, with less informed grade school or high school graduates being replaced by informed college alumni. Controlling for education would reveal this effect by indicating relatively little change by educational level. This control is presented in Table 2.5, which clearly shows that educational upgrading does not explain the shift in perceptions. Awareness has increased at all educational levels.

In fact, the disparities in perceptions among persons of varying schooling have tended to lessen, particularly in regard to identifying the Democrats as the liberal party. This effect was most marked in the 1964 campaign; in that year, on every issue, respondents with only a grade school education were clearer in their perceptions of the parties than college graduates were in 1956. The educational gap widened slightly in 1968, but the level of awareness remained substantially higher in all educational strata. In one sense, therefore, the political events of this period provided a tax-free learning substitute for the political education that might otherwise have occurred in high school and college classrooms. (The vocational implications for political science faculty members might best be left aside.)

A final control may be made for region and race, as in Table 2.6 since the changed perceptions noted above may have been concentrated in particular segments of the population. Such differences are evident in Table 2.6, although the changes are also apparent in both the North and South, and among

TABLE 2.5
**Perceptions of Parties on Policy Issues, by Education**

| | Existence of Party Differences | | | | | | | | | | | |
|---|---|---|---|---|---|---|---|---|---|---|---|---|
| | Aid to Education | | | | Medical Care | | | | Job Guarantee | | | |
| Group | '56 | '60 | '64 | '68 | '56 | '60 | '64 | '68 | '56 | '60 | '64 | '68 |
| | *(Percentages of those With Opinions Perceiving Party Differences)* | | | | | | | | | | | |
| Elementary School | 45.7 | 51.8 | 61.6 | 56.1 | 49.2 | 53.4 | 76.0 | 70.7 | 59.9 | 65.3 | 68.8 | 63.7 |
| High School | 52.2 | 55.4 | 61.6 | 53.0 | 50.0 | 60.0 | 80.6 | 68.0 | 52.3 | 71.2 | 65.5 | 61.4 |
| Some College | 49.0 | 58.2 | 66.9 | 61.7 | 57.0 | 63.8 | 84.3 | 68.9 | 48.1 | 56.4 | 71.2 | 68.1 |
| College Graduate | 65.2 | 60.2 | 73.2 | 67.4 | 61.7 | 63.9 | 87.8 | 84.1 | 55.2 | 56.5 | 71.9 | 74.9 |
| | Fair Employment | | | | School Integration | | | | Foreign Aid | | | |
| Group | '56 | '60 | '64 | '68 | '56 | '60 | '64 | '68 | '56 | '60 | '64 | '68 |
| | *(Percentages of those With Opinions Perceiving Party Differences)* | | | | | | | | | | | |
| Elementary School | 47.2 | 45.9 | 68.2 | 62.5 | 50.0 | 35.2 | 63.3 | 61.9 | 40.2 | 39.0 | 51.0 | 46.3 |
| High School | 49.1 | 36.3 | 67.7 | 61.2 | 54.1 | 37.3 | 61.3 | 57.1 | 43.1 | 35.5 | 54.8 | 47.5 |
| Some College | 46.5 | 48.3 | 67.5 | 63.1 | 51.7 | 34.4 | 66.7 | 60.2 | 47.1 | 42.3 | 55.7 | 42.2 |
| College Graduate | 44.3 | 44.4 | 65.8 | 57.6 | 51.8 | 41.2 | 58.9 | 61.7 | 62.0 | 36.5 | 68.3 | 51.6 |
| | Consensus on Party Positions | | | | | | | | | | | |
| | Aid to Education | | | | Medical Care | | | | Job Guarantee | | | |
| Group | '56 | '60 | '64 | '68 | '56 | '60 | '64 | '68 | '56 | '60 | '64 | '68 |
| | *(Percentage of those Perceiving Difference Selecting Democrats as Liberal)* | | | | | | | | | | | |
| Elementary School | 65.7 | 71.8 | 86.4 | 75.0 | 70.9 | 75.3 | 92.7 | 84.0 | 68.8 | 78.0 | 90.1 | 82.0 |
| High School | 62.3 | 73.9 | 77.6 | 70.3 | 75.5 | 85.0 | 90.3 | 87.0 | 69.9 | 83.6 | 87.2 | 76.2 |
| Some College | 67.5 | 78.9 | 77.4 | 71.6 | 82.9 | 81.1 | 89.4 | 86.4 | 65.0 | 80.0 | 85.6 | 79.2 |
| College Graduate | 75.8 | 88.7 | 86.9 | 75.8 | 89.0 | 93.9 | 95.4 | 92.0 | 72.2 | 82.9 | 90.0 | 84.4 |
| | Fair Employment | | | | School Integration | | | | Foreign Aid | | | |
| Group | '56 | '60 | '64 | '68 | '56 | '60 | '64 | '68 | '56 | '60 | '64 | '68 |
| | *(Percentage of those Perceiving Difference Selecting Democrats as Liberal)* | | | | | | | | | | | |
| Elementary School | 49.7 | 53.7 | 91.6 | 79.7 | 45.5 | 51.5 | 87.2 | 84.8 | 46.5 | 47.8 | 88.4 | 84.8 |
| High School | 53.0 | 63.8 | 88.5 | 81.3 | 44.5 | 41.7 | 91.2 | 83.3 | 40.6 | 58.2 | 86.0 | 83.5 |
| Some College | 39.2 | 44.0 | 85.3 | 83.6 | 51.0 | 36.7 | 87.0 | 87.7 | 51.0 | 40.5 | 83.6 | 84.3 |
| College Graduate | 46.5 | 39.5 | 91.3 | 88.9 | 56.0 | 35.8 | 96.6 | 87.0 | 56.0 | 54.8 | 97.2 | 86.4 |

## TABLE 2.6
## Perceptions of Parties on Policy Issues, by Region and Race

Existence of Party Differences

| Group | Aid to Education | | | | Medical Care | | | | Job Guarantee | | | |
|---|---|---|---|---|---|---|---|---|---|---|---|---|
| | '56 | '60 | '64 | '68 | '56 | '60 | '64 | '68 | '56 | '60 | '64 | '68 |
| | (Percentages of Those With Opinions Perceiving Party Differences) | | | | | | | | | | | |
| North White | 48.0 | 57.3 | 61.1 | 58.0 | 51.2 | 53.6 | 81.1 | 71.5 | 52.4 | 63.2 | 66.4 | 65.2 |
| North Black | 66.7 | 80.0 | 71.8 | 72.6 | 61.5 | 57.9 | 83.3 | 79.2 | 75.0 | 79.0 | 78.8 | 77.0 |
| South White | 51.0 | 49.3 | 68.8 | 50.2 | 54.6 | 57.6 | 78.3 | 65.3 | 61.5 | 62.2 | 69.8 | 61.0 |
| South Black | 62.4 | 50.8 | 80.8 | 87.7 | 54.7 | 45.7 | 83.3 | 88.1 | 64.5 | 68.3 | 81.8 | 90.9 |

| Group | Fair Employment | | | | School Integration | | | | Foreign Aid | | | |
|---|---|---|---|---|---|---|---|---|---|---|---|---|
| | '56 | '60 | '64 | '68 | '56 | '60 | '64 | '68 | '56 | '60 | '64 | '68 |
| | (Percentages of Those With Opinions Perceiving Party Differences) | | | | | | | | | | | |
| North White | 43.2 | 44.2 | 63.5 | 59.2 | 49.5 | 37.3 | 59.2 | 57.6 | 43.3 | 36.2 | 53.2 | 45.0 |
| North Black | 79.5 | 73.2 | 88.2 | 87.5 | 57.5 | 57.2 | 85.7 | 81.2 | 43.5 | 50.9 | 57.8 | 45.1 |
| South White | 52.7 | 36.4 | 67.4 | 56.1 | 57.0 | 30.6 | 64.3 | 56.0 | 49.7 | 39.1 | 57.9 | 44.9 |
| South Black | 70.0 | 60.0 | 89.3 | 89.9 | 58.5 | 46.0 | 82.2 | 88.1 | 61.8 | 38.1 | 63.3 | 75.0 |

Consensus on Party Positions

| Group | Aid to Education | | | | Medical Care | | | | Job Guarantee | | | |
|---|---|---|---|---|---|---|---|---|---|---|---|---|
| | '56 | '60 | '64 | '68 | '56 | '60 | '64 | '68 | '56 | '60 | '64 | '68 |
| | (Percentage of Those Perceiving Difference Selecting Democrats as Liberal) | | | | | | | | | | | |
| North White | 66.4 | 75.9 | 81.2 | 68.0 | 74.8 | 81.7 | 93.1 | 87.0 | 66.0 | 78.8 | 88.8 | 79.0 |
| North Black | 77.2 | 84.4 | 100.0 | 95.0 | 81.2 | 91.0 | 97.5 | 100.0 | 76.0 | 91.1 | 97.3 | 96.0 |
| South White | 63.8 | 80.8 | 74.3 | 70.0 | 81.9 | 79.3 | 83.6 | 79.0 | 67.4 | 82.5 | 81.3 | 72.4 |
| South Black | 75.0 | 53.3 | 98.4 | 100.0 | 82.3 | 71.4 | 98.7 | 98.2 | 80.0 | 86.1 | 98.6 | 100.0 |

| Group | Fair Employment | | | | School Integration | | | | Foreign Aid | | | |
|---|---|---|---|---|---|---|---|---|---|---|---|---|
| | '56 | '60 | '64 | '68 | '56 | '60 | '64 | '68 | '56 | '60 | '64 | '68 |
| | (Percentage of Those Perceiving Difference Selecting Democrats as Liberal) | | | | | | | | | | | |
| North White | 47.1 | 78.8 | 88.8 | 81.1 | 54.2 | 48.3 | 91.2 | 84.0 | 45.2 | 52.2 | 89.5 | 84.1 |
| North Black | 65.7 | 83.7 | 98.0 | 100.0 | 60.8 | 32.1 | 100.0 | 100.0 | 70.0 | 57.1 | 84.6 | 86.9 |
| South White | 34.8 | 48.0 | 79.0 | 75.0 | 34.4 | 37.4 | 77.5 | 79.6 | 45.7 | 41.4 | 83.2 | 82.4 |
| South Black | 60.6 | 53.8 | 100.0 | 100.0 | 35.3 | 17.6 | 100.0 | 100.0 | 61.5 | 43.8 | 100.0 | 100.0 |

whites as well as blacks. Southern whites particularly stand out. Their perceptions varied widely over the course of the four elections, but the net result has been relatively little change in their awareness of party differences or in their ideological identifications of the parties. They changed almost exclusively in their identification of the Democrats as the more liberal party on issues of civil rights. These changing perceptions may well be related to the growth of Republican voting in the white South.[23]

Blacks' opinions also varied widely, but the net result has been a substantially increased awareness of party differences and a clear identification of the Democrats as the liberal party. While this change is most dramatically evident on the civil rights issues, and among southern blacks, it is not confined to these issues or to the former Confederacy. Negroes of both regions also became more cognizant of differences between the parties and of Democratic liberalism on economic issues. It is interesting to note, moreover, that within each region in all years, blacks tended to be more conscious of political differences than whites. Given their perceptions of increasing differences between the parties, it is not surprising that blacks now overwhelmingly identify with and vote for the Democrats.[24]

There is no obvious demographic cause for the changed awareness of party differences by the electorate. Neither the passing of generations, nor improved education, nor regional and racial variations provides a simple explanation. The fact remains that, during these twelve years, all segments of the population displayed considerable political learning (or misperception, depending on one's view of the "real" character of the parties). The alternative to a demographic explanation is a directly political one: the events and campaigns of the 1960s, I suggest, made politics more relevant and more dramatic to the mass electorate. In the process, party differences were developed and perceived. Democrats divided from Republicans, Democrats became more liberal, and voters became more aware.

There are many correspondences between the events of the political world and the voters' perceptions of the parties. In the 1960 campaign, John Kennedy and Richard Nixon, and the Democratic and Republican platforms, differed on federal aid to education[25]—and the voters became more likely to regard the Democrats' position on the issue as the more liberal. Medicare became a major partisan issue during the Kennedy administration, resulting in a series of partisan Congressional roll calls on the issue, and a platform conflict during the 1964 campaign. Perceiving this disagreement, the voters were much more likely in 1964 to see a difference between the parties on the issue of medical care and to identify the Democrats as more favorable to governmental action on the issue. When a Republican administration acted vigorously to promote school integration, as in Little Rock, the voters tended to believe that the G.O.P. was more favorable to this policy. This opinion was particularly common in 1956 and 1960 among Southerners and blacks. When a Democratic administration came to support new civil rights legislation, when it sent marshals and National Guardsmen to desegregate the University of Alabama and the University of Mississippi, when it reacted sympathetically to the protests of Martin Luther King in Birmingham and Selma, the voters drew the conclusion that there was a difference between the parties and identified the Democrats as more favorable to the cause of the Negroes. When the Republican party adopted a ''Southern strategy'' in 1968 and its candidate largely ignored the issue of civil rights, the voters continued to hold this position and clearly to distinguish the parties.[26]

The most important electoral event of this period appears to be the 1964 Presidential campaign. Senator Barry Goldwater consciously sought to clarify and widen the ideological differences between the parties. The evidence presented here indicates that he accomplished his goal, although it did not benefit the Republican party. Voters, previously unable to see differences between the parties, learned the lesson of ''a choice, not an echo.'' They accepted the Senator's characterization of the Republicans as conservative and the Democrats as liberal, and, on the specific issues involved, they preferred the liberal alternative.[27] This process of education was not confined to the insightful young, or to the formally trained college population, or to committed white segregationists and black integrationists. This political education was general and apparently persistent. The party characteristics which had been so clearly marked in 1964 remained relatively evident to the voters four years later. The lessons remained learned even though differences between the candidates had narrowed considerably, and although some of the previous issues, such as aid to education and medical care, had been partially resolved. Differences were not perceived as clearly in 1968 as in 1964, but they were far more apparent to the voters than in the Eisenhower years.

## Implications of the Data

The data developed in this article lead to three implications. First, the central importance of the 1964 campaign lends support to the supposition that this election was a critical election, initiating a new political era in the United States, rather than the aberrant event it appeared at the time. A critical election, such as that of the New Deal, is one in which a deep and enduring cleavage in the electorate becomes evident.[28] Characteristic of such elections is increased voter consciousness of policy questions, and the later electoral persistence of group divisions based on the policy questions raised in the critical election.[29] These hallmarks of a critical period are evident in the upsurge of mass perceptions of party differences in 1964 and the persistence of these perceptions in 1968. While the voters did not respond ideologically in the full sense of the term, they did respond to the specific issues presented to them, and they did align their partisan loyalties far closer to their policy preferences. Such readjustments occur rarely, but they are the decisive moments in American political history.

Research at the time of the 1964 election led to the conclusion the electorate did not respond primarily in ideological terms,[30] although there already were signs available that deeper forces were moving the voters.[31] Subsequent work by younger scholars, perhaps less committed to prevailing commonplaces, has shown the growth of ideological constraints and divergent "party images" during the turbulent decade of the 1960s.[32] Moreover, the most current controversies are tending to emphasize the ideological division between the parties. Partisan conflicts on such issues as national health insurance, federal revenue sharing, or enforcement of equal employment opportunities are likely to reinforce the popular belief that Democrats favor increased federal government action and Republicans prefer private or state governmental action.[33] Perceptions of party differences are therefore likely to be confirmed and extended.

Confirming evidence is needed to demonstrate a critical election in 1964. Such evidence would include shifts in party identification among substantial groups of voters and the emergence of new issues. The data presented here do not speak to these questions. Indeed, they deal only with issues already evident in 1956. We do find, however, increased coherence of policy positions within each party following, and new sharp cleavages associated with racial issues. These findings are congruent with those expected in a period of realignment.

Clarification and realignment of the parties' policy positions leads to a second implication, the possible development of a "responsible two-party system" in the United States. Such a system was advocated by a committee of the American Political Science Association in 1950.[34] That committee, however, expected more of voters than was possible at the time. To effectuate the system of party government advocated in the APSA *Report*, the voter must perceive a relationship between his policy preferences and his partisan choices. Furthermore, for the parties to serve as links between voter preferences and public policies, their programs must be perceived as somewhat distinct and reasonably clear. These are necessary but not sufficient conditions for developing a responsible party system in which parties put forth programs, receive popular approval of these programs, and then carry out the popular mandate.

That these conditions did not exist at the time of the APSA *Report* is indicated by our data for the 1956 election. On most issues, the voters did not relate their policy preferences to their partisan affiliations nor did they see a difference between the parties, nor did they agree on the relative positions of the two parties. In recent years, however, the situation has changed. There is a sizeable statistical correlation now between party identification and policy preference on the particular issues studied. Voters now do see a difference between Democrats and Republicans and agree on their ideological character.

Parties can now meaningfully stand as "groups of like-minded men" offering particular stances toward public issues. Their victories in elections can now reasonably be interpreted as related to the mass choice of one set of issue positions over another. To this extent, the conditions for a responsible party system have been fulfilled.

Other necessary conditions, however, have not been met. Greater voter awareness of party differences does not in itself create a mandating election system. It would also be necessary to show that votes are actually cast *because of* issue preferences. Moreover, a responsible party system requires not only a responsible electorate to provide direction, approval, or castigation for the parties. It also requires coherent, effective, and relatively disiplined parties. In fact, both in the APSA *Report* and in the British party system which its authors cited with admiration, party government is crucially dependent on the internal discipline of the parties, even more than on the electorate.[35] There is comparatively little evidence of the development of cohesive parties in the United States.[36] Many developments in fact have tended in the opposite direction, such as the diffusion of party power to wealthy individuals, media specialists, and campaign managers; the challenge to entrenched party leaders through party primaries and the decentralizing reforms of national conventions; and the separation of national, state, and local elections. The electorate is more ready today than in the 1950s for a responsible party system, but the parties may be too weakened for the task.

The final implication of the data relates to the study of American voting behavior. Because of the excellence with which the Michigan studies have been conducted and presented, we have tended to overgeneralize the findings of such studies as *The American Voter*. We have assumed that this superb analysis of the 1950s is a study of the electorate of all time. Because voters of the Eisenhower period did not respond to the parties in ideological terms, we have often concluded that they could not respond in such terms. Yet, Key reminded us that "the voice of the people is but an echo. . . . The people's verdict can be no more than a selective reflection from among the alternatives and outlooks presented to them."[37] If the parties do not emphasize issues, or do not present distinct and clear positions, the voters are unlikely to invent party programs. When there *are* party positions and differences, the voters can perceive them. Students of electoral behavior must be sensitive to these changing stimuli and reactions.

In observing electoral behavior and mass ideology, we particularly must beware of our own ideological biases. It is instructive to remember that *The*

*American Voter* was written at the time of "the great American celebration," when the dominant academic ideology was that the United States had reached the "end of ideology" through a consensual agreement on twentieth-century liberalism.[38] It was therefore comforting and appropriate to find that ideology was absent among the mass public. In the absence of ideology, basic social change was difficult to imagine. The existing political system was therefore seen as stable and relatively insulated from change. Throughout the Michigan studies, the emphasis is on the inertial elements of American politics, an emphasis that, in keeping with the tone of the era, plays down the possibility and desirability of basic social change.[39]

In the last decade, after a series of political shocks, ideological conflict has been resurrected, and consensus has been severely disrupted, if not destroyed. Basic issues have been raised again, and the electorate has shown itself able to comprehend and respond to such conflicts. Furthermore, an emphasis on ideological passivity is itself seen to be ideological. Earlier findings on the electorate remind us of the dangers of overgeneralization from data derived from a limited temporal or spatial context.

More generally, we must remember to be aware of the political context of voting behavior. Perhaps the major fault of the Michigan studies has been the comparative neglect of the political environment as an independent variable. The methodology of survey research has brought an overemphasis on the individual behavior of isolated respondents. The influences upon these respondents have been studied only indirectly, through the voters' personal perceptions and actions.[40] But voters in fact are not isolated, for they are affected by their environment,[41] the mass media, the economic system, and the prevailing ideology. More attention must be devoted to these shaping influences.

Most critically, we must emphasize in this context the effect upon voters of the stimuli they receive from the parties and other electoral actors. If these stimuli are issueless and static, as they largely were in the 1950s, the citizenry is likely to respond in the manner described in *The American Voter*. If these stimuli are more ideological and dynamic, we are likely to see different perceptions and behavior, such as that evidenced in the 1964 and 1968 elections.[42] "In the large the electorate behaves about as rationally and responsibly as we should expect, given the clarity of the alternatives presented to it and the character of the information available to it."[43] Confused voters reflect confused parties; clarity among the voters follows from clearheaded parties.

## Notes

1. The most important past works are, chronologically: Paul Lazarsfeld, Bernard Berelson, and Helen Gaudet, *The People's Choice*, 2nd ed. (New York: Columbia University Press, 1948); Bernard Berelson, Paul Lazarsfeld and William

McPhee, *Voting* (Chicago: University of Chicago Press, 1954); Angus Campbell, Gerald Gurin and Warren Miller, *The Voter Decides* (Evanston: Row, Peterson, 1954); Eugene Burdick and Arthur Brodbeck, eds., *American Voting Behavior* (New York: The Free Press, 1959); Campbell, Philip Converse, Warren Miller, and Donald Stokes, *The American Voter* (New York: Wiley, 1960); Ithiel de Sola Pool, Robert Abelson and Samuel Popkin, *Candidates, Issues and Strategies* (Cambridge: MIT Press, 1964); Philip Converse, "The Nature of Belief Systems in Mass Publics," in David Apter, ed., *Ideology and Discontent* (New York: The Free Press, 1964); and Campbell, Converse, Miller and Stokes, *Elections and the Political Order* (New York: Wiley, 1966).

2. V. O. Key, Jr., *Public Opinion and American Democracy* (New York: Knopf, 1961), chap. 4; Campbell et al., *The American Voter*, p. 174.
3. Campbell et al., *The American Voter*, p. 249.
4. Campbell et al., *The American Voter*, chap. 9.
5. Herbert McClosky, Paul J. Hoffman, and Rosemary O'Hara, "Issue Conflict and Consensus among Party Leaders and Followers," *American Political Science Review* 54 (June 1960), p. 419. Among party leaders, by contrast, differences existed on 23 of 24 issues.
6. Campbell et al., *The American Voter*, pp, 182–84.
7. Campbell et al., *The American Voter*, p. 544.
8. James M. Perry, *The New Politics* (New York: Clarkson Potter, 1968), p. 213.
9. Berelson, chap. 14.
10. V. O. Key, Jr., *The Responsible Electorate* (Cambridge: Harvard University Press, 1966), p. 7.
11. Arthur Goldberg, "Discerning a Causal Pattern among Data on Voting Behavior," *American Political Science Review* 60 (December 1966): 913–22; "Social Determinism and Rationality as Bases of Party Identification," *American Political Science Review* 63 (March 1969): 5–25.
12. Norman Luttbeg, "The Structure of Beliefs among Leaders and the Public," *Public Opinion Quarterly* 32 (Fall 1968): 398–409.
13. Steven R. Brown, "Consistency and the Persistence of Ideology," *Public Opinion Quarterly* 34 (Spring 1970): 60–68.
14. Robert Lane, *Political Ideology* (New York: The Free Press, 1960).
15. See John Plamenatz, "Electoral Studies and Democratic Theory: I. A British View," *Political Studies* 6 (February 1958): 9.

> A choice is reasonable, not because the chooser, when challenged, can give a satisfactory explanation of why he made it but because, if he could give an explanation, it would be satisfactory. The reasoning that lies behind the choice is often made in private language which the chooser never learns to translate into words intelligible to others because there is ordinarily no need for him to do so.

16. J. O. Field and R. E. Anderson, "Ideology in the Public's Conceptualization of the 1964 Election," *Public Opinion Quarterly* 3 (Fall 1969): 380–398. While the coding in this research differs somewhat from that of *The American Voter*, the changes were essentially those made necessary by new procedures of the Survey Research Center.
17. John G. Pierce, "Party Identification and the Changing Role of Ideology in American Politics," *Midwest Journal of Political Science* 14 (February 1970):

25–42. Confirming evidence is found in the recent work of David E. RePass, "Issue Salience and Party Choice," *American Political Science Review* 65 (June 1971): 389–400. Using responses to open-ended questions, RePass finds considerable mass concern for issues, an increase in issue awareness from 1960 to 1964, a close relationship between issue position and partisanship, and a significant partial correlation of .23 in 1964 between issue partianship and vote, controlling for candidate image and party identification.

18. The differences in wording consisted largely of changes in form. In 1956 and 1960, the questions were asked as statements with which the respondent could agree or disagree (and also indicate the intensity of his opinion), e.g., "If cities and towns around the country need help to build more schools, the government in Washington ought to give them the money they need." In 1964 and in 1968, the respondent was offered a choice between two policies, each of which was advocated by "some people," such as—"the government in Washington should help towns and cities provide education," or "this should be handled by the states and local communities." There are two differences in wording of possible substance. In 1956 and 1960, the question dealing with full employment asks whether or not "the government in Washington ought to see to it that everybody who wants to work has a job and a good standard of living," while the later alternative does not include "who wants to work." In the earlier surveys, the question on racial equality asks whether, "If Negroes are not getting fair treatment in jobs and housing, the government should see to it that they do," while in later years the question is more narrowly presented as dealing with jobs alone. I believe the basic thrust of these questions is not affected by these changes. The questions used are, by deck and column numbers, in 1956: 3/12, 3/18, 3/21, 3/24, 3/33, 3/54; in 1960: 4/59, 4/67, 4/55, 4/63, 4/72, 4/61; in 1964: 4/45, 4/56, 4/61, 5/11, 5/14, 4/67; in 1968: 4/54, 4/58, 4/60, 4/74, 4/76, 5/29. The surveys of 1948 and 1952 could not be used because questions were insufficiently comparable.
19. The answers of 1956 respondents can be found in Table 8–3 of Campbell et al., *The American Voter*, p. 182. It might be argued that 1956 voters were far more issue-conscious than the data reveal, but that they were thinking about different issues than those raised by the parties or the survey. This argument seems hardly plausible, since it would require a degree of ideological originality for which there is no evidence among any mass public.
20. Campbell et al., *The American Voter*, p. 182.
21. The perceptions of party are asked in different ways in the four surveys, so the data must be handled differently, In 1956, respondents were asked which party "is closer to what you want." To locate those who believe the Democrats are liberal on federal aid to education, for example, one must combine those who favor the policy, and think the Democrats are closer to their own position, with those who oppose the policy, and think the Republicans are closer. In 1960, 1964, and 1968, the question was asked in a straightforward manner, which party is likely to favor federal aid to education. These data are located, in 1956: two columns to the right of the policy question; in 1960: in decks and columns 4/60, 4/70, 4/56, 4/64, 4/75, 4/62; in 1964: 4/45, 4/60, 4/63, 5/13, 5/18, 4/69; in 1968: immediately after the policy questions except for party stands on school integration, 4/79.
22. On the method of cohort analysis, see Neal E. Cutler, "Generation, Maturation and Party Affiliation: A Cohort Analysis," *Public Opinion Quarterly* 33 (Winter 1969–70): 583–92.

23. See Bernard Cosman, "Republicanism in the South," *Southwestern Social Science Quarterly* 48 (June 1967): 13–23; Philip Converse, Warren Miller, Jerrold Rusk, and Arthur Wolfe, "Continuity and Change in American Politics: Parties and Issues in the 1968 Election," *American Political Science Review* 63 (December 1969), esp. 1095–1101. The Wallace Campaign in 1968 did not substantially affect the perceptions of the major parties' positions on civil rights. In noting the parties' stands, a respondent could answer that there was no difference between the major parties, but Wallace did represent a distinctive position. Few respondents chose this option; those who did were included in this analysis with the "no difference" group.
24. Of the 1968 SRC sample, only 3 of the 149 blacks identified themselves as Republicans, and only 3 voted for Nixon.
25. Kirk Porter and Donald Johnson, *National Party Platforms*, 3rd ed. (Urbana: University of Illinois Press, 1966), pp. 590–614.
26. On the development of medicare, civil rights, and other programs in this period, see James L. Sundquist, *Politics and Policy* (Washington: Brookings Institution, 1968).
27. Also see Lloyd Free and Hadley Cantril, *The Political Beliefs of Americans* (New Brunswick: Rutgers University Press, 1967), chap. 2.
28. V. O. Key, Jr., "A Theory of Critical Elections," *Journal of Politics* 17 (February 1955): 3–18. The concept and its significance have been deeply researched in Walter Dean Burnham, *Critical Elections and the Mainsprings of American Politics* (New York: Norton, 1970).
29. The point is elaborated well in Everett C. Ladd, *American Political Parties* (New York: Norton, 1970), pp. 1–10, and illustrated historically in the body of this book.
30. See Philip Converse, Aage R. Clausen, and Warren E. Miller, "Electoral Myth and Reality: The 1964 Election," *American Political Science Review* 59 (June, 1965): 330–35.
31. See: Walter Dean Burnham, "American Voting Behavior and the 1964 Election," *Midwest Journal of Political Science* 12 (February 1968): 1–40; John Kessel, *The Goldwater Coalition* (Indianapolis: Bobbs Merrill, 1968), pp. 301–08; Gerald Pomper, *Elections in America* (New York: Dodd, Mead, 1968), chap. 5; David Segal, "Partisan Realignment in the United States: The Lesson of the 1964 Election," *Public Opinion Quarterly* 32 (Fall 1968): 441–44; RePass, "Issue Salience and Party Choice," 398–400.
32. See David Nexon, "Hacks, Fanatics, and Responsible but Dense Voters" (Unpublished M.A. thesis, University of Chicago, 1970); and Rick S. Piltz, "Mass Support for the Policial Parties: Bases for Realigment," (Ph.D. dissertation, University of Michigan).
33. See the roll calls listed in *Congressional Quarterly Weekly Report*, 29 (January 29, 1971), 220–22, dealing with the 91st Congress.
34. American Political Science Association, Committee on Political Parties, "Toward a More Responsible Two-Party System," *American Political Science Review* 44 (September 1950): Supplement.
35. On the British electorate, see David Butler and Donald Stokes, *Political Change in Britain* (New York: St. Martin's Press, 1969), esp. Part IV.
36. Sundquist, however, in *Politics and Policy*, chaps. 9 and 12, argues that Democratic party actions in the 1950s and 1960s already constituted the creation of a responsible party system. In contrast, see Donald E. Stokes and Warren E. Miller, "Party Government and the Saliency of Congress," in *Elections and the*

*Political Order*, chap. 11. Originally published in 1962, the latter work shows the absence of conditions for responsible parties, at least before the possibly critical election of 1964.

37. Key, *The Responsible Electorate*, p. 2.
38. Daniel Bell, *The End of Ideology* (New York: The Free Press, 1960); Louis Hartz, *The Liberal Tradition in America* (New York: Harcourt, Brace and World, 1955).
39. For example, note the concluding chapter of *The American Voter* or chaps. 2, 8, 10, 12 of *Elections and the Political Order*, which are largely reprints of earlier articles.
40. Note the criticisms of Kenneth Prewitt and Norman Nie, in "Revisiting the Election Studies of the Survey Research Center," a paper prepared for delivery at the 1970 meeting of the American Political Science Association, p. 18:

> The SRC group has written persuasively regarding the implications for American politics of the findings about citizen information and awareness. They have less critically discussed the implications for voter rationality of their findings about election processes and alternatives.

41. Warren Miller recognized this point in "One Party Politics and the Voter," *American Political Science Review* 50 (Sept. 1956): 707–25.
42. The recent work of the Survey Research Center has given more emphasis to dynamic elements. See Donald Stokes, "Some Dynamic Elements of Contests for the Presidency," *American Political Science Review* 60 (March 1966): 19–28; and Converse et al., "Continuity and Change in American Politics."
43. Key, *The Responsible Electorate*, p. 7.

# 3

# From Confusion to Clarity: In Retrospect

My family were immigrants, passionately proud of American democracy. They prized their right to vote at least as much as a Pilgrim descendant. If they were better educated, they would have described voting as the epitome of responsible and rational citizenship.

Children see the world as variations of their parents, so I believed that all Americans considered electoral choices this seriously. When I began to study political science, however, the conventional wisdom of the discipline was that most voters were a sorry lot: uninformed, uninterested, neglectful of issues, and incapable of connecting ideas. These findings clashed both with my preferences for a more rational electorate and my personal experiences. I wanted voters to be politically smart, and I had known a lot of smart voters. Still, who was I to disagree with my academic mentors and betters?

Came the 1960s. Whatever the political science literature said, issues were being debated, and voters seemed to be responding to questions of civil rights, social welfare, and foreign policy. Inspired by the posthumously published work of V. O. Key,[1] a number of us began to uncover evidence that parties had some ideological firmness, that voters were aware of policy issues, and that electoral decisions were connected to policy preferences. My own contribution was to show that, in contrast to the 1950s, voters could now recognize policy differences between Democrats and Republicans and that their own party loyalties were correlated to these distinctions between the major parties. To draw some attention, I summarized the change in the title of this article as: "From Confusion to Clarity."

This line of research did not win immediate acclaim, since it challenged past assumptions. An attack on my own article, for example, was ill-manneredly titled: "From Confusion to Confusion."[2] Yet, the evidence mounted. The presidential elections of 1964, 1968, and 1972 were strongly affected by voters' preferences, respectively, on government social programs, civil rights, and the Vietnam War. A major book arguing the thesis of increased voter rationality was accorded the Woodrow Wilson prize, the discipline's highest research award.[3] The research questions shifted. No longer did political scientists see voters as unconcerned and unaffected by policy questions, or repeat the old clichés that the political parties were no more different than Tweedledum and Tweedledee. The analytical questions became ones of specifying the degree, conditions, and permanence of the newly discovered qualities of the electorate. This has led to the emergence of entirely different models of voting behavior, as illustrated particularly in the work of Fiorina.[4]

I can think of several reasons for the frequent citation of the article. It was a small part of an important shift in thinking on a vital element in democratic politics. Thus, research of this sort had both an intellectual and a utilitarian appeal. Furthermore, the article was published as the first contribution to a five-author symposium in the most prestigious journal in the discipline, giving it considerable visibility. Using only simple statistics and being, I believe, well written, it could be understood by most readers and used in their own work. Finally, I suspect that its optimistic conclusions about the quality of the American electorate were congenial to political scientists: many of us had immigrant parents.

## Notes

1. V. O. Key, Jr., and M. C. Cummings, *The Responsible Electorate: Rationality in Presidential Voting, 1936–1960*. (Cambridge: Harvard University Press, 1966).
2. M. Margolis, "From Confusion to Confusion," *American Political Science Review* 71(1977):31–43.
3. N. H. Nie, S. Verba, and J. Petrocik, *The Changing American Voter*. (Cambridge: Harvard University Press, 1976).
4. M. P. Fiorina, *Retrospective Voting in American National Elections* (New Haven: Yale University Press, 1981).

# 4

# Variability in Electoral Behavior

*Co-Authored by Mark A. Schulman*

Electoral studies increasingly have sought the elaboration of relationships among ever more sophisticated survey variables. A proliferation of concepts and methods have been employed to refine or reformulate hypotheses or to describe the character of specific elections. Theoretical emphasis has shifted from initial sociological and psychological models which conceived of voting almost as a "deterministic" act,[1] to those which stressed the electorate's essentially "rational" predispositions.[2] Cross-tabulation methods have been supplemented by new techniques, such as computer simulation, multidimensional scaling, and spatial analysis.[3]

Much of this research, however, has been based upon cross-sectional survey data, limited to a single time period (i.e., "synchronic" data). Reliance on survey data derived from one election presents three related dangers. The most general problem is that such analyses tend to provide a view of society "suspended at a given moment, giving the illusion of a static structure that may be quite at variance with both theory and reality."[4] Different behaviors existing in different temporal circumstances cannot be discovered. Thus, time itself is disregarded as a variable of possible explanatory power.

This problem is illustrated by contrasting findings of time series data with those of cross-sectional surveys. The former, or "diachronic," studies have indicated a high degree of voter dynamism and responsiveness, with perhaps half of American presidential elections considered "deviating."[5] Yet analyses of single surveys have cast aspersions on the ability of the electorate to think coherently and understand issues, to discern party differences on issues, and to free itself from traditional party loyalty.

These contrasting conclusions point to the second danger of reliance on synchronic data, that of overgeneralization from time-bound data. The tendency to draw longitudinal inferences from such data is evident in *The American Voter*, whose authors concluded that "the relationships in our data reflect primarily the role of enduring partisan commitments in shaping attitudes toward politics."[6] Yet, as one of these authors later mused, such conclusions may have been a product of "investigator's misfortune" in choosing campaigns in which the tides of change were weak.[7] The original finding, while accurate for 1952 and 1956, may well have been a time-bound description rather than an enduring truth. Static description inadvertently can become commingled with general explanation.[8]

A third problem is the tendency for methodological innovation to be conjoined with synchronic data. Spurred both by the late V. O. Key's normative concerns as well as by recent political ferment, revisionists have seriously challenged notions of the mass public's "inherent limitations."[9] These recent endorsements of voter rationality have often been based on new methodologies. Thus, RePass argues that preworded, preselected issue questions used in previous studies may have depressed issue-voting relationships existing in the data.[10] However, much of this revisionist research is based on data collected since the 1964 election. The innovative findings, therefore, may reflect changed temporal circumstances, rather than improved methodologies.

With the extensive accumulation of surveys, these problems can be met. Surveys can serve, to some extent, as a diachronic data source to test hypotheses in varying empirical situations. Theory can then be focused on the analysis of stability and change in survey variable relationships over time. As the election itself becomes the unit of analysis, replication becomes a means of establishing longitudinal data.

Prerequisites for such time-series analysis are comparable techniques and comparable data sets. Methodological and conceptual changes in survey procedures and questions, in addition to inevitable changes in salient events, limit comparative survey analysis.[11] Since election data sets are never precise duplicates of one another, variables must be carefully selected and strategies must be chosen which enhance comparability or, at least, explicate possible distorting effects caused by differences in the data. In the following analysis of three recent presidential elections, we seek both to promote longitudinal research and to illustrate how some specific problems of survey comparability were satisfied.

## Causal Modeling of Presidential Elections

Processes of electoral continuity and change can be examined through the causal modeling of survey data. By using the same technique in three different empirical contexts, we can begin to generalize about variability in voter behavior. Comparative causal modeling provides a convenient summary of complex, linear, multivariate relationships, relating variables frequently used in electoral research. For each election, considered separately, it promotes analysis of developmental relationships in that period. By comparing elections, the method then permits specification of the variables as relatively stable or relatively changeable in their effects over time.[12]

For this study, the presidential elections of 1956, 1964, and 1972 have been employed. The 1956 election was, in many respects, the model election in *The American Voter* and related analyses.[13] The 1964 election has been equally important in the research of latter-day revisionists, some of whom, including Burnham, have suggested that it might be a "critical election."[14] The 1972 results provide the most recent time point, and are of intrinsic interest because of the apparent disequilibrium they reveal. By analyzing three elections with varying substantive outcomes, and which span sixteen years of intensive scholarly research, we hopefully avoid concentration on the unique characteristics of isolated events.

The variables and method employed generally parallel those of Arthur Goldberg.[15] Seven variables are included:

1. Family Socioeconomic Partisan Predispositions: Derived from a dummy variable regression analysis of five demographic variables on the party identification of that parent who is more politically interested.[16] The five demographic variables are race, religion, region of residence, place of residence, and subjective social class.
2. Family Party Identification: Using the more interested parent, Republicans were scored 1, Democrats 0, and Independents 0.5.
3. Respondent's Socioeconomic Partisan Predispositions: Operationalized in a manner similar to the family index.
4. Respondent's Party Identification: Operationalized in a manner similar to the family partisanship.
5. Candidate Evaluation: An arithmetic sum of pro-Republican and anti-Democratic candidate evaluations *minus* the total of pro-Democratic and anti-Republican candidate evaluations.[17] References to issues and parties are excluded from the measure.
6. Partisan Issue Index: Derived from a dummy variable regression analysis of the five most frequently mentioned issues in each election upon the respondent's vote.
7. Respondent's Vote: The dependent variable was scored 1 for a Republican, and 0 for a Democratic vote.[18]

The issue variable presented the greatest problem in this analysis. We sought to construct a measure which included issues salient to each election, which was comparable among elections, and which was least subject to voter rationalization. Open-ended inquiries on the salient issues were not available in all of the surveys. Similarly, scales measuring the "proximity" of respondents and the candidates are another recent innovation, and may be affected by respondent rationalization[19] as well. Limiting ourselves to those few questions asked in all three surveys could result in the inclusion of past issues that have faded from the "zone of relevance"[20] and the exclusion of such vital, but latter-date, questions as Vietnam. To include all questions asked would be excessive, while still excluding issues not included in the interview schedule.

The approach we adopted established an issue selection criterion based upon the five issues mentioned most frequently in a series of open-ended questions, common to all three surveys, about what the respondent likes and dislikes about candidates and parties. The Partisan Issue Index was then constructed from the respondent's position on the closed-ended equivalents of those issues. The selection criterion therefore achieves comparability over time, with the issues selected being clearly salient to each election.[21] Furthermore, by use of the respondent's actual issue position, the index specifically excludes rationalization, where the voter projects his own issue stand upon the candidate he favors. An artificial inflating of the correspondence between issue position and the vote is avoided.[22]

The variables are ordered as follows: (1) Family Socioeconomic Political Predispositions; (2) Family Party Identification; (3) Respondent's Socioeconomic Political Predispositions; (4) Respondent's Party Identification; (5) Partisan Issues Index; (6) Candidate Evaluation; (7) Respondent's Vote. While the correct ordering of variables cannot be determined by statistical derivation,[23] the variable ordering follows established practice and theory. Party identification temporally precedes the issues and candidates of a particular election, as has been shown in past electoral research and socialization studies.[24] Issues, in turn, tend to be more longstanding than the particular candidates running in a given election.[25] In our particular cases, moreover, some of the issues are present in more than one election, while there was no overlap of candidates.

After ordering the variables, the paths in the model were solved through a series of multiple regressions, with nonsignificant relationships eliminated.[26] Each variable is treated as a dependent variable in a multiple regression, with the independent variable being all variables in the model for which there is a single direct path to that dependent variable.

## From 1956 to 1972

Figure 4.1, a causal model of the 1956 election using standardized regression coefficients or beta weights, reflects the "dual mediation" model developed by Goldberg. The model has several distinctive features. First, party identification is the "pivotal encapsulator" of prior political socialization, with no direct links between background socioeconomic characteristics and the respondent's vote. As Goldberg notes, the omission of direct causal links between these variables and voting behavior, as well as the omission of such a link between childhood sociological characteristics and adult party identification "certainly justify the qualms of the authors of *The American Voter*'s about the sociological explanations of voting behavior."[27]

Second, Goldberg reported a "dual mediation" of the respondent's vote by party identification and a Partisan Political Attitudes index. However, the attitude index was one of the more unsatisfactory aspects of Goldberg's work because it combined both candidate evaluations and issues. In light of current interest in issue voting, the effects of these two variables were calculated separately in Figure 4.1. The result indicates that the preponderance of Goldberg's RPA path to the vote (.596 in his model) is accounted for by candidate evaluations, with both the direct and indirect (through CE) paths from the issue index to vote being very weak.[28] Reviewing the link between party identification and the vote, both RPI's direct path (.448) and its indirect path through candidate evaluations (.200) remain strong. At the same time, the path between respondent's party identification and the issue index, while significant (.235), must engender support for those researchers who have emphasized the often "nonrational" nature of party identification.

In summary, the 1956 election may still be viewed as being dominated by a dual mediation process. However, the dual mediators are party identification and candidate evaluation, with issues only weakly linked to the vote. The model seemingly comports well with *The American Voter*'s conclusion, cited previously, that "the relationships in our data reflect primarily the role of enduring partisan commitments in shaping attitudes toward politics."[29]

The 1964 model, in Figure 4.2, using variables identical with those in the 1956 analysis, reveals a pattern quite distinct from 1956. For the most part, moreover, these differences continue to be evident in the 1972 model, in Figure 4.3, indicating that the contest between Johnson and Goldwater was not a completely unique event. Three implications are suggested by these new patterns.

First, we see an evident breakdown in the New Deal's socioeconomic party coalitions. The older generation shows a rather stable effect of demographic characteristics on party identification, measured as the path from FSPP to FPI. However, this relationship is fast diminishing among current voters. The relationship between socioeconomic variables and partisanship weakens from one election to the next, as shown in the very low beta weight in 1972 for RSPP-RPI.

A shift in the nature of the partisan coalitions is also shown by the falling into insignificance in 1972 of the path between FSP and RSPP. Compound path analysis reveals the same conclusions, showing that most of the transmission of partisanship between the generations now occurs through FPI, by tradition itself, rather than by the replication of the relationship of demographic variables to the current electorate's loyalty.[30]

Second, the importance of issues to the vote has been enhanced considerably. This development is evident in 1964 both in terms of the direct impact of

**FIGURE 4.1**
**Causal Model of the 1956 Presidential Election**

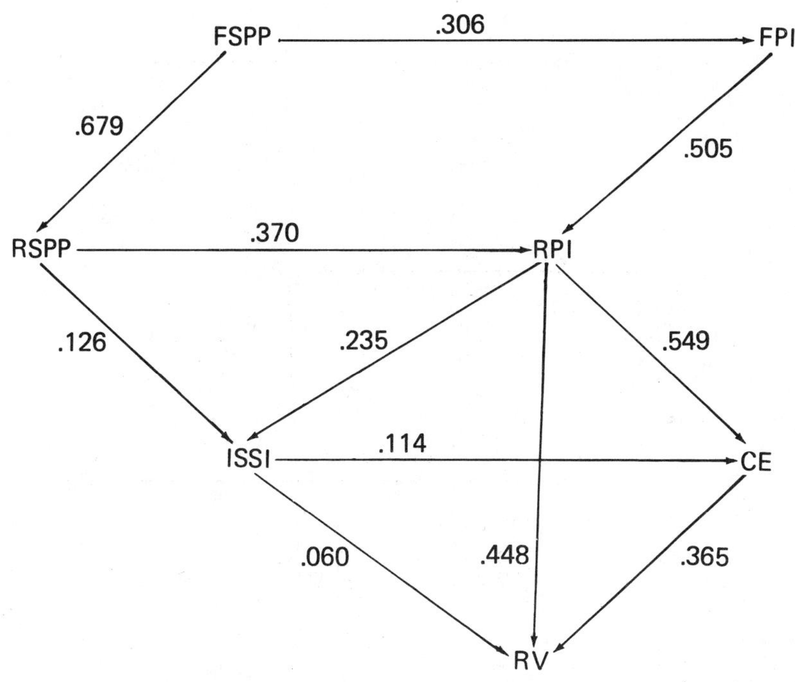


Significance Level = .001
N = 763
$R^2$ = .548

Key:
FSPP: Family Socioeconomic Partisan Predispositions
FPI: Family Party Identification
RSPP: Respondent's Socioeconomic Partisan Predispositions
RPI: Respondent's Party Identification
ISSI: Partisan Issues Index
CE: Candidate Evaluation
RV: Respondent's Vote

**FIGURE 4.2**
**Causal Model of the 1964 Presidential Election**

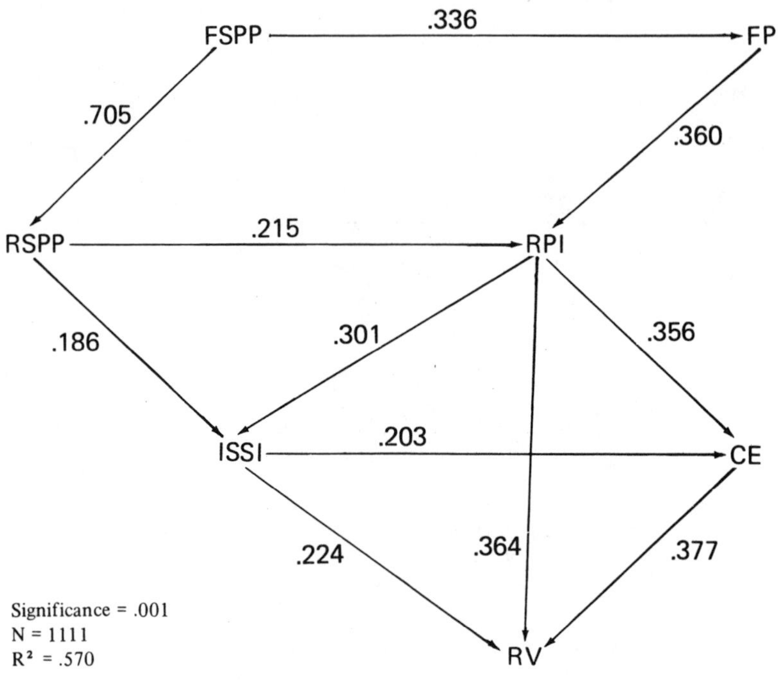


issues (.244) and their indirect path through candidate evaluation (.076). In 1972, the impact of issues was still greater, both marginally in a direct fashion (.233) and particularly as issues affect the evaluation of candidates and the resultant vote (.114).

Concurrently, there has been a decline in the impact of partisanship on the vote. This decline is evident in the simple path from party loyalty to the vote, where there is a continuous drop in weight from 1956 to 1964 and, again, from 1964 to 1972. The decline is evident as well in the complex paths. Candidate evaluations have become far more independent of party loyalty, while the controlled influence of such evaluations on the vote has remained largely

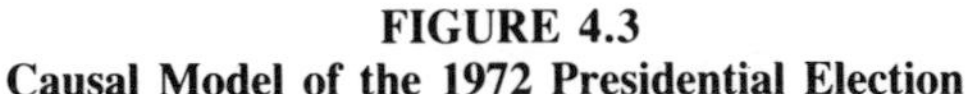

**FIGURE 4.3**
**Causal Model of the 1972 Presidential Election**

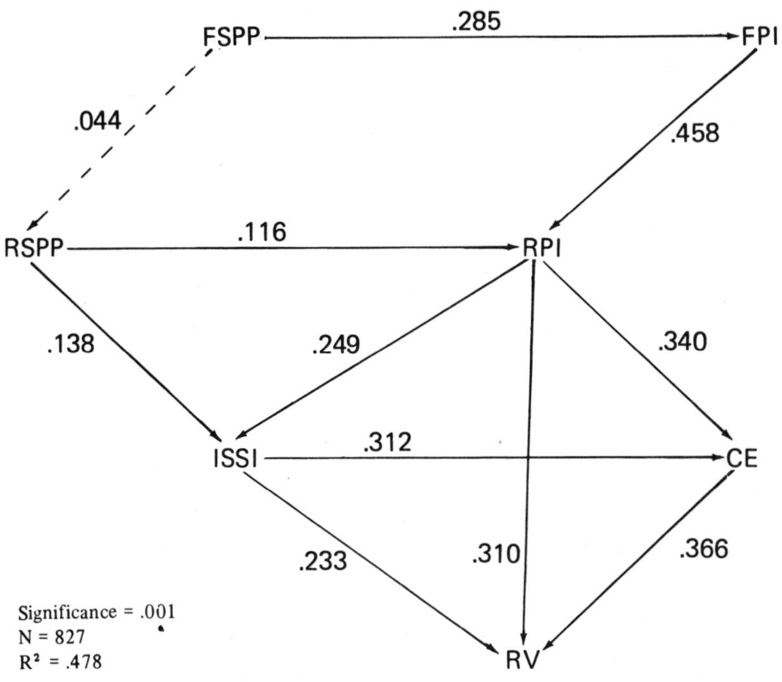


unchanged. The importance of party identification remains, but it is seemingly more than a simple reflection of traditional loyalty. An increasing proportion of its impact is through the relationship with issue preferences.

The relative importance of the political variables can be gauged by analysis of the compound paths between respondent's party identification and the vote. While the direct path between the two variables remains primary, as seen in Table 4.1, the contribution of the indirect paths through the issue index has risen considerably. Excluded from the model are those issue preferences which influence party identification itself. Therefore, the total impact of issues on the vote in these years is underestimated.[31]

**TABLE 4.1**
**Compound Path Coefficients to Respondent Vote**

| Path | 1956 Coeff. | 1956 Relative Importance* | 1964 Coeff. | 1964 Relative Importance* | 1972 Coeff. | 1972 Relative Importance* |
|---|---|---|---|---|---|---|
| Direct: | | | | | | |
| RPI/RV | .448 | 66.6 | .364 | 61.8 | .310 | 59.5 |
| Through Candidate: | | | | | | |
| RPI/CE/RV | .200 | 29.8 | .134 | 22.8 | .125 | 23.9 |
| Through Issues: | | | | | | |
| RPI/ISSI/RV | .014 | 2.1 | .067 | 11.4 | .058 | 11.1 |
| Through Issues and Candidate: | | | | | | |
| RPI/ISSI/CE/RV | .010 | 1.5 | .023 | 3.9 | .028 | 5.4 |
| Total | .672 | 100.0 | .588 | 99.9 | .521 | 99.9 |

*Figures in this column are the percentages of the total relationship between RPI and RV which are explained by the given paths.

## Alternative Explanations

The most obvious difference in these elections is the apparently greater importance of issue preferences in 1964 and 1972. The vote has become less determined by sociological characteristics and traditional loyalties and is more affected by the electorate's position on public policy and its corresponding evaluation of the candidates. Such influences bring results as disparate as the Democratic landslide of 1964 and the overwhelming Nixon triumph eight years later.

To explain these changes in the level of issue voting since 1956, one might hypothesize that a new, issue-oriented younger generation in 1964 and 1972 replaced older, less issue-conscious cohorts.[32] To examine generational shift, the magnitudes of issue-voting paths for 1956 age cohorts were compared, in Table 4.2, to those of their generational cohorts in 1964 (age in 1956 + 8 years) and in 1972 (age in 1956 + 16 years). If common generational learning experiences were responsible for low levels of issue voting in 1956, simi-

**TABLE 4.2**
**Direct Paths from Partisan Issue Index to Respondent Vote, by Generational and Maturational Cohorts**

| Generational Cohort | Age in 1956 | Age in 1972 | 1956 | 1964 | 1972 |
|---|---|---|---|---|---|
| | | 18–25 | | | .244 |
| | | 26–33 | | .220 | .162 |
| 1 | 18–25 | 34–41 | .121 | .277 | .323 |
| 2 | 26–33 | 42–49 | .116 | .279 | .217 |
| 3 | 34–41 | 50–57 | .074 | .169 | .168 |
| 4 | 42–49 | 58–65 | .039 | .258 | .206 |
| 5 | 50–57 | 66 & Older | .016 | .253 | .268 |
| 6 | 58–65 | | −.008 | .123 | |
| 7 | 66 & Older | | .035 | | |

larly low levels should be evident within the same cohorts across the three elections. Little variation would appear, then, in the rows of Table 4.2. If a new issue-oriented generation is changing global voting behavior, the highest coefficients would be evident in the first entry in each column.

Data in Table 4.2 soundly disconfirm the generational shift hypothesis. While new voters in 1964 and 1972 demonstrate greater issue responsiveness than the older 1956 cohorts they presumably replaced, a substantial increase in issue voting is evident across time in all generational cohorts (rows in Table 4.2). In fact, viewing each election separately, it is not necessarily the new voters who demonstrate the greatest influence of issues on their votes. Although the aged might be considered inflexible by some, they show more responsiveness to issues, particularly in 1972, than do many younger cohorts.

Parenthetically, the data also permit us to draw some inferences about life-cycle or maturational effects on voting behavior. If the life cycle is a predominant influence, relatively little variation should be present along the diagonal lines of Table 4.2, which indicate the same life-cycle age groupings. Furthermore, if aging reduces susceptibility to issue influences, as is implied in *The American Voter*,[33] the coefficients across the horizontal rows should diminish. Precisely the opposite conclusions must be drawn from the data. There is a wide variation along the diagonals and a general increase along the horizontal rows. Maturity does not mean rigidity.[34]

The generational shift hypothesis fails to explain the heightened association between issue preferences and the vote. To pursue the subject, an analysis of variance was undertaken. Of the total variance, 74.5 percent is explained by the elections (columns in Table 4.2), and the degree of explanation is even higher when we compare the 1956 cohorts to either 1964 or 1972 alone. Voting behavior appears quite distinct in these latter two contests.[35]

A second possible reason for upward shifts in issue voting might be the increasing educational achievement among the electorate from 1956 to 1972. Table 4.3 presents the results of controlling for level of education. Substantial increases in issue voting are apparent at every level in 1964 compared to 1956, and this development generally continues in 1972. Interestingly, issue voting was more pronounced in 1964 and 1972 among respondents in the lowest educational categories than among college-educated voters in 1956. The electorate in the latter two elections was responding quite differently than in 1956, and the transformation is evident throughout the national sample. We must therefore reject the hypothesis that educational upgrading explains these results.

**TABLE 4.3**
**Direct Paths from Partisan Issue Index to Vote, by Education Levels**

| Education Level | 1956 | 1964 | 1972 |
|---|---|---|---|
| Grades 0 thru 8 | .008 | .158 | .213 |
| Grades 9 thru 12 | .094 | .189 | .217 |
| College | .109 | .295 | .258 |

Given the inability of demographic variables to account for heightened issue voting, the most obvious explanation must be offered, namely, politics itself—the contrasting circumstances and styles of the three elections and their impacts on the electorate. In 1956, according to Kelley, both Eisenhower and Stevenson described their policy positions in terms so general that "their statements lacked any clear relation to issues on which voters had to decide."

> Both were for peace, social welfare, full justice for farmers, honest government, a strong national defense, the expansion of civil liberties, full employment, the development of individual talents, a vigorous economy, a flourishing world trade, and a large number of other objectives of similarly general appeal . . . (A)t no time did either candidate declare himself to be opposed to any statement of fundamental belief that his opponent had advanced.[36]

What major differences which may have existed did not transform themselves into affective and cognitive links with the voters.

By contrast, the 1964 and 1972 campaigns surely marked a departure from "Tweedledum-Tweedledee" politics. Offering "a choice, not an echo," the Johnson-Goldwater contest presented the electorate with two clearly different sets of domestic and foreign blueprints, with Goldwater representing a challenge to the New Deal legacy of "positive government." Sharp differences between the candidates were also evident in 1972, and were perceived as such by the voters. Regardless of their own positions on the issues, the electorate saw McGovern as quite dovish and welfare-minded, and Nixon as more aggressive in Vietnam and economically conservative.[37] With a choice available, the voters chose.

## Conclusions

Using comparable survey variables and causal modeling techniques, we have sought to gain a longitudinal perspective on two divergent sets of hypotheses on voting behavior, both of which were derived largely from synchronic, cross-sectional survey analysis. The first hypotheses stress continuity and stability, with the electorate viewed as the captive of "inherent limitations." The second, which might be termed, after Key, the "voters-are-not-fools" hypotheses, find the electorate capable of acting responsibly. Three elections, spanning sixteen years, each featuring an incumbent president, were compared.

The 1956 election comported well with the continuity paradigm exemplified by *The American Voter*: (1) party identification was the "pivotal encapsulator" or prior political socialization, with a strong linkage between parents' partisan attachments and those of the voter; (2) links between party identification and issue positions were not as strong as in 1964, raising questions about the ability of political parties to aggregate issues meaningfully for purposes of electoral competition; (3) the voting decision was mediated primarily by party identification and candidate evaluations; (4) issues were only weakly associated with the voting decision, indicating the electorate's inability to discern them.

The 1964 and 1972 elections, by contrast, present portraits of the electorate which better conform to the "voters-are-not-fools" model. The findings indicate that: (1) the linkages between demographic factors and family tradition to offspring's partisanship diminished considerably; (2) while party identification was still a significant indicator of the vote, it remained so partially because of the greater weight of the paths from partisanship through issues; and (3) issues played a meaningful role in the voting decision. These changes cannot be explained by generational or educational alterations in the electorate.

Thus, the voters are capable of a wide range of behaviors and are not "inherently limited." In the appropriate circumstances, such as the intense contests of 1964 and 1972, the electorate will respond to issue differences between the candidates. We do not believe that the finding of increased issue voting can be explained simply by the use of new methodological and conceptual tools. The relationship of issues to the vote was not constant during this period, nor disguised by flawed techniques. Rather, actual changes in the level of issue voting may now be inferred from 1956 through 1964 and 1972.

Finally, our most general conclusion is that theory generated from any single election must, necessarily, be incomplete and static. Voters must be studied comparatively, in a variety of empirical and temporal contexts. In doing so, we have found reason to support Key's view that "the electorate behaves about as rationally and responsibly as we should expect, given the clarity of the alternatives presented to it and the character of the information available to it."[38]

## Notes

1. Paul Lazarsfeld, Bernard Berelson, and Helen Gaudet, *The People's Choice* (New York: Columbia University Press, 1948); Berelson, Lazarsfeld, and William McPhee, *Voting* (Chicago: University of Chicago Press, 1954); Eugene Burdick and Arthur Brodbeck, eds., *American Voting Behavior* (New York: Free Press, 1959); Angus Campbell et al., *The American Voter* (New York: Wiley, 1960).
2. V. O. Key, Jr., *The Responsible Electorate* (Cambridge: Harvard University Press, 1966); Richard Boyd, "Popular Control of Public Policy: A Normal Vote Analysis of the 1968 Election," *American Political Science Review* 66 (June 1972): 429–49; Norman Nie and Kristi Andersen, "Mass Belief Systems Revisited: Political Change and Attitude Structure," *Journal of Politics* 36 (August 1974): 540–91.

3. William R. Shaffer, *Computer Simulations of Voting Behavior* (New York: Oxford University Press, 1972); Jerrold Rusk and Herbert Weisberg, "Perceptions of Presidential Candidates: Implications for Electoral Change," *Midwest Journal of Political Science* 16 (August 1972): 388–410; Samuel Kirkpatrick, "Political Attitudes and Behavior: Some Consequences of Attitudinal Ordering," *Midwest Journal of Political Science* 14 (February 1970): 1–24; Benjamin Page and Richard Brody, "Policy Voting and the Electoral Process: The Vietnam War Issue," *American Political Science Review* 66 (September 1972): 979–95.
4. Matilda White Riley and Edward Nelson, "Research on Stability and Change in Social Systems," in Bernard Barber and Alex Inkeles, eds., *Stability and Social Change* (Boston: Little, Brown, 1971), p. 408.
5. Richard Merelman, "Electoral Instability and the American Party System," *Journal of Politics* 32 (February 1970): 115–39.
6. Campbell et al., *The American Voter*, p. 135.
7. Donald Stokes, "Some Dynamic Elements of Contests for the Presidency," *American Political Science Review* 60 (March 1966): 19.
8. Ronald Brunner and Klaus Kiepelt, "Data Analysis, Process Analysis, and System Change," *Midwest Journal of Political Science* 16 (November 1972): 538–69.
9. Philip E. Converse, "The Nature of Belief Systems in Mass Publics," in David Apter, ed., *Ideology and Discontent* (New York: Free Press, 1964), pp. 206–61.
10. David RePass, "Issue Salience and Party Choice," *American Political Science Review* 65 (June 1971): 389–400; John C. Pierce, "Party Identification and the Changing Role of Ideology in American Politics," *Midwest Journal of Political Science* 14 (February 1970): 25–42; John Field and Ronald Anderson, "Ideology in the Public's Conceptualization of the 1964 Election," *Public Opinion Quarterly* 33 (Fall 1969): 380–98.
11. John H. Kessel, "Comment: The Issues in Issue Voting," *American Political Science Review* 66 (June 1972): 459–65.
12. We do not seek to compare the absolute magnitudes of the coefficients over time. Such comparisons are inappropriate when using standardized coefficients.
13. Reliance on the 1956 data is evident both in *The American Voter* and the subsequent work by Campbell et al., *Elections and the Political Order* (New York: Wiley, 1966).
14. Walter Dean Burnham, "American Voting Behavior and the 1964 Election," *Midwest Journal of Political Science* 12 (February 1968): 1–40.
15. Arthur Goldberg, "Discerning a Causal Path Among Data on Voting Behavior," *American Political Science Review* 60 (December 1966): 913–22.
16. Langton has found that the more politicized parent tends to have relatively more "pulling power" with regard to the transmission of party identification to offspring. In "ties" between the parents, the father's identification is employed. See Kenneth Langton, *Political Socialization* (New York: Oxford University Press, 1969), chap. 3.
17. For a similar measure, see Stanley Kelley, Jr. and Thad Mirer, "The Simple Act of Voting," *American Political Science Review* 68 (June 1974): 572–91. In the 1956 election model, FPI was established on the basis of data from a second wave with the same panel, in 1958. In 1972, only "Form 1" respondents could be employed.
18. Four important modifications have been made in Goldberg's analysis. Mothers, as well as fathers, are included in family characteristics. Independent voters are in-

cluded. The voters' evaluations of candidates and policy questions have been separated. A separate issue index has been constructed.

19. Richard Brody and Benjamin Page, "Comment: The Assessment of Issue Voting," *American Political Science Review* 66 (June 1972): 450–58.
20. V. O. Key and Frank Munger, "Social Determinism and Electoral Decision: The Case of Indiana," in Burdick and Brodbeck, pp, 281–99.
21. In 1964 and 1972, a comparison of the responses to the "salient issue" and "like-dislike" questions shows high correspondence in the issues selected. This result heightens our confidence in the salience of the issues employed. Cf. RePass.
22. In contrast, others have emphasized subjective rationality through the use of proximity indices. In our view, indices constructed from proximity measures do not gauge if the voter has any information about the issue or if he perceives candidate or party differences correctly. See Michael Shapiro, "Rational Political Man: A Synthesis of Economic and Social-Psychological Perspectives," *American Political Science Review* 63 (December 1969): 1106–19; Arthur Miller et al., "A Majority Party in Disarray," *American Political Science Review* 70 (December 1976): 753–78.
23. Hugh Forbes and Edward Tufte, "A Note of Caution in Causal Modelling," *American Political Science Review* 62 (December 1968): 1258–64; Hubert Blalock, Jr., *Causal Models in the Social Sciences* (Chicago: Aldine Atherton, 1971).
24. Campbell et al., *The American Voter*, chap. 7; Fred Greenstein, *Children and Politics* (New Haven: Yale University Press, 1965), chap. 4.
25. Stokes, "Some Dynamic Elements," pp. 20–22.
26. The significant paths ($p < .001$) were the same in each of the three elections, with the exception in 1972 of FSPP/RSPP. This path is retained as a dashed line in the 1972 diagram solely for comparability.
27. Goldberg, "Discerning a Causal Path," p. 919.
28. In this case, the indirect path is obtained by multiplying the following: ISSI/CE. CE/RV.
29. Campbell et al., *The American Voter*, p. 135.
30. Compound path coefficients are calculated as the product of the simple path coefficients. With RPI as the dependent variable, the following compound relationships result:

| | FSPP/RSPP/RPI | FSSP/FPI/RPI |
|---|---|---|
| 1956 | .251 | .155 |
| 1964 | .152 | .121 |
| 1972 | .005 | .131 |

31. See H. Daudt, *Floating Voters and the Floating Vote* (Leiden: Stenfert Kroese, 1961).
32. See Riley, "Aging and Cohort Succession: Interpretations and Misinterpretations," *Public Opinion Quarterly* 37 (Spring 1973): 35–49; Neal E. Cutler, "Generation, Maturation and Party Affiliation: A Cohort Analysis," *Public Opinion Quarterly* 33 (Winter 1969–70): 583–92.
33. Campbell et al., *The American Voter*, p. 165.
34. This conclusion is in keeping with new findings in developmental psychology, where many heretofore hypothesized "maturational" differences, such as cognitive abilities and intellectual levels, are now viewed as products of "generational" differences. See K. Warner Schaie and C. R. Crother, "A Cross-

Sectional Study of Age Changes in Cognitive Behavior," *Psychological Bulletin* (1968): 671–80.

35. The correlation ratio is .770 for 1956–1964 and .784 for 1956–1972. It is a stark zero for the comparison of 1964–1972, indicating the great similarity of results within age cohorts in this pair.
36. Stanley Kelley, Jr., *Political Campaigning* (Washington: Brookings Institution, 1960).
37. McGovern was seen as more "dovish" on the 1972 "Vietnam action scale" and more inclined to "social solutions" on the "urban unrest scale" by a majority of respondents in every response category. Cf. Miller et al., "A Majority Party in Disarray."
38. Key, *The Responsible Electorate*, p. 7.

# 5

# Sex, Voting, and War

Sex is obvious. To be a woman or a man is a permanent and distinctive identity. If behavior is determined, the causal agent may well be found in the chromosomes that fix individual gender. "Biology is destiny," decreed Freud, and his dictum might apply to politics as much as psychology. Probably from the days of Lesbos and Sparta, discussion of female participation in government has implicitly assumed that the matter of their sex would have some unique effects on political participants.

The argument over female suffrage itself was based on a deterministic assumption that women's participation in balloting would make a substantive difference. The more optimistic advocates of equality in the voting booth expected it would "abolish poverty, protect family life, and raise educational cultural standards; an international society made up of nations in which women had the suffrage would not tolerate war."[1] Concerning the first presidential election in which women fully participated, Democrats "hoped that women voters in 1920 would save the party from electoral defeat on the issue of the League of Nations."[2] In the contemporary United States, the major parties maintain distinct women's sections in their organizations, draft platform planks specifically addressed to women, and tailor their campaigns to attract female votes.

Contrary to these great expectations, women's participation in the vote has had quite limited substantive impact. Despite biological differences between the two sexes, virtually all investigations show no political differences between men and women that can be attributed to the factor of sex itself. "With few exceptions, opinion patterns have been associated with the same social and demographic factors among both sexes."[3] In the vote itself, "if we take a large variety of other social characteristics into account, there are no residual differences in partisanship between men and women."[4]

There are some limited exceptions to the lack of sexual differentiation in politics, and we will investigate two of the outstanding differences. Yet, at the outset, it is important to realize that these are exceptions. Even on questions directly related to sex distinctions, differences between men and women are neither large nor consistent. For example, as recently as 1969, men were more willing than women to vote for a female candidate for president, while a 1972 poll shows women more accepting of a nominee of their own sex. In both cases, the difference between the two groups was 9 percent; this limited and inconsistent margin hardly provides evidence of sexual conflict.[5]

Political differences between men and women have been limited because necessary conditions for such differences have been absent. The most important prerequisite of political distinctiveness is "an economic division of labor or a physical separation or a social differentiation in the population such that people of unlike characteristics are affected in different ways by a single political policy. . . . It would be difficult in contemporary America, for example, to maintain strong voting differences by sex, because there are few policy issues persisting over a period of time that affect men and women differently."[6] Given the absence of this condition, the sexes have been quite similar politically.

In the 1970s, however, the situation may have changed. Sexual differentiation in politics is possible as a result of the women's liberation movement; its causal antecedents, such as the changed occupational structure and the spread of effective contraceptives; and the rise of sex-related issues, such as job discrimination, abortion, and child care. Therefore, one observer predicts: "For the elections of the 1970's female voters and activists will differ from male groups primarily because of their link to the developing women's liberation. For the first time we are witnessing on the American scene a woman's movement which is self-interested, coming into consciousness along with new racial, ethnic, religious and student groups."[7]

The full development of political divisions between the sexes remains to be seen; it hardly seems likely that these differences will reach the level of racial conflict or even class polarization in the United States because social separation is unlikely to be very great. Biology certainly will continue to bring men and women together physically. The economic division of labor between the sexes is narrowing, not increasing, as women leave the drudgeries of housework for schools and for jobs similar to those of men. The sexes are not segregating themselves, but coming together—in sports, colleges, on the job, and in their leisure.

Although new issues have arisen that might form the basis of a sexual politics, positions on these issues do not correlate very highly with gender. Even on an issue like abortion, the only difference is a slight tendency for men to favor the practice more than women. A more general opinion is that on "women's place," but there is virtually no sex difference on a seven-point scale that ranges from "women and men should have an equal role" to "women's place is in the home."

Politically, then, "vive la difference!" is largely an empty slogan, for most attitudes are not sex-determined. As we have mentioned, though, there are some variations, and we will devote most of this chapter to two of them. The first is the relatively lower participation of women in the voting act. The second is sex difference on a small range of opinions relating to war and the use of force. For the most part, these sex differences reflect particular circumstances of the sexes and are subject to change in different situations. The portrait of the responsive voter can be drawn as either a man or a woman.

## Sex and Voting Turnout

One of the few aspects of female electoral behavior to receive scholarly attention has been participation in voting itself. The most publicized struggles involving women in politics have been over suffrage, and considerable notice has been given to the frequency with which they have exercised this power over the past half-century.

The consistent conclusion from this research has been that women participate less than men in the vote.[8] In the first American study of the subject, only a third of women were found to vote in the Chicago mayoral election of 1923, compared to twice as many men.[9] We can also see this relationship historically. National voting turnout dropped considerably in 1920, the first presidential election after passage of the 19th Amendment, and has never since reached the levels attained during the period of exclusively male suffrage. Surveys of individual voters have also substantiated this conclusion. Dealing with the decade of the 1950s, the authors of *The American Voter* found "the vote participation rate among women in our samples is consistently 10 percent below that of men as an over-all estimate."[10]

The primary psychological cause of these differences in turnout is to be found in sex role typings. Whether enforced by men and/or expressed by women, a significant proportion of female adults have believed that "politics is a man's business." In the early Chicago election, 13 percent of the females expressed such sentiments as "All our family troubles are caused by our women folks getting away from the ways of living in previous and former years."[11] Even in more contemporary periods, we find that women have less interest in politics, tend to define their roles in less political terms, believe they are less efficacious politically, and feel less of a citizen's obligation to vote.[12]

We would expect lessened sex differences in turnout in recent years. The women's liberation movement is one indication that past sex typings are no longer widely accepted, and more general opinion data supports this supposition. Among both sexes there is increased acceptance of the idea of a woman as president and of female activity in politics generally.[13] Demographic change will further this trend. Reluctance to participate in politics has been concentrated among older women of lower education and of immigrant background.[14] As the sexes become equal in education and as new native-born generations mature, past role definitions will alter.

Nationally, these expectations have been largely fulfilled. A Census Bureau report on the 1972 presidential election found only the slightest difference in turnout between the sexes. While 73.1 percent of males were registered and 64.1 percent claimed an actual vote, the figures for females were very similar: 71.6 percent registered and 62.0 percent voting.[15] Even these small differences were eliminated among younger respondents, where women in fact tended marginally to outvote men. In the University of Michigan study, the sex differential remains somewhat higher, about 5 percent more of men voting. Even this difference, however, is only half of that observed in the 1950s.[16] In total participation, then, the nation has moved toward sexual equality at the ballot box.

This overall similarity may well disguise differences among subgroups. We can observe the changing effect of role definitions by concentrating on three demographic variables, which previously have been found to be related to lower female turnout: age, education, and region. Older, less educated, and southern women have been particularly unlikely to vote, as they were more likely to adhere to traditional conceptions of women's restricted political role. We would expect the sex differential in turnout to diminish as new generations enter politics, as the level of schooling increases among women, and as the cultural patterns of the nation diffuse through the more isolated South.

In Table 5.1, the voting turnout of men and women is compared within age, education, and regional groupings.[17] In 1972, in the North, the first two variables have only weak effects. While male turnout is still relatively higher among older voters and the less educated, large differences are found only when these two factors combine. A statistically significant difference in voting participation is found exclusively among persons who are 55 years or older and who also have no more than grade school education. In contrast to this group are the younger and more educated persons, where a slight feminine lead is found. In the North, we may conclude that women have been largely liberated in regard to electoral participation.[18]

In the South, sex differences in turnout remain. Disparities exist particularly among older and less educated persons, as in the rest of the nation, but the differences tend to be larger. Among the two lower educational strata, we find a growing sex effect on turnout as we pass from younger to older age groups. There also is an independent effect of education, with more equal voting rates evident as we climb the educational ladder. The southern woman with a college education is quite unusual. She participates more in 1972 than a comparable man, and also, relative to males, votes more than her northern sister.[19]

**TABLE 5.1**
**Sex Differences in Voting Turnout, 1972***

| | Non-South Education | | | | South (White)** Education | | | |
|---|---|---|---|---|---|---|---|---|
| Age | Grade School | High School | College | Average | Grade School | High School | College | Average |
| Less than 35 | 4.4 | − 8.4 | − 5.6 | − 2.8 | −15.1.a | 11.9 | 6.4 | 11.6 |
| | (14) | (205) | (305) | (525) | (23) | (88) | (131) | (242) |
| 45-54 | 9.0 | 4.7 | − 0.1 | 3.2 | 20.6 | 22.4 | − 5.8 | 9.5 |
| | (56) | (228) | (254) | (538) | (35) | (76) | (63) | (174) |
| 55 and Over | 22.2 | 13.4 | 4.9 | 15.0 | 30.2 | 15.2 | −27.5 | 7.2 |
| | (177) | (161) | (105) | (443) | (80) | (73) | (53) | (207) |
| Average | 16.3 | 3.4 | − 2.1 | | 19.8 | 16.0 | − 5.9 | |
| | (248) | (596) | (667) | | (138) | (241) | (249) | |

*The percentage in each cell is a subtraction of the proportion of women in the category voting for president from the same proportion among men. Positive percentages indicate greater male turnout; negative percentages indicate higher female turnout. The number in parenthesis refers to the number of cases.

**Previous and current restrictions on black voting in the South complicate historical as well as contemporary analysis of the independent effect of sex on turnout. Race must therefore be considered separately.

a The small number of cases in this cell make the finding of greater female voting in this group of no significance.

There evidently has been some movement toward equality in voting between the sexes. A particularly dramatic change has occurred among those in the South with only grade school education. When this group was largely aged 35–54 (in the 1950s), there was a 53 percent sex disparity in voting rates; in 1972 the disparity of the group over 55 is reduced to 30 percent. Since we are dealing in the South only with white voters, this change cannot be due to legal innovations such as civil rights legislation. The cause is more probably found in general modifications in social and political attitudes.

While disparities have lessened throughout the nation, a regional discrepancy remains. The areal difference in turnout can be found in all of the elections of the past two decades. In the North, women are actually outvoting men by 1962, while men continue their predominance in the South up to the present. When we further subdivide the northern samples, there is no consistent pattern of male or female advantage in turnout. Evidently the norm of participation has been diffused throughout the population. In the South, during all of this period, there is a consistent pattern: the highest sex difference is always found among those of grade school education, while male predominance is always lowest or absent among those who are college educated. The norm of political equality has reached especially those white southerners most exposed to the modern influences that pervade the other regions.

The distinctiveness of the South in female turnout is a descriptive fact. To explain this fact, we can pursue two lines of investigation. The first is to follow the apparent evidence of a distinctive regional culture, as we shall below. The second is to attempt to explain the South by analyzing other population characteristics that happen to be unusually frequent in the South. Level of education, for example, is closely related to voting turnout and to sexual equality. Regions with higher levels of education, such as the non-South, can be expected to evidence more sexual equality. The disparity in southern turnout might therefore be due only to its lower levels of education, not to any unique feature of the region as a cultural and geographic entity. However, the data already presented show that southern distinctiveness largely remains even with a control for education.

Another explanation of this distinctiveness might be the more rural character of the South. Divergent sex roles and female abstention from politics are more characteristic of a rural society. Therefore, the lesser participation of southern women might be related to the residential patterns of the area.[20] Again, the data do not support this hypothesis. In 1972, men did outvote women in the rural areas of both the South and the rest of the nation, but the difference is the South was 15.4 percent, compared to 10.0 percent in the North.[21] The demographic features of the South do not provide a sufficient interpretation of the area's patterns of turnout.

Another indication of a true regional effect can be found by examining the effect of parental status on turnout. The most enduring sex role of women, or course, is that of mother. As women are held primarily responsible for child rearing, we might expect that this task would have some effect on voting participation. In fact, mothers do appear at the polls somewhat less frequently than either childless women or fathers, as the presence of children tends to emphasize differences in sex roles. In an early Chicago election, women were four times less likely than men to vote because they were "detained by a helpless member of the family," and this explanation was most commonly offered by females aged 30–39, the mothers of young children. Illustrative of this problem was "Mrs. Palek, aged thirty-eight, who said she had eight small children and had no time for voting. She added that if her husband voted and she took care of her children she was doing her duty for her country."[22]

Role differences in the care of children are complicated, however, by regional factors. The care of children has its greatest impact when the youngest child is of a preschool age and requires the most attention. Among parents of such children, sex differences between the regions are virtually equal. Both northern and southern women vote about 8 percent less than men at this stage of the life cycle. When the children are older, however, areal effects become apparent. In the North, even when there are still school-age children in the home, women's turnout increases and becomes equal to that of men. When the children are past high school age, or there are no children, northern women actually outvote men. In the South, by contrast, women's turnout barely changes with the status of children. Since men do vote more as they age, the sexual differential in turnout increases.[23]

**TABLE 5.2**
**Sex Differences in Nonvoting, by Parental Status and Region, 1968**

| | North | | South | |
|---|---|---|---|---|
| | **Male** | **Female** | **Male** | **Female** |
| Preschool Children | 21.8<br>(101) | 28.6<br>(90) | 34.2<br>(35) | 43.3<br>(53) |
| School-Age Children Only | 20.3<br>(86) | 18.8<br>(125) | 20.0<br>(45) | 41.4<br>(58) |
| No Children, or Over 18 | 27.9<br>(215) | 16.0<br>(256) | 22.1<br>(104) | 41.5<br>(135) |

*The entry in each cell is the percentage of the group not voting for president in 1968. The number in parenthesis is the total number in the group.

## Women and Southern Tradition

Rather than in demography, we must seek the cause of southern nonvoting of women in the distinctive attitudes of the region. Biology does not determine women's place in the home or out of the voting booth, but regional disparities in turnout can be attributed to contrasts between defined sex roles in the more modernized North and the more traditional white South. Both women and men below the Mason-Dixon line are more inclined to agree that women should stay out of politics. Moreover, in the South there is a noticeble sex difference. Only 47 percent of the area's men and 55 percent of its women favor more female political activity, while in other regions at least 55 percent of both sexes support such involvement. Only in the South, in addition, is a reduction in women's political role supported by even a tenth of the females.[24]

A regional effect is evident also when sex role definitions are compared directly to turnout. Regional differences in the behavior of men and women continue, whether they believe that women are fully equal or that they belong in the home. To show this effect, attitudes on "women's place" have been collapsed into three categories of egalitarian, moderate, and traditional role definitions. In Table 5.3, sex differences in turnout are presented within categories of these definitions and education. In the North, marked disparity in

TABLE 5.3
Sex Differences in Turnout, by Role Definitions, 1972

| | Non-South Role Definitions | | | White South Role Definitions | | |
|---|---|---|---|---|---|---|
| Education | Equality | Moderate | Traditional | Equality | Moderate | Traditional |
| Grade School | 11.6<br>(83) | 12.2<br>(66) | 21.8<br>(99) | 5.3<br>(48) | 20.5<br>(22) | 27.5<br>(57) |
| High School | 7.6<br>(253) | 0.5<br>(162) | 0.3<br>(181) | 19.5<br>(84) | 32.5<br>(49) | 11.2<br>(96) |
| College | − 4.1<br>(395) | 0.4<br>(138) | 1.8<br>(134) | − 0.1<br>(130) | −16.5<br>(54) | − 5.7<br>(59) |
| Total | 2.8<br>(731) | 6.5<br>(287) | 8.1<br>(414) | 5.8<br>(262) | 8.0<br>(125) | 12.2<br>(212) |

*The form of this table is similar to that of Table 4.1.

voting is seen only among the few grade school educated with traditional role definitions. In the South the effect of role precriptions on turnout is evident among high school graduates as well as those with lesser education. Comparison between regions shows that southerners more frequently accept traditional role definitions, but that a regional difference is evident even within the other role categories. Unliberated southerners show more sex distinction in voting than their northern brothers and sisters who agree that women's place is in the home. Even southerners who speak for sexual equality do not evidence it as strongly as northerners in the voting booth. An important exception again is found among college graduates, where the southern woman is at least as strong as her northern sister in maintaining her active franchise.

Another index of traditional attitudes is found in the frequency of church attendance. The aphoristic description of women's role as "kinder, küche, kirche" illustrates the presumptive link between adherence to organized religion and a restricted female role. When we analyze voting by church attendance, we find the effect of religious observance different in the two regions. Outside of the South, there is no regular relationship with male or female predominance in turnout. Even among regular churchgoers with only a grade school education, women vote more frequently than men by 1968.

If religion was once restrictive of female political activity, northern women have been liberated from these bonds. In the South, by contrast, there is a definite effect of religious traditionalism, particularly among those whites of lower education. The quality of southern religion apparently has been more closely related to confining sex typings. It is not simply that churchgoing itself is more common in the South. The very nature of that traditional behavior is more inhibitive of female political activity.[25]

We must conclude that the South has a more traditional culture, which defines the sex role of women in such a manner that they are less likely to participate in voting than their regional brothers or their sisters elsewhere. More than in other areas of the nation, the southern woman has been placed on a pedestal above the mundane world of conflict and politics. This attitude has persisted in the region from the antebellum era, when women's separate place became symbolic of southern virtue.

> She was the South's Palladium, this Southern woman—the shield-bearing Athena gleaming whitely in the clouds, the standard for its rallying, the mystic symbol of its nationality in face of the foe. She was the lily-pure maid of Astolat and the hunting goddess of the Boeotian hill. And—she was the pitiful Mother of God.[26]

This role provided a protected, but dependent, position for the southern white woman and also promoted ''yet more precious notions of modesty and decorous behavior for the Southern female to live up to.[27] In political activity, these ideals served to reduce women's participation. That effect continues, albeit with lessened impact, to the present.

We can further illustrate this effect of southern tradition by comparing two groups of southerners. More traditional attitudes would be expected among those who have lived most of their lives in the South, and therefore have been most fully exposed to the political culture of the region. Liberation would be more likely among women who have immigrated after childhood. To examine this hypothesis, we compare turnout rates among southern whites who have lived in their present state at least since the age of ten and those who grew up elsewhere.[28]

The data confirm the hypothesis fully. In both 1968 and 1972, there is a sharp sex difference in turnout among those who have remained in the same state since the age of ten. Turnout of men is 14 to 20 percentage points higher than among women. Among the mobile voters, however, there is virtually no sex difference. The effect of static residence is notable in the South—but not in the rest of the nation.

While the number of cases is small, these differentials also tend to remain when we control for age and education, factors that might be disguised as geographical mobility. A further indication of the effect of continued contact with southern tradition is evidenced when we control for sex role definitions. Whatever their characterization of ''women's place,'' long-term southern residents show more of a sex difference in turnout. Thus, long-term residents who believe women's place is in the home evidence this belief in an 18.3 percent turnout differential. Migrants with the same traditional view, however, show a mere 1.8 percent difference in their vote. Traditional southern-bred women stay at home even on election day. Traditional migrants venture outside at least once a year.

The controlled effect of the sex-related variables on turnout can be measured through the technique of multiple regression. Such analysis leads to the unoriginal conclusion that men and women voters are considerably different—even in the factors that bear on voting. For both sexes there is a large effect of education, and its weight is increased among women in 1972. But females are additionally affected by region and the presence of young children in the household, while these factors do not consistently correlate with male turnout. These special influences on women are clearly reflections of role differences, for southern tradition and the duties of parenthood have served to limit women's turnout in that region. By 1972, however, the disparities are reduced considerably. The effect of education now becomes predominant for both sexes; children equally affect men and women; and the differential effect of region is reduced to a marked degree.[29]

This detailed analysis has shown a definite, but diminishing, effect of sex roles on turnout. To a limited extent, the suffragettes' hopes for equal participation of men and women in the political process have been unfulfilled. However, the gap is slight and the trends are clearly toward closing that gap completely. Those demographic characteristics associated with equality in the voting booth are ever more prevalent. The increase of education, movement away from rural areas, and passing of generations continue. Even the cultural gap of southern tradition appears to be fading. Among college-educated southerners in 1972, women voted more frequently than men, and this was true even of long-term residents. Higher education is one means by which modern conceptions of women's place are replacing the southern chivalric myths. Migration is another such means, with new residents of the South carrying new conceptions of women's political equality in their baggage.

Sex, the basic biological fact, does not determine voting turnout. At least in this aspect of their lives, men and women do not depend on their bodies. Appearing at the polls instead is related to the views they hold of their proper place in society, and the conditioning effects of their circumstances. The trends in America are toward reduced differences in these conditioning factors and toward greater equality between the sexes in their ability to react to the events and issues of their times. The responsive voters will soon be unidentifiable by their genders.

## The Politics of the Sexes

Does sex really matter in voting? Once in the voting booth, do women act differently from men? Deterministic descriptions of women as the "gentler sex" predict their political views on the basis of inherent characteristics. Responsive women, like responsive men, on the other hand, would not have predestined attitudes, but would react to the stimuli of their times. For the remainder of this chapter, we will consider variations in the opinions and electoral behavior of the sexes.

The earliest European study of female voting found that women were more likely to support bourgeois over socialist parties, and to reject both left- and right-wing extremists in favor of clerical and moderate parties.[30] Given these findings, gross generalizations about inherent female conservatism have been accepted.[31] However, these studies were conducted in the early period of woman suffrage, when participation among the working class was restricted. It is quite possible that the supposed conservative character of the "weaker sex" was really a reflection of the class interests of the bourgeois women who voted.[32]

Among Americans, there is no evidence of a more conservative character among women—but some slight indication of the opposite. In party identification, in the more distant period of 1952, there was a slight tendency for more women than men to be Republicans (29.8% identifying with the GOP, compared to 25.8% of the males). By 1968, the marginal sex difference has shifted toward the Democrats (48.4% of the women identifying with the more liberal party, compared to 43.0% of the men, while similar proportions of each sex considered themselves Republicans). The Democratic leanings of women further developed in 1972, as seen in Table 5.4.

The sex differene in identification is located in particular groups. Most importantly, women under the age of thirty are far more likely than men to be Democrats, by proportions of 38.7 percent to 23.7 percent. This sexual disparity existed in 1968 as well, but became even more exaggerated in 1972. Young males do not compensate by disproportionate support of the Republicans, but rather by an Independent posture. In the other age groups, a substan-

**TABLE 5.4**
**Party Identification by Sex, 1972**

| | Male | Female |
|---|---|---|
| Strong Democrat | 15.5 | 14.7 |
| Weak Democrat | 22.0 | 29.1 |
| Independent | 39.4 | 31.9 |
| Weak Republican | 13.2 | 13.4 |
| Strong Republican | 9.9 | 10.9 |
| (N) | (1152) | (1507) |

*Percentages add vertically by columns to 100 percent.

tial sex difference is found among those over sixty, where women are more likely than men to be Republicans. Only in that passing generation is the alleged conservatism of women evident.

In the vote, American women have not evidenced any special fondness for conservative or Republican candidates. Any early tendencies in this direction could be explained by the disproportionate frequency of voting among wealthier and white women. By 1952, contrary to the stereotypes of the time, women did not fall prey to the glamorous appeal of General Dwight Eisenhower,[33] nor, until 1972, did their votes differ appreciably from those of men in any other presidential election.

In 1968, Nixon drew virtually the same vote from men (37.9%) and women (37.1%), while Humphrey's slightly greater appeal to women (32.9%) than men (31.0%) is statistically insignificant.[34] A marked sex difference was evident in support of Governor Wallace, however, with nearly twice as many men voting for him (12.1% as against 6.3%). The lower female support for Wallace cannot be explained by regional factors, even though his vote was concentrated in the South, where women vote less than men, nor by any other demographic influence.

In 1972, for the first time in available survey research, a significant sex difference was found in the two-party vote, as 7 percent more of men voted for Richard Nixon. The difference between the sexes was particularly important among the youngest voters. Reflecting their Democratic partisanship, women below 30 preferred McGovern by a 12 percent margin and actually gave him a majority of their vote. Further analysis indicates that the senator's advantage was concentrated among white northern women with a college education. This is the youth vote that McGovern strategists had expected to provide the core of his electoral majority.[35] The strategy was half effective, reaching particularly the female members of the new generation.

Women and men voted differently in 1972. This difference could not be predetermined, for it is contrary to the alleged conservatism of females. In contrast to the past, women in 1972 were more closely identified than men with a liberal party and voted in greater proportions for a liberal candidate. They were responding here not to biological necessity, but to the policy issues of the time.

War policy has been most significant in recent times, and the fact of war relates to the fact of sexual difference in the vote. From the time of Aristophanes to the torment of Vietnam, women have been viewed as more pacific. Defending his continued intervention in Southeast Asia, President Johnson insisted that he would not take a weak, womanly position; and, as Halberstam has pointed out, "the advocates of force were by the very nature of Johnson's personality taken more seriously, the doubters were seen by their very doubts as being lesser men."[36] Opinion data support this common belief that women have been more opposed to war. As American soldiers applied brutal force in Vietnam, these views became critical to the 1968 and 1972 voting choices.

From the beginning, women were more opposed than men to the American intervention in Southeast Asia. In 1968, over two-thirds of women regarded U.S. involvement as a mistake, compared to somewhat more than half of the men. While men were more active on the issue, the feminine population registered greater opposition[37] when asked its preferences on a seven-point Vietnam Action Scale ranging from withdrawal to the use of unlimited force. In both 1968 and 1972, as seen in Table 5.5, women are more dovish, although the difference between the sexes narrowed between the two elections. The proportion of male hawks in 1972 drops to the level of females in 1968. In the interim, however, women became even more opposed to the use of force.[38] Yet, there is no male predominance in the emphasis given to the intervention question by the two sexes. Among both men and women in 1968, 44 percent consider the issue the most important issue or very important in influencing their vote. By 1972, more women consider the war as an important issue than men, and more women (49% to 44%) give first priority to ending the war.[39]

Women's more pacific views are persistent. The degree of sex-association, however, varies with political circumstances. In 1968, gender is a major influence upon views about Vietnam, while party loyalty is of no assistance in understanding these attitudes. By 1972, the independent effect of sex is considerably reduced, and partisanship becomes the best predictor of opinion on the war. In the intervening four years, as detailed later in Table 5.7, an issue that caused a social division separating men and women was transformed in great part to a political issue distinguishing Democrats and Republicans.

**TABLE 5.5**
**Vietnam Action Scale by Sex, 1968 and 1972***

| | Male | | Female | |
|---|---|---|---|---|
| **Scale Position** | **1968** | **1972** | **1968** | **1972** |
| 1. Withdrawal | 11.8 | 18.4 | 15.4 | 23.4 |
| 2. | 6.7 | 9.0 | 9.9 | 10.4 |
| 3. | 6.5 | 13.9 | 9.4 | 13.3 |
| 4. | 26.3 | 24.4 | 33.0 | 25.5 |
| 5. | 11.2 | 13.0 | 10.3 | 11.4 |
| 6. | 12.0 | 7.0 | 7.0 | 5.7 |
| 7. All Force | 25.5 | 14.3 | 15.1 | 10.2 |
| (N) | (552) | (1018) | (690) | (1260) |

*Percentages add vertically by columns to 100 percent, except for rounding errors.

The immediate cause of this change was the transfer of power and responsibility for the war from Lyndon Johnson to Richard Nixon. The doves could now concentrate in the Democratic party. The different views of the sexes could thereby be absorbed into the system of party competition. Deterministic factors, such as gender, influence opinion when political alternatives are incoherent. Their influence lessens when the parties provide an opportunity for responsive voters to express their views politically.

The sex difference on the use of force explains the sex difference in political choice. The effects of gender and opinion on the vote are specified in Ta-

TABLE 5.6
Opinion on Vietnam and Vote, by Sex, 1968 and 1972*

| | Humphrey, 1968 McGovern, 1972 | | Nixon 1968-72 | Wallace 1968 | (N) |
|---|---|---|---|---|---|
| | | Men | | | |
| **1968—Less Interest** | | | | | |
| Doves | 35.3 | | 52.9 | 11.8 | (34) |
| Hawks | 44.6 | | 45.8 | 9.6 | (83) |
| (Gamma) | | (.09) | | | |
| **1968—More Interest** | | | | | |
| Doves | 51.7 | | 43.1 | 5.2 | (58) |
| Hawks | 27.9 | | 45.0 | 27.1 | (129) |
| (Gamma) | | (.42) | | | |
| **1972** | | | | | |
| Doves | 56.3 | | 43.7 | | (272) |
| Hawks | 11.7 | | 88.3 | | (239) |
| (Gamma) | | (.62) | | | |
| | | Women | | | |
| **1968—Less Interest** | | | | | |
| Doves | 49.3 | | 46.5 | 4.2 | (71) |
| Hawks | 35.5 | | 59.7 | 4.8 | (62) |
| (Gamma) | | (.12) | | | |
| **1968—More Interest** | | | | | |
| Doves | 54.7 | | 43.4 | 1.9 | (106) |
| Hawks | 28.6 | | 53.3 | 18.1 | (105) |
| (Gamma) | | (.40) | | | |
| **1972** | | | | | |
| Doves | 57.4 | | 42.6 | | (371) |
| Hawks | 15.7 | | 84.3 | | (235) |
| (Gamma) | | (.55) | | | |

*Percentages add horizontally by rows to 100 percent. "Doves" are those at positions 1-3 on Vietnam Action Scale; "Hawks," those at positions 5-7.

ble 5.6, which compares the ballots of those less or more interested in Vietnam in 1968 and those of all electors in 1972. Among the less interested voters in 1968, whether men or women, there is little relationship between opinion and vote. Among the more interested voters, a significant relationship is found, but at about the same level for both sexes. However, a small sex difference does remain, with even hawkish women being less ready to support George Wallace. In the simpler policy choice of 1972, the relationship of Vietnam positions and the vote is unusually high for both sexes. Men and women taking dovish views give similar majorities to McGovern, while the only (statistically insignificant) sex difference is the marginal tendency of women to support the less aggressive candidate. The relationship of opinion on Vietnam to the vote also remains when partisanship is controlled.

Because women are more opposed to war, they will also vote more for candidates whom they believe to be opposed to war. The greater feminine vote for McGovern in 1972 is a direct result of this association. Like males, females saw the South Dakotan as holding a dovish position on Vietnam. Because more women were themselves doves, more of them voted for McGovern. Women's vote is not a direct, dependent consequence of their femininity, but of politically responsive views women hold.

## Women and Force

Sex differences on Vietnam are a rare instance of distinctiveness between the opinions of men and women. Previous research has not found consistent sex differences on most issues of public policy, such as economic regulation, foreign aid, or civil rights. While women have shown some inclination to concentrate on local and reformist matters, they have generally been less interested in political issues, rather than distinctive.[40] One historic issue that did divide the sexes was prohibition. In elections from Illinois to Scandinavia, women were consistently found to be more favorable than men toward banning the bottle.[41] For this reason, woman suffrage was often favored by prohibitionists and opposed by liquor interests.[42] As one female opponent of both prohibition and woman suffrage is reported to have complained: "her husband got drunk on moonshine and beat her so she left him. She blames woman suffrage for this and for all other political evils."[43]

Of greatest contemporary significance is the persistent sexual difference on war. After World War II, men and women largely agreed on foreign policy issues, except that females were less likely to have an opinion at all and were also more likely to take "idealistic" or "internationalist" attitudes, such as a preference for action by the United Nations, rather than military means, to achieve national security.[44] More generally,

> differences between the sexes have pertained to attitudes on the use of military force and the implementation of policies regarded as risking U.S. involvement in war. Females were more likely to view our entry into the two world wars and the Korea and Vietnam conflicts as a mistake than were males. Women have been more likely to support U.S. withdrawals from wars already entered into and to be less receptive to the idea of "peacetime" conscription. . . . Support for the defense establishment, military aid, and collective security arrangements has been less as well among the fair sex.[45]

These general sex differences were specifically evident in regard to the American intervention in Korea from 1950 to 1953. Women were consistently more dovish on this first Asian war, although they were also less willing to express an opinion. "Women generally are less favorable to escalation than men, but only slightly more opposed to it; and women are less opposed to withdrawal than men, but only slighly more in favor of it."[46] Responding to the election survey of 1952, in the middle of the Korean conflict, women were significantly less inclined than men to believe the United States had been correct in intervening in the conflict (gamma = .26). In regard to future policy, almost two-thirds of females preferred the relatively dovish alternatives of withdrawal or negotiation, while close to half of the males were more hawkish, favoring the use of additional force (gamma = .22). Even today, after both Korea and Vietnam, the contrast between the sexes continues concerning use of force. When Congress passed the War Powers Resolution in 1973, inhibiting the use of military force by the president, 85 percent of women favored the act, compared to 76 percent of the men.[47]

Tenaciously, women raise their voices against war. Perhaps women are indeed the "gentler sex," and inevitably take a more humanitarian and more moral position. Undoubtedly some husbands and Elizabethan historians would dispute this global characterization. Nevertheless, there *is* a persistent sex distinction on one aspect of social policy, the use of force. Beyond the issue of war, there are other indications that women consistently are less willing to employ coercion in the settlement of group conflicts. To that extent, women may be entitled to credit as more humanitarian than men.

Race issues are illustrative of the character of women's humanitarian attitudes. Favoring programs to aid minorities certainly would be considered the humanitarian position, but women do not consistently show stronger support for such programs than men. Thus, in 1972, more women than men (39% to 32%) favored spending for poverty programs, but men were more willing (by 28% to 22%) to spend money to aid cities, and there was no sex difference in attitudes toward welfare spending.[48] In the 1972 election survey, women were slightly more favorable to school integration and government guarantee of equal public accommodations, but slightly more in favor of housing and social segregation—yet none of these relationships were statistically significant.

When the use of force is involved in civil rights, sex again does make a difference. To assess these attitudes, an Urban Unrest Scale has been established suggesting alternative means of dealing with the problem, ranging from "solve the problems of poverty" to "use all available force." In both 1968 and 1972, women were more likely to express the less aggressive opinions, and in both years almost twice as many females as males are at the very softest point. Between the two elections, both sexes moved toward more liberal positions, but the difference between them remained.[49] Overall, by 1972, a slim majority of men tended toward social solutions, while almost two-thirds of women approved of these gentler methods.

Men and women saw the issue differently, but they viewed the candidates similarly. To both sexes, Humphrey, as well as McGovern, seemed inclined to deal with urban unrest through solving the problems of poverty, and this evaluation was shared by persons on both sides of the issue. George Wallace was also perceived quite distinctly, no fewer than five of every six voters seeking him at the forceful end of the scale. Distortion of the candidate's position occurred only in assessments of Richard Nixon, who was seen by liberals of both sexes as advocating social solutions and by hardliners as favoring the use of force. The former president alone came close to meeting the traditional political formula of seeming to be "all things to all men"—and all women.[50]

Candidate perceptions were sufficiently distinct on the issue to permit a direct effect on the presidential vote. In 1968, the association between opinion and vote is apparent even among those less interested in the issue, and becomes quite pronounced when we consider those more interested. Among all voters in 1972, there remains a substantial correlation (.38 for men, .34 for women) between position on this issue and the vote, although it is less robust than the effect of Vietnam. Once their opinions are taken into account, however, women do not differ from men in the vote. Among those advocating peaceful solutions, 56 percent of the men and 58 percent of the women voted for Humphrey in 1968. Four years later, McGovern received the support of 43 percent of these liberal males and 48 percent of the liberal females.

In all of these cases, there is a slight but consistent inclination on the part of women to take the less hard alternative. Thus, women who favor the use of force still are less willing than men to support Wallace in 1968 or Nixon in 1968 and 1972. On both Vietnam and urban unrest, women advocate the use of force less than men and are also less likely to carry through on their forceful convictions in voting for candidates perceived as taking a more militant position.

Other data reinforce the evidence of a sex distinction in behavior related to differential readiness to employ force. For example, women tend to be more favorable to strict gun control than men.[51] Another example is found in the 1972 issue of campus unrest and the use of force in quelling college disturbances. While women do not favor students more than men do, they are less willing to use force to repress campus unrest (51.8% of women, compared to 59.3% of men). There is a high correlation between position on this issue and the vote. McGovern wins the vote of 65 percent of the relatively few men and 71 percent of the small number of women favoring students, while Nixon wins 80 percent of the men compared to 73 percent of the women advocating the use of force. Again, we find the pattern of women being somewhat more inclined to support the gentler candidate, with men more consistently inclined to back the perceived advocate of force.

The factor of sex has a consistent influence on political opinion, but the effect changes with political circumstances. The variation is revealed by regression analysis of the two vital issues in the elections of 1968 and 1972: Vietnam and urban unrest. In regard to urban unrest, sex is an important predictor of opinion in both years, and in 1972 it is more important than party identification and as important as the critical variable of race. Opinion on Vietnam is related to sex in 1968 but, as we have seen, becomes a more partisan issue in 1972.

Political developments explain these contrary movements. Between the two presidential contests and with the decrease of civil disorders, the urban issue became less salient. Opinions were therefore less tied to the political world, and political clues such as partisanship were made less relevant to opinion, while basic social influences such as sex could become more influential. The Vietnam issue remained salient in 1972 and was more closely related to party feelings, which came to substitute for underlying social memberships.

Women and men respond to the electoral environment. While women are

**TABLE 5.7**
**Sex and Opinion on the Use of Force***

| Variable | Vietnam 1968 | Vietnam 1972 | Urban Unrest 1968 | Urban Unrest 1972 |
|---|---|---|---|---|
| Party Identification | .00 | .19 | .11 | .07 |
| Sex | .17 | .08 | .12 | .14 |
| Education | −.06 | −.02 | −.12 | −.05 |
| Age | −.03 | .04 | .03 | .18 |
| Race | .16 | .14 | .26 | .14 |
| Region | .09 | .12 | .10 | .13 |

*Positive coefficients indicate that approval of the use of force is dependent on Republican party identification, male sex, higher education, greater age, white race, and southern residence.

indeed gentler in their approach to national problems, their compassion cannot always find an appropriate political expression. In such cases, opinions will be particularly related to the fixed characteristic of gender. When the parties present programs relevant to the opinions of women and men, however, biological determinism is replaced by political responsiveness.

## The Future of Sexual Politics

The contemporary tremors in the established terrain of America may change its political landscape. One possible result of present upheavals would be a sexual politics, with men and women facing each other across partisan fissures. The analyses in this chapter provide little reason, however, to anticipate such a future. There are few issues that are primarily related to a person's gender, and opinions on such matters as job discrimination actually do not polarize men and women. Nor is social segregation between the sexes likely as long as hormones do their pleasant work.

The one longstanding behavioral difference between the sexes—in voting turnout—is likely to be totally eliminated very soon. A lag is evident only in limited populations where traditional restraints on female participation continue. These restraints will be removed shortly and cannot stand against the impact of the education of women, the eased burdens of motherhood, and the diffusion of egalitarian norms.

In regard to opinions and voting, we have found relatively few differences between the sexes. In 1972, women showed greater support of the Democratic party and candidate, but this difference can largely be explained by their greater opposition to the Vietnam war. The permanent construction of sexual alignments partially depends on the future salience of issues involving war and force, as well as on the sources of women's greater reluctance to employ coercion to settle social conflict. Alternative speculations are available to comprehend these variations by sex. Deterministic theories find them inherent and unchanging, while cultural theories allow more autonomy to contemporary men and women.

One deterministic theory finds biological origins for sex differences. Recent anthropological research has pointed to the inheritance not only of physical features, but also of learned human behavior. Through the processes of natural selection, people have evolved with certain characteristic behaviors that enabled them to survive the many dangers of the race's history. It is possible that these characteristics necessary for survival included a relative aggressiveness on the part of men and a relative aversion to force on the part of women. For most of their time on earth, humans were hunting and migratory animals. A division of labor was efficient, in which one group hunted for food and defended the group, while another group attended the young and helpless, and maintained domestic life. Since women bore the children, theirs became the latter role, increasing their concern for survival of the group and their reluctance to risk lives in war. Women who were adapted to a nonaggressive role would survive longer and reproduce greater numbers. For men, aggressive qualities would serve better in the hunt and defense, and forceful men therefore would be favored in the evolutionary struggle. Over the long period of human existence, these differential characteristics could become fastened onto the very germ plasms of the species.[52]

Inherently, it is impossible to test this theory, since we have no relevant records of the preliterate history of man and obviously cannot conduct controlled experiments. Nor can we refute it by noting that the human race is no longer primarily a hunting species. The "civilized" life of man has been very short, less than one percent of the species' time on the planet. If certain behavioral characteristics were imprinted in the genes of primitive man, they would still affect our responses today.

The principal difficulty with this theory for social science is its deterministic and static quality. If behavior is greatly affected by inherited characteristics, we cannot expect significant changes in this behavior in a short period of years, or indeed for the imaginable future. We must become passive in regard to the control of our fate and any changes in our predestined lives. On the microscopic level of changes in opinion, deterministic theories do not explain the shifts that occurred in support of the Vietnam war from 1968 to 1972. Clearly, genetic transformations do not account for the increased dovishness of men or for the narrowing of the sex difference in this period.

A second theory, relying on the effect of childhood socialization, is also deterministic, but allows for greater change. According to this theory, differences in adult political behavior are related to the sexes' divergent experiences in childhood. For example, Gorer argues that American boys are compelled to demonstrate their masculinity by forceful behavior. "To prove to himself, and to the world that he is a real 'he-man' (the reduplication of the term is itself suggestive) the little boy has to be more strident, shout and boast more, call more attention to himself than his sister need."[53] Therefore, we should expect more aggressive behavior and attitudes among these boys grown to men.

The more common argument today is that of the women's liberation movement, which emphasizes the socialization of girls, rather than boys. Sex differences exist not because boys are socialized to be aggressive, but because girls are taught to be submissive.[54] Girls are kept from rough play as children, and are expected to be passive and restrained. The models they are presented with are those of a politically neuter housewife or, in the occupational world, of women in less competitive or more humanitarian activities, such as nursing and teaching. These influences in the girl's immediate environment of home and school are then reinforced in the mass media.[55]

We cannot consider these arguments in any detail here, but at least two doubts about them must be raised. First, it has not been demonstrated that socialization does produce the stated differences in boys and girls, in relation to politics itself. While we have overwhelming evidence on sex stereotypes in textbooks, the media, and other sources, there is not corresponding evidence that these influences produce differential attitudes when children are considered as potential citizens. That girls are personally less aggressive than boys does not necessarily mean they are taught to disapprove of the use of force by others, such as adult males. Furthermore, while there is no specific finding that children are different in their attitudes on the use of force in politics, girls tend if anything to have more positive affect toward the wielders of authoritative force, such as presidents and policemen.[56]

A second point is more vital. Whatever the differences in the socialization of children, the connection has not been made between these experiences and mature attitudes. In fact, it is no more than an unverified hypothesis that the political actions of men and women are directly determined by their childhood influences. Recent research has cast in doubt the influence of even the most salient political attitude learned in childhood, identification with a political party; and other research has found almost no differences between boys and girls in political interest, affect, and activity.[57] The alleged ties between early learning and adult opinion are tendentious.

These arguments approach absurdity in Gorer's examples, or when the Vietnam War is virtually attributed to sex standards that "force" men "into the continued pursuit of policies associated with aggressiveness, determination and presumed bravery after these policies have proven fruitless and damaging to the nation and the world."[58] Such explanations cannot account for behavior and particularly fail to explain changes in male opinion. To argue that men support the use of force in Vietnam because boys play with wooden rifles is not political science, but only cocktail party rambling.

Rather than being determined by evolution or in childhood, sex differences on public issues may be related to contemporary attitudes and role definitions. Although boys and girls are raised to be different, these expectations can change fairly quickly, as has been occurring recently in the United States. As the prescribed roles of men and women alter, their positions on other questions may also change, including their views on the use of force. One limited finding along this line suggests that if women become "more assertive so that they can compete in a male-oriented society, a correlative result may be to make them more hawkish on war and foreign policy."[59]

Our data provides a better test of the effect of sex role definitions. In Table 5.8 the difference between men and women on the use of force remains evident among the liberated and unliberated alike. Moreover, on the questions of both Vietnam and urban unrest, feminists who hold egalitarian views are still more opposed to the use of force than those who accept their place in the home. Similarly, egalitarian males also are more opposed to the use of force. The two issues are clearly related, but women especially continue to show a reluctance to use force to settle conflicts. Thus, feminism does not mean severity, since females generally do favor milder policies.

Women's persistent opposition to the use of force can be politically relevant. When issues of war and social coercion are raised, the truly gentler sex is particularly likely to be on the side of pacific settlement. Political leaders therefore have an available constituency in women, one that is increasing in size and relative participation. If candidates and parties offer less aggressive policies, they are likely to hear an augmented response from the feminine section of the collective popular voice.

The source of women's more moderate temperament cannot be located deterministically in their genes or their unconscious. It is more likely to be found in their contemporary lives as mothers and wives, lives grounded in biological inheritance but conditioned by social norms. While men plan abstract strategies, women worry about the safety of individuals they love. While men praise fallen heroes, women weep at the deaths of sons and husbands. We cannot fully explain this difference between the sexes, but we can

**TABLE 5.8**
**Sex Role Definitions and the Use of Force***

| | Sex Role Definitions | | | | | |
|---|---|---|---|---|---|---|
| | Equality | | Moderate | | Traditional | |
| **Policy Attitude** | Men | Women | Men | Women | Men | Women |
| **Vietnam** | | | | | | |
| Doves | 45.8 | 54.5 | 35.0 | 39.0 | 34.2 | 41.2 |
| Moderates | 22.2 | 23.3 | 33.9 | 31.1 | 23.6 | 25.8 |
| Hawks | 31.9 | 22.2 | 31.1 | 29.9 | 42.3 | 33.1 |
| (N) | (504) | (589) | (180) | (264) | (284) | (357) |
| | G = −.18 | | G = −.05 | | G = −.15 | |
| **Urban Unrest** | | | | | | |
| Solve Problems | 58.7 | 67.8 | 54.7 | 61.0 | 45.5 | 62.1 |
| Moderates | 16.0 | 13.9 | 17.3 | 18.0 | 24.1 | 13.7 |
| Force | 25.4 | 18.4 | 28.0 | 21.0 | 30.4 | 24.2 |
| (N) | (213) | (267) | (75) | (100) | (112) | (153) |
| | G = −.18 | | G = −.13 | | G = −.24 | |

*Percentages add vertically by columns to 100 percent, except for rounding errors. The moderate opinion is position 4 on the scales of women's equality, Vietnam, and urban unrest, with positions 1-3 and 5-7 collapsed into the other two categories.

respect it. For those seeking more peaceful solutions to the problems of society, this quality is worthy of preservation among women and of development among men.

## Notes

1. Gabriel A. Almond and Sidney Verba, *The Civic Culture*, abridged ed. (Boston: Little, Brown, 1965), p. 325.
2. Martin Gruberg, *Women in Politics* (Oshkosh: Academia Press, 1968), p. 7.
3. Alfred Hero, "Public Reaction to Government Policies," in John P. Robinson et al., *Measures of Political Attitudes* (Ann Arbor: Institute for Social Research, 1968), p. 52.
4. Angus Campbell, Philip Converse, Warren Miller, and Donald Stokes, *The American Voter* (New York: Wiley, 1960), p. 493.
5. Hazel Erskine, "The Polls: Women's Role," *Public Opinion Quarterly* 35 (Summer 1971): 278 f; Louis Harris and Associates, *The 1972 Virginia Slims American Women's Public Opinion Poll* (1972), p. 35.
6. Bernard Berelson, Paul Lazarsfeld, and William McPhee, *Voting* (Chicago: University of Chicago Press, 1954), p. 74.
7. Marjorie Lansing, "Women: The New Political Class," a paper presented at the annual meeting of the American Political Science Association (1971), p. 5.
8. The pioneering study is Herbert Tingsten, *Political Behavior* (Totowa: Bedminister Press, 1963), pp. 10–36. This book was first published in 1937.
9. Charles E. Merriam and Harold F. Gosnell, *Non-Voting* (Chicago: University of Chicago Press, 1924), p. 7.
10. *The American Voter*, p. 484.
11. Merriam and Gosnell, pp. 37, 114.
12. *Voting*, pp. 25–28; Robert E. Lane, *Political Life* (New York: The Free Press, 1959), pp. 211–13; Angus Campbell, Gerald Gurin, and Warren Miller, *The Voter Decides* (Evanston: Row, Peterson, 1954), pp. 191, 197.
13. Erskine, p. 277ff.
14. Merriam and Gosnell, p. 44; Lansing, pp. 9–19.
15. U.S. Bureau of the Census, "Voter Participation in November 1972," *Current Population Reports*, P-20, No. 244 (December 1972).
16. The census figures are likely to be more accurate than those of the University of Michigan study, since they are based on a larger sample and are factually closer to the actual turnout. However, the Michigan figures are only slightly less accurate and can be employed confidently for the examination of subgroups. For analysis of the sources of error, see Aage R. Clausen, "Response Validity: Vote Report," *Public Opinion Quarterly* XXXII (Winter 1968-69): 588–606, and U.S. Bureau of the Census, "Voting and Registration in the Election of November 1970," *Current Population Reports*, P-20, No. 228 (October 1971), p. 6.
17. Table 5.1 is a deliberate replication of the analysis of 1952–56 data as reported in *The American Voter*, p. 486.
18. Similarly, no sex difference in turnout was found in two northern presidential primaries in 1968—Austin Ranney, "Turnout and Representation in Presidential Primary Elections," *American Political Science Review* LXVI (March 1972): 26. Greater activity among black women compared to black men is found by John C.

Pierce et al., "Sex Differences in Black Political Beliefs and Behavior," *American Journal of Political Science* XVII (May 1973): 422–430.

19. This disparity may be unique to the 1972 election. In 1968, college-educated southern women voted 12 percent less than men, while the disparity in the North was an insignificant 1.6 percent. All other results in 1968 evidenced the same pattern as in 1972. However, even in 1952–56, college-educated southerners were distinctive in their sexual equality.
20. *The American Voter*, p. 487. Tingsten first noted this areal affect in *Political Behavior*, p. 14ff.
21. In 1968, the regional difference was even greater. In the North, women actually outvoted men by a small margin in the outlying areas. In the outlying areas in the South, however, 41 percent of women did not vote, compared to only a quarter of the men.
22. Merriam and Gosnell, pp. 37, 44, 76.
23. The 1972 data could not be analyzed on this point because no question was asked on the age of children in the home. The only relevant question asked if there were any school-age (5–18) children in the household. Even these poor data do show some slight sex difference. Men are not affected at all in turnout by the presence or absence of children. Women without school-age children are more likely to vote.
24. *Virginia Slims Poll*, p. 18.
25. Similarly, a study twenty years ago found southerners and women less tolerant of nonconformity, and a control for churchgoing could explain neither the sex nor the regional difference. See Samuel A. Stouffer et al., *Communism, Conformity and Civil Liberties* (Garden City: Doubleday, 1955), pp. 140–149. Another indication of the particularly strong influence of southern religion is found in the 1960 presidential election. See Angus Campbell, Philip Converse, Warren Miller, and Donald Stokes, *Elections and the Political Order* (New York: Wiley, 1966), pp. 88–93, 112–122.
26. W. J. Cash, *The Mind of the South* (New York: Knopf, 1941; reprinted by Doubleday Anchor), p. 97.
27. *Ibid.*, p. 137.
28. The latter group includes those who have moved only within the South, and therefore have not experienced other cultural influences directly. By including intraregional migrants within out "mobile" group, we make it even more difficult to establish our hypothesis.
29. Separate regressions were performed for men and women. The relevant beta weights in 1968 are: education, .33 for males, .26 for women; region, .01 for males, .21 for females; age of children, −.10 for men and .09 for females. In 1972 they are: education, .28 for males .33 for females; region, .10 for males and .13 for females; age of children, .05 for both sexes. Other variables included in the regression are age, residential area, race, and geographical mobility. Only for age is there a significant beta weight.
30. Tingsten, pp. 42–47.
31. As in Almond and Verba's summary, p. 325.
32. Tingsten, p. 72, found higher Republican votes in Illinois, where ballots were separated, in 1916 and 1920; but class and race bias can explain these results. Cf. Robert Lane, *Political Life* (New York: The Free Press, 1959), p. 214.
33. *The Voter Decides*, pp. 71, 75. On 1948, see *Voting*, p. 319f.

34. This finding contradicts Lansing, p. 7, who does not support her assertion that "women voted in greater percentages for Senator Humphrey than for Nixon."
35. Frederick G. Dutton, *Changing Sources of Power* (New York: McGraw-Hill, 1971), chaps. 2, 3.
36. David Halberstam, *The Best and the Brightest* (New York: Random House, 1972), p. 532.
37. An independent study conducted in March 1967, found "men were almost twice as likely as women to be hawkish on the war in Vietnam, and they were about twice as likely to be active *vis-à-vis* the war"—Sidney Verba and Norman Nie, *Participation in America* (New York: Harper and Row, 1972), p. 287.
38. The gamma correlation of opinion and sex decreases from .25 to .12 from 1968 to 1972.
39. *Virginia Slims Poll*, pp. 68, 74.
40. James G. March, "Husband-Wife Interaction over Political Issues," *Public Opinion Quarterly* XVII (Winter 1953–54): 461–470. Other differences be tween the sexes are summarized in *The American Voter*, pp. 489–493, and Kirsten Amundsen, *The Silenced Majority* (Englewood Cliffs: Prentice-Hall, 1971), pp. 134–138.
41. Tingsten, pp. 12–24, 72.
42. Alan Grimes, *The Puritan Ethic and Woman Suffrage* (New York: Oxford University Press, 1967); and Peter Odegard, *Pressure Politics* (New York: Columbia University Press, 1928).
43. Merriam and Gosnell, p. 113.
44. Gabriel A. Almond, *The American People and Foreign Policy* (New York: Harcourt, Brace, 1950), p. 121.
45. Hero, p. 53.
46. John E. Mueller, *War, Presidents and Public Opinion* (New York: Wiley, 1973), p. 146. The finding is confirmed by Louis Harris, *Is There a Republican Majority?* (New York: Harper, 1954), p. 111.
47. The Gallup poll, reported in *The New York Times*, November 18, 1973.
48. *Virginia Slims Poll*, p. 93.
49. G = .20 in 1968, .18 in 1972.
50. Cf. Gerald Finch, "Policy and Candidate Choice in the 1968 American Presidential Election," Ph.D. dissertation (University of Minnesota, 1971), and Arthur Miller, Warren Miller, Alden Raine, and Thad Brown, "A Majority Party in Disarray," *American Political Science Review* 70 (December 1976).
51. *Virginia Slims Poll*, p. 79.
52. Although not explicitly argued in these terms, suggestions along these lines may be found in Robert Ardrey, *The Territorial Imperative* (New York: Atheneum, 1966); Lionel Tiger, *Men in Groups* (New York: Random House, 1969); and Robin Fox, "The Evolution of Human Sexual Behavior," *The New York Times Magazine* (March 24, 1968), p. 32ff.
53. Geoffrey Gorer, *The American People* (New York: Norton, 1949), p. 94.
54. See Naomi Weisstein, " 'Kinder, Küche, Kirche' as Scientific Law: Psychology Constructs the Female," in Robin Morgan, ed., *Sisterhood is Powerful* (New York: Random House, 1970), pp. 205–20.
55. For a review of sex stereotyping, see Amundsen (above, n. 40), chap. 6.
56. See Fred I. Greenstein, *Children and Politics* (New Haven: Yale University Press, 1965), chap. 6; David Easton and Jack Dennis, *Children in the Political System* (New York: McGraw-Hill, 1969), pp. 335–43; Almond and Verba, pp.

332–35; M. Kent Jennings and Kenneth P. Langton, "Mothers Versus Fathers: The Formation of Political Orientations among Young Americans," *Journal of Politics* XXXI (May 1969): 329–58; Robert D. Hess and Judith V. Torney, *The Development of Political Attitudes in Children* (Chicago: Aldine, 1967).

57. On the transmission of partisanship, see Donald D. Searing et al., "The Structuring Principle: Political Socialization and Belief Systems," *American Political Science Review* LXVII (June 1973): 415–32. For recent research showing the absence of sex differences in children's political attitudes, see Anthony M. Orun et al., "Sex, Socialization and Politics," *American Sociological Review* XXXIX (April 1974): 197–209, and the references cited there.
58. Amundsen (above, n. 40).
59. This tentative conclusion follows from a survey taken during the Korean War, in which women with more liberal sexual attitudes were found to be more willing to use atomic weapons than their traditional sisters. Cf. Mueller, p. 147.

# 6

# Ethnic and Group Voting in Nonpartisan Municipal Elections

Although nonpartisan elections are now employed in almost two-thirds of American municipal elections,[1] only limited analysis has been made of their actual political effect.[2] There has been considerable theoretical discussion of the assumed values of this electoral system,[3] but Lee's study on California municipalities is the only substantial book on this subject.[4] Other investigations have appeared in the form of doctoral dissertations and journal articles, the most outstanding being the work of Adrian.[5]

In the existing literature, the major focus has been on the activities of candidates, political parties, and interest groups. Freeman examined voter preferences in a city with a local two-party system separate from the national alignment.[6] Williams and Adrian studied relationships between the votes for candidates in partisan and nonpartisan elections.[7] Both these articles are concerned with the involvement of the national parties in local, legally nonpartisan elections. To supplement these studies, it may be useful to analyze the votes in such contests directly, testing the assertion that "the nonpartisan ballot will not lead to new and unwanted irrelevancies influencing local voting decisions."[8] This study of two elections in Newark, New Jersey—one nonpartisan and one on a party ballot—is an attempted step in this direction.

## Socio-Political Background

Newark, the largest city in New Jersey, leads a double life in politics. In municipal affairs, it is governed by a strong mayor and council, the latter consisting of four councilmen elected at large and five chosen from wards. All officials are chosen for four-year terms in a nonpartisan election held separately from state and local contests.[9] At the same time, Newark is deeply involved in the partisan politics of its county and state. Elections for the county board, which controls great areas of patronage and policy, are highly competitive. The size of the Democratic Party margin in Newark is the key to victory in these contests. The county, in turn, is extremely important in state politics, since it casts 15 percent of the New Jersey vote.

**TABLE 6.1**
**Distribution of Social Groups in Newark, by Wards**

| | *Ward* | | | | |
|---|---|---|---|---|---|
| *Group* | *North* | *East* | *West* | *Central* | *South* |
| "Italian" | *† | * | * | * | |
| Negro | * | * | * | *† | * |
| "Irish" | * | | *† | | |
| Jewish | | | | | *† |
| "East European" | | *† | | | |

* Group present in this ward in significant numbers.
† Group particularly concentrated in this ward.

Although county and city are organizationally distinct, both involve the same constituency. For our purposes, the unique aspect of this constituency is its ethnic, religious, and racial variety. In 1960, fully a third of the Newark population was of foreign stock, that is, either of foreign birth or the children of immigrants. More than another third was Negro, making Newark the northern city with the largest proportion of nonwhites in its population.[10] Even among the remaining native whites, ethnic identifications retained some significance, since the grandchildren of immigrants might still consider themselves members of a distinct cultural group.[11]

We are concerned here with the voting behavior of these different groups. Exact figures on their relative size in the electorate cannot be obtained for a number of reasons: (1) The proportion of a group in the population and in the electorate differ because of variations in age and turnout; (2) the proportion of Negroes may have been underestimated in 1960 and has increased significantly since; (3) ethnic identifications of immigrants beyond the second generation are not determined; and (4) religious identifications are not reported, making it impossible to distinguish, for example, between Polish Catholics and Polish Jews. Similar problems exist when we seek to determine the proportions of different groups in smaller units, such as the five wards or 209 precincts of the city. The difficulties are increased by the fact that there is no correspondence in the boundaries of census tracts or other statistical areas and the precincts.[12]

Because of these factors, it is not possible to derive statistical correlations between the votes for particular candidates and the group characteristics of the voters. We can, however, use other procedures. The relative size and geographical concentration of the different groups can be estimated to provide useful background information.[13] In Newark as a whole, those of Italian descent clearly comprise the largest group in the electorate, including some 40 to 45 percent of all voters. Negroes comprised about a third in 1962. Those of Irish descent, once dominant politically, had largely departed to the suburbs by this time, and constituted about a tenth of the electorate. Jews and Eastern European groups each totaled less than a tenth.[14] These groups are somewhat separated geographically within Newark. Their distribution is summarized in Table 6.1, which is meant to be suggestive rather than definitive.

## Method

The method employed here does not depend on the accuracy of these estimates. We will not attempt to correlate the votes for various candidates with the social characteristics of the voters, since data on the latter factor are inexact. Instead, we will rely on the data that are available, the votes received by the various candidates. Analysis of the two elections is accomplished by correlating the votes for pairs of candidates. We attempt to find whether some candidates are closely associated with one another in their support. If such associations are found, we can then seek explanations.

For all significant contenders, the percentage of the vote for that office received in each of Newark's 209 precincts was calculated. Then, within each ward, the precincts were ranked, from those giving a candidate his highest percentage to those giving him his lowest. A Spearman rank-order correlation coefficient between various pairs of candidates was then calculated in each ward. There are, of course, well-known logical difficulties in drawing conclusions about individual voters from aggregate statistics. However, the units of analysis—precincts with an average of 500 voters—are quite small, making our conclusions more valid.[15]

We must assume that there is some reason for the relationships that become evident through this procedure. A high positive coefficient would indicate that a given pair of candidates was receiving support from a distinct group of voters; a high negative figure, that those voting for one did not support the other; and a low coefficient, that no definite relationship existed between the support of the two candidates. Our analysis can then concentrate on the nature of the voters involved.

## The Municipal Nonpartisan Contest of 1962

In the first election to be investigated, a total of fifty candidates obtained places on the ballot. For the mayoralty, only two were significant entries—the incumbent, Leo Carlin, and Congressman Hugh Addonizio. In the analysis, only the vote for the latter was ranked, since the ranking of Carlin's vote was simply the mirror image of his competitor's. In the balloting, Addonizio won by a 3 to 2 margin.

The voters' choice was far more cloudy in the races for city council. For the four at-large seats there were nineteen candidates. For each of the five ward seats there were from three to eight aspirants. All candidates who received a significant vote are included in this analysis, a total of twenty-two contenders. Only two candidates, both contesting ward seats, won an absolute majority of the votes and thereby secured a council chair. The remaining seven legislators were chosen in later runoff elections.

In Table 6.2, correlation coefficients are listed of the votes for Addonizio and the significant candidates for councilmen-at-large, as well as correlations between selected pairs of candidates for the at-large positions. Pairs involving candidates for ward councilmen are presented in Table 6.3.

In seeking underlying common characteristics of the paired candidates to explain the listed correlations, four possibilities may be suggested: (1) Although the ballot is formally nonpartisan, the voters selected candidates of the same party; (2) the voters ignored party lines but voted for the "slates" of allied candidates; (3) the voters chose candidates who represented similar positions on policy issues; (4) the voters chose candidates of the same ethnic background.

1. The election results do not evidence any relationship to the party affiliations of the candidates. Although the vote for Addonizio is closely related to that for Guiliano or Villani, the only prominent Republicans contesting for

**TABLE 6.2**
**Rank-Order Correlation Coefficients of Pairs of Candidates for Mayor and Councilmen-at-Large, Newark, 1962**

| | *Ward* | | | | |
|---|---|---|---|---|---|
| *Candidate Pair* | *North* | *East* | *West* | *Central* | *South* |
| Addonizio–Payne | −.33 | −.16 | .37 | .08 | .73 |
| Addonizio–Trugman | −.58 | −.59 | −.36 | −.30 | −.42 |
| Addonizio–Brady* | −.96 | −.93 | −.79 | −.35 | −.84 |
| Addonizio–Callaghan* | −.95 | −.87 | −.72 | −.15 | −.68 |
| Addonizio–Bontempo* | .72 | .53 | .28 | .12 | −.62 |
| Addonizio–Coppola | .82 | .42 | .23 | .11 | .09 |
| Addonizio–Guiliano* | .81 | .54 | .38 | −.10 | −.72 |
| Addonizio–Marmo | .84 | .74 | .25 | −.01 | −.10 |
| Addonizio–Villani | .87 | .66 | .86 | .39 | −.26 |
| Payne–Trugman | .39 | .44 | .37 | .09 | −.67 |
| Brady*–Callaghan* | .96 | .82 | .89 | .56 | .59 |
| Brady*–Bontempo* | −.69 | −.57 | −.04 | .50 | .67 |
| Bontempo*–Guiliano* | .79 | .79 | .67 | .47 | .59 |

* Incumbent.

councilmen-at-large, it is also closely correlated with the votes for such known Democrats as Bontempo and Marmo. Of the seven major Democratic candidates for the council, Addonizio's vote is positively correlated with the vote for three candidates, negatively related to three others, and variably associated with the last. Similarly, the votes for Democrats Bontempo and Brady show no consistent relationship, but there is such a relationship between the votes for Bontempo and Guiliano, although they were prominent members of opposing parties.

It is not surprising that party was not determining in the election. No identifying label existed on the ballot, of course.[16] Moreover, both candidates for mayor, and most of those for councilmen, were Democrats, so a direct partisan choice was not possible. The party organizations did not even attempt to offer organized alternatives. In the council races, there was no formal activity by the parties. While they did play a role in the mayoralty contest, it was in too incoherent a manner to offer much guidance to the electorate. Addonizio, although a well-known Democrat, was supported by most activists in the five Republican ward organizations. Carlin had the formal endorsement of the

**TABLE 6.3**
**Rank-Order Correlation Coefficients of Pairs of Candidates for Mayor, Councilmen-at-Large, and Ward Councilmen**

| Candidate Pair | Ward | | | | |
|---|---|---|---|---|---|
| | *North* | *East* | *West* | *Central* | *South* |
| Addonizio–leading "loyalist" | −.14 (Gerard) | .22 (Gordon) | .75 (Addonizio)* | −.36 (Marshall) | −.53 (Cooper) |
| Addonizio–leading "insurgent" | .44 (Iacobucci) | −.52 (Stolowski) | −.34 (Reilly) | .46 (Turner) | −.42 (Bernstein) |
| Addonizio–leading "ethnic candidate" | −.17 (Melillo) | .67 (DiBella) | .75 (Addonizio)* | .46 (Turner) | .68 (Kilgore) |
| "Ethnic ticket"–at-large and ward | −.10 (Bontempo–Melillo) | .52 (Bontempo–DiBella) | .29 (Brady–Reilly) | .64 (Payne–Turner) | .78; .88 (Trugman–Bernstein; Payne–Kilgore) |

* Frank Addonizio (no relation to the mayoral aspirant).

Democratic county chairman and four of his party's ward chairmen. These endorsements did not mean actual support, however. The county chairman made it clear that his support was only personal.[17] In a primary contest, control of the North Ward Democratic organization was assumed by insurgent Addonizio supporters. In the other wards, defections to Addonizio were widespread, involving three-fourths of the precinct workers in at least one ward, according to its Democratic chairman.

2. Similarly, there is no evidence of voting for nonparty slates of allied candidates. Generally, no such slates existed, as candidates avoided mutual endorsements in order to prevent the alienation of any potential support. The only such alliance involving candidates for mayor and councilmen-at-large was one between Carlin and Callaghan. As might be expected if voting by slates existed, there is a high negative correlation of the votes for Addonizio and Callaghan. However, the vote for Addonizio and Brady, who were not formally opposed, shows an even higher negative relationship in every ward.

There were some isolated cases of informal alliances between candidates for mayor and ward councilman. In the North Ward, Addonizio was opposed by Gerard. In the South, he was supported by Bernstein. The voters, however, were apparently unaware of or unimpressed by these alliances. In both cases, there is a negative correlation between the paired candidates. In fact, as will be seen in Table 6.3, there is more of a negative correlation between the votes for Addonizio and his supporter, Bernstein (−.42), than between Addonizio and his opponent, Gerard (−.14).

Slate making was more apparent in the Central Ward, which was effectively organized by a Negro "machine" led by ward councilman Turner. There is a relatively high correlation between the votes for Addonizio and Turner (.46), who were openly allied. On the other hand, there is a substantial negative correlation between the support for Turner and that for Bontempo (−.55), despite the endorsement of Bontempo by Turner. Even in the bailiwick of Newark's most efficient "machine," slate voting was not fully apparent. These few cases are the only instances of candidate slates in the election.

3. It is equally difficult to explain the observed relationship between the candidates' votes in terms of policy agreements. If policy constitutes the basis for vote correlations, at least three conditions must be met: the candidates must take policy positions of some clarity and significance, the voters must be cognizant of these positions, and the voters must cast their ballots because of policy considerations. The evidence does not indicate that these conditions were met.

For the most part, candidates did not take definite positions on the issues and the dissemination of their views to the voters was limited. Only in the mayoralty contest were issues argued, as Addonizio attacked the incumbent administration's policies on crime, race relations, urban renewal, and taxes,[18] while Carlin defended his plans for a "New Newark."[19] These views were frequently reiterated and widely publicized.

Such was not the case for councilmanic candidates. A questionnaire was distributed by the League of Women Voters to all aspirants and the answers reprinted in the local newspapers. These answers constituted the fullest expression of the candidates' views available to the voters, but ten candidates did not even return the questionnaire. Among the more specific "platforms" were pledges to formulate "sound and effective policies," to "attract industry and shopping," and to place traffic stop signs on all streets.[20] An exhaustive examination of newspapers for the six-month period before the election revealed scarcely any meaningful programs advanced by the major contenders in this period. The candidates were largely ignored by the press and the voters. A city-wide meeting in the final week of the campaign, to which all councilmanic candidates were invited, was the voters' only opportunity for direct confrontation and comparison of the candidates, but only 25 voters out of 150,000 bothered to attend.[21] In these circumstances, the common aspirant preferred "to take no stand at all, or an ambiguous one, or to discuss irrelevancies. He would rather try to be all things to all people."[22]

Nevertheless, it is still possible that issue preferences of a general nature affected the voters and account for the observed correlations. Voters did have a choice between candidates generally supporting existing municipal policies and those generally attacking these programs. This, of course, was the fundamental difference between Addonizio and Carlin in the mayoralty race and the voter might be aware of this difference in councilmanic candidates also. With some injustice, but for the sake of simplicity, we can characterize those attacking city policies as "insurgents" and those defending them "loyalists."[23] The most obvious "insurgents" were Addonizio for mayor and Payne and Trugman for councilmen-at-large. All the incumbent councilmen-at-large, as well as Villani, were basically "loyalists." The same was generally true of the incumbent ward councilmen, with the exception of Turner. In the election, there are mixed results. While the voters decisively rejected the incumbent mayor, and thereby presumably indicated some disapproval of past policies, they also returned seven "loyalists" to the council. Protest voting apparently existed in the mayoralty contest; it was not expressed in the elections for the city council.[24]

Analysis of candidate pairs also shows no policy coherence in the voting. If the electorate were casting its ballots on the basis of issues, there should have been a high correlation between the votes for Addonizio, Payne, and Trugman and a negative correlation in the votes for Addonizio and most incumbent councilmen. This does not exist. The correlations between Addonizio, Payne, and Trugman are erratic. The vote for Addonizio is negatively correlated with that for a "loyalist" such as Brady, but highly related to that of others, such as Bontempo and Guiliano. Similarly, the votes for incumbent ''loyalists'' Bontempo and Brady are generally not related.

4. The only explanation of the vote which can be supported is that which emphasizes ethnic considerations. Regardless of party, slate, or policy positions, the votes for candidates of the same stock are closely related, especially in those wards populated by members of that stock. Other factors become significant only in wards in which few persons of the particular ethnic group live.

The vote for ''Italian'' candidates is illustrative. The closest correlates to the vote for Addonizio are the votes for others of the same ethnic group, particularly when one considers wards in which large numbers of ''Italians'' live. Almost invariably, the correlation of votes for paired ''Italian'' candidates decreases as one examines in order the North, East, West, Central, and South wards. This is also the order of decreasing ''Italian'' population by wards.[25]

Ethnic considerations go far toward explaining the lack of relationships between candidates on the basis of party, slates, or policy positions. Addonizio's vote is closely correlated with that for both a Republican, Guiliano, and a Democrat, Bontempo, because all were ''Italian.'' Payne and Trugman, Negro and Jewish respectively, to take another example, were alike in many of their policy positions, but the votes for them were closely related only in wards that had relatively few of their ethnic fellows. Where the voters could feel a group kinship, this became more important to them, apparently, than policy considerations.

Generally, candidates received disproportionately high support from areas populated by members of their own ethnic groups. This is apparent if we examine the actual votes received, rather than rankings. Trugman received close to half his votes from the South ward, although only 22 percent of all ballots were cast in this area. Payne received 60 percent of his support from the South and Central wards, but little more than a third of the total electorate resided in these areas. The ''Irish'' candidates received about a third of their support from the West ward and the ''Italians'' a third from the North ward. Each of these areas contained less than a quarter of all votes, however.[26]

Addonizio alone had a political appeal that extended significantly beyond his own ethnic group. Addonizio won in all wards, and actually received his highest percentage in the predominantly Negro Central ward. Nevertheless, Addonizio's appeal also was an ethnic one. It differed from that of other candidates in that it was an ethnic appeal to Negroes as well as to his own ''Italian'' group. A great part of Addonizio's congressional career had been devoted to performing services for his many nonwhite constituents, and he maintained a personal organization in the Negro districts. In the election, the vote for Addonizio was closely related to that for Negroes like Payne in nonwhite areas, as well as to that for other ''Italians'' in the other districts.

A brief analysis of the elections for ward councilmen gives further evidence of the importance of ethnic factors. For each ward four different kinds of pairs are compared: (1) Addonizio and the most prominent "loyalist" among the ward councilmanic candidates; (2) Addonizio and the leading "insurgent" candidate for ward councilman; (3) Addonizio and the principal "ethnic candidate," that is, the leading "Italian" or Negro among the ward candidates; (4) an "ethnic ticket," created by the author, of leading candidates of the same ethnic group for councilman-at-large and ward councilman. (Two such "tickets" are listed in the South ward.)

As seen in Table 6.3, ethnic factors clearly influenced the vote in the East, West, and South wards. Addonizio's vote is most closely related to that for others with a similar ethnic appeal, whether they be "Italians" or Negroes. There are substantial negative relationships between the votes for Addonizio and for other "insurgents," but more of a relationship between the votes for Addonizio and for the "loyalists." There is generally a close relationship between votes for members of the "ethnic tickets."

The North and Central wards are different. In the North ward, all candidates were "Italian," and the ethnic factor was controlled. In the Central ward, all local candidates were Negro. Moreover, Turner was both an "insurgent" and the leading "ethnic candidate." The correlation between the votes for Addonizio and Turner, therefore, cannot be said to be based on ethnic factors alone. It is noteworthy, nevertheless, that there is a still higher correlation between the votes for Payne and Turner, both Negroes.

It is possible, of course, that these correlations are accidental or that they reveal some relationship other than ethnicity not accounted for by our three alternative explanations. Ethnicity as a causal factor, however, is consistent with the private statements of politicians and with their campaign activities. All respondents agreed that the major factor in the election was ethnicity, variously expressed by them as "race," "nationality," "the elements," and "gutter politics." Candidates sought their major support through ethnic organizations such as the Italian Federation or the Negro churches. Almost no advertisements were run in Newark's city-wide newspapers, as candidates concentrated their expenditures in the neighborhood publications, where more specific appeals could be made to different groups. Typical of such appeals were pamphlets endorsing Addonizio. Incumbent city officials were pictured as "Carlin's lily-white administration," while promises were made of appointments of Negroes to public office.[27]

As a final indication of the influence of ethnicity in this election, we can attempt to measure its impact with other factors controlled. We need not and cannot control for party or slate, since there were only a handful of cases involving Republican candidates or nonparty slates. We can, however, attempt to assess the relative importance of ethnic affiliation and policy position in the following way: The 58 coefficients measuring the rank-order correlations between Addonizio and candidates for the at-large and ward seats are ordered from + 1 to − 1, and then divided into quartiles.[28] Each of the 58 candidate pairs is then placed in one of four descriptive categories on the basis of ethnicity and issue position: (1) Addonizio and the other candidate have a similar ethnic appeal and also take the same general issue position, i.e., they are "insurgents"; (2) the two candidates share the same issue position but represent different ethnic appeals; (3) the two candidates disagree on the issues, but represent the same ethnic appeal; (4) the two candidates disagree on both the issue and their ethnic appeal.

The resulting table (Table 6.4) indicates the relative importance of these two factors. The crucial categories are the second and third. High positive or negative correlations for candidate pairs in agreement or disagreement both on issues and ethnic appeal do not discriminate between the two influences. However, if issue position is more significant than ethnicity, positive correlations should be concentrated in the second category. If ethnicity is more important, then positive correlations should be concentrated in the third group.

Table 6.4 clearly indicates the greater importance of ethnicity. Most of the high positive correlations come from pairs of similar ethnic appeal but of opposed policies. The negative correlations show a disproportionate number of candidate pairs agreed on policy but of contrasting ethnic appeals. Reading the table horizontally, we see the same pattern.

**TABLE 6.4**
**Correlation Coefficients of Addonizio and Councilmanic Candidates, by Quartiles and Ethnic and Issue Appeals**

| *Appeal of Addonizio and Candidates* | *Quartile* | | | |
|---|---|---|---|---|
| | *1* (*.96 to .46*) | *2* (*.44 to −.01*) | *3* (*−.10 to −.42*) | *4* (*−.42 to −.96*) |
| Issues and ethnicity | 2 | 1 | | |
| Issues, but not ethnicity | 1 | 2 | 6 | 4 |
| Ethnicity, but not issues | 12 | 10 | 5 | 2 |
| Neither issues nor ethnicity | | 1 | 3 | 9 |
| Total | 15 | 14 | 14 | 15 |

In summary, ethnic considerations appear to have influenced the Newark municipal contest. In making their choices, voters seem particularly inclined to vote for candidates of their own groups. Considerations of party, electoral alliances, and policy are apparently subordinated. The goal of nonpartisanship is fulfilled, as party identification does not determine the outcome. In the place of party, ethnic identification is emphasized, and the result is "to enhance the effect of basic social cleavages."[29]

## The State Assembly Contest of 1961

The second election to be considered was conducted on a county-wide partisan basis. Each of the major parties presented a full slate of nine candidates, formally nominated through a direct primary, but actually named by the county leadership through a "screening committee." Each party took care to present a "balanced ticket," including all major ethnic groups.

To assess the influences in this election, five members of each party's slate were chosen for rank-order correlation analysis. In both parties the selected candidates included the first name on the ticket, in both cases men of remote Irish ancestry; one "Italian"; one Jew; one Negro; and the last man on the ticket, who in both cases was Jewish.[30] Correlations were computed between the vote for the ticket leader and each of his running mates and then correlations were derived, across party lines, of the votes for persons of the same ethnic stock.

The purpose of the analysis in this section is to gauge the relative influence of the voters' party affiliations, and the policy positions implied by party, as compared with their ethnic affiliations. Correlations of the votes for different candidates cannot be conclusive proof, but they can provide an indicative pattern. If party voting were predominant, there should be high positive correlations in the first two groups of figures in Table 6.5, representing the Democratic and Republican candidates. The absence of ethnic influences on the vote would be shown by high negative correlations in the last group, representing interparty comparisons along ethnic lines. On the other hand, if ethnic considerations are more important, the reverse would be true.

Evidently, party voting is the more important factor. In every case, there are positive correlations of the votes for members of the same party, and these are high in all but one case. Conversely, correlations of votes for candidates of the same ethnic group but of different parties are always negative and generally highly negative. While we cannot prove that party sentiment formed the basis for the voters' choices, it should certainly be apparent that ethnic considerations cannot explain the revealed pattern. Moreover, it is difficult to imagine any factor other than party that could explain such high and consistent relationships between the paired votes.

**TABLE 6.5**
**Rank-Order Correlation Coefficients of Pairs of Candidates for State Assembly, Newark, 1961**

| *Candidate Pair* | *Ward* | | | | |
|---|---|---|---|---|---|
| | *North* | *East* | *West* | *Central* | *South* |
| Democratic Party: | | | | | |
| Matthews–Policastro | .75 | .72 | .91 | .79 | .96 |
| Matthews–Mandlebaum | .97 | .87 | .97 | .93 | .65 |
| Matthews–Richardson | .96 | .84 | .94 | .79 | .86 |
| Matthews–Poll | .97 | .87 | .93 | .85 | .66 |
| Republican Party: | | | | | |
| Bate–Sarcone | .63 | .90 | .90 | .87 | .98 |
| Bate–Lindeman | .99 | .98 | .98 | .95 | .66 |
| Bate–Tate | .94 | .87 | .88 | .82 | .81 |
| Bate–Warner | .97 | .96 | .97 | .91 | .12 |
| Interparty pairs: | | | | | |
| Matthews–Bate | −.95 | −.93 | −.97 | −.90 | −.87 |
| Policastro–Sarcone | −.19 | −.52 | −.69 | −.59 | −.92 |
| Mandlebaum–Lindeman | −.95 | −.95 | −.97 | −.95 | −.32 |
| Richardson–Tate | −.89 | −.69 | −.78 | −.58 | −.30 |

There is only scattered evidence of an ethnic influence on the vote. The support for two "Italian" candidates, Policastro and Sarcone, shows only a low negative correlation in the North ward. It is possible that a great many "Italian" voters bolted their party tickets to choose a candidate "of their own kind." There were similar defections by Negroes in the South ward.[31]

The most significant deviation from party voting apparently involved Jewish voters in the South ward. Here Warner ran far ahead of his Republican colleagues. This seems to have resulted because Democratic voters selected Warner in place of Poll, the last name on the Democratic ticket. This preference cannot be explained on ethnic grounds, since both candidates were Jewish. Rather, a Newarker known for his activity in Jewish and civic affairs was preferred over a suburbanite with little personal appeal to Jewish voters. Factors of personality and residence, aside from ethnicity, were involved.

It is evident that "bolting" of the party ticket was generally restrained in this election. Similarly, there was less "cutting" or "single-shot voting" in this contest than in the nonpartisan municipal election. In the latter case, only

75 percent of the maximum number of ballots were cast, as the average voter made only three of a possible four choices for councilman-at-large.[32] In the Assembly contest, 87 percent of the maximum ballots were cast, as the average voter made eight of a possible nine choices.

The most significant conclusion one can draw from analysis of the Assembly election is the reduced appeal of ethnicity with a party ballot. Voters generally do not seek out candidates of their own ethnic stock nor do they deliberately vote against candidates of other groups. Different group identifications are promoted by the different ways in which politics is conducted under the two systems.[33] Under nonpartisanship in Newark, politics is largely individual, disorganized, and incoherent. Election organizations exist only for the duration of the campaign, possessing no permanency, traditions, or responsibility for policy.[34] Financing is strictly the responsibility of the candidates, and no effective control or publicity exists.

In the partisan Assembly elections, the parties act to bridge ethnic differences and to achieve unified support of their candidates. Nominations are strictly controlled. Campaigning is conducted for a slate, not for individuals, and the parties largely manage the conduct and financing of the election contest. While ethnic appeals exist, they are subordinated to pleas for a vote for the party ticket, and it is considered improper for a candidate to seek votes for himself alone rather than for the entire list.

Because the parties wield effective control of nominations, they have sanctions available with which to enforce these canons of political behavior. Furthermore, elections are conducted on a county-wide basis and the candidate needs the party organization to reach all voters. Even more than organization, however, he needs the appeal and traditional support of the party label. With this, he can overcome the putative defect of membership in a minority ethnic group. Without it, membership even in a large ethnic group will be of limited political value.[35]

In this system, the individual candidate is not a free agent. He is subject to the discipline of the state and county party. This control is occasionally arbitrary or dictatorial, but the party can then legitimately be held responsible for the conduct of public affairs. The voters are presented with an organized choice between two relatively cohesive groups. In Assembly elections, the parties approximate the ideal model of groups which "put forward candidates for office, advocate particular courses of governmental action, and if their candidates win, create enough of a sense of joint responsibility among various officials to aid them in the fulfillment of a group responsibility for the direction of government."[36] No such groups exist in Newark's municipal nonpartisan elections. Whether city affairs have benefited from their absence remains a moot question.

## Discussion

Ethnic loyalties have long been an influence in American society. They have accounted both for the richness of American "cultural pluralism" and for the inherent racism of past immigration policies. The results in Newark's nonpartisan election show the continuing importance of these factors. Some specific cases underscore this general point. The strongest negative correlations exist in pairs of "Italian" and "Irish" candidates, indicating the persistence of an established pattern of social conflict.[37] Jewish voters, although generally considered the most liberal of any ethnic group, evidence sharp antagonistic reactions to a Negro councilmanic candidate such as Payne in the South ward. These reactions might be related to population movements within Newark, with the Negro lower-middle class gradually occupying formerly Jewish areas. Voting may be a silent and peaceful means of expressing resentment at the change.

In a partisan election, these loyalties are only slightly apparent. Interestingly, they become most observable in middle-class areas—among Jews and Negroes of the South ward and "Italians" of the North. Ethnicity apparently does not disappear with class mobility, as some have expected.

The effect of nonpartisan elections is to change the lines of electoral cleavage in Newark. Instead of being based on party loyalties, politics comes to emphasize more the ethnic affiliations of the voters. As Freeman suggests, "Insofar as legal devices may have some effect in disrupting the durable and persistent relationship between national and local party identifications, the foundations of the local [political] system will be altered in the direction of the dominant social divisions in the community."[38]

The influence of ethnicity should be considered as part of the longstanding debate on nonpartisanship. In one sense, nonpartisanship has succeeded in Newark. The goal of its advocates—to "emancipate" municipal elections from "the tyranny of the national and state political parties"[39] has been fulfilled. On the other hand, nonpartisanship has not succeeded in creating a model electorate, one which makes its decisions free of any group influences. The reformers rely "on the ability of the individual voter to discern the worth of individual candidates." In fact, the displacement of party ties may simply result in the substitution of other influences. "These ties may be as far from the rational, individual deliberation conceived by the nonpartisan advocate as would a 'blind party vote.' "[40]

The substitution of ethnic identifications for party loyalties is no advance toward the idealistic goal of a rational electorate. To be sure, ethnic affiliations will influence voting even in partisan elections, and they partially account for national party loyalties.[41] In some cases, ethnic voting may actually be the most rational form of voting, as when Negroes vote as a group on the basis of the civil rights issue. It is therefore doubtful whether ethnic factors will be entirely eliminated from American politics, regardless of the form of the ballot or other purely legal changes.

The real question is not whether, but how, ethnic factors are to influence the political system. Competition for office is a basic prerequisite for democratic control, but competition may be organized on various grounds. Ethnic factors may become the chief basis of political division, or they may be incorporated into more general cleavages. Nonpartisan elections tend toward the former alternative, partisan elections toward the latter.

Potentially, the political process is a means of overcoming the very great differences between ethnic groups. Common programs, compromises of differences, and mutual accommodation can be fostered. It is much more difficult to achieve these purposes, however, when the political system itself is based on ethnic differences. In such a case, political and ethnic differences simply reinforce one another, making reconciliation less likely. The voters' identification with their separate ethnic groups is strengthened, while their attachment to integrating, common groups is weakened. An increase in community incohesion is a likely result.

The partisan system of election tends to overcome these problems. Ethnic considerations remain, but they become part of a generalized party appeal, rather than the major basis of political division. The total effect is "to repress divisive issues."[42] Parties in Newark do not eliminate ethnicity as a political factor. Instead, they *manage* it, providing "unifying forces to integrate the wide-ranging interest groups and to establish the basic lines of political argument for the voters who must make the ultimate decisions."[43]

The basic party device for managing ethnicity is the "balanced ticket." Through the nomination of a slate comprising members of all ethnic groups, and through the practice of joint campaigning and centralized discipline, the parties are able to combine ethnic differences into an integrating and general appeal. The principle is further realized in "balanced" appointments to administrative positions.

Such devices help to bring all groups within the political system, fostering their consent to its rules and limitations. Political opportunities are consequently increased, and the channels for the recruitment of leadership are broadened. A "balanced ticket" also serves the function of promoting intergroup tolerance in the electorate and of helping, if only marginally, to remove some of the group tensions that pervade urban society. Individuals will vote for persons of an ethnic group other than their own because they are of the same party. The form of the election changes the identifications emphasized by the voters. The divisive factor of ethnicity is replaced by the unifying factor of party.

The argument for nonpartisan elections has generally emphasized rationality, "good government," and similar reformist slogans. This study presents only minimal evidence, to be sure, limited as it is to Newark, and to only two elections in that city. Undoubtedly, the political situation is different in other cities, and the particular Newark elections analyzed here may not even be typical of Newark. Recognizing these limitations, we can still conclude that ethnic factors were crucial in the outcome of the nonpartisan election analyzed here, while they were managed and subordinated in the partisan contest. It may be proper to suggest that the basic question raised is the real effect of any political device on the social life of the community, not its presumed rational quality. To judge by this case, nonpartisan elections do not contribute to an integrated civic life.

## Notes

1. *Municipal Year Book, 1962*, Chicago, International City Managers' Association, 1962, p. 103.
2. The subject is virtually ignored in the major textbooks on political parties. A representative treatment is Howard R. Penniman, *Sait's American Parties and Elections*, 5th ed. (New York: Appleton-Century-Crofts, 1952), pp. 296–97, 370–71.
3. See, for early examples, National Municipal League, *A Municipal Program* (New York: Macmillan, 1900); and Charles Beard, "Politics and City Government," *National Municipal Review* 6 (March 1917): 201–06.
4. Eugene C. Lee, *The Politics of Nonpartisanship* (Berkeley: University of California Press, 1960).

*5. Charles Adrian, "The Nonpartisan Legislature in Minnesota" Minneapolis, University of Minnesota, 1950, Ph.D. dissertation; "Some General Characteristics of Nonpartisan Elections," *American Political Science Review* 46 (1952): 766–76; "A Typology for Non-Partisan Elections," *Western Political Quarterly* 12 (1959): 449–58. See also Charles E. Gilbert, "Some Aspects of Nonpartisan Elections in Large Cities," *Midwest Journal of Political Science* 6 (1962): 345–62; Marvin Harder, *Nonpartisan Election: A Political Illusion?* (New York: McGraw-Hill, 1960) Oliver P. Williams and Charles Adrian, "The Insulation of Local Politics under the Nonpartisan Ballot," *American Political Science Review* 53 (1959): 1052–63.

6. J. Leiper Freeman, "Local Party Systems: Theoretical Considerations and a Case Analysis," *American Journal of Sociology* 64 (1958): 282–89.
7. Williams and Adrian.
8. *Ibid.*, p. 1052. The authors find that their data do not permit examination of this claimed merit of nonpartisanship.
9. In terms of Adrian's typology, Newark most nearly falls into the third category of nonpartisan elections, "where slates of candidates are supported by various interest groups, but political party organizations have little or no part in campaigns, or are active only sporadically." However, even group slates are not always present or meaningful. See Adrian (1959), p. 454.

*(Ph.D. thesis, University of Minnesota, 1950)

10. *U.S. Census of Population, 1960: General Social and Economic Characteristics, New Jersey*, Final Report PC (1)-32C, 1962, pp. 266, 278.
11. I have used "ethnic" as a general term, meaning not only national origin, but also religion and race. If not technically correct, this usage is at least common, convenient, and understood. See Robert Lane, *Political Life* (Glencoe: Free Press, 1959) p. 235.
12. Robert Dahl analyzes these problems in *Who Governs?* (New Haven: Yale University Press, 1961) Appendix B, section VIII.
13. These estimates are based on a combination of methods, particularly analysis of the distribution of the foreign-born, and personal interviews with some twenty political leaders in Newark, including a majority of the city council and professional politicians of all factions. Their estimates are largely in agreement, but the statistical evidence that follows does not depend on their accuracy. All other information not specifically documented is based on these interviews.
14. The "Italian vote" of course comprises far more than the first and second generation Italians enumerated by the Census Bureau. For the sake of simplicity, the various groups are referred to as "Italian," etc. It should be understood that these terms are meant in a strictly neutral manner to refer to "Americans of Italian descent," etc. (see Dahl, p. 36).
15. The Spearman correlation coefficient is calculated by the formula $p = 1 - (6\Sigma D^2/n\ [n^2 - 1])$, in which $D$ refers to the difference in rank between paired items, and $n$ to the number of paired comparisons. The voting returns were obtained from the official canvass by the Newark City Clerk.
16. Moreover, as indicated by George W. Pearson, "Predictions in a Nonpartisan Election," *Public Opinion Quarterly* 12 (1948): 112–17, the voters' preferences are not likely to change even when they are made aware of the candidates' parties.
17. *Newark Evening News*, Jan. 25, 1962.
18. *Ibid.*, Jan. 7, 1962.
19. *Ibid.*, Mar. 4, 1962.
20. *Ibid.*, April 26, 1962; April 27, 1962.
21. *Ibid.*, May 2, 1962.
22. Adrian (1952), p. 773.
23. These terms are meant only to be relative and descriptive, and imply no assessment as to individual ability. Generally, incumbents are considered "loyalists" unless they frequently dissented from city policies during their incumbency. Other candidates are judged on the basis of their past political careers, the sources of their support in the election, and their statements.
24. This is predicted by Adrian (1952), p. 773. Of the seven "loyalists," six were incumbents, as was one of two "insurgents."
25. There are two exceptions, involving one pairing of Addonizio and Villani, and one of Bontempo and Guiliano. In both cases, the pair includes a former incumbent in municipal or county office, and this background may have given these candidates a wider appeal. For the record of former incumbents and other features of nonpartisan elections, see Charles E. Gilbert and Christopher Clague, "Electoral Competition and Electoral Systems in Large Cities," *Journal of Politics* 24 (1962): 342–43.
26. Uneven geographical distribution of the vote from one area to another may be taken as a general indicator of a "particularistic" influence on the vote. In national politics sectionalism is similar in its effects on the vote to ethnic influence on the local level. See. E. E. Schattschneider, *The Semi-Sovereign People* (New York: Holt, Rinehart and Winston, 1960), chap. 5.

27. *Newark Evening News*, April 29, 1962, p. 15.
28. There are 45 correlations of the vote for Addonizio and that for each of 9 candidates for councilman-at-large in each of the 5 wards. There are 13 additional correlations of the vote for Addonizio and that for individual candidates for ward councilman. The quartiles cannot contain exactly the same number of coefficients, but there is no significant change in the pattern found if the groupings are altered.
29. Freeman, p. 285.
30. To clear any doubts, Matthews and Bate are the ticket leaders, Policastro and Sarcone are "Italian" Richardson and Tate are Negro, and the others are Jewish. The ethnic affiliations of the candidates were known in the community. The candidates were selected for their party tickets, in part, because they had the "right" names or had received recognition in Negro civil rights organizations, Jewish philanthropies, etc.
31. In all ethnic groups, there were probably more defections by Democrats, simply because the large majority of all Newark voters are Democrats. Williams and Adrian also suggest that Republicans tend to be more ideologically consistent in their votes.
32. Lee, pp. 64*n*, 142, also finds "single-shot voting" in nonpartisan elections. The figure for "maximum number of ballots" is derived simply by multiplying the vote for the head of the ticket by the number of legislative seats to be filled.
33. See David B. Truman, *The Governmental Process* (New York: Knopf, 1951), chap. 2 and Angus Campbell *et al.*, *The American Voter* (New York: Wiley, 1960), chap. 12, for general discussions of the influence of group memberships on political behavior.
34. See Lee, pp. 119–31, for a general discussion of campaigning in nonpartisan elections.
35. The party's power was demonstrated in the Assembly election of 1963. Richardson, the Negro Democrat, became objectionable to the party leadership, partly because of his militancy on civil rights, and was dropped from the ticket. He then ran as an independent. Despite great civil rights agitation and a 20 percent nonwhite county population, Richardson received only 5 percent of the vote.
36. V. O. Key, *Southern Politics* (New York: Knopf, 1950), p. 298.
37. See Duane Lockard, *New England State Politics* (Princeton: Princeton University Press), 1959, chap. 11 and Dahl, pp. 33–51.
38. Freeman, p. 289.
39. National Municipal League, pp. 144–45.
40. Lee, p. 183. That this is still the hope of the reformers is indicated by a Citizens Union statement opposing party slates: "It has been made all too easy for voters to vote a party line blindly, when if they had to look at the names they might have recognized an unqualified candidate" (*New York Times*, June 20, 1963. p. 40).
41. For an historical example, see Lee Benson, *The Concept of Jacksonian Democracy* (Princeton: Princeton University Press), 1961. A general discussion is found in Lawrence H. Fuchs, "Some Political Aspects of Immigration," *Law and Contemporary Problems* 21 (Spring 1956), pp. 270–83.
42. Gilbert, p. 361.
43. *Government Organization for Metropolitan Cleveland*, Cleveland Metropolitan Services Commission, 1959, cited by Lee, p. 37n.

# 7

# The Impact of *The American Voter* on Political Science

"A teacher affects eternity," according to an old adage with which academics console themselves while facing recalcitrant students. If that is true, a major book affects even more people, for it reaches many teachers, many student bodies, and many populations. Clearly *The American Voter* is such a book. Although this book has never been revised, it is still relevant in describing the behavior of contemporary voters, some of whom were not even born when this research was conducted. It has been seminal in the development of research on electoral behavior particularly and on political science generally. Indeed, it can be viewed as a "paradigmatic" work, setting the boundaries and standards for subsequent research.[1]

Scholars—especially the four authors of this volume—would agree, however, that any book must be subject to continual examination and reappraisal. Now that *The American Voter* has reached voting age, it is an appropriate time to analyze its impact, evaluate its limitations, and suggest new directions in research.

One measure of its impact, if not necessarily its truth, is supplied by the marketplace. The book has sold nearly 100,000 copies in clothbound and paperback editions.[2] It has now been officially certified as a classic by the recent republication of the hardcover edition by the University of Chicago Press.

Its academic impact can be gauged from textbooks and scholarly journals. Standard textbooks in American government and politics rely heavily on its conclusions. Illustratively, even as late as 1975, Burns and Peltason cite *The American Voter* and its descendants ten times, while the first edition of Sorauf's parties text referred to these works in twenty of fifty footnotes.[3] Even a deliberately critical book such as Dye and Zeigler is dependent on these sources, using them for fifteen of its forty-two citations.[4] Journal articles have shown the same respect to the original work. In a symposium on voting behavior in the *American Political Science Review*, there were sixty-two references to the Michigan research. A later discussion, although centered on other studies, added fifty-nine more references.[5]

Specialists in the field of electoral research have been made into academic catatonics. It is hardly an exaggeration to say that there was but one other original work on American electoral behavior for all of fifteen years after the publication of the work of Campbell, Converse, Miller, and Stokes—the "fearsome foursome," as one of my students described them. Such works as were published were essentially summaries and restatements of the basic findings of the original research.

The one possible exception to the deference paid to this work was V. O. Key's posthumous work, *The Responsible Electorate*.[6] Yet Key sought in that important work to refute what he regarded as distortions of *The American Voter*, not to challenge the original findings. In fact, he praised the book quite fully upon its publication.[7] Moreover, in handwritten notes for the projected final chapter of his own work, he concluded that his research "probably confirms the significance of Angus Campbell's model built on party identification."[8]

## Sources of the Impact

To explain the impact is somewhat more difficult than to demonstrate its existence. Obviously some of the influence of the Michigan work is due to its scholarly merits, the care with which the investigations were conducted, the detail and elegance of its presentation, and the revealing truths of its findings. However, good research is not always its own reward; many a village Hampden rests unnoticed in the country churchyards of scholarship. Aside from quality, there were other reasons for the renown of *The American Voter*. These reasons are to be found in the fit between the book itself and the nature of the times in which it was researched, published, and distributed.

When we speak of the "behavioral revolution" in political science, we speak specifically of the decade of the 1950s, and perhaps of the preceding and following five years. The discipline sought to capture the glamour of science, highest after the end of World War II, for itself. It arose in the period of the cold war, when ideological controversy was subordinated to national consensus, encouraging political science to neglect normative questions and to concentrate instead on value-free analyses.[9] The technology of high-speed digital computers had been developed, opening up the possibilities of manipulating large sets of quantitative data. The means to obtain such data had already been demonstrated by the sociologists in two important works, *The American Soldier* and *The People's Choice*.[10] The application of these methods to the study of mass politics was an obvious, indeed inevitable, step.

*The American Voter* rode the crest of the behavioral revolution, and was in fact its most prominent example. Techniques of sampling were now available to investigate not only the small groups of college students previously favored by psychologists and not only the individual communities probed by

Lazarsfeld and Berelson.[11] The entire nation could now be represented by fewer than 2,000 carefully drawn respondents. Findings could no longer be dismissed as representative only of Sandusky, Ohio, or Elmira, New York.

This research, moreover, was not only at the right time but also at the right intellectual place. Voting behavior is a subject particularly likely to interest others. As someone has said, everybody is an amateur political scientist, and every political scientist is an amateur voting specialist. Almost all political scientists vote—and think they know something about what happens in the process. Additionally, casting a ballot is the most common political activity of Americans generally, and the fame and fortunes of politicians, advertisers, consultants, interest groups, and others directly depend on accurate knowledge of mass electoral behavior. A large scholarly and national audience therefore was available for an insightful work on voting.

*The American Voter* was not only insightful, it was insightful in the right way. It appropriately rejected two other modes of interpretation, that is, appropriately for the intellectual climate of its time. It rejected the tradition of armchair speculation on voting, which could be traced back at least to Plato's comments about the misguided actions of an inexpert population. Instead of speculation, this book presented hypotheses. In place of personal examples, it presented representative data. Rather than moral exhortations, it presented behavioral regularities. Illustratively, armchair speculation had championed the nonpartisan, independent voter, rationally choosing between competing issues and candidates. The virtues of behavioral research were exemplified in the SRC description of the so-called Independent voter. With what joy we empiricists read of the deficiencies of that erstwhile paragon of the civics textbooks![12]

Secondly, the book rejected the sociological interpretation of voting, and thus saved the self-respect of political scientists. Empirical research on voting to this date had been conducted by sociologists invading our turf. With the appearance of *The American Voter*, electoral analysis became again the province of political scientists, even if, like the Michigan authors, they had to be recruited from social psychology or mathematics. No longer would politics be seen as only a reflection of social position, nor need we any longer believe, with Lazarsfeld, that "a person thinks, politically, as he is socially."[13] Instead, we would now examine "the politically relevant in surveys," in Key's phrase. The satisfaction, even relief, felt in the discipline is exemplified in the work of Daudt, who had completed a severe criticism of voting studies in 1960. Upon publication of *The American Voter*, he wrote an epilogue, fulsomely praising the new book as the answer to his previous criticisms of sociological determinism.[14]

Material and organizational factors also help to explain the impact. The significance of the first work of the Survey Research Center led to grants for further research, which in turn led to more findings, more impact, more grants, etc. By making their data readily available, the Michigan group certainly advanced the cause of scholarship. Their generosity was a signal service to all social scientists, perhaps most of all those young persons needing to publish quickly to gain promotion. The latent function of the availability of grant funding and the data, however, was to create a national corps of SRC disciples, who would have little intellectual choice but to accept the basic premises and methods of SRC.

As Michigan drew, trained, and placed the most outstanding graduate students in this subfield, these premises and methods would become the standard explanation of voting throughout the classrooms of America's colleges and universities. This development was furthered by the creation of the Inter-University Consortium for Political Research, which began its valuable work as a distribution center for the results of the national voter surveys. Data were now available to all, for a once-modest fee, and would be imbibed directly by impressionable undergraduates. The summer training programs then brought faculty and graduate students to Ann Arbor for personal contact with the "fearsome foursome" and for socialization into their axioms and techniques.

In no way do I mean to suggest that these efforts were ill-conceived, deleterious, or conspiratorial. The important work of conducting national surveys necessarily had to be centralized, and Michigan was the appropriate place to locate the enterprise. It has been done openly, seriously, and conscientiously. The entire discipline has benefited enormously. My point is that the inevitable effect was to create an intellectual quasi-monopoly in thinking about voting behavior. This effect is similar to that of the Bell system in telephone service. Here too a quasi-monopoly is technologically determined. It results in the best telephone service in the world, but it is also a constraint on trade—appropriate, useful, and not conspiratorial, but still a constraint.

We may also look to the overall tone of the volume to explain its impact. There is a distinct elitist appeal to this work. It uses modern statistical methods, comprehensible to the trained specialist but somewhat mysterious to the average voter. In so doing, it reinforces the claims of social scientists to be expert professionals, a guild with secrets unknown to the uninitiated. Moreover, the findings are not basically complimentary to the democratic elector. He, and apparently more often, she,[15] is not well informed, has poorly developed attitudes toward politics, and is heavily dependent on traditional loyalties in making voting decisions. Exceptions to these general descriptions are found principally among the well-educated, that is, among political scientists. To be sure, the book was not written by snobs or as an effort to promote snobbism, but its appeal may partially lie in its elitist implications.[16]

Finally, in one effort to be fair, one must acknowledge that the impact of *The American Voter* is also due simply to its scholarly merits. Its authors accumulated their data carefully. They allowed, even encouraged, criticism by making that data available to persons of different outlooks. They provided the basis for extended comparisons across time by accumulating a unique time-series archive, and across space by pursuing similar studies in other nations. In contrast to some later interpreters, their conclusions were stated precisely and with many necessary qualifications. Building on their sound empirical work, they went on, at least in their concluding chapters, to attempt the development of empirical theories. By providing these model elements of good scholarship, their impact has been not only great, but good.

## The Present Challenge

The influence of a work of scholarship can also be gauged by the controversy it creates and the responses it stimulates. By this test, *The American Voter* is currently being born again, which is perhaps appropriate in the present context of American politics. At least five major works have been published in the last two years which are direct challenges to the original volume.[17] The most prominent of these new books takes its title, *The Changing American Voter*, directly from the Michigan study and is actually dedicated to those four authors.

These books, and a multitude of journal articles, directly challenge or refute many of the specific findings of *The American Voter*. A brief canvass of this literature provides the following list of twenty-five disputed propositions drawn from the original work, grouped under four headings.[18]

### *Partisanship*

1. Since citizens are largely supportive of the political parties, party identification is the principal determinant of the vote.[19]
2. Independents are less knowledgeable and politically active than partisans.[20]
3. Most voters consistently identify with the same party across time.[21]
4. Party images are consistently distorted by the respondent's party identification.[22]
5. The likelihood of defection in the vote is inversely related to the strength of partisanship.[23]
6. In any given election, the bulk of the vote is from standpatters who consistently choose the same party, with change coming predominantly from less interested voters.[24]
7. Party identification is largely an affective, psychological, and traditional attachment rather than a choice based on policy agreement.[25]
8. Partisan loyalty increases steadily with age.[26]

*Issues*

9. The parties present no clear ideologies or set of policy stances to the electorate.[27]
10. Issue orientations are of relative insignificance in the voting decision.[28]
11. No more than a tenth of the voters, even using generous criteria, can describe the parties in ideological terms.[29]
12. The policy bases of the parties and the vote consist primarily of economic issues originating in the Depression of the 1930s.[30]
13. Ideologies, or coherent patterns of belief across issue areas, are largely absent in the mass electorate.[31]

*Social Factors*

14. Social class has steadily declined as an influence on the vote.[32]
15. Farmers are the least politically involved of all occupational groups.[33]
16. Social mobility is not associated with changes in party identification.[34]
17. Class-based voting is most evident among persons with strong party identification.[35]
18. Religion has little independent effect on party vote.[36]
19. Level of education is the basic explanation of coherent political attitudes.[37]
20. Low psychological motivation among Negroes (not blacks) is a partial explanation for low levels of political activity.[38]

*Electoral Trends*

21. Party realignments occur infrequently and as the result of deep, catastrophic, social crises.[39]
22. Elections can be explained by six relatively independent components of the voting decision.[40]
23. Aside from voting, Americans barely participate in political activities.[41]
24. Elections carry no policy mandates.[42]
25. There was a sharp break in the direction of party loyalties occasioned by the Great Depression.[43]

Admittedly, all of these propositions are not equally important and all of them have not been falsified by more recent research. In their entirety, however, they represent a significant part of the findings of *The American Voter*, while the contradictory research cited is of sufficient scope and depth to make the original work largely irrelevant except as a historical monument. We would therefore expect it to be of diminishing impact. New works are likely to take over the intellectual leadership of the field. The republication of the original hardcover edition may therefore be honorific, but in a way analogous to the erection of a gravestone.

However, reports of the death of *The American Voter* are probably exaggerated. Although I have cited twenty-five propositions of doubtful validity drawn from its pages, many would argue that these propositions are still true, and certainly many of them continue to be repeated in textbooks[44] and ingested by students. This book provided us with our basic socialization into the study of voting behavior and it is difficult to change one's early beliefs. Inertia alone will ensure a continued hold on our minds of these ideas. Moreover, the quality of the work and the skill of its authors will further strengthen that hold.

Yet, we cannot overlook the weaknesses of *The American Voter* if we are to carry forward the scholarly inquiry these authors initiated. Beyond the truth or falsity of any specific propositions, we should be aware of three general points of attack.

First, the research was weak in concept definition. The most basic variable, party identification, is illustrative. There is no clear basis in *The American Voter*, or later research, for asserting that the responses to the standard questions on party loyalty actually reach a basic psychological attachment to the Republicans or Democrats. The only test of this concept has been behavioral regularity in voting, but the concept is claimed to be distinct from that behavior. Furthermore, partisanship is claimed to be an ordinal variable, ranging from strong Democrat through a variety of Independents to strong Republicans. In fact, there are few clear indicators of ordinality in this measure. Indeed, the concept is so much in need of redefinition that a national conference has been convened for precisely this purpose.

Lack of clarity in concepts has led many researchers into difficulty when they attempt to replicate the findings of *The American Voter* or to extend their methods to the analysis of later elections. Thus, the original partitioning of the electorate into four levels of conceptualization was a brilliant individual effort by Philip Converse.[45] But his lesser successors have found it difficult to retrace his steps, or to verify his results.[46]

A second defect of this work was its time period. As the authors have since acknowledged, the 1950s were a time of unusual political quiescence. The passive, compliant, nonideological voter they portrayed was probably at one extreme of a possible scale of political activity.[47] Of course, we cannot fault them for living and doing their research in that particular decade. But there was more to the problem than simply the accident of time. The findings, and particularly the overall conclusions, of *The American Voter* were not presented as the results of a given era, but as relatively long-term truths about the characteristic quality and behavior of the United States electorate. The possibilities of change were hardly discussed, and the brief consideration of such possibilities was only in the context of unexpected catastrophies such as civil war or a major depression.

The book was static in its very outlook, providing no basis even for speculation about change. This work would have led one to predict not black political resistance in the South—but its opposite. It would have led one to predict not voting shifts on the basis of a foreign war—but its opposite. It would have led one to predict not voter responsiveness to the initiatives of political leaders—but its opposite. Given their static stance, these authors could not predict, or expect, or explain "changes in the quality of political life, changes in political leadership, and changes in patterns of voting" until long after these changes were startlingly evident.[48]

This problem is related to a more general one of behavioral research, of which *The American Voter* is a leading example. The emphasis of this research is necessarily and properly on observable and preferably measurable phenomena. The movement has done much to make the study of politics more scientific, to make theories explicit and testable, and to remove many false notions and "ghosts" from the field. The discipline is certainly better for its influence.

But the concentration of research on the observable also means that many important questions may be slighted. Nonobservable behaviors are not only not observed; they are also not considered or drawn into speculation. The Civil Rights movement of the 1960s could not be observed in the 1950s, but a speculative mind might have dwelt on the possible significance of the Montgomery bus boycott of 1956. The Vietnam protests could not have been observed when no American soldier had touched foot on that land, but one might have considered more fully the implications of the vote for Eisenhower in the midst of the Korean War.[49] Certainly a behavioral work need not be unimaginative, but the nature of the enterprise does not encourage a futuristic outlook. Prediction will tend to be based on the continuity of the observable present. Yet, when change is the most certain factor, such predictions are likely to be as fallible as those of *The American Voter*.

A final problem with this work is that basically it has no theoretical foundation. Its famous "funnel of causality"[50]—significantly omitted from the paperback edition—is essentially a classification of variables, rather than a set of causal propositions. To quote a critic, "The SRC substituted a *strategy* for a *theory*. . . . Researchers have operated with a few empirical regularities and proceeded to report a large number of high correlations among them. They failed to consider either alternative or comprehensive theories."[51]

The absence of theory from the Michigan work has restricted its impact. While studies of American voting behavior have been embarrassingly dependent on this source, it has had very little influence beyond this one field. One might have thought, for example, that this major work on voting would have some spillover to the study of political parties. Yet it is hardly cited in the textbook chapters on parties, even in the same books that rely heavily on its discussions of voting. Strikingly, the best textbook in the field cited the SRC more frequently than any other source in regard to voting, but provides not a single reference to the Center's work when it deals with parties.[52]

Similarly, one would have thought that a major work on American politics would be of interest in other countries and in the development of theories of comparative politics. It seems significant, however, that *The American Voter* had never been translated into a foreign language and that its foreign sales are less than 5,000 over its publishing life. Rarely, if ever, will one find a reference to the work in journal articles on other political systems or in works of empirical theory.

To be sure, *The American Voter* has had its influence in studies of the politics of other nations. The Michigan authors themselves have been prominent in the extension of survey research around the world, and we have increased our knowledge of comparative politics through their research in Great Britain, France, Norway, and elsewhere.[53] Yet, even while the methods of the original work are imitated around the globe, its basic premise of the importance of party identification is disputed. Even as we accumulate more data on voting behavior in a variety of nations, we do not approach a general theory of politics.

The result of these accumulated deficiencies has been a theoretical attack on *The American Voter*, based on both its normative and empirical theories. The authors have been criticized as antidemocrats.[54] The attack is unfair, I believe, but they presented others with the opportunity because they seemed uninterested in the ultimate normative import of their findings. More convincing has been the attack on the empirical theory, or lack of theory, in the work of the SRC.[55] Since these authors did not deal with theory sufficiently, others have now attempted to fill the gap. This is probably the most important next step in the development of voting research.

## Future Directions

It is now time to move beyond *The American Voter*. It has had an immense impact, but it may now be retarding development of the field. If we continue to look backward to this monument of the past, we may stumble over future paths. Those paths are reasonably clear, and the way in fact is being trod by some of the original four authors.

Methodologically, we need to develop more complex measures and to ground these measures on clearer definitions of concepts. A new index of party loyalty should be more fully tied to behavior, and should be multidimensional. The concept of political efficacy needs to be subdivided into separate concepts of subjective competence and systemic responsiveness, as suggested by Converse.[56] Issue voting can be better analyzed through proximity measures than by the simple cross-classifications originally used.[57]

These changes need to be made part of a recognition of the dynamic character of elections, and of the importance of events and leadership on mass response.[58] Part of this new recognition will be acknowledgment of the importance of issues to voting, a concession that voting decisions are, like other political decisions, about policies and their effects on groups and individuals. An acceptance of the importance of issues to the voters, if not grudging or churlish, will also do much to revive the legitimacy of democratic participation, at least in the minds of academicians.

Most generally, we need to see voting again as part of a political system, rather than as only an individual-level behavior. We must be more cognizant of its effect on the total system. We also need to view it more within a general system. Methodologically, this may mean more awareness of the impact of areal variables on individual behavior, in the tradition of Durkheim. It means as well more consciousness about large social trends, such as the movements of blacks and women, or the cultural effects of a postindustrial society. Ultimately, it means a consistent concern for theory.

Whatever the new trends in voting research, we can be sure that *The American Voter* has had and will have an impact. It has been indeed a seminal work; and if there have been failures, we should remember that only one sperm in ten million achieves fertility. I suspect that future voting analysts visiting Ann Arbor will come with the reverential and nostalgic attitude that once was true of behaviorists visiting Charles Merriam's haunts at the University of Chicago. They may even offer a poetic remembrance to the pioneering days in which *The American Voter* was written:

> Joy was it in that day to be alive—
> But to be young was very heaven.

## Notes

1. W. Lance Bennett, "The Growth of Knowledge in Mass Belief Studies: An Epistemological Critique," *American Journal of Political Science* 21 (August 1977): 465–500.
2. This information has been supplied by Mr. Wayne Anderson, political science editor of the publisher. The book under consideration is Angus Campbell et al., *The American Voter* (New York: Wiley, 1960).
3. James M. Burns et al., *Government by the People*, 9th ed. (Englewood Cliffs, N.J.: Prentice-Hall, 1975); Frank Sorauf, *Party Politics in America* (Boston: Little, Brown, 1968).

4. Thomas Dye and L. Hermon Zeigler, *The Irony of Democracy*, 2nd ed. (Belmont, Calif.: Wadsworth, 1972).
5. *American Political Science Review* 66 (June 1972): 415–70; *American Political Science Review* 70 (September 1976): 753–849.
6. V. O. Key, Jr., *The Responsible Electorate* (Cambridge: Harvard University Press, 1966).
7. V. O. Key, Jr., "The Politically Relevant in Surveys," *Public Opinion Quarterly* 24 (Spring 1960): 54–61.
8. Key, *Responsible Electorate*, p. 150.
9. This point is made by Walter Dean Burnham, "Contributions of the SRC to the Development of Voting Theory" (paper presented at American Political Science Association Annual Meeting, San Francisco, Calif., September 1975), p. 7.
10. Samuel Stouffer, *The American Soldier* (Princeton: Princeton University Press, 1949); Paul Lazarsfeld et al., *The People's Choice*, 2nd ed. (New York: Columbia University Press, 1948).
11. See Bernard Berelson et al., *Voting* (Chicago: University of Chicago Press, 1954).
12. Campbell et al., *American Voter*, p. 143.
13. Lazarsfeld et al., *People's Choice*, p. 27.
14. H. Daudt, *Floating Voters and the Floating Vote* (Leiden: Stenfert Kroese, 1961).
15. Sexism might be suspected in the choice of interviews illustrating voter levels of conceptualization: For the "higher" levels A and B, six men and six women are selected. For the "lower" levels C and D, only two men but nine women are presented. See Campbell et al., *American Voter*, pp. 228–49.
16. See Jack Walter, "A Critique of the Elitist Theory of Democracy," *American Political Science Review* 60 (June 1966): 285–95.
17. Herbert Asher, *Presidential Elections and American Politics* (Homewood, Ill.: Dorsey Press, 1976); David Knoke, *Change and Continuity in American Politics* (Baltimore, Md.: Johns Hopkins University Press, 1976); Warren Miller and Teresa Levitian, *Leadership and Change* (Cambridge, Mass.: Winthrop Publishers, 1976); Norman Nie et al., *The Changing American Voter* (Cambridge: Harvard University Press, 1976); Gerald Pomper, *Voter's Choice* (New York: Harper & Row, 1975).
18. In footnotes 19–43, the first reference is to the original statement of the proposition in *The American Voter* (hereafter cited AV). The next references are to recent research disputing that proposition.
19. *AV*, chap. 6; Miller and Levitian, *Leadership and Change*, chap. 5; Arthur Miller et al., "A Majority Party in Disarray," *American Political Science Review* 70 (September 1976): 753–78; Nie et al., *Changing American Voter*, chap. 4.
20. *AV*, pp. 134–35; Walter Dean Burnham, *Critical Elections and the Mainsprings of American Politics* (New York: Norton, 1970), pp. 123–31; Pomper, *Voter's Choice*, pp. 31–35; William Flanigan and Nancy Zingale, *Political Behavior of the American Electorate*, 3rd ed. (Boston: Little, Brown, 1975), chap. 3.
21. *AV*, p. 148; Edward C. Dreyer, "Change and Stability in Party Identifications," *Journal of Politics* 35 (August 1973): 712–22.
22. *AV*, pp. 128–36; Pomper, *Voters' Choice*, chap. 7; Richard Trilling, *Party Image and Electoral Behavior* (New York: Wiley, 1976), chap. 8.
23. *AV*, pp. 136–42; Theodore Macaluso, "Parameters of 'Rational' Voting: Vote Switching in the 1968 Election," *Journal of Politics* 37 (February 1975): 202–34.

24. *AV*, chap. 4 and p. 148; Key, *Responsible Electorate*, chap. 2.
25. *AV*, pp. 146–50; Samuel Popkin et al., "Comment: What Have You Done For Me Lately? Toward an Investment Theory of Voting," *American Political Science Review* 70 (September 1976): 790–92.
26. *AV*, pp. 161–67; Paul Abramson, "Generational Change in American Electoral Behavior," *American Political Science Review* 68 (March 1974): 93–105.
27. *AV*, pp. 179–87; Gerald Pomper, "From Confusion to Clarity," *American Political Science Review* 66 (June 1972): 415–28.
28. *AV*, pp. 256–65; Nie et al., *Changing American Voter*, chap. 10; David Repass, "Issue, Salience and Party Choice," *American Political Science Review* 65 (June 1971): 389–400.
29. *AV*, chap. 10; John Pierce, "Party Identification and the Changing Role of Ideology in American Politics," *Midwest Journal of Political Science* 14 (February 1970): 25–42; J. O. Field and R. E. Anderson, "Ideology in the Public's Conceptualization of the 1964 Election," *Public Opinion Quarterly* 33 (Fall 1969): 380–98.
30. *AV*, chap. 10; Miller and Levitian, *Leadership and Change*, chap. 4; Alden Raine, *Change in the Political Agenda* (Sage Professional Papers in American Politics, 1977); Richard Boyd, "Popular Control of Public Policy," *American Political Science Review* 66 (June 1972): 429–49.
31. *AV*, chap. 9; Nie et al., *Changing American Voter*, chap. 8; James Stimson, "Belief Systems: Constraint, Complexity and the 1972 Elections," *American Journal of Political Science* 19 (August 1975): 393–418.
32. *AV*, pp. 345–61; Robert Alford, *Party and Society* (Chicago: Rand McNally, 1965), chap. 8; Richard Hamilton, *Class and Politics in the United States* (New York: Wiley, 1972), chap. 12.
33. *AV*, pp. 404–08; Michael S. Lewis-Beck, "Agrarian Political Behavior in the United States," *American Journal of Political Science* 21 (August 1977): 543–65.
34. *AV*, p. 45; James A. Barber, Jr., *Social Mobility and Voting Behavior* (Chicago: Rand McNally, 1970), chap. 6.
35. *AV*, pp. 365–68; Pomper, *Voters' Choice*, chap. 3.
36. *AV*, pp. 301–07; Knoke, *Change and Continuity in American Politics*, chap. 2.
37. *AV*, pp. 250–56; Norman Nie and Kristi Andersen, "Mass Belief Systems Revisited," *Journal of Politics* 36 (August 1974): 566–71; Walter Dean Burnham, "Theory and Voting Research," *American Political Science Review* 68 (September 1974): 1002–23.
38. *AV*, p. 279; Donald Matthews and James Prothro, *Negroes and the New Southern Politics* (New York: Harcourt, Brace and World, 1966), chap 10; Sidney Verba and Norman Nie, *Participation in America* (New York: Harper & Row, 1972), chap. 10; Paul Beck, "Partisan Realignment in the Postwar South," *American Political Science Review* 71 (June 1977): 477–96.
39. *AV*, pp. 531–38; Everett C. Ladd, Jr., and Charles Hadley, *Transformation of the American Party System* (New York: Norton, 1975), pp. 332–44; James Sundquist, *Dynamics of the American Party System* (Washington, D.C.: Brookings Institution, 1973), chaps. 1, 13, 14.
40. *AV*, pp. 128–36; William Shaffer, "Partisan Loyalty and the Perceptions of Party, Candidates and Issues," *Western Political Quarterly* 25 (September 1972):424–33.

41. *AV*, pp. 91–93; Verba and Nie, *Participation in America*, chap. 2.
42. *AV*, pp. 541–48; Gerald Pomper, *Elections in America* (New York: Dodd, Mead, 1968), chaps. 7, 8; Boyd, "Popular Control of Public Policy"; John Sullivan and Robert O'Conner, "Electoral Choice and Popular Control of Public Policy," *American Political Science Review* 66 (December 1972); 1256–68.
43. *AV*, pp. 150–60; Kristi Andersen, "Generation, Partisan Shift, and Realignment: A Glance Back to the New Deal," in Nie et al., *Changing American Voter*, chap. 5; Philip Converse, *The Dynamics of Party Support* (Beverly Hills: Sage, 1976), 132–35.
44. E., Judson James, *American Political Parties in Transition* (New York: Harper & Row, 1974), pp. 153–54 on ideology and voting.
45. Campbell et al., *American Voter*, chap. 10.
46. See David Repass's paper, "Levels of Rationality Among the American Electorate" (paper presented at the American Political Science Association Annual Meeting, Chicago, Ill., September 1974).
47. Donald Stokes, "Some Dynamic Elements of Contests for the Presidency," *American Political Science Review* 60 (March 1966): 19; Philip Converse, "Public Opinion and Voting Behavior," in Fred Greenstein and Nelson W. Polsby, *Handbook of Political Science*, vol. 4 (Reading, Mass.: Addison-Wesley, 1975), pp. 89–111.
48. Miller and Levitian, *Leadership and Change*, p. 60.
49. Data for this examination could be found in the earlier SRC work by Angus Campbell et al., *The Voter Decides* (New York: Row, Peterson, 1954).
50. Campbell et al., *American Voter*, chap. 2.
51. Peter B. Natchez, "Images of Voting: The Social Psychologists," *Public Policy* 18 (Summer 1970): 586–87.
52. Sorauf, *Party Politics in America*. Burns et al., *Government by the People* (note 3) make but three such references in their chapter on parties; Dye and Ziegler, *Irony of Democracy* (note 4) make none.
53. Among the leading examples are Angus Campbell et al., *Elections and the Political Order* (New York: John Wiley, 1966); David Butler and Donald Stokes, *Political Change in Britain* (New York: Macmillan, 1969). For an extended analysis, see I. Budge, I. Crewe, and D. Farlie, eds., *Political Identification and Beyond* (New York: John Wiley, 1976).
54. Walker, "A Critique of the Elitist Theory of Democracy"; Peter Bachrach, *The Theory of Democratic Elitism* (Boston: Little, Brown, 1967).
55. Popkin, "Comment"; Burnham, "Contributions of the SRC to the Development of Voting Theory."
56. Philip Converse, "Change in the American Electorate," in Angus Campbell and Philip Converse, *The Human Meaning of Social Change* (Beverly Hills, Calif.: Sage, 1972), pp. 302–37.
57. David Kovenock et al., *Explaining the Vote*, Institute for Research in Social Sciences, University of North Carolina (Chapel Hill, N.C., 1973), Part 1, pp. 1–30.
58. The importance of these factors had indeed been recognized by the Michigan authors in recent works, such as Converse, *The Dynamics of Party Support*; Miller and Levitian, *Leadership and Change*; and Stokes, "Some Dynamic Elements of Contests for the Presidency."

# PART II
# Elections

# *Part II: ELECTIONS*

Elections are the means of collective decision making in a democracy. They can be as meaningless as an uncontested Soviet celebration of the power of the Politburo, or as meaningful as the replacement of Jimmy Carter by Ronald Reagan. Their true significance depends on the quality of the voters, which was considered in the previous section, and on the structure of the party system, which will be analyzed in the next group of essays.

Elections' significance also depends on the interpretation of analysts. Some scholars have seen elections as no more than rituals, means by which the citizenry falsely believes that it affects public policy, and therefore quietly accepts the acts of government as reflections of democratic majorities. Campaign specialists also tend to minimize the importance of elections, seeing them more as occasions for practicing manipulative skills than as means for popular decisions. Politicians, too, are affected by these interpretations. If elections are denigrated by the experts, they are likely also to be disregarded by the holders of power.

In these essays, elections are seen as meaningful. Ritual, manipulation, and cynicism surely exist in elections, even as they are evident in the deepest human relationships, such as parenthood. Yet, the true significance of elections is no more found in these negative aspects than the true significance of parenthood is found in mothers' techniques and fathers' complaints. Rather, elections are meaningful in three senses: there is a rationality in voters' choices; there are intelligible patterns; and there are significant effects.

This interpretation is based on the realistic but still optimistic view of voters presented earlier. I do not expect voters to be objective philosophers, tirelessly considering the public good. I do expect them to have their own interests in mind, and to devote relatively little time from busy lives to public affairs. At the same time, I insist that voters also are concerned with the nation's welfare, and that a significant part of their own experiences inform them about public affairs. As Morris Fiorina has elegantly theorized, the electorate's decisions are intelligible reflections of its past political experiences, retrospective evaluations of governmental performance, and evaluations of future policy actions.[1] To this extent, voters are politically rational.

Elections are obviously based on voting, but they are different from opinion surveys, and more than collections of individual views. Elections are about power, not preferences. They are choices among alternative politicians, the personal qualities that they embody, and the public policies that they advocate. To find patterns in elections, we must look beyond individuals to the interactions among citizens.

Seeing elections as interactions emphasizes their dynamic elements. There is a dynamic of voter response. Voters react to the actual alternatives offered by candidates and parties, and these reactions vary as the offered choices vary. Further, there is a dynamic of politicians' response to voters. The alternatives they present reflect past decisions made by voters and those anticipated in the present and future. Finally, there is a dynamic over time. Each election, however unique, is part of a series of elections. It is influenced by previous voting results, and exerts an influence over future contests.

After the ballots are counted, elections have diverse effects. Most obviously, they bring some people to office and deny power to others. Policies are affected, as the victors attempt to fulfill their promises. Institutions, such as the presidency, Congress, and the political parties, are also affected by the actions of those who are chosen as their leaders. These different effects are discussed in the following essays.

We begin with an analysis of philosophic theories involving elections. The thesis of the first essay is that elections have been viewed differently by the friends and foes of democracy. Properly understood, elections should be seen as beneficial devices by which citizens protect their interests, rather than as dangerous interventions by an ill-informed mass public. When judged by the former criterion, the accumulated evidence on voter behavior[2] justifies the expectations of democratic theorists.

In retrospect, I would place more emphasis on the participatory benefits of elections claimed by some of these theorists. Following John Stuart Mill, significant contemporary writers have argued that, aside from any direct advantages, citizens' involvement in government through elections improves their character, moral understanding, and self-esteem.[3] However, these benefits remain less tangible and less demonstrable than the protective aspects emphasized in my original essay.

The interaction between leaders and followers in elections becomes more specific in the second essay, an analysis of political party platforms in the modern era. In the conventional literature, platforms have been disregarded as empty and vague. This essay shows quite the opposite, using detailed content analysis. In reality, platforms are relatively specific; they focus on the record of the party in power, and they include a considerable proportion of meaningful pledges for future action. Moreover, other research has shown that these pledges are taken seriously, and much of the party program is actually carried out.[4] Electoral choice also affects policy choice.

The original research on the party platforms covered the period from 1944 to 1964. Later, this material was updated and revised, largely by Susan Lederman, the co-author of the chapter included here. This later analysis reveals changes in the electoral system. The parties have come to stress newer issues, and have become less cohesive and less able to redeem their promises. These changes in the platform therefore reinforce other indications of party realignment.

Realignment itself is the subject of the following essay. It reviews all U.S. presidential contests, and develops methods for identifying realigning elections, when there is a fundamental shift in the party system. The methods are of interest in themselves, and have been extended in others' work.[5] Substantively, the most interesting finding in this essay was the suggestion that Lyndon Johnson's victory in 1964 was a critical election, converting the base of the Democratic party, while continuing it as the nation's majority party.

As acknowledged in the introduction to the first section, this conclusion was faulty to the extent it predicted Democratic interparty dominance. In respect to intraparty realignment, however, the changes of 1964 continue to the present. The Democrats have lost much of their traditional support among white southerners, but have partially compensated by strong gains among blacks.[6] The net result is a closely competitive party system throughout the nation. Such alterations of the parties' coalitions, and subsequent policy actions, are a major effect of elections.

Realignment has been particularly evident in the South. This area is the subject for the next chapter, which is also the only one in the book to deal with congressional elections. Although the methodology is primitive, this article accurately predicted the growth of southern Republicanism, more moderate racial attitudes on the part of Democratic representatives from Dixie, and increased influence of black legislators in the Congress. Today, these conclusions are obvious: Republicans have won state-wide elections for either governor or senator in every former Confederate state; most southern Democrats voted for the extension of the Civil Rights Act in 1982; and the number of blacks in Congress has nearly quintupled. The emergence of these trends is additional evidence of the adaptability of the voters and of the impact of elections on government.

Elections also affect the structure of government. In the following essay, I deal with the significance of Richard Nixon's 1972 reelection for the institution of the presidency. The brief argument is that the White House has become isolated from the normal controls of partisan politics, and that this isolation is dangerous for American democracy. Shortly after its publication, the Watergate investigations demonstrated these points far more emphatically. While I am gratified that the dangers have become more recognized, I am still concerned that the basic problem of institutional linkages has not been resolved. The recent Iran-Contra fiasco further substantiates the argument.

The final essay in this section brings us up to date, with a description and analysis of the presidential election of 1984. Examining four explanations of the contest, I reject interpretations of the Reagan landslide as either a triumph of personality or as a policy mandate. Instead, I argue that the vote was a retrospective endorsement of the president's conduct in office, and the possible continuation of long-term party realignment. This last note on realignment thus concludes a theme that has been sounded throughout this section and, indeed, through much of political science in the past two decades. Like other observers, I await the election of 1988 for further data.[7]

## Notes

1. Morris Fiorina, *Retrospective Voting in American National Elections* (Cambridge: Harvard University Press, 1981).
2. See Fiorina; Norman Nie, Sidney Verba, and John Petrocik, *The Changing American Voter* (Cambridge: Harvard University Press, 1976); Jeffrey Smith, *American Presidential Elections: The Role of Trust* (New York: Praeger, 1980).
3. *Elections in America*, 2d ed. (New York: Longman, 1980), pp. 23–25.
4. *Elections in America*, chap. 8; Paul T. David, ''Party Platforms as National Plans,'' *Public Administration Review* 31 (May, June 1971); and, in Great Britain, Richard Rose, *Do Parties Make a Difference?* (Chatham, N.J.: Chatham House, 1980), chap. 4.
5. Walter Dean Burnham, *Critical Elections and the Mainsprings of American Politics* (New York: Norton, 1970); Jerome Clubb, William Flanigan, and Nancy Zingale, *Partisan Realignment* (Beverly Hills: Sage Publications, 1980).
6. See Harold Stanley et al., ''Partisanship and Group Support over Time,'' *American Political Science Review* 80 (September 1986): 969–76; Robert Axelrod, ''Presidential Election Coalitions in 1984,'' *American Political Science Review* 80 (March 1980): 281–84.
7. In a growing literature, see Everett C. Ladd, ''As the Realignment Turns,'' *Public Opinion* 7 (January 1985): 2–7; David Brady and Patricia Hurley, ''The Prospects for Contemporary Partisan Realignment,'' *PS* 18 (Winter 1985): 63–68; Barbara Farah and Helmut Norpoth, ''Trends in Partisan Realignment, 1976–1986'' (Washington: paper delivered to American Political Science Association, 1986).

# 8

# The Concept of Elections in Political Theory

Popular elections are generally assumed to be the crucial element of democratic governments, but the significance of elections is so widely assumed that it is rarely examined. Although studies of voting behavior abound, there are relatively few theoretical or empirical investigations of the effects of voting on the total political system. To clarify our thinking, and as a preliminary to contemporary discussion, it may prove helpful to reexamine some major works of premodern European and American political thought.

### The Benefits of Elections

Some, but few, writers have seen wisdom as the result and chief benefit of elections. Rousseau was probably the most optimistic in his assessment of popular competence. Under suitable conditions, he believed, "The general will is always right and tends to the public advantage."[1] Most often, the advantages of elections have been found largely apart from the content of public decisions. The emphasis rather has been on their benefits to the processes and functioning of government. Elections would improve the workings of politics, even if they would not ensure the quality of the resulting product.

A principal procedural benefit claimed has been the achievement of legitimate government. The legitimacy of elective government has been grounded on a moral premise. "The liberty of man in society is to be under no other legislative power but that established by consent in the commonwealth," declared Locke, "nor under the dominion of any will, or restraint of any law, but what the legislature shall enact according to the trust put in it."[2]

While consent has been defended as morally necessary, theorists have also tried to show that legitimacy is the empirical result of popular elections. In such governments, said Aristotle, the voters "have the power of electing the magistrates and calling them to account; their ambition, if they have any, is thus satisfied."[3] By contrast, argued eighteenth-century Americans, the denial of electoral power would "create division among the people and make enemies of all those who would be excluded."[4]

Another advantage claimed for elections is more intangible. Participation in government, of which voting is the most common means, is said to contribute to the personal development of the electors. To Locke, self-determination is held essential to human development, and consent is essential to political man. "He who would get me into his power without my consent would use me as he pleased when he had got me there, and destroy me too when he had a fancy to it."[5] For Mill, personality develops furthest when a man "either is, or is looking forward to becoming, a citizen as fully privileged as any other."[6]

Probably the most important virtue of elections is protection, or a check on power. Only with the ballot for self-defense can citizens be secure. "Men, as well as women," summarized Mill, "do not need political rights in order that they may govern, but in order that they not be misgoverned."[7] While government is necessary, protection is also essential. Machiavelli and Madison share this basic premise. One "must start with assuming that all men are bad and ever ready to display their vicious nature, whenever they may find occasion for it."[8] Those who provide a role for elections do so because of a certain pessimism or realism about the possible misdeeds of governors. "If angels were to govern men, neither external nor internal controls on government would be necessary," but it their absence, it becomes necessary to restrain power, and "a dependence on the people is, no doubt, the primary control."[9]

To be effective, Mill wrote, control must be exercised directly by those needing protection. Given the character of governors, their good intentions are an uncertain reliance. The vote makes the expression of popular demands effective.

> The rights and interests of every or any person are only secure from being disregarded when the person interested is himself able, and habitually disposed, to stand up for them. . . . Rulers and ruling classes are under a necessity of considering the interests of those who have the suffrage; but of those who are excluded, it is in their option whether they will do so or not, and however honestly disposed, they are in general too fully occupied with things which they *must* attend to, to have much room in their thoughts for anything which they can with impunity disregard.[10]

Popular protection is achieved in two distinctive, but related ways. As stated by Madison: "As it is essential that the government in general should have a common interest with the people, so it is particularly essential that the [legislature] should have an immediate dependence on, and intimate sympathy with, the people. Frequent elections are unquestionably the only policy by which the dependence and sympathy can be effectually secured."[11]

"Dependence" suggests the direct control of legislators by the voters, who are alert to their representatives' actions and prepared to punish any misdeeds.

"Do the members of Congress, says he, displease us, we call them home, and they obey. . . . Let these members know their dependence on the people and I say it will be a check on them, even if they were not good men."[12]

Elections also serve as a check on power because of the "sympathy" between representatives and their constituents. This quality does not refer to the personal feelings of the legislator, but to the similarity between his social position and that of the voters. A representative would sympathize with his constituents because he would be of the same geographical area, occupation, and status. For this reason, Aristotle characterized election by lot as the most democratic method.[13] The principle survives today in the militant Negro demand for "black power."

Protection becomes more complex when society is seen as comprising many different and divergent interests. The representative no longer can be the embodiment of the whole community, but is likely to be more aware of some interests than others. With a variety of groups, conflicts between interests become likely. Government is no longer the only threat; it is also a means by which a group can advance and achieve its demands.

In this situation, elections serve a different function from negative protection. They may also be the positive means by which groups seek their particular goals. That representatives would promote specialized interests has been widely accepted. Most of the controversies over suffrage in American history have been based on the tacit or explicit recognition that legislators would advance the special interests of their electors.

The advancement of particular interests, however, could also be dangerous. When representatives are no longer a "random sample" of the population, some groups may be forgotten, Melancton Smith warned of an oligarchy: "A substantial yeoman, of sense and discernment, will hardly ever be chosen. From these remarks it appears that the government will fall into the hands of the few and the great."[14] If the representative is no longer identified with the community, "sympathy" becomes less of a control, which must come largely from the "dependence" on the voters. At the same time, this dependence carries its own dangers. Important interests, perhaps essential to the common good, might be disregarded in the electoral process. There are dangers as well as benefits in the electoral process.

## The Dangers of Elections

Writings on the reputed dangers of elections concentrate on the wisdom and content of political decisions.

Elitism is clearly undemocratic. The elitists hold that certain discoverable abilities are needed to participate in government, that only a severely limited number of persons have these skills, and that all others should be excluded from politics. Specialists are necessary not only for the technical positions of a civil service; they are regarded as exclusively able to conduct all affairs of government.

Plato remains the most persuasive proponent of the elite position. Since government was a specialized skill, he argued, it was madness to entrust it to the general public. Choosing leaders by elections is comparable to navigating a doomed ship:

> The sailors are quarrelling over the control of the helm; each thinks he ought to be steering the vessel, through he has never learnt navigation and cannot point to any teacher under whom he has served his apprenticeship; what is more, they assert that navigation is a thing that cannot be taught at all, and are ready to tear in pieces anyone who says it can.[15]

The crucial problem is bringing the true elite to power. In the *Republic*, Plato provides only for the perpetuation, not initiation, of the philosophers' rule, through the control of public opinion and training of the rulers. To establish good government, and as an alternative to his ideal plan, Plato later suggested an elaborate system of laws and elections for a new commonwealth. On the principle of specialization, the electorate was to be severely restricted and there were high qualifications of age, property, and character for most officers.[16]

This system is meant as a second-best substitute for the ideal rule of the philosopher-king. The ideal still remains, and Plato returns to it. At the end of the *Laws*, he provides for a Nocturnal Council of the elderly wise men of the community, to whom is entrusted the education of new rulers and revision of the constitution. Plato puts his final trust in the Council. Elections may be guarded, carefully constructed, and controlled, but they are a poor substitute for the rule of the wise.

Furthermore, elections have been held harmful because they actually promote the unqualified. As Mill remarked, "The natural tendency of representative government, as of modern civilization, is toward collective mediocrity; and this tendency is increased by all reductions and extensions of the franchise, their effect being to place the principal power in the hands of classes more and more below the highest level of instruction in the community."[17]

Critical theorists have also attempted to delineate the unwise decisions expected in elective governments. The recurrent fear is the asserted disregard of minority demands, the imposition of majority tyranny, and the consequent destruction of the state. "The instability, injustice and confusion introduced into the public councils have, in truth, been the mortal diseases under which popular governments have everywhere perished," wrote Madison. "Measures are too often decided not according to the rules of justice and the rights of the minor party, but by the superior force of an interested and overbearing majority."[18]

Theorists have agreed that elections can be used to promote the particular interests of social groups, but have differed in their evaluations of this effect. Promotion of self-interest could be regarded as proper or as morally reprehensible. Calhoun saw the elective system as a suitable protection to the majority. At the same time, in a society of inevitable conflict, elections would contribute to the destruction of the rights of the minority. "There must, of necessity, be a governing and a governed,—a ruling and a subject portion. . . . The minority, for the time, will be as much the governed or subject portion, as are the people in an aristocracy, or the subjects in a monarchy."[19]

Those fearful of election tend to bolster their arguments by reference to a presumed "general welfare." "It does not follow that the public decisions are equitable," admitted Rousseau. On occasion, "the people is seduced by private interests, which the credit or eloquence of clever persons substitutes for those of the State; in which case the general will, will be one thing, and the result of the public deliberation another."[20]

Commonly, the general welfare is identified with the interests and rights of particular minorities. Elections provide no protection for these groups; indeed they only strengthen the position of the majority. To prevent oppression, theorists have endorsed a number of devices. Mill favored proportional representation, plural voting, and open ballots. Madison relied on social pluralism and governmental mechanisms such as the separation of branches and a variety of national checks and federal-state balances. Calhoun sought to institutionalize his "concurrent majority" through sectional equality in the Senate or a second President with full veto power.

Without some checks, it was feared, the policy decisions of elective governments would be unjust and destructive of vital interests. Ultimately, it is claimed, unrestricted elections are dangerous to all, leading to instability and the destruction of the state. The principal cause of instability is the inability of the majority to restrain itself. Eventually, it infringes on some basic rights and intense beliefs of the minority, or one faction of the majority turns on another. The government no longer commands loyalty; its legitimacy is destroyed; consent eventually gives way to force. Ultimately, representation by tyrannical rulers is substituted for popular controls. "That freedom which knew no bounds must now put on the livery of the most harsh and bitter servitude, where the slave has become the master."[21] The final danger of elections is the end of all elections.

## The Argument over Elections

The primary basis of the argument over elections has been the different premises and criteria on which various theories have been based. The argument against elections has been focused on the ends of government, the achievement of wise decisions, and the content of policy. The fundamental premise has been that there is a basic public good, and that this good can be ascertained and achieved by wise rulers. Given this emphasis, broad popular participation is acceptable only if the voters have the competence to discern the public good. It is only the most optimistic theorists who have believed that the general electorate was wise enough to achieve the ideal. Rousseau is striking in his optimistic appraisal of popular competence.

More commonly, an emphasis on the content of government policy leads to disparagement of elections. Wise policy cannot be achieved through popular control, for the voters lack capacity. The inevitable results are wrong decisions, disregard of public welfare, and depredations of the minority. "A government which is exposed to the hasty action of a people is the worst and not the best government on earth," according to a common argument.[22]

The position favoring elections has been grounded on different premises. In this theory, liberal in tradition, the basic goal of political institutions is to prevent oppression. Elections are highly evaluated because they are effective means of providing protection for society and control over government. Decisions might be better or worse, but this consideration is not central. Elections, and democracy, are "no more than well-tried and, in the presence of a widespread traditional distrust of tyranny, reasonably effective institutional safeguards against tyranny."[23]

The argument over elections has therefore not been a true debate, for each side has began on different premises and pursued different points. Opponents have seen the principal aim of politics to be the realization of wisdom, and have feared elections as giving power to the inexpert. Proponents have seen the primary purpose as protection and control of government, and have praised elections for their contributions to these ends.

To be sure, the debate has sometimes been directly joined. Democratic theorists have occasionally argued that competence is more likely to be achieved through the election of rulers, rather than by some ascriptive method such as hereditary succession. They have also held that the promotion of his self-interest by each individual would also result in substantively better policy, for only the individuals affected could truly know the consequences of public policy. Elitists have also claimed that the real interests of a society would be better guarded by a talented aristocracy than by mass intervention. Nevertheless, the thrust of each argument is in a different direction.

Some theorists have tried to combine the values of competence and protection. Madison and Mill provide various means to permit the achievement of the public interest, while not derogating the power of the electorate. Inevitably, the two values come into conflict. The promotion of equality threatens esteemed minority interests, while providing special protections for the minority violates the principle of equality.[24] Two different values are involved in the argument over elections. They must be distinguished logically and, in a practical situation, one must often be preferred over the other.

The threat of majority tyranny has been based on the same difference in premises, and is indeed not a real issue in many ways. Majority tyranny can only be a threat if the majority in elections make policy. Tocqueville probably expressed this fear most graphically; "When an individual or a party is wronged in the United States, to whom can he apply for redress? If to public opinion, public opinion constitutes the majority; if to the legislature, it represents the majority and implicitly obeys it; if to the executive power, it is appointed by the majority and serves as a passive tool in its hands."[25]

The support of elections, however, is rarely based on the policies which will result from the direct action of the majority. Rousseau is again distinctive in this regard. "Every law the people have not ratified in person is null and void—is, in fact, not a law," he declared.[26] Putting this principle into practice, the American Progressives favored direct election of all officials, the initiative, and referendum.

Most supporters of elections have not spoken of majorities as having definable policy preferences. They have been concerned with the protection of the community as a whole, as with Locke, or with the protection of distinct interests within it, as with Mill. The policy content of elections eventually becomes resolved into another value difference. The protection of interests results in particular policies. Popular elections will tend to protect some of these interests more than others, giving greater weight to the interests of numerically larger groups than those of lesser factions. Empirically, it is doubtful that any of these groups will constitute a majority of the entire nation, and even the smaller interests have manifold opportunities—through lobbying, campaign contributions, and personal influence—to win their points. Elections still make a difference, by requiring government to pay greater attention to unorganized, mass groups and comparatively less to elite groups of smaller numbers.

Protection is desired by both supporters and opponents of elections, but the more democratic position is concerned with the protection of broad social groups, and the opposition with smaller groups and their pursuit of "property, status, power or the opportunity to save mankind."[27] Each argument assumes some interests should be advanced, and some retarded by government; the dispute is over which interests deserve more attention—a value question answered differently by different persons. These value differences are the core of the argument over elections.

## Elections in Contemporary Thought

This survey of some classical political theorists is generally relevant to the current debate about democracy. There is a defensiveness apparent in the arguments of many modern democrats. They wish to retain and extend democracy, yet are hard pressed to find logical support for their personal preferences. Modern experience and social science findings have combined to raise problems about "the revolt of the masses," "irrational man," and the "escape from freedom." The universal extension of the suffrage has not produced ideal society, by any means. Racial prejudice, nationalistic frenzy, and cultural degeneration are apparently major characteristics of the contemporary world. While no totalitarian regime has yet won a free election, large proportions of the voters in many nations have supported Nazi, Fascist, and Communist movements.

In the United States, social scientists find large proportions of the citizenry opposed to presumably "fundamental principles of democracy"[28] The picture of democratic man that is drawn in our extensive studies of voting is one of a generally uninformed, and only intermittently interested voter, responding to politics largely on the basis of vague symbols of party, issues, and candidates.[29] An election is far less than a public debate on issues and a reasoned choice of candidates. "The vocabulary of the voice of the people consists mainly of the words 'yes' and 'no'; and at times one cannot be certain which word is being uttered."[30]

A full examination of these findings is unnecessary here. The reaction among contemporary writers is more pertinent. One reaction is to deprecate and seek to revise the "traditional" theory of democracy. "Theories of consent, majoritarianism, the role of elites, the nature of individual and collective will, and theories of social contract are areas which would need radical revision if the findings of the voting studies on the nature of political man and political participation are accurate."[31] Some brave souls have even attempted to begin this building of a new theory of democratic politics, accepting the deficiencies of the modern voter as a basic premise.[32]

The other common reaction is to deprecate the findings of social science and to insist on the essential truth of the "traditional" theory of democracy. The voting studies are therefore deplored as irrelevant, deterministic, or methodologically unsound. Empirical findings about the apathy of large numbers of citizens are attacked as prescriptive statements in favor of apathy, while hopes for a democratic revival are ritually reiterated.[33]

Both of these responses are based on a false view of the theory of democracy, at least insofar as it relates to the theory of elections, described above. The assumption in these modern writers is that voters are expected to make policy in elections. Since the evidence strongly indicates that voters do not make policy, the modern writers attack either the voters or the evidence. Yet, in accepting this assumption, they are also accepting the premises and criteria of the very persons who opposed elections. It was those who feared elections and democracy who considered wise policy and the competence of the citizenry the tests of good government. In judging modern voters by these standards, we accept the basis of their argument. It was Plato after all, not

Mill, who measured the quality of a government by the wisdom of its rulers and the absolute truth of its decisions.

The agonizing reappraisal of democratic theory, then, is possibly unnecessary. We tend to apply the tests of the antidemocrats to democratic practice. After granting the premise that the proper test of an electoral system is the competence of the electors, it becomes difficult to remain a democrat. Admittedly, modern democracy has not yielded philosopher-kings, or a utopian society. To this extent, the critics of elective government have been vindicated.

Those who supported elections, however, rarely expected these results. Even when the democratic voter was given a policy role, "these writers never claimed to be describing existing reality, for they were elaborating, at least in part, a set of ideals for a democratic society, which were also meant to be operative ideals for their own time."[34] In practice, elections would normally not meet these ideals, but would still serve important functions.

If we are to appraise the effects of elections in the light of modern experience, it may be more appropriate to judge by the criteria of those who regarded elections as beneficial. These theorists have seen elections as a means of dealing with a problem of high priority to them—controlling the government as the governed wished it to be controlled. Elections would give the voters a means of protection, a method of intervention in politics when their vital interests were being threatened. By their very existence, they would act as a restraint on government, and tend to bring representatives to further the needs and wants of their constituents. Have elections provided protection for society and control over government? These seem the most appropriate questions to ask. By these criteria, there is no convincing reason to despair of modern democracy. A full appraisal is clearly impossible here, but there are some interesting threads of evidence.

One such thread is in the voting studies themselves. These have been employed to show the inability or unwillingness of the voters to choose public policy. Yet, the studies also show the capacity of the voters to protect themselves through elections. Only 15 percent of the American electorate finds broad policy differences between the parties, and only smaller minorities can correctly make detailed policy the basis of their votes. On the other hand, 45 percent see the parties as a means of advancing group interests, and another 23 percent react to the parties in terms of the "nature of the times"—as a means of applauding or condemning the effects of policy.[35] Self-protection of this sort is not irrational, unless rationality is bounded by the absolute truths of the idealist philosopher. This is the practical qualification which Aristotle found in the general electorate: "There are some arts whose products are not judged of solely, or best, by the artists themselves, namely those arts whose products are recognized even by those who do not possess the art."[36] Only the wearer knows if the shoe pinches.

Do the voters get the protection they want? There are some further threads of evidence that politicians in democracies, although not philosopher-kings, are responsive to those demands. Even if we suspend moral judgments, we may still draw some tough-minded conclusions from recent history. No freely elected leader has made the disastrous decisions of a Hitler to engage in a suicidal war, of a Stalin to virtually destroy his nation's defense, or of a Sukarno to impoverish a richly endowed country. Leaders in democracies have not necessarily been wiser or more moral. Outrageously immoral or disastrous actions are less likely in democracies only because leaders must win public favor in an election. They are thereby restrained from violating the beliefs of any large group of voters or the general beliefs of the community.[37] That these restraints are imperfect is logically obvious. Entire nations can go mad—but probably less often than rulers. So long as some substantial portion of the community remains sane, rulers must give some attention to sanity.

It is difficult to prove that voters are protected by elections. In a direct sense, protection is a negative concept. Voters are protected so long as they are not oppressed, yet it is probably impossible fully to know what governments might have done, but did not do, and why they were restrained. Still, a final thread of evidence is the changes in the actions of rulers when a new group of voters appears. Policies previously unconsidered or rejected now come to be deemed proper by elected officials. Civil rights policies in the United States have closely paralleled the voting status of the Negro. Upon Emancipation, the Republican Party championed the rights of the ex-slaves and the new voters. When the southern states succeeded in disenfranchising the Negro again, the G.O.P. lost interest in his problems. After the Second World War, with the settlement of millions of black voters in the North, both parties became favorable to racial equality. Today, as Negroes vote in the South, sheriff candidates like Alabaman Al Lingo, who once freely clubbed and cursed them, now politely hear and respond to their demands.[38]

These threads do not constitute a fully woven fabric of democratic theory. Admittedly, many other theorists not included here have also discussed elections, and they provide different views and further facets of the subject. It is certainly valuable to reexamine democratic political theory,[39] and elections are still subject to the criticisms of their detractors. Any modernized theory cannot reject the evidence of the twentieth century, and need not reject all of classical theory. Ultimately, the choice of democracy is based upon value premises, one of which is the preference for a political system in which protection of the citizens is considered of higher priority then the possible attainment of wise policy by elite rulers. Elections have been seen by theorists as a contribution to public protection, and empirical evidence provides no contradiction. A modern theory of democratic elections need claim no more and a modern democratic state can seek no less.

## Notes

1. J. Rousseau, *The Social Contract and Discourses* (New York: Dutton, 1950), p. 27.
2. John Locke, *Of Civil Government* (New York: Dutton, 1943), Book II, p. 127.
3. Aristotle, *Politics* (Modern Library ed., New York, 1943), Book VI, 1318b.
4. John Rutledge, in Max Farrand, ed., *The Records of the Federal Convention of 1787* (New Haven, 1911), Vol. II, p. 205.
5. Locke, p. 125.
6. John Stuart Mill, *Considerations on Representative Government* (New York, 1958), p. 53.
7. *Ibid.*, p. 144.
8. Niccolo Machiavelli, *Discourses* (Modern Library ed., New York, 1940), p. 117.
9. James Madison, *The Federalist*, No. 51 (Modern Library ed., New York, 1941), p. 337.
10. Mill, pp. 43, 131.
11. *The Federalist*, No. 52, p. 343.
12. General Thompson of Massachusetts, in Jonathan Elliot, ed., *Debates on the Adoption of the Federal Constitution*, 2nd ed. (1888) (New York, Burt Franklin Research Source Series, 109), Vol. II, p. 16.
13. Aristotle, *Politics*, Book IV, 1300a-b.
14. In the New York convention, Elliot, II, pp. 246–47.
15. Plato, *The Republic*, trans. Francis Cornford (New York, 1945), Book VI, 488.
16. Plato, *Laws*, trans B. Jowett (New York, 1937), 753–68.
17. Mill, p. 114.
18. *The Federalist*, No. 10, pp. 53–54.
19. John C. Calhoun, *A Disquisition on Government* in *Works*, Vol. I (New York, 1854), p. 23.
20. Rousseau, p. 291.
21. Plato, *The Republic*, Book VIII, 569.
22. Massachusetts Senator Hoar, in the classic defense of indirect Senate elections, *Congressional Record*, Vol. 25, 53rd Cong., special sess. (1893), p. 103.
23. Karl R. Popper, "Plato as Enemy of the Open Society," in Thomas L. Thorson, ed., *Plato: Totalitarian or Democrat?* (Englewood Cliffs, 1963), p. 71.
24. See Robert Dahl's analysis of the logic and illogic of Madison's position in *A Preface to Democratic Theory* (Chicago, 1963), chap. 1.
25. Alexis de Tocqueville, *Democracy in America*, ed., Phillips Bradley (New York, 1954), Vol. I, p. 271.
26. Rousseau, p. 94.
27. Dahl, p. 31.
28. See James W. Prothro and Charles M. Grigg, "Fundamental Principles of Democarcy," *Journal of Politics* 22 (May 1960): 276–94; Herbert McClosky, "Consensus and Ideology in American Politics," *American Political Science Review* 58 (June 1964): 361–82.
29. The best studies are Angus Campbel *et al.*, *The American Voter* (New York, 1960) and V.O. Key, jr., *The Responsible Electorate* (Cambridge, 1965).
30. V. O. Key, jr., *Politics, Parties and Pressure Groups*, 5th ed. (New York, 1964), p. 544.
31. Eugene Burdick, "Political Theory and the Voting Studies," in Burdick and Arthur Brodbeck, *American Voting Behavior* (Glencoe, 1959), p. 141.

32. Notable is Bernard Berelson, *Voting* (Chicago, 1954), chap. 14.
33. See Walter Berns, ''Voting Studies,'' in Herbert Storing, ed., *Essays on the Scientific Study of Politics* (New York, 1962); Jack L. Walker, ''A Critique of the Elitist Theory of Democracy,'' *American Political Science Review* 60 (June 1966): 285–95, and the rebuttal by Robert Dahl, *ibid.*: 296–305. A particularly peevish and inaccurate attack on the voting studies is Berns' ''Defending Politics,'' *Commentary* 42 (August 1966): 62–64.
34. Graeme Duncan and Steven Lukes, ''The New Democracy,'' *Political Studies* 11 (June 1963): 161.
35. See Campbell *et al.*, *The American Voter*, chaps. 8, 10.
36. Aristotle, *Politics*, Book III, 1282a.
37. See Dahl, pp. 132–33.
38. *The New York Times*, April 4, 1966, p. 27.
39. Among the works emphasizing democracy as a system of controlling governors are A. D. Lindsay, *The Modern Democratic State* (London, 1943), and Henry B. Mayo, *An Introduction to Democratic Theory* (New York, 1960).

# 9

# "If Elected, I Promise": American Party Platforms

*Revision Co-Authored by Susan S. Lederman*

An election rarely is a policy referendum or a mandate for designated future actions. The voters largely make their decisions on the basis of party loyalties rather than issues. Direct control over policy is therefore unlikely. Indirect influence on policy is still possible, through voters' judgment of party performance. There is an inevitable fusing of party and policy, and therefore an inevitable programmatic result from elections. Voters cannot choose either a program or a party alone, but must select both simultaneously, even unwittingly or unwillingly.

Parties are the crucial links between the voters' interests and the activities of government. The electorate approves or disapproves of policy by its choice of a party. Democrats and Republicans support particular programs in their quest for office and become identified with particular actions through their conduct in office. The initiatives and commitments of parties and candidates are vital in the determination of public policy.[1]

These commitments are found in the national platforms. Adopted by their only general bodies, the nominating conventions, and presented to the voters as the presidential election approaches, they most fully represent the parties' intentions.

Indirect voter influence over policy can be facilitated in two ways through the platforms. First, the documents may provide a means by which the voters choose parties and their policies. The electorate makes its judgments on the basis of the past performance of the parties and their promised group benefits. Meaningful platforms would aid such decisions. Second, the platform may be significant even if not widely read. The campaign manifesto may reflect program initiatives made by parties in anticipation of voter needs and demands. If the platform commits politicians to relatively specific actions, the electorate's choice of a party would also become a choice of policies.

In both cases, platforms must be specific, policy-oriented, and relevant to the voters' concerns. The conventional view, however, is that platforms are meaningless, and the party document has received more scorn than attention. According to one hoary cliché, "A platform is to run on, not to stand on." The classic condemnation of platforms is Ostrogorski's:

> The platform, which is supposed to be the party's profession of faith and its programme of action is only a farce—the biggest farce of all the acts of this great parliament of the party. The platform represents a long list of statements relating to politics, in which everybody can find something to suit him, but in which nothing is considered as of any consequence by the authors of the document, as well as by the whole convention. . . . The platform has just as little significance and authority for Congress. Its members consider themselves in no way bound to the programs laid down in the convention, for they know perfectly well under what circumstances and with what mental reservations it has been promulgated.[2]

If platforms are meaningless, it seems odd that they should bring, as they have, severe intraparty disagreement, and the attention of interest groups, mass media, and practical politicians. Platform conflicts have occasioned convention walkouts by southern Democrats in 1948; physical confrontations among Republican factions in 1964; and a series of controversies in recent Democratic conclaves, most notably in 1972. Rather than neglect platforms, politicians seem to regard them as significant factors in the quest for voter support.[3]

## The Rational Platform

One means of exploring the impact of platforms would be an assessment of their *rational* character. Defined in instrumentalist terms, rationality is any means that furthers the goals of voters and parties. Traditional critics of platforms consider them nonrational because they do not contribute to the realization of voters' goals. The party documents, it is claimed, do not help the voter to make informed policy choices and are unrelated to the party's policy positions. Conversely, a platform that is rational would provide a guide to party commitments, help the voter in making his decision, and link the programmatic appeals made in campaigns to the actions of government. By examining platform rationality, we can test these assertions and the policy significance of party manifestos.

Two kinds of rationality are involved. Derived from the theory of Anthony Downs,[4] they can be designated voter-rationality and party-rationality. Platforms provide for voter-rationality if they help an individual select the party that will bring the greatest individual benefit or "utility income." The voter's concern for individual protection and gains has been noted in chapter 8. Benefits are not only material gains but all things valued by the voter, such as psychic satisfactions or altruistic actions. Platforms promote party-rationality if they contribute to the victory of their authors. Considerations of the wisdom or morality of individual benefits or party actions are not independently involved in this model—although wise and moral actions are likely eventually to have an effect.

A particular action may serve neither, either, or both kinds of rationality. For a party to ignore its pledges consistently, for example, serves neither end, because it confuses voters and also results in distrust of the party, to its ultimate detriment. Honoring of pledges, by contrast, in most cases is rational for parties and an aid to voters. To take a different situation, it may be rational in a two-party system for a party to be vague on important issues, for it can thereby gain support from diverse groups in the electorate. Such vagueness does not contribute to voter-rationality, however, since electors will find it difficult to make an informed choice.[5]

Let us specify some of the qualities of a party platform that would aid the voters. A rational platform would have five qualities:

1. It would be concerned, in considerable degree, with questions of public policy and would be precise enough to be meaningful to the voter.
2. Since voters tend to make their party choices on the basis of performance, it would facilitate a comparison of the two parties' past positions and actions, with special attention to the merits and defects of the incumbents' record. The platform would thereby provide a judgement on the "nature of the times."
3. It would indicate future positions of the party, specifically enough to be meaningful to the voter, particularly in policy areas of greatest benefit to the voter. Such statements are needed partially as an aid to voting in the impending election, providing a guide to the group benefits available through each party. Statements on future policy also are needed for the next election, as a means of judging the party's reliability in keeping pledges.[6]
4. The party would be highly consistent in its positions from one platform to the next.
5. If victorious, the party would carry out its indicated platform positions to the best of its ability.

Platforms would need to meet a somewhat different set of standards if they were to be considered a contribution to the party's rational goal of election. The parties would attempt to anticipate the voters' policy interests. For a two-party system, we can suggest the following criteria:

1. The content of the platform would vary in accord with the party's campaign strategy. It would deal with policy questions only insofar as this discussion contributed to victory.
2. The past records of the parties would be presented as a favorable comparison of the party with its opposition, to win voters concerned with the "nature of the times."
3. In regard to future policies, the party would promise group benefits, but its pledges would vary in specificity according to the political situation. In detail: (*a*) The party would specifically accept any policy known to be intensely favored by a majority of voters. (*b*) The party would specifically accept any policy favored by a minority of voters and not opposed by a substantial minority. (*c*) Where voter preferences are uncertain or politically unimportant, the party position would tend to be vague. (*d*) Where opposing positions on an issue are held by two or more minorities of voters, the party position would tend to be vague. (*e*) In certain cases, despite the foregoing propositions, the party might specifically accept a minority position on an issue. This action would occur if the party were attempting to enlist the support of a "passionate minority" (i.e., a minority for which support on one particular issue was more important than the party's stands on all other issues).

Party-rationality would also require consistency and party performance, as in propositions 4 and 5 above.[7]

It is important to realize that it is not necessary to the achievement of either kind of rationality that there always be differences between the parties, as advocated by proponents of "responsible party government."[8] Complete disagreement would be nonrational, for it would lead to the collapse of the political system, a disadvantageous result for almost all voters. Disagreements on issues on which there is a decided majority preference would also not be rational. It would lead either to the selection of a party opposed to most voters' wishes or to the continuous defeat of one party, and the foreclosure of choice.

For the parties, issue differences where there is an intense majority preference would be nonrational, probably resulting in defeat of the party sponsoring the minority position. On other issues, differences result from uncertainty or from dissimilar strategies. Uncertain of public preferences, the parties may advance differing positions, hoping they have correctly gauged public sentiment. Alternately, the parties may be aware of preferences but attempt to appeal to different or opposed "passionate minorities," again resulting in conflicting policies. This can be a rational course, but it is also logical for the parties to agree in their appeals to minorities, as well as to majorities.

Do the American platforms fit this "model" of rationality? Through an analysis of major party platforms from 1944 to 1976,[9] it is possible to test some of these propositions and thereby gain an indication of the policy significance of platforms. It is not necessary to substantiate in detail the propositions on the consistency of party platforms. There is manifest continuity in each party from one election to the next. Changes of emphasis and of specificity, as noted below, are evident. In the last decade, party platforms have become longer and broader in scope, as each party attempts to promise to meet the individual needs of its constituent groups. The thrust of those promises, however, changes little from one quadrennium to the next. We will confine our analysis to the first three major propositions on both voter- and party-rationality, as revealed in the eighteen major party platforms of the last three score years.

The method used for this purpose is content analysis. "Content analysis is a term used to describe a wide variety of research techniques, all of which are used for systematically collecting, analyzing, and making inferences from messages."[10] The purpose of these methods is to reduce the multiplicity and ambiguity of verbal communications to a relatively small number of comparable categories. Quantitative techniques can then be applied to reveal patterns and trends. There are three major steps in this technique: (1) selecting a unit of analysis; (2) establishing categories; and (3) providing clear standards for classification within these categories.[11]

The unit of analysis selected here is the sentence in the platform. (In other cases, words, paragraphs, or inches of printed material might be used.) Where distinct ideas are included in a compound sentence, each idea is counted separately, and transitional sentences are excluded. There are some possible distortions in this method, for important qualitative differences may be disregarded. One sentence explicitly pledging, "We will repeal the draft" is considered equal to one of vague rhetoric, such as, "America is the land of opportunity." College students would probably dispute the equivalence. These distortions are acceptable, however, for pledges tend to be short, and rhetoric to be long-winded. We are therefore making it more difficult to show policy significance in platforms.

Each sentence was placed in one of three principal categories, which were then further divided into eleven minor categories. These categories follow the typical organization of platforms, which proceed from the general to the specific, and from discussion of the past to proposals for future action. The categories used are listed below, together with examples from the 1976 platforms.[12] Specific standards of definition will be found in the Appendix for this chapter.

## 1. Rhetoric and Fact

"Ethnic Americans have enriched this nation with their hard work, self-reliance, and respect for the rights and needs of others." (Rep.)

''As a nation, we are blessed with rich resources of land, water, and climate.'' (Dem.)

### 2. Evaluation of the Parties' Records and Past Performance

a. *General Approval*: ''The Democratic Party's concern for human dignity and freedom has been directed at increasing the economic opportunities for all our citizens and reducing the economic deprivations and inequities that have stained the record of American democracy.'' (Dem.)
b. *General Criticism*: ''During the past 25 years, the American economy has suffered five major recessions, all under Republican administrations.'' (Dem.)
c. *Policy Approval*: ''Our confidence in the people of this nation was demonstrated by initiating the Revenue Sharing Program.'' (Rep.)
d. *Policy Criticisms*: ''The Democratic Congress has created no new federal judgeships since 1970: we deplore this example of playing politics with the justice system.'' (Rep.)

### 3. Statements of Future Policies

There are six minor categories, intended to be arranged in increasing order of commitment and specificity. A rational voter should find it increasingly easy to understand the party's intentions as he or she progresses through the pledges in the different categories.

a. *Rhetorical Pledges*: ''The United States must always stand for peace and liberty in the world and the rights of the individual.'' (Rep.)
b. *General Pledges*: ''The next Democratic administration will commit itself to move vigorously against anti-competitive concentration of power within the business sector.'' (Dem.)
c. *Pledges of Continuity*: ''We will continue our consistent support of Israel, including sufficient military and economic assistance to maintain Israel's deterrent strength in the region, and the maintenance of U.S. military forces in the Mediterranean adequate to deter military intervention by the Soviet Union.'' (Dem.)
d. *Expression of Goals and Concerns*: ''Increased part-time and flexible-hour work should be encouraged whenever feasible.'' (Rep.)
e. *Pledges of Action*: ''We pledge to support effective voluntary family planning around the world, as well as at home, and to recognize officially the link between social and economic development and the willingness of the individual to limit family size.'' (Dem.)
f. *Detailed Pledges*: ''We will seek repeal of Section 14(b) of the Taft-Hartley Act which allows states to legislate the anti-union shop.'' (Dem.)

The pledges of future action were also classified separately by topic, as well as by content. Nine policy areas were distinguished and are detailed in the

Appendix. The topics are (1) foreign policy, (2) defense, (3) economic policy, (4) labor, (5) agriculture, (6) resources, (7) social welfare, (8) government, and (9) civil rights and ethnic policy.

## Judgments of the Party Records

We are now able to assess the rational quality of platforms. A basic concern of voters is the past performance of the parties. In judging the "nature of the times," a party manifesto that consisted only of rhetoric would be of little help to the electorate. It would derive more benefit from the documents if they concentrated on evaluations of the parties, particularly the incumbents' record of performance. Table 9.1 summarizes the percentage distribution of platform statements, with evaluations of the parties' records further subdivided into the four minor categories.[13] This distribution of platform statements indicates a greater contribution to voter-rationality than is commonly supposed. Platforms are not principally vague paeans to God, mother, and country. The first category, including factual statements as well as "hot air," tends to comprise less than a quarter of all statements, and the average is one of six statements.

Almost one-third of the platform statements represent evaluations of the parties' records providing abundant material for those crucial voters who cast their ballots on the basis of past performance. In their manifestos, parties respond to the electorate's concern for past performance. The patterns in this category are further indications of the national character of the platforms. Statements relating to policy actions always predominate over general approvals and criticisms. This pattern holds for each party in each of the nine election years. In reading the platform, therefore, the citizen would be able to make comparisons of the parties on the basis of the issues and actions of the preceding period. Its relatively specific statements on past policy also commit a party to future action.[14]

The discussion of the past focuses on the actions of the incumbent party in the White House. Less attention is given to the actions of the party out of the Presidency, even when it controls Congress, as in 1948, 1956–60, and 1968–72. The 1976 Republican platform is a notable exception. The party, striving to disassociate itself from the Watergate debacle, specifically and repeatedly attacked the actions of the "Democrat Congress" as the cause of the nation's malaise. In figure 9.1, we compare the approvals and criticisms of the incumbents and their opponents. The frequencies of platform statements tend to assume the following order: approvals by the in-party, criticisms by the out-party, approvals by the out-party, and criticisms by the in-party. The debate is one over the record of the executive party. It is not a contrast between two different sets of policies argued during the past four years.[15] A further indication of the emphasis on the in-party's record is the greater frequency with which the in-party makes any policy evaluations, whether approving or disapproving. These patterns are in accord with the voters' own emphasis on the incumbents' record.

A focus on the record of the incumbents is further promoted by the nature of the American political system. Presidential government and the lack of an authoritative spokesman for the other party focus attention on the chief executive's program. A two-party system, moreover, tends to reduce political conflict to a simple alternative of continuity or change in present policies without equal consideration of the opposition's alternatives. It is also simpler to concentrate on the known record of the incumbents than on the hypothetical performance of the opposition.

Platforms also serve the cause of party-rationality. Democrats and Republicans anticipate the voters' reactions in their campaigning, seeking to emphasize electoral perceptions of partisan benefit. Without direct control, the voters are thereby influencing politicians' behavior. The distribution of statements is not random but in accord with the apparent strategy of each party in the campaign. Three platforms, illustratively, are prominent in the emphasis given to statements of rhetoric and general approval of the party: the Democratic in 1944, the Republican in 1956, and the Democratic again in 1964. In each, the party attempted (successfully) to win on the strength of the personal popularity of the incumbent. In each year, the opposition party presented a

**TABLE 9.1**
**Content Distribution of Party Platforms**
**(in percentages of designated platform)**[a]

| | *1944* | | *1948* | | *1952* | | *1956* | |
|---|---|---|---|---|---|---|---|---|
| *Category* | *Dem.* | *Rep.* | *Dem.* | *Rep.* | *Dem.* | *Rep.* | *Dem.* | *Rep.* |
| Rhetoric | 22 | 11 | 12 | 23 | 18 | 9 | 14 | 15 |
| Evaluation | | | | | | | | |
| General approval | 23 | 3 | 11 | 3 | 11 | 3 | 5 | 15 |
| General criticism | 0 | 7 | 3 | 4 | 1 | 18 | 11 | 4 |
| Policy approval | 13 | 2 | 10 | 8 | 16 | 11 | 9 | 26 |
| Policy criticism | 0 | 10 | 8 | 1 | 3 | 14 | 17 | 2 |
| Future Policy | 42 | 68 | 56 | 61 | 51 | 45 | 44 | 38 |
| Number of Statements | 92 | 177 | 205 | 159 | 419 | 345 | 596 | 538 |

[a] *Percentages add vertically to 100%, except for variations due to rounding. Percentages are of the number of statements in each platform.*[13]

sharply contrasting platform, emphasizing partisan and policy criticism, and future policies. Accepting the incumbent's popularity, the opposition sought to shift the focus of the campaign.

A stress on rhetoric and general approval was also somewhat evident in the 1968 Democratic and more strongly apparent in the 1976 Republican platform. Again, the party attempted to succeed on the basis of its White House accomplishments. In 1968 the incumbent President gave up the mantle to his vice-president, and Humphrey found the President's record more a hindrance than a help. The 1976 Republican platform is notable for the unusually high percentage of rhetorical statements. The platform, supporting incumbent President Ford, had to be circumspect about reminding the voters of President Nixon's actions. Though the party wished to continue the administration's economic and foreign policies, the Republicans had to focus on the achievements without calling attention to the former President associated with those polices.

Parties also devote varying proportions of their platforms to evaluations of the past, depending on the course deemed most likely to succeed. Opinion polls provide some guide to public sentiment and the likely outcome of the election. If the record of the party has been well received and victory seems likely, it will tend to emphasize that record. If the public is dissatisfied with

**TABLE 9.1**
***Continued***

| *1960* | | *1964* | | *1968* | | *1972* | | *1976* | |
|---|---|---|---|---|---|---|---|---|---|
| *Dem.* | *Rep.* | *Dem.* | *Rep.* | *Dem.* | *Rep.* | *Dem.* | *Rep.* | *Dem.* | *Rep.* |
| 20 | 21 | 20 | 11 | 15 | 8 | 14 | 20 | 17 | 29 |
| 4 | 7 | 14 | 5 | 12 | 3 | 1 | 3 | 1 | 1 |
| 7 | 1 | 1 | 12 | 1 | 6 | 4 | 3 | 4 | 3 |
| 4 | 13 | 48 | 2 | 15 | 1 | 1 | 29 | 2 | 6 |
| 11 | 1 | 1 | 25 | 1 | 11 | 9 | 5 | 7 | 4 |
| 53 | 56 | 15 | 44 | 56 | 71 | 72 | 40 | 70 | 56 |
| 795 | 519 | 941 | 414 | 822 | 556 | 1,103 | 1,094 | 863 | 966 |

past action, even if the record is "objectively" good, the rational course for the party is clearly to neglect the "nature of the times" and make more promises or resort to vagueness.

The distribution of platform statements conforms to these expectations of party strategy. In the elections of 1944, 1952, 1956, 1964, and 1972, the winner was predicted early in the campaign. The underdogs, possibly in an attempt to overcome their disadvantage, put less emphasis on their record and more on what they would do in the future. The 1960 election was generally expected to be close, and the distribution of platform statements was similar for the two parties. In 1948, an exception, the Democrats were universally expected to lose, but still stressed the past record more than the Republicans. This discrepancy was offset by the greater specificity of Democratic pledges, discussed below.

## Future Pledges in Platforms

The future pledges in platforms can also be examined to assess their contribution to rationality. Voter-rationality and indirect policy influence would be

**FIGURE 9.1**
**Distribution of Platform Statements on Parties' Records**

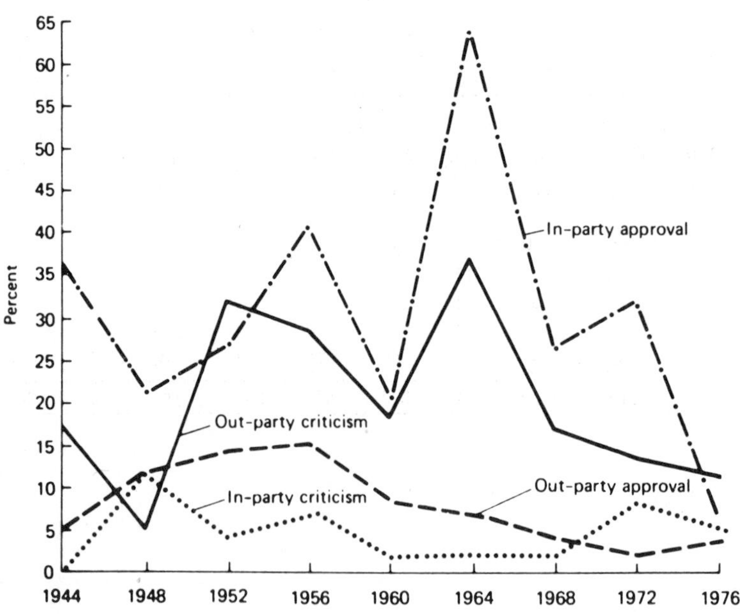

promoted if the large proportion of citizens concerned with group benefits could find some guide to these benefits in the platforms. Alternately, by making meaningful promises of future action, the parties would be initiating proposals to protect the electorate's vital interests. Victory for the party would then mean endorsement as well for a set of programs.

Analysis of the 5,470 future pledges in the eighteen platforms reveals some meaningful patterns. The topical distribution, presented in table 9.2, is largely the result of the definition of the topics. There is a concentration in the areas of foreign policy, economic policy, and social welfare, because these to pics are broadly defined. Variations among the topics are more significa nt and reveal the responsiveness of the parties to voter concerns. Over the three and a half decades, there has been a definite decline in the a ttention given to issues of general economic policy and to agriculture, an indication of the decreasing salience of the New Deal ideological division between the parties, and of the reduced political importance of the farm vote. Greater stress has come to be placed on issues of welfare and government, as they have become more important to the voters and more politically profitable to the parties.

The degree of specificity evident in future pledges varies considerably among topics and platforms. The content distribution of future pledges is presented in table 9.3. An inspection of the table demonstrates that, although there are many rhetorical and vague statements, a majority of pledges almost invariably fall in the four more specific categories, giving some meaningful guide to future action. It is also true that the degree of specificity varies by topic. To make comparisons simple, it is helpful to have a single measure of specificity.

A "pledge weight" has been constructed for this purpose. This figure is simply a weighted average of the pledges in any platform and topic.[16] If all pledges were rhetorical, the figure would be 1.0. If all promises were detailed, it would be 6.0. The average for all pledges is actually 3.4. The data are presented in table 9.4.

This measure shows platform pledges to be politically rational. Specificity in platform pledges is particularly conducive to voting on the basis of promised group benefits, the most common criterion employed by the voters. The parties in turn construct their platforms in order to appeal to these popular interests.

Historically, there have tended to be two distinct groups of topics, as measured by the "pledge weight." There has been a low specificity in foreign, defense, economic policy, government, and civil rights pledges, but more detailed pledges in labor, natural resources, and social welfare policies, and agriculture has tended in the same direction. There has been a decrease in the level of specificity in the pledges in these policy arenas, but the distinction in the level of specificity remains significant.

## TABLE 9.2
## Topical Distribution of Future Pledges, by Platforms (in percentages of designated platform)[a]

| | *1944* | | *1948* | | *1952* | | *1956* | | *1960* | |
|---|---|---|---|---|---|---|---|---|---|---|
| *Topic* | *Dem.* | *Rep.* | *Dem.* | *Rep.* | *Dem.* | *Rep.* | *Dem.* | *Rep.* | *Dem.* | *Rep.* |
| Foreign | 18 | 17 | 18 | 22 | 15 | 19 | 13 | 15 | 19 | 14 |
| Defense | 8 | 6 | 5 | 6 | 4 | 8 | 4 | 10 | 4 | 10 |
| Economics | 23 | 18 | 17 | 20 | 16 | 12 | 12 | 15 | 15 | 14 |
| Labor | 5 | 9 | 7 | 2 | 4 | 2 | 6 | 5 | 5 | 5 |
| Agriculture | 18 | 14 | 12 | 7 | 11 | 10 | 12 | 17 | 7 | 9 |
| Resources | 8 | 11 | 10 | 9 | 14 | 14 | 16 | 11 | 13 | 8 |
| Welfare | 8 | 8 | 17 | 12 | 17 | 10 | 17 | 6 | 18 | 19 |
| Government | 8 | 11 | 8 | 17 | 8 | 17 | 11 | 12 | 10 | 10 |
| Civil rights | 5 | 7 | 6 | 5 | 11 | 8 | 11 | 8 | 7 | 11 |
| Number of Pledges | 39 | 120 | 114 | 97 | 213 | 154 | 261 | 205 | 425 | 289 |

[a] *Percentages add vertically to 100%, except for variations due to rounding. Percentages are of the number of pledges in each platform.*

## TABLE 9.3
## Content Distribution of Future Pledges, by Platforms (in percentages of designated platform)[a]

| | *1944* | | *1948* | | *1952* | | *1956* | | *1960* | |
|---|---|---|---|---|---|---|---|---|---|---|
| *Category* | *Dem.* | *Rep.* | *Dem.* | *Rep.* | *Dem.* | *Rep.* | *Dem.* | *Rep.* | *Dem.* | *Rep.* |
| Rhetorical | 18 | 23 | 11 | 20 | 22 | 30 | 18 | 23 | 22 | 12 |
| General | 23 | 11 | 19 | 34 | 20 | 16 | 16 | 13 | 16 | 18 |
| Continuity | 8 | 4 | 15 | 4 | 15 | 4 | 13 | 21 | 7 | 12 |
| Goals | 26 | 24 | 7 | 16 | 8 | 19 | 14 | 16 | 19 | 22 |
| Actions | 20 | 18 | 24 | 21 | 23 | 20 | 22 | 14 | 18 | 17 |
| Details | 5 | 19 | 24 | 5 | 11 | 11 | 16 | 13 | 18 | 19 |
| N Platform | 39 | 120 | 114 | 97 | 213 | 154 | 261 | 205 | 425 | 289 |

[a] *Percentages add vertically to 100%, except for variations due to rounding.*

*Continued*

| *1964* | | *1968* | | *1972* | | *1976* | | *Total* | *Total* |
|---|---|---|---|---|---|---|---|---|---|
| *Dem.* | *Rep.* | *Dem.* | *Rep.* | *Dem.* | *Rep.* | *Dem.* | *Rep.* | *(1944–76)* | *(1968–76)* |
| 11 | 26 | 14 | 15 | 12 | 11 | 25 | 25 | 17 | 17 |
| 10 | 20 | 8 | 4 | 4 | 8 | 7 | 4 | 7 | 6 |
| 13 | 11 | 13 | 16 | 9 | 17 | 11 | 12 | 15 | 13 |
| 11 | 3 | 4 | 5 | 6 | 4 | 6 | 3 | 5 | 5 |
| 6 | 7 | 8 | 6 | 5 | 3 | 4 | 3 | 9 | 5 |
| 9 | 5 | 7 | 6 | 7 | 8 | 9 | 7 | 7 | 7 |
| 24 | 8 | 24 | 25 | 26 | 24 | 17 | 25 | 17 | 24 |
| 8 | 13 | 16 | 20 | 25 | 14 | 16 | 16 | 13 | 18 |
| 8 | 7 | 4 | 2 | 8 | 11 | 5 | 5 | 7 | 6 |
| 145 | 183 | 463 | 396 | 791 | 434 | 599 | 542 | 5,470 | 3,225 |

*Continued*

| *1964* | | *1968* | | *1972* | | *1976* | | *Total* | *Total* |
|---|---|---|---|---|---|---|---|---|---|
| *Dem.* | *Rep.* | *Dem.* | *Rep.* | *Dem.* | *Rep.* | *Dem.* | *Rep.* | *(1944–64)* | *(1968–76)* |
| 17 | 16 | 21 | 25 | 18 | 23 | 17 | 22 | 20 | 21 |
| 21 | 22 | 27 | 21 | 22 | 27 | 27 | 23 | 18 | 25 |
| 16 | 6 | 7 | 3 | 3 | 17 | 7 | 12 | 11 | 8 |
| 19 | 15 | 18 | 22 | 23 | 13 | 25 | 21 | 17 | 20 |
| 16 | 23 | 15 | 13 | 18 | 12 | 12 | 13 | 19 | 14 |
| 11 | 17 | 12 | 16 | 17 | 8 | 12 | 10 | 15 | 13 |
| 145 | 183 | 461 | 396 | 791 | 434 | 599 | 542 | 2,245 | 3,225 |

On topics in the first group, the voter is likely to be uninformed. Vague platform pledges are a sufficient appeal in these cases. In the second group of topics, however, voters are more likely to be knowledgeable. Pledges dealing with these topics consequently must be specific to convince the electorate. The gains to be obtained from a given foreign policy, for example, are usually cloudy, but a "senior citizen" is apt to have the skill of an actuary in calculating the advantage of a change in old-age retirement provisions. Parties respond to these differences by being more or less explicit in their promises.

Variations in specificity are also related to the voters' interests and political perceptions. We have learned that relatively few voters are concerned with issues of general policy or ideology.[17] Platform provisions dealing with such issues are likely to receive less popular attention. While the topics evidencing low specificity are of general importance, the special advantage to particular individuals or groups is uncertain. Thus, all voters certainly gain from a successful foreign policy, or honest government, but the advantage to a particular voter is difficult to see. The benefits are general, or "nondistributive" to individuals. In the absence of some obvious failure, a voter need not be too concerned about party policy in these areas. The social benefits of government action will probably occur without voter attention, and one voter will gain as much as another. Since voters are not apt to be concerned about these topics, the parties need be less concerned about popular reactions and can resort to vagueness.

A minority of voters are concerned with general questions. Pledges even to

**TABLE 9.4**
**"Pledge Weights," by Topics and Platforms**

| | *1944* | | *1948* | | *1952* | | *1956* | | *1960* | |
|---|---|---|---|---|---|---|---|---|---|---|
| *Topic* | *Dem.* | *Rep.* | *Dem.* | *Rep.* | *Dem.* | *Rep.* | *Dem.* | *Rep.* | *Dem.* | *Rep.* |
| Foreign | 3.8 | 2.4 | 3.8 | 2.2 | 2.9 | 2.5 | 3.2 | 3.3 | 2.8 | 3.0 |
| Defense | 3.7 | 2.6 | 2.2 | 3.0 | 1.5 | 2.0 | 3.3 | 2.9 | 3.3 | 3.3 |
| Economics | 2.4 | 3.9 | 2.4 | 2.7 | 2.9 | 2.8 | 3.4 | 3.5 | 3.5 | 3.4 |
| Labor | 3.5 | 3.4 | 5.2 | 3.0 | 4.1 | 4.3 | 4.9 | 3.9 | 3.9 | 4.0 |
| Agriculture | 3.4 | 3.8 | 3.9 | 3.0 | 3.3 | 3.9 | 3.8 | 2.9 | 3.2 | 3.8 |
| Resources | 3.0 | 4.5 | 4.2 | 4.0 | 3.4 | 4.1 | 3.3 | 3.3 | 3.9 | 4.1 |
| Welfare | 3.3 | 4.0 | 4.6 | 3.3 | 4.1 | 3.6 | 4.3 | 3.6 | 4.2 | 4.2 |
| Government | 3.3 | 3.8 | 2.7 | 3.0 | 2.8 | 3.1 | 2.8 | 3.8 | 3.0 | 3.7 |
| Civil rights | 3.0 | 4.0 | 4.7 | 4.4 | 3.0 | 3.3 | 2.6 | 2.7 | 3.8 | 4.1 |
| *Platform means* | *3.2* | *3.6* | *4.0* | *3.0* | *3.2* | *3.2* | *3.6* | *3.2* | *3.5* | *3.7* |
| *N* Platform | 39 | 120 | 114 | 97 | 213 | 154 | 261 | 205 | 425 | 289 |

these voters need not be specific. The satisfactions to voters in such cases are psychic and ideological, not personal, and promises to them can be hazy but still effective in winning their loyalty. A voter who considers foreign policy, defense, or economic issues important is likely to be satisfied with general commitments such as mutual security, American nuclear superiority, or maintenance of the free-enterprise system.[18]

The bulk of the electorate is concerned with narrower policies and group benefits. Republican and Democratic candidates are evaluated according to the particular or "distributive" benefits they seem to offer workers, businessmen, the aged, the young, and the urban or rural poor. Pledges to win these voters must be specific to be effective. The advantages of higher minimum wages to a worker or price decontrol to an oil company are definite. They are of decided interest to those affected and are likely to have a direct influence on their electoral decisions.[19]

The parties respond to the particular interests of the voters by including specific pledges on these topics in their platforms. Such pledges are the documentary expression of their concern for popular needs. Not all, but some voters are likely to become aware of these pledges. Evasive statements are difficult in regard to distributive benefits. Because of the importance of these pledges to those involved, they will be more knowledgeable about the topic and able to demand more from the parties. The writers of the campaign manifesto will act to win this support, even anticipating group demands before they arise. Moreover, an organized interest group is likely to exist, making explicit

**TABLE 9.4**
***Continued***

| *1964* | | *1968* | | *1972* | | *1976* | | *1944–76 Topic* | *1944–76* |
|---|---|---|---|---|---|---|---|---|---|
| *Dem.* | *Rep.* | *Dem.* | *Rep.* | *Dem.* | *Rep.* | *Dem.* | *Rep.* | *Mean* | *N* |
| 3.5 | 3.7 | 3.0 | 3.5 | 3.1 | 2.7 | 3.3 | 2.8 | 3.0 | (925) |
| 2.9 | 3.5 | 2.2 | 3.3 | 2.4 | 1.4 | 3.4 | 3.0 | 2.9 | (354) |
| 2.4 | 3.3 | 3.2 | 3.3 | 3.5 | 2.9 | 2.9 | 3.4 | 3.2 | (726) |
| 3.8 | 3.8 | 4.3 | 3.1 | 4.2 | 2.6 | 3.3 | 3.2 | 3.8 | (269) |
| 3.7 | 3.9 | 3.9 | 2.8 | 3.1 | 3.3 | 3.1 | 3.7 | 3.5 | (382) |
| 3.8 | 4.0 | 3.8 | 4.1 | 2.9 | 3.6 | 3.3 | 2.7 | 3.7 | (499) |
| 3.3 | 4.4 | 3.4 | 3.4 | 4.0 | 2.7 | 3.2 | 3.0 | 3.7 | (1,085) |
| 2.9 | 3.0 | 2.6 | 2.8 | 3.2 | 3.2 | 3.3 | 3.3 | 3.1 | (852) |
| 2.8 | 2.2 | 3.5 | 2.1 | 4.2 | 3.2 | 3.1 | 2.6 | 3.3 | (378) |
| *3.3* | *3.6* | *3.3* | *3.2* | *3.8* | *2.8* | *3.2* | *3.1* | *3.4* | |
| 145 | 183 | 463 | 396 | 791 | 434 | 599 | 542 | | |

demands on the party's platform drafters, who in turn are quite receptive to any group with a plausible claim on voter loyalties. For all of these reasons, specificity increases on those issues of distributive benefit. Voters indirectly affect policy through partisan pledges of group gains.

Even within the topics of relatively low specificity, there are some more detailed pledges. It seems significant that these latter pledges also tend to emphasize distributive benefits, their focus evidently on a specific group. Thus, many of the foreign policy pledges in the third through sixth categories deal with U.S. relations toward Israel, in obvious attempts to win the votes of American Jews. Specific pledges on defense or government often relate to the living or working conditions of servicemen or civil servants, rather than the broader issues within the policy area. Similarly, specific economic pledges are directed toward discrete groups, such as shipbuilders, small businessmen, airlines, or retailers. More basic issues of government regulation of the economy are dealt with vaguely.

Party strategy also accounts for these differences in specificity, as campaigners react to their perceptions of the electorate. The rational party will specifically support any policy definitely favored by a majority of voters or by an unopposed minority, while it will be less specific when it deals with issues on which voter opinion is unknown, unimportant, or divided. The issues on which we have found low specificity are of the latter variety. Aside from ideological positions, there is no clear consensus among American voters on issues such as foreign policy, economic controls, and government. On other questions, such as territorial government, the group affected is politically unimportant. In another group of issues, such as regulation of the economy, opinion exists but is divided. In all of these cases, a political party will commonly seek to appeal to all views, the necessary result being an unspecific pledge.

Even within policy areas of low specificity, however, some pledges will be detailed, where an apparent majority opinion exists or where there is an unopposed minority. Although foreign policy planks tend to be vague, both parties had, through 1964, specifically and continuously pledged nonrecognition of Communist China in the belief this was the strong preference of a voting majority. Similarly, voter opinion since 1944 has clearly favored the social security system. Acting rationally in response to a majority preference, both parties have continuously pledged highly specific improvements in benefits. On issues such as agriculture and resources, or support of Israel, a highly interested minority has not been strongly opposed, and party pledges could be relatively precise.

Labor represents a different case. Pledges on this topic are highly specific, even though opinion is often strong and conflicting. Specificity here is the result of the alliance of each of the parties to one or the other of the opposing camps. The Democratic identification with labor unions, and Republican estrangement, has been so strong that neither party has attempted to muddle its positions on these issues.[20]

Civil rights is a unique topic. The "pledge weight" here lies between the two groups, although closer to that of lower precision. The variation in specificity from one election to the other, however, is extremely high, indicating its unusual character. As an issue, civil rights is peculiarly tangible as well as ideological, involving both distributive and general benefits. Some voters may be satisfied with imprecise statements, such as praise of equality; others demand detailed pledges, such as the abolition of literacy tests for voting. Neither the nature of the subject nor the expectations of the voter provide a sure guide to the parties.

Civil rights is also peculiar in the nature of voter opinion on the subject, and the consequent influences on party strategy. Aside from a shared ideological commitment to "equality," citizens have been divided and have felt more intensively on both sides of this issue than on any other topic.[21] Parties could attempt to appeal to both sides by taking an ambiguous position. Thus, in reacting in 1956 to the school desegregation decisions, the Democrats merely recognized "the Supreme Court of the United States as one of the three Constitutional and coordinate branches of the Federal Government," while the Republicans were so bold as to declare that "the supreme law of the land is embodied in the Constitution, which guarantees to all persons the blessings of liberty, due process and equal protection of the laws."[22]

Civil rights issues in the 1960s and '70s were considerably broadened to include the right to bilingual education, the right to recognition of the unique cultural contributions of ethnic groups, and an expanded emphasis on the rights of women. Both parties remained concerned with school desegregation, but the focus was more specific: court-ordered busing. The Democrats, though in support of the desegregation of schools according to the 1954 Supreme Court order, suggested that "mandatory transportation of students beyond their neighborhoods for the purpose of desegregation remains a judicial tool of the last resort for the purpose of achieving school desegregation." The Republicans, much more specific, noted that "segregated schools are morally wrong and unconstitutional. However, we oppose forced busing to achieve racial balance in our schools."[23]

The example of school busing indicates the conditions under which parties shun ambiguity. When opinion is intense, a party can also attempt to win a "passionate minority" to its side by clearly endorsing its position. If one party takes a specific position, the most rational course for the other party is also to take a precise position, or else lose votes from both sides. Thus, in 1948 and 1960 both parties took highly detailed and similar stands on civil rights.[24] These similarities are further indications of the parties' rational attempt to capture votes on these issues and of the consequent indirect influence of voters on policy.

## Party Variations

In the previous sections, we have seen that platforms often can serve as an aid to voter-rationality and thereby help provide an indirect policy influence to elections. Platforms aid a retrospective judgment on past performance and provide indications to the voter of the benefits he or she may expect in the future, especially those benefits of a distributive character.

The actions of the party are crucial in providing these aids to the voter. In writing their platforms, parties respond to the perceived political demands of the electorate. Both Democrats and Republicans adjust their strategy to the peculiarities of each election, evaluate the past records of the parties, and promise definite gains to identifiable interests. There are also variations between the parties in the specificity of their pledges. These differences also can be related to the parties' perceptions of the demands of the voters.

We have earlier found that the party trailing in a particular campaign tends to emphasize future pledges. Similarly, the party expected to lose the presidential election is always more specific. It is as if the underdog, trailing in polls and predictions, attempts to win converts by making more detailed promises. The leading party needs only to protect its advantage, which can be done best by not antagonizing any group and by holding to relatively ambiguous positions. The best example of these presumptive strategies is the 1972 campaign, in which the two parties produced both the most and least specific platforms.

The Democrats, following George McGovern's banner, forged the longest platform in modern history, with hundreds of specific promises for their constituent groups. The rights of youth, blacks, women, Indians, the elderly, the mentally and physically handicapped, and other disadvantaged groups were affirmed, and various specific remedies pledged. The Republicans, with Nixon as incumbent, were confident of victory and focused on their party's executive leadership of the past four years. The greater specificity of the likely loser is evident in 1944, 1948, 1956, and 1968. In 1948 the incumbent President Truman, faced with what seemed inevitable defeat, and the Democrats sought to recoup by a variety of explicit promises of mainly distributive benefits. The relationship is less clear in 1960, 1968, and 1976, when no winner could be predicted confidently in advance. The level of specificity of pledges in those years is almost identical for each party.

Further variations attributed to party strategies may be sought by examining the stress placed on different topics. In seeking support through its pledges, a party could devote a larger proportion of its platform to those policy areas it believes politically profitable. A second tactic would be greater specificity in these pledges. To gain a general measure of the emphases of the parties, therefore, we must combine the adjusted percentage share of each policy area with its "pledge weight." The resulting figure is called an index of "attention." In general, this figure is comparable to the "pledge weight." It can vary from 2.0, the lowest degree of specificity, to 7.0, the level of the most detailed pledges.[25]

The graphs of figure 9.2 picture the "attention" given by the parties to the various topics. They also serve to summarize much of the previous discussion. Taken as a whole, the slope (upward or downward) of the graphs is an indication of the changing importance of different topics. Measured against the average of all indexes, 4.4, each graph also indicates the relative specificity of the topic depicted.

Party differences also become evident. Republicans are seen to place more emphasis on defense and governmental issues, and Democrats on labor and welfare. In the terms used earlier, the GOP relies more on nondistributive benefits, whereas the Democratic emphasis is on those issues of differential significance to social groups and individuals. These variations are in accord with the images of the parties held by the voters. Although there have been some recent changes, Republicans have tended to be regarded as better managers of the government and to be more trusted on issues of war and peace. Democrats have been regarded more highly in terms of domestic policy and group benefits.[26] The parties emphasize their areas of strength. By responding to voter preferences, they again demonstrate the impact of elections on policy. Republican victory will mean more emphasis on nondistributive issues: Democratic success will bring particularistic gains.[27]

In any given year, rather than all years, the parties usually differ in their relative emphasis, as each stresses those topics it finds to its advantage. A party's stress is related to its campaign strategy in a particular election. Thus the Democrats were attentive to social welfare, government, and civil rights questions and focused considerable attention on labor problems in an attempt to win support of all disadvantaged groups in society. The Republicans in 1976 voiced concern over continued inflation and urged specific reforms on Congress.[28]

The content of the pledges within the categories has also changed significantly. Welfare concerns have been broadened substantially. The federal government has, in the past score of years, assumed an increased responsibility for public education. The platform pledges reflect this role in their specificity of concern over education of all groups including the handicapped, bilingual, urban, rural, undergraduate, adult, poor, and middle-income learners. The decreased interest in labor and agriculture policies is reflective of the decreased importance of union members and farmers in American society as a result of their decreased representation in the total population.

The scope of defense concerns has shifted since 1964. A large part of the Democratic platform's attention to defense questions revolved around arms control and reduction of expenditures for new weapons, whereas Republicans urged modernization programs for the navy and air force.

For Democrats, 1972 was a special case. The focus on foreign policy dropped significantly, and increased attention centered on welfare and government policy. The government category by 1968 became imbued with "law and order" issues. For the McGovern Democrats, reform of government structure was a means to provide distributive benefits to their constituent groups. The historically high level of platform focus on government (25 percent of future pledges; 5.1 attention index) is a reflection of that convention's concern with representative democracy and open decision making. Further, as the federal government has enlarged its areas of concern, it has become the focus of distributive benefits—from funds for education and housing to revenue sharing for local governments to use at discretion. Given this expansion of the scope of the federal sector, it is not surprising that the manner in which government is structured and the procedures that federal agencies use come under increased scrutiny in platforms.

The Republican campaign of 1964 also differed from past patterns. Some particular pledges of the past were discarded. High levels of specificity were achieved in six of the nine topics. Moreover, the amount of attention devoted to different subjects was quite at variance with the past. Less attention was devoted to all forms of distributive benefits than in 1960, and the civil rights plank drew the least notice of all eighteen studied. Foreign policy and defense questions reached unequaled levels of both percentage of the total platform (a combined total of 46 percent) and "attention" (5.2 and 6.4, respectively). This platform, like the Goldwater campaign, may have been directed either at previous nonvoters who might be stirred by a changed content, or at creating a winning coalition of "passionate minorities," each willing to support the party on the basis of its most intense beliefs.[29] The measurement of "attention" thus confirms the peculiar character of the 1964 Republican effort.

## The Influence of Platforms

We have attempted to gauge the contribution platforms make to voter-rationality and party-rationality. Platforms can aid the voter's retrospective judgment and quest for government benefits. They include considerable discussion of policy questions, often with a meaningful degree of specificity. They also include a great share of rhetoric and vagueness. As a summary measure of voter-rationality in platforms, it is useful to combine categories. Rhetorical statements, general approvals and criticisms, and rhetorical or general pledges will be considered "nonrational" elements in the platform (from the voter's viewpoint). The remaining statements, since they have some meaningful content, will be considered "rational." Of the eighteen platforms, as indicated in table 9.5, only seven had a majority of "nonrational" statements. The distribution between these two groupings is fairly constant over time, with most platforms tending toward a slight predominance of "rational" statements. Although much in platforms is not helpful to the rational voter, there would appear to be sufficient material to help him or her to make an informed choice.

In judging the past records of the parties, platforms are again of partial assistance. The record of the incumbent party, the one more crucial to the voter, is roundly debated, and this debate is conducted principally in terms of policy actions. The alternative policies of the opposition are not given the same consideration. A rational choice on the basis of the incumbents' record is facilitated, but a true comparison of the two parties is not feasible.

The parties present rather full descriptions of their future policy objectives and intentions and tend to be relatively specific. Their future pledges are most explicit in those policy areas involving distributive benefits, of most interest to voters with limited time and knowledge. The platforms also match the images voters hold of the parties in terms of "group benefits" and the "nature of the times," the most common voter conceptions. They are therefore a contribution to voter-rationality. However, the parties do not stress the same issues in most elections, and direct comparison of their positions becomes difficult. Although not overwhelming, the considerable proportion of meaningless pledges is also an impediment to the voter.

The platforms fall short of the full standards of voter-rationality because they are party instruments, serving the cause of party-rationality. The content of the platform varies with the strategy of the party. A policy emphasis and specificity in future pledges is sometimes consonant with partisan success. In such cases, platforms serve both party-rationality and voter-rationality. At other times, when a party is relying on the personality of its candidate, the party loyalty of the voters, or an apparent tide in its favor, it will have less cause to detail its policy actions and intentions.

In choosing their issues, parties act rationally, emphasizing the policy areas of their strength and neglecting the strong points of their opponents. They tend to be specific on these issues of direct, distributive benefit to the voters and to resort to rhetoric or vagueness where voters are unclear, uninterested, or divided. Policies favored by a majority of voters are endorsed by the parties, as are those supported by an unopposed minority. Where opposing minorities exist, the party rationally evades a policy choice. The parties do not often disregard majority preferences in an appeal to "passionate minorities." When they do make such appeals, as in civil rights, the parties are likely to imitate one another in the specificity and direction of pledges. These responses probably contribute to political stability by deemphasizing the most intense social conflicts.

**TABLE 9.5**
**Percentage Distribution of All Platform Statements**

| | *1944* | | *1948* | | *1952* | | *1956* | | *1960* | |
|---|---|---|---|---|---|---|---|---|---|---|
| | *Dem.* | *Rep.* | *Dem.* | *Rep.* | *Dem.* | *Rep.* | *Dem.* | *Rep.* | *Dem.* | *Rep.* |
| "Rational" | 38 | 56 | 57 | 38 | 48 | 50 | 55 | 52 | 48 | 54 |
| "Nonrational" | 62 | 44 | 43 | 62 | 52 | 50 | 45 | 48 | 52 | 46 |

Rationality is evident in platforms. They provide one means by which a party can pursue victory while serving popular interests. To be sure, convention delegates do not consciously consider platforms in these terms, or calculate "pledge weights." The significant finding, however, is that there are logical explanations to behavior which outwardly resembles only a circus—and one at which all the animal cages have been unlocked.[30] Similarly, platforms promote voter-rationality, although it would be foolish to claim that more than a small minority reads the entire document. The statements made in the platform reach the voter less directly, through interest groups, mass media, candidates' speeches, party controversy, and incomplete popular perceptions. A campaign is a contest for incremental votes, not for total support, and the platform is one of the means by which marginal voters make decisions. Interested "issue publics" may become aware of salient points, and an alleged broken promise may affect voters of even limited conceptual insight sufficiently to turn an election.[31] Even if the electorate does not read it, the platform functions to shape future action. The party becomes identified with certain policies, although all voters do not recognize the identification. In foreseeing the interests of voters and making appeals to these interests, the parties provide an indirect means of electoral influence on policy. Voters do not control government, but parties are restrained in their actions by their need to win votes.

The platform is a campaign document. Its characteristics are rationally derived from the party's goal of victory. In order to win elections, the party must also promote, in part, the cause of voter-rationality. The attention to the presumed interests of voting groups in the platforms provides a policy significance to elections. These documents are reasonably meaningful indications of the party's intentions. By their strictures about the past and pledges for the future, a party becomes committed to particular policies. The voter, by conferring legitimacy on these programs, intervenes significantly in the process of government. Platforms provide assistance to voters and indirect policy influences on the parties. Platforms indeed are to run on, not to stand on—but

TABLE 9.5
*Continued*

| | 1964 Dem. | 1964 Rep. | 1968 Dem. | 1968 Rep. | 1972 Dem. | 1972 Rep. | 1976 Dem. | 1976 Rep. | (1944–76) Total |
|---|---|---|---|---|---|---|---|---|---|
| "Rational" | 59 | 55 | 45 | 51 | 53 | 54 | 48 | 42 | 50.2 |
| "Nonrational" | 41 | 45 | 55 | 49 | 47 | 46 | 52 | 58 | 49.8 |

they also can reflect and affect the pace, direction, winner, and meaning of the race.

## Appendix

The following standards were used in classifying platform sentences among the content categories:

### 1. Rhetoric and Fact

Approval of commonly accepted values; appeals to "valence" issues without any specific context; support of diffuse symbols; citation of truisms and clichés. All purely factual statements, if not in a particular context, are also included.

### 2. Evaluations of the Parties' Records and Past Performances

All statements referring to past actions, policies, leaders, and conduct of the parties, including references to historical events which are attributed to the parties. There are four minor categories included here:

a. *General Approval:* Favorable citation of the party or its leaders; nonspecific citation of achievements and personnel; reference to national achievements (not government policies) in the context of praise for the given party.
b. *General Criticism:* Unfavorable citation of the opposite party or its leaders in statements analogous to *a*.
c. *Policy Approval:* Reference to designated policy actions of the party or its leaders of alleged social benefit. A definite policy must be cited to justify inclusion in this category, but no proof of the benefits of the policy is necessary.
d. *Policy Criticism:* Unfavorable reference to designated policy actions of the opposite party or its leaders, in statements analogous to *c*.

## FIGURE 9.2
## "Attention" of Platform Pledges

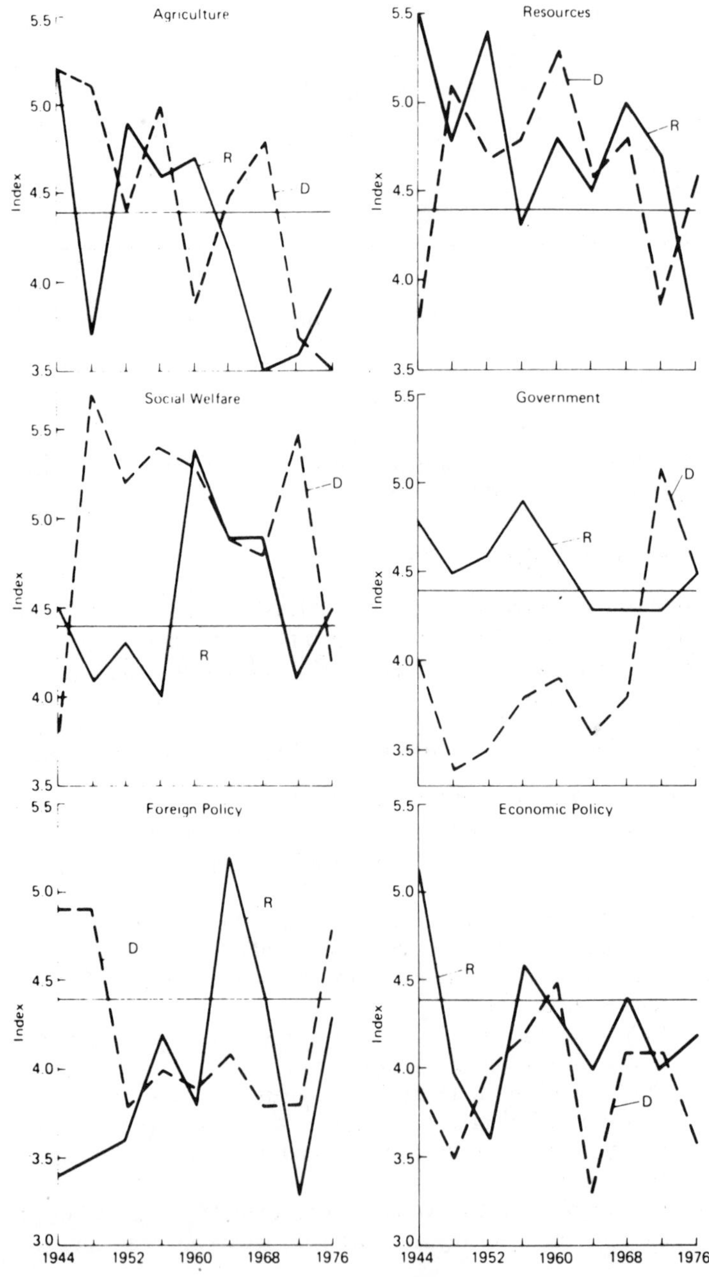

**FIGURE 9.2**
**(continued)**

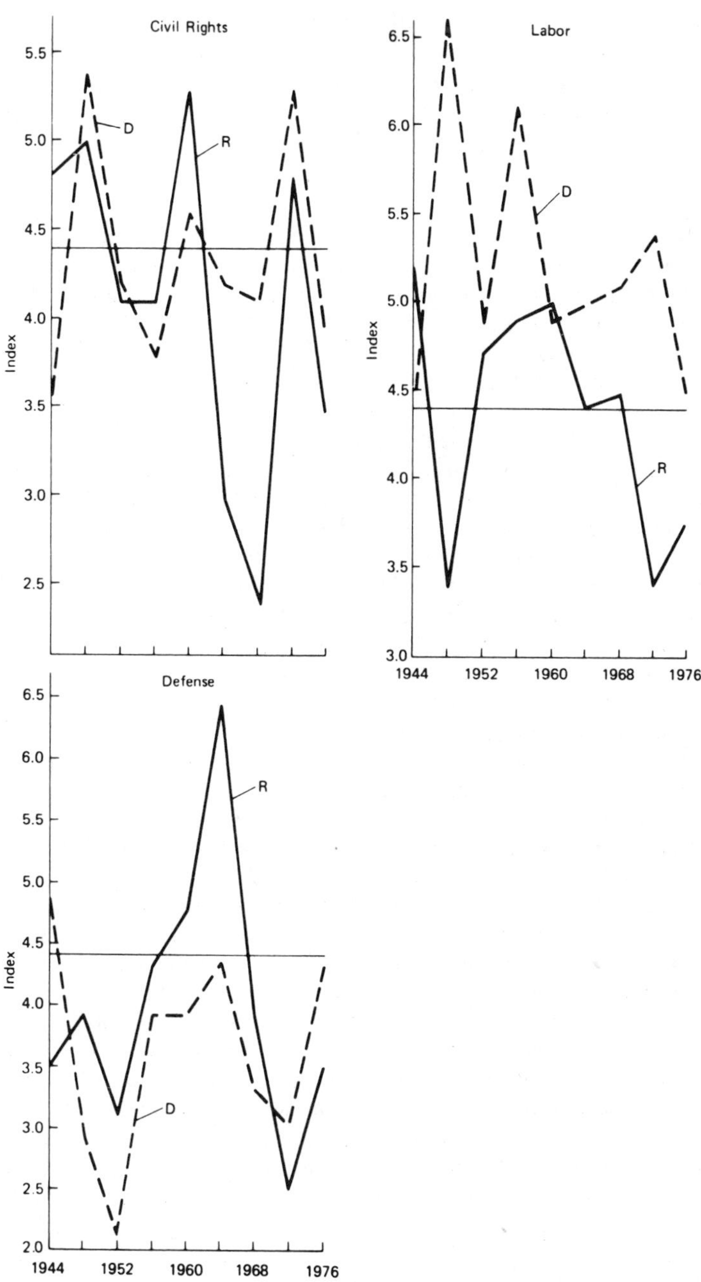

## 3. Statements of Future Policies

The six minor categories are in order of increasing commitment and specificity. The degree of party commitment is judged by the verbs employed, and the degree of specificity by the character of the sentence object. Pledges to oppose or refrain from an action are considered as relevant as positive promises. Since the categories are constructed on more than one criterion, these categories are nominal classifications and do not constitute a continuous, unidimensional scale.

a. *Rhetorical Pledges:* Future support of commonly accepted values, "valence" issues, truisms, and clichés. A simple test of a sentence in this category is to state the opposite. If the resulting sentence is absurd and could not be a logical policy, the pledge of future support is only rhetorical. A pledge that is not logically required, even though politically necessary, such as support of social security, is not rhetorical and is not included here.
b. *General Pledges:* Statements with a policy content unspecified or unclear, but not logically necessary. Typically, these statements could be made by either major party, and a reader would find it difficult to attribute the pledge to one party or the other. Unlike the rhetorical pledges, there is some relation to governmental action but, like the former, it is difficult to measure performance on pledges in this group.
c. *Pledges of Continuity:* A pledge to maintain present governmental policy, but without specification of its character, or with reference only to the general nature of a program. Verbs such as "continue," "support," "renew," "press," and "strengthen" are used, followed by indefinite objects. Although the details of future policy are unclear, a pledge in this category would provide the voter with a notion of future actions, if he were informed of present policies.
d. *Expressions of Goals and Concerns:* Stated intentions to meet a specific problem or to achieve a particular goal, but without specification of the means to be employed, or without complete commitment to the goal; recognition of a need or statements of concern, without the promise or possibility of government action. Verbs used in this category include "aid," "foster," "develop," "promote," "seek," "encourage," "endeavor," and their opposites. Object nouns may be qualified by adjectives such as "feasible," "reasonable," "sound," and "constitutional."
e. *Pledges of Action:* Definite promises of the direction of policy, as well as of the problems to be considered, although detailed provisions are not included. Pledges in this category dealing with government finances or other quantitatively measurable policies indicate the direction, but not the amount, of intended changes. These provisions include verbs such as "insist," "offer," "favor," "oppose," "resist," "extend," "increase," "restrict," and "decrease." Object nouns tend to be unqualified or modified by adjectives of quantity, such as "additional," "greater," "decreased," and "reduced."

f. *Detailed Pledges:* The character of the action pledged, as well as its direction, is stated. A specific bill or executive action may be mentioned, or its context explicated. Pledges to continue specific past policies or to exact quantitatively defined policies are included as well. Even in this category, however, specificity must be understood as considerably less than the details of an actual law. Verbs such as "endorse," "recommend," "pledge," and "commit" are followed by a definite object, often modified by strengthening adjectives such as "immediate," "prompt," "complete," and "full."

The following topics were included in the nine policy areas. These areas roughly correspond to the functions grouped in cabinet departments before 1964 and the groupings used in legislative analysis by *Congressional Quarterly:*

1. *Foreign Policy.* Diplomacy; the United Nations; foreign aid; collective security agreements unless exclusively military in character; policy toward Israel or other specific nations; East-West Center.
2. *Defense.* Conduct of war and military strategy; the draft; living conditions of military personnel; weapons systems; military research; civil defense; United Nations armed forces; disarmament and testing of nuclear weapons.
3. *Economic Policy.* Control of business cycles; federal fiscal policy and taxation; regulation of business; distribution of military procurement contracts; science and nonmilitary research; transportation, including mass transit and rivers and harbors; depressed areas.
4. *Labor.* Regulation of labor unions; employment conditions and minimum wages; occupational safety and health; retraining programs; employment services; equal pay for women; farm workers; standards in government contracts other than nondiscrimination.
5. *Agriculture.* Farm commodity; storage, loan, and income policies; food reserves; foreign distribution of agricultural surpluses; agricultural research; production and marketing controls; food stamp programs; school lunches; fisheries; rural electrification.
6. *Resources.* Policies relating to minerals, fuels, and other raw materials; energy policy; depletion allowances; water, forest, and game policy; air and water pollution; conservation and recreation; atomic energy for domestic purposes; regional development; electrical and hydroelectric power policy, excluding rural electrification.
7. *Social Welfare.* All programs related to health, hospitals, education, and social welfare; social security, including unemployment insurance and supplemental income assistance; Medicare and Medicaid; programs for the aged, handicapped, bilingual persons, and youth; consumer protection; housing, urban and regional planning and renewal other than transportation; veterans; arts and humanities.

8. *Government.* Administration; government efficiency including sunset laws and zero-based budgeting; loyalty programs and civil liberties; management of the civil service; intergovernmental relations; federalism in general terms, including programs of federal, state, and local grants-in-aid, tax adjustments and revenue sharing; federal budgeting and spending levels apart from particular programs; the national debt; statehood, government of territories and the District of Columbia; regulation of elections and the electoral college; legislative apportionment; congressional procedures other than Senate cloture.
9. *Civil Rights and Ethnic Policy.* All provisions related to discrimination against blacks, including desegregation of schools, armed forces, and so forth; social welfare programs specifically designed to deal with racial, ethnic, and sexual discrimination; affirmative action; constitutional rights of poor, veterans, youth; Senate cloture; immigration policy; American Indians; equal rights of women.

## Notes

1. A good treatment of the effect of commitments is Norton Long. "After the Voting is Over," *Midwest Journal of Political Science* 6 (May 1962): 183–200. See also Theordore Sorensen, *Decison-Making in the White House* (New York: Columbia University Press, 1963).
2. M. Ostrogorski, *Democracy and the Organization of Political Parties* (Garden City, N.Y.: Doubleday Anchor, 1964), vol. 2, pp. 138–39.
3. Studies of platform drafting include Edward F. Cooke, "Drafting the 1952 Platforms," *Western Political Quarterly* 9 (September 1956): 699–712; Paul Tillett, ed., *Inside Politics: The National Conventions, 1960* (New Brunswick: Rutgers University, 1961), chaps. 6–9; and Denis G. Sullivan et al., *The Politics of Representation* (New York: St. Martin's, 1974), chap. 4.
4. Anthony Downs, *An Economic Theory of Democracy* (New York: Harper & Row, 1957). Related important works include J. M. Buchanan and G. Tullock, *The Calculus of Consent* (Ann Arbor: University of Michigan Press, 1962); Duncan Black, *The Theory of Committees and Elections* (Cambridge, England: Cambridge University Press, 1958); and Donald E. Stokes, "Spatial Models of Party Competition," *American Political Science Review* 57 (June 1963): 368–77.
5. Downs, *Economic Theory*, pp. 135–39.
6. Downs, especially in ibid., chap. 3, emphasizes that the voter must rely on past actions of the parties rather than future promises. If future pledges are relatively specific, and discounted by the voters, it is then rational for them to consider them in making their choices. In any case, Downs sees a need (on p. 106) for future promises so that the party can be measured in the next election as a faithful or faithless keeper of its word.
7. These propositions are derived, with some modification, from Downs, ibid., propositions 2, 3, 4, 8, 14, 15, 23, and 24; and from chaps. 3, 4, 7, 8, and 13. Cf. Robert Dahl's brilliant analysis, *A Preface to Democratic Theory* (Chicago: University of Chicago Press, 1956), esp. chaps. 3–5.
8. See American Political Science Association, Committee on Political Parties. "Toward a More Responsible Two-Party System," in *American Political Science*

*Review* 44 (September 1950): supplement; and James MacGregor Burns, *The Deadlock of Democracy* (Englewood Cliffs, N.J.: Prentice-Hall, 1963).

9. The platform are collected in Donald B. Johnson, *National Party Platforms 1840–1976* (Urbana: University of Illinois Press, 1978), 2 vols.
10. Robert C. North et al., *Contest Analysis* (Evanston: Northwestern University Press, 1963), p. 50.
11. Content analysis is discussed further in Bernard Berelson, *Contest Analysis in Communications Research* (Glencoe: Free Press, 1962); and Ithiel de Sola Pool, *Trends in Content Analysis* (Urbana: University of Illinois Press, 1959). Among works using this method in the study of American politics are Elmer E. Cornwell, *Presidential Leadership of Public Opinion* (Bloomington: Indiana University Press, 1965); John W. Ellsworth. "Rationality and Campaigning: A Content Analysis of the 1960 Presidential Campaign Debates," *Western Political Quarterly* 18 (December 1965): 794–802; and Ira Sharkansky, "Four Agencies and an Appropriations Subcommittee," *Midwest Journal of Political Science* 9 (August 1965): 254–81.
12. Johnson, *National Party Platforms*, 2:915–46, 965–94.
13. The data for 1968 differ slightly from those published in a previous analysis of the platforms in Gerald M. Pomper, "Controls and Influence in American Elections (Even 1968)," *American Behavioral Scientist*, November 1969, pp. 215–30. The percentage distribution of platform pledges was inaccurate due to an apparent inversion of numbers. The thesis and conclusions of the article remain valid and are, in fact, enhanced by the correction.
14. In 1964 the Democrats issued two platforms. The first was a conventional platform, the second a long "Accounting of Stewardship, 1960–1964," detailing and praising the record of the Kennedy-Johnson administration, and comparing its achievements to the platform promises of 1960. Because of this separation, the percentage of statements of policy approval is markedly above normal, and that for future policies is markedly below normal. If the first platform alone is analyzed, the percentages, reading vertically in table 9.1, would be 25, 7, 2, 8, 1, 56.
15. There are important exceptions to these tendencies. The 1976 Republican platform was somewhat subdued in its lauding of the executive record. The Watergate legacy suggested prudence in calling attention to the Republican performance in the White House. The Republicans in 1976 thus urged comparison to *future* policies: "You are about to read the 1976 Republican Platform. Compare. You will see basic differences in how the two parties propose to represent you" (Johnson, *National Party Platforms*, 2:903). In 1972 the McGovern Democrats spent little time praising traditional Democratic party virtues in their platform. And in 1948 the Republicans disdainfully declared, "We shall waste few words on the tragic lack of foresight and general inadequacy of the Democrats: they have lost the confidence of all parties" (ibid., 1:451). In 1948, it may be recalled, the Republicans were so certain of victory that they allocated cabinet positions before the election. Their platform, perhaps, is therefore more typical of an in-party. More typical behavior is described by Cooke, "Drafting the 1952 Platforms," p. 706, who reports that the incumbent Democrats in 1952 deliberately discarded statements critical of the opposition from the original platform drafts and instead concentrated on approval of their own records.
16. The method is simple. The content categories from "rhetorical" to "detailed." are assigned arbitrary weights from 1 to 6. The number of pledges in each category is then multiplied by the appropriate weight, and the total of the products is

divided by the total number of statements. Algebraically, $f_1$, $f_2$, etc., being the number of pledges in each category:

$$\text{``Pledge Weight''} = \frac{\Sigma f_1 + 2f_2 + 3f_3 + 4f_4 + 5f_5 + 6f_6}{N}$$

17. See Angus Campbell et al., *The American Voter* (New York: Wiley, 1960).
18. A similar analysis is applied to incentives in organizations by Peter B. Clark and James Q. Wilson, "Incentive Systems: A Theory of Organization," *Administrative Science Quarterly* 6 (September 1961): 129–66; and by Mancur Olson, *The Logic of Collective Action* (Cambridge: Harvard University Press, 1965).
19. For similar reasons, Downs, *Economic Theory*, pp. 254–56, observes that the tangible interests of producers are likely to be preferred in democratic government over the more generalized interests of consumers.
20. Cooke, "Drafting the 1952 Platforms," p. 704, notes the different reception given to labor and business representatives in the platform-drafting committees. The difference between the parties on issues of labor regulation is also evident in Congress.
21. See Herbert McClosky, "Consensus and Ideology in American Politics," *American Political Science Review* 58 (June 1964): 361–82; and William Brink and Louis Harris, *Black and White* (New York: Simon and Schuster, 1967).
22. Johnson, *National Party Platforms*, 542–54.
23. Ibid., 2:927, 974.
24. See Downs, *Economic Theory*, pp. 55–56. If the two "passionate minorities" were of equal voting power, it would be rational for both parties to take specific but opposing positions. The stances of the candidates, but not the platforms, were such in 1964 on civil rights. The election results were in direct response to these strategies, Johnson winning 94 percent of the black vote and Goldwater carrying five states of the Deep South. In electoral payoff, however, the former was more important, and the Goldwater strategy was therefore irrational. Since then, the Republican party has been less specific in its civil rights promises than the opposition.
25. The percentage devoted to each topic is greatly dependent on the way in which the categories have been constructed. To adjust the percentage in a given year, we divide it by the percentage devoted to that topic in all years. If no particular emphasis is placed on this topic in the given year, the resulting ratio will be 1. Increased or decreased emphasis will be reflected in ratios above or below 1. This ratio is then added to the "pledge weight" for that year to obtain the index of "attention."
26. Campbell et al., *American Voter*, chap. 3. See also Donald E. Stokes, "Some Dynamic Elements of Contests for the Presidency," *American Political Science Review* 60 (March 1966): 19–28; and Gerald Pomper, *Voters' Choice* (New York: Harper & Row, 1975), chap. 7.
27. Party differences on economic policy are shown by Edward Tufte, *Political Control of the Economy* (Princeton: Princeton University Press, 1978), pp. 71–74.
28. The voters' response corresponded to these emphases. See Arthur Miller and Warren Miller, "Partisanship and Performance: 'Rational' Choice in the 1976 Presidential Election" (paper presented at the meetings of the American Political Science Association, 1977), esp. pp. 42–52.

29. On the 1964 Republican effort, see Richard Rovere, *The Goldwater Caper* (New York: Harcourt Brace Jovanovich, 1965); and John Kessel, *The Goldwater Coalition: Republican Strategies in 1961* (Indianapolis: Bobbs-Merrill, 1968).
30. For an analysis of the logic of national nominating conventions, see Nelson Polsby and Aaron Wildavsky, *Presidential Elections*, 4th ed. (New York: Scribners, 1976), chaps. 2–4.
31. See Philip E. Converse, "The Nature of Belief Systems in Mass Publics," in David E. Apter, ed., *Ideology and Discontent* (London: Free Press, 1964), pp. 245–46, and Campbell et al., *American Voter*, pp. 234–49.

# 10

# Classification of Presidential Elections

The accumulation of voting research in the United States[1] has provided a foundation from which we can investigate more than the unique candidates, issues, and events of a specific election. Rather, we can focus on the similarities between different elections, attempt to classify them, and abstract some patterns from the historical realities. This chapter presents certain methods of classification using aggregate voting statistics, and offers a tentative categorization of presidential elections.

Comparisons between elections can perhaps most usefully be focused on the enduring factors in American politics, the parties, and their sources of support. V. O. Key stimulated such study in "A Theory of Critical Elections." Key pointed to "a category of elections . . . in which the decisive results of the voting reveal a sharp alteration of pre-existing cleavages within the electorate. Moreover, and perhaps this is the truly differentiating characteristic of this sort of election, the realignment made manifest in the voting in such elections seems to persist for several succeeding elections."[2]

Building on this concept, the authors of *The American Voter* suggested classifying elections into three categories: Maintaining, Deviating, and Realigning.[3] In the first two types of elections, there is no change in the basic patterns of party loyalty. In a Maintaining election, the "normal" majority party wins its expected victory; in Deviating cases, the minority party wins a short-lived tenure because of temporary factors, such as a popular candidate. In the Realigning election, much as in Key's critical election, the basis of voter cleavage is transformed.[4]

There are three important differences between these approaches: (1) Key's *scope* is narrower, as he is concerned principally with the unusual balloting, while the Michigan researchers attempt a classification of all contests, and tend to emphasize the importance and stability of party loyalty. (2) The *methods* are quite distinct. Key employs electoral data from geographic areas, such as towns in New England or counties or states in the rest of the nation. Campbell and his collaborators use national sample surveys. (3) Because of the last difference, the *historical period* considered differs. While the survey method allows greater precision, reliable data of this kind are lacking for the period before 1936. Electoral data, on the other hand, are available in some usable form for most of American history.[5]

Various methods may be employed in analysis of presidential elections which combine elements of these two schemes. Electoral data for geographic areas, states, are employed here in a fourfold categorization based on that of the Survey Research Center. The SRC classification cannot be used without change. As noted by Irish and Prothro,[6] the Michigan typology is based on two different dimensions which are not clearly distinguished. One of these dimensions is power, i.e., continuity or change in the party controlling the White House. The second dimension is electoral support, i.e., continuity or change in voter cleavages. Four combinations of these factors are possible, but the basic Michigan scheme includes but three.

The deficiency is due to ambiguous use of the Realigning category, applied to elections in which "the basic partisan commitments of a portion of the electorate change, and a new party balance is created."[7] This definition confuses two distinct effects: change in partisan commitments, and change in the party balance. Both results are evident when the former majority is displaced, as was the case in the period around the New Deal. It is also possible, however, that the reshuffling of voters can retain the same majority party, although it is now endorsed by a different electoral coalition. Partisan commitments change, while the party balance continues the same party as the majority.

The election of 1896, perhaps the classical critical contest, illustrates the problem. The Republican Party was the majority both before and after this watershed year, winning six of eight presidential elections in each interval. The basis of its support changed significantly in 1896, even though the party balance was not affected. Given the ambiguities of their classification, the Michigan authors find it difficult to deal with this election. At one point, the contest is included in a series of Maintaining elections but, in the space of a few pages, it is discussed as Realigning.[8]

The classification represented in Figure 10.1 separates the two aspects of elections. The horizontal axis is the power of the "normal" majority party. The horizontal is continuity or change in electoral cleavages.[9] The terms Maintaining and Deviating are used in a manner similar to that employed by the SRC. Realigning is reserved for elections in which a new majority party comes to power as the electorate substantially revises its loyalties. If the invention of a new label may be excused, Converting is offered as a term for elections in which the majority party retains its position, but there is considerable change in its voter base.

The problem is one of assigning given elections to the proper category. The horizontal dimension presents no difficulties. There are only two possible outcomes, victory or defeat of the majority party, and these are historical facts.

Complexities arise in regard to the vertical dimension, in knowing whether a particular result signifies electoral continuity or change. Since both are partially present in every contest, there can be no simple solution. Some reasonable means is needed to locate critical elections, by distinguishing a Maintaining from a Converting victory of the majority party, and discriminating between Deviating and Realigning triumphs of the minority. To deal with these questions, various statistical procedures are applied here to presidential state voting results. If these techniques are valid, they should be applicable to more extensive and detailed studies, using elections for other offices and using data more detailed than the state-wide results employed here.

## Methods of Classification

A change in the parties' bases of support would be evidenced in various changes in the election returns. The geographical distribution of each party's vote would be different from the past: traditional strongholds would fall, while new areas of strength would become evident. Statistically, the vote in a critical election would not be closely associated with previous results. In individual states, each party's vote would likewise tend to diverge measurably from traditional levels. Taking all states together, each party would experience both gains and losses. The Democratic percentage of the vote, for example, would increase in erstwhile rock-ribbed Republican areas, but would decline in previously Democratic geographical bastions.

**FIGURE 10.1**
**A Classification of Presidential Elections**

| | | MAJORITY PARTY | |
|---|---|---|---|
| | | *Victory* | *Defeat* |
| ELECTORAL CLEAVAGE | *Continuity* | "Maintaining" | "Deviating" |
| | *Change* | "Converting" | "Realigning" |

Figure A
*A Classification of Presidential Elections*

*Correlation of Successive Elections*

The first method employed here is linear correlation of the state-by-state results in paired presidential elections. Linear correlation will indicate the degree to which the results in two elections are similar. The basic data were the Democratic party's percentage of each state's total vote from 1824 and 1964.[10] Each election constituted a variable, and the Democratic percentage in each state was a case of that variable. Each election, or variable, was then paired and correlated with that in every other election. An additional problem is created by the presence of significant third parties in many presidential elections. The possibility exists that these splinter groups are receiving votes which ordinarily would be cast for the Democrats. To deal with this possibility, separate correlations were made. The third-party percentage was added to the Democratic share, and the totals for the given year then constituted a new variable, to be correlated with every other election. In all there are 47 variables, and a total of 46 + 45 . . . + 1 pairings, or 595 totally.[11] The resulting coefficients provide a measure of the association of the geographical distribution of votes in paired elections.

Correlation analysis will indicate the relative degree of electoral continuity or change. If there is high geographical continuity between two elections, regardless of partisan victory or defeat, the correlation coefficient should be high. If there is change, even if the same party wins both elections considered, we should find a relatively low coefficient.[12] The basic assumption here is that change in the electorate's party preferences will be revealed by changes in the various states' support of the Democrats.[13]

Figure 10.2 pictures the correlation of the Democratic vote in successive elections. The peaks of the diagram indicate that Democratic support in the designated election was highly related to that in the preceding presidential contest. The valleys indicate a change in the sources of support.[14] Significant change in electoral cleavages appear to have occurred five times in American history: (1) Van Buren's victory in 1836; (2) the Civil War and Reconstruction period, with the elections of 1864 and 1872 particularly significant; (3) the Populist and Bryan period of 1892–96; (4) the time of the Great Depression, particularly in the contests of 1928 and 1932; and (5) the current era, most prominently the Kennedy and Johnson victories of 1960 and 1964. Questions can be raised about each of these, but a fuller discussion can be postponed until the other methods of classification have been presented.

*Correlation With Average Democratic Vote*

Each election is inevitably unique and will always differ somewhat from its predecessor and its successor. A given election may stand out not because it is

**FIGURE 10.2**
**Correlation of Successive Presidential Elections, 1828–1964**
**(Graphed at Latter Year)**

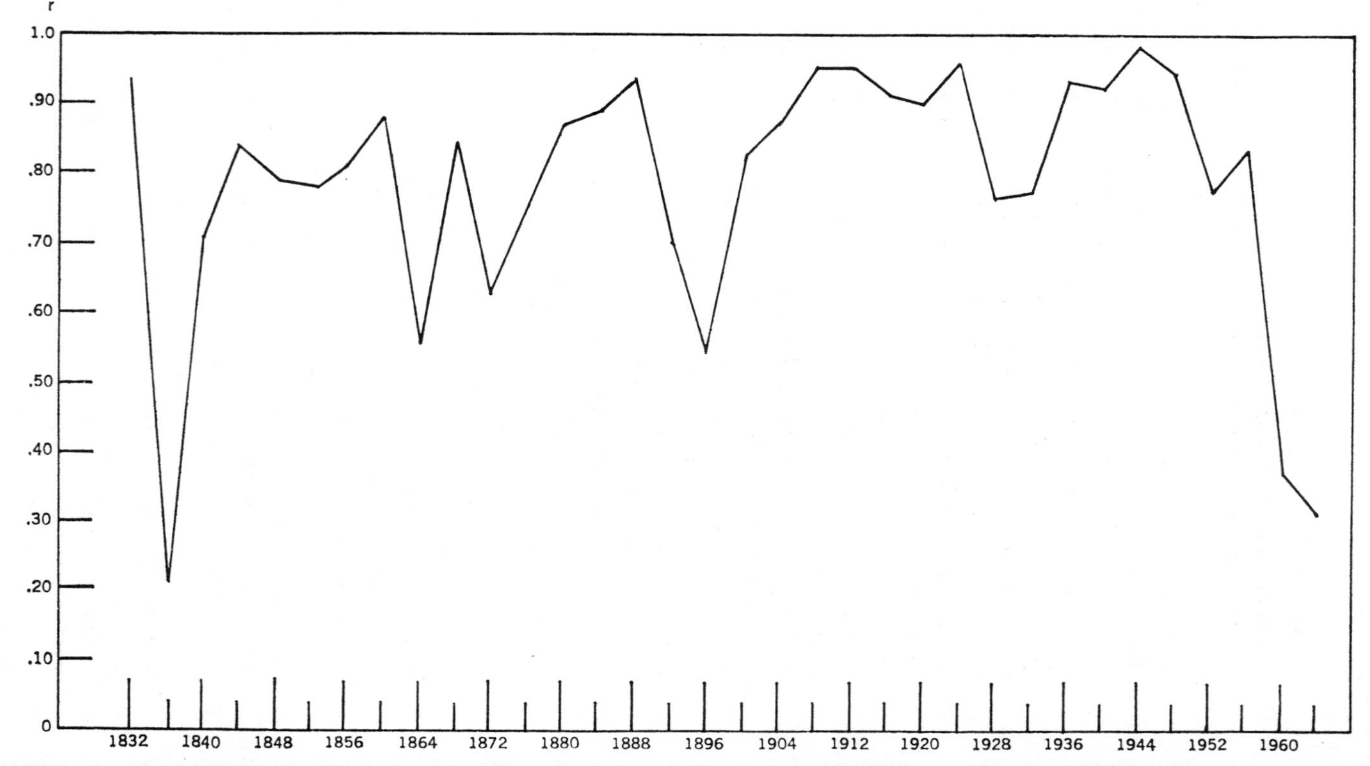

truly a critical election, marking the end of one era and the beginning of another, but only because of temporary peculiarities. Thus, MacRae and Meldrum, analyzing shifts in the vote between successive elections, show increased dispersion in 1920 and 1940, although there is no reason to believe that these elections revealed any basic change in the electorate.[15]

One means of moderating such eccentricities is to average the party's state votes in past elections. The mean Democratic vote in the four preceding elections is taken here to be the "normal" or traditional party vote. Four elections were chosen as sufficient to eliminate influences due solely to particular candidates or similar factors, while avoiding the inclusion of too many elections, and thereby making it difficult to detect significant changes.[16] In a second operation, the Democratic state-by-state vote in each election was then correlated with the averages for each state's vote. Separate calculations were again made for those years in which significant third parties existed. Because of the various combinations of third parties possible, an additional 99 correlations result.

Figure 10.3 represents the correlations between the Democratic vote by states in the designated years and the "normal" party vote. The pattern is similar to that in Figure 10.2, with the same dates indicated as critical elections, but there are some refinements. In general, the electoral eras pictured are more distinct from one another. Certain erraticisms are eliminated. The low correlation for 1872 is seen as due largely to the peculiarities of the previously paired contests of 1868 and 1872, rather than any enduring change in the 1872 election itself. In the New Deal period, the election of 1928 stands out as the time of change. In our own time, realignment beginning in 1952 is made more apparent, with the uniqueness of the 1964 election heavily emphasized.

### *Correlation Matrices*

Emphasizing single elections, even critical ones, can be misleading. We cannot assume that all contests between two critical elections are similar, or that no change occurs between them. Instead of focusing on individual results, we can seek to identify periods of voter stability, or electoral eras. These eras are identified by correlations of nonsuccessive elections.[17]

When a stable, persistent voter coalition is established, the vote in nonsuccessive elections will be highly correlated. To identify such eras, the correlation coefficients of the Democratic vote in paired elections over a period of years are placed in a matrix.[18] To be considered in a stable era, the vote in a given year must be related not only to the immediately following or preceding election, but to *every other* consecutive election in that era. Even in a period of change, a large proportion of the voters retain their party loyalty, and spuri-

**FIGURE 10.3**
**Correlation of Presidential Vote in Designated Years, With Average of Previous Elections, 1832–1964**

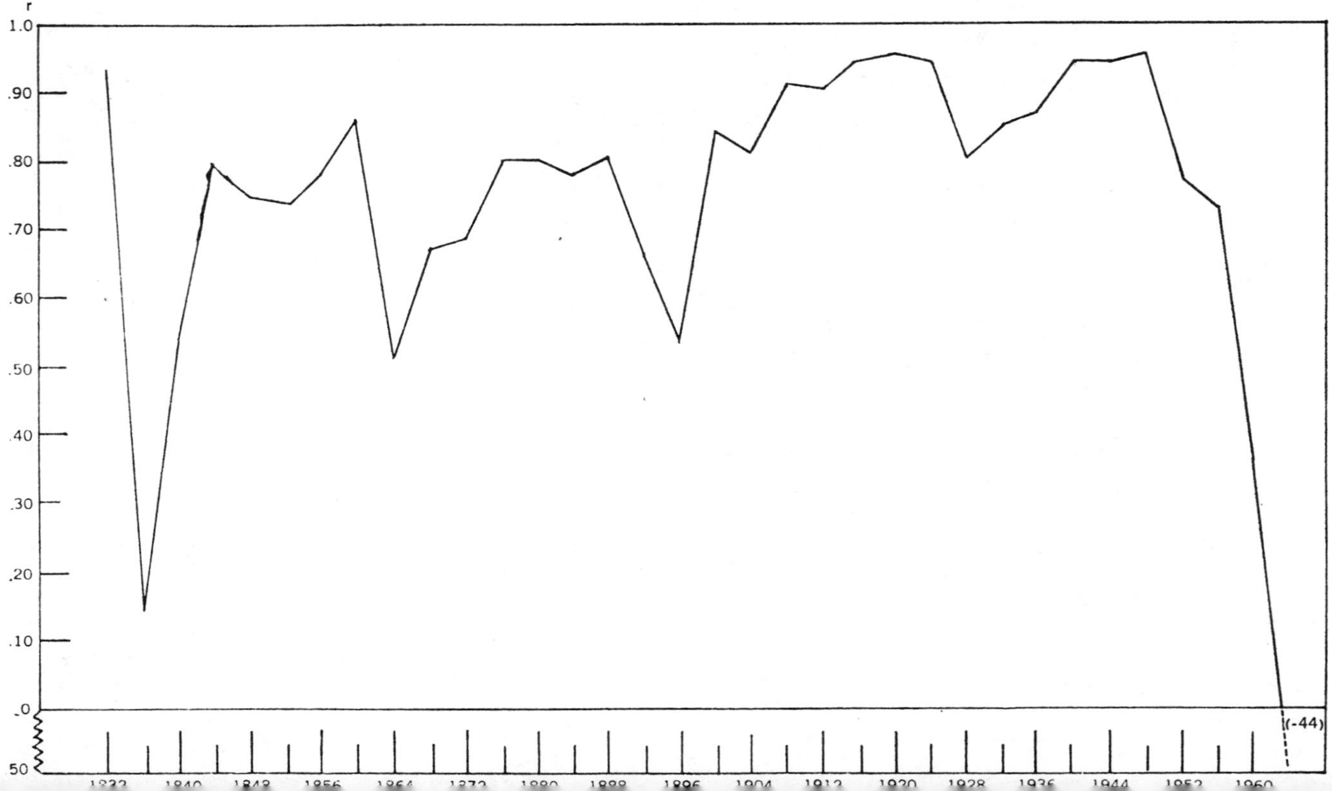

ous correlations may result. Requiring high correlation to a series of elections should avoid inclusion of votes with such meaningless correlations in the designated eras.[19]

Table 10.1, a matrix of the Democratic vote in paired elections from 1924 to 1964, illustrates the method. The core or stable electoral era is the period from 1932 to 1948. Each election in this period is related to every other at a high level, no coefficient being lower than .84. Correlation with the earlier elections of 1924 and 1928 falls below this level, indicating differences in the Democratic party's geographical sources of support from one period to the next. Correlations with the Eisenhower elections are too low to be included in the core period as well, the 1952–56 votes apparently constituting the postscript to the New Deal Democratic period. A changed basis of support is sharply evident in 1960 and 1964.

Correlation matrices for overlapping earlier periods are presented in reverse chronological order in Tables 10.2, 10.3, and 10.4. The previous stable period seems to be 1900–1920, with the lowest coefficient of any pair of elections .87, a very high degree of association. The coefficients are somewhat lower for 1924, particularly if the Progressive vote is added to the Democratic, and lower still in 1928. Another grouping is found in the period

**TABLE 10.1**
**Correlation of Democratic Vote in Presidential Elections, 1924–1964***

| | Election Years | | | | | | | | | |
|---|---|---|---|---|---|---|---|---|---|---|
| | *1928* | *1932* | *1936* | *1940* | *1944* | *1948* | *1952* | *1956* | *1960* | *1964* |
| *1924* | .77 | .79 | .78 | .88 | .86 | .88 | .72 | .54 | .18 | –.59 |
| | (.79) | (.95) | (.93) | (.87) | (.84) | (.88) | (.57) | (.59) | (.07) | –.73 |
| *1928* | | .78 | .76 | .80 | .82 | .85 | .58 | .43 | .22 | –.56 |
| *1932* | | | .93 | .86 | .84 | .90 | .58 | .64 | .09 | –.73 |
| *1936* | | | | .93 | .91 | .90 | .66 | .66 | .15 | –.74 |
| *1940* | | | | | .98 | .94 | .78 | .64 | .27 | –.67 |
| *1944* | | | | | | .94 | .80 | .67 | .30 | –.68 |
| *1948* | | | | | | | .77 | .71 | .21 | –.68 |
| | (–.43) | (–.29) | (–.32) | (–.36) | (–.41) | (–.33) | (–.16) | (–.08) | (.16) | (.65) |
| *1952* | | | | | | | | .84 | .56 | –.39 |
| *1956* | | | | | | | | | .38 | –.47 |
| *1960* | | | | | | | | | | .32 |

*Row figures in parentheses refer to the combined Democratic and Progressive vote in 1924 and the vote of Truman alone in 1948.

1876–88, with all paired elections evidencing a coefficient of .70 or better. A similar relationship is found for the elections from 1844 to 1860. Coefficients for elections in the nineteenth century tend to be lower than in later periods, perhaps partially because of the changing number of states in each contest.[20] However, the median coefficient in the 1876–88 period is .86 and, in 1844–60, it is .79.

Of the total of 35 presidential elections since the initiation of broad popular participation, we can classify twenty as included within four eras of electoral stability. Critical elections are not usually part of these stable periods, but serve as breaking points, ending one era and leading to the next. Other contests represent transitional elections before and after critical times. The last stable period ended in 1948 with Truman's victory. Since then, we have seen four transitional elections significantly different in the geographical distribution of the vote from the preceding period. This last conclusion is seemingly in conflict with the results of voting surveys, which posit considerable stability in the voters' partisan predispositions. We will return to the consideration of this important question after discussing two other methods of analysis and surveying the overall results.

### *Variations From State Averages*

The remaining methods concern the variations in state votes from "normal" Democratic percentages. Even in periods of stability, the state-by-state vote will vary from one election to the next. In periods of substantial alteration in voting cleavages, however, the changes will be larger and more geographically dispersed. For each year, the absolute difference between each state's vote and its "normal" Democratic percentage was calculated. These state differences were then averaged to yield a single national figure. The expectation was that changes from past voting habits would be reflected in a correspondingly higher national mean.[21]

The results of this procedure are charted in figure 10.4. The regular pattern of the earlier graphs is not evident here, with relatively high means, or apparent voter change, recorded not only in predictable years such as 1896, but also in such unlikely times as the 1916 election.[22] These anomalies indicate the deficiencies of the mean alone as a measurement of change. High means will exist in critical elections, but may also occur even when there is no basic change in the electorate. In a Deviating election, there is likely to be considerable change from past voting habits, although the change does not persist. Thus, in 1916, the peace issue, the reforms of the first Wilson administration, and the remaining Progressive defections induced a crucial marginal group of voters to defect from the normally dominant G.O.P. This change, however, constituted no essential change in voter loyalties and was short-lived.[23]

## TABLE 10.2
### Correlation of Democratic Vote in Presidential Elections, 1896–1928*

| | Election Years | | | | | | | | |
|---|---|---|---|---|---|---|---|---|---|
| | *1900* | *1904* | *1908* | *1912* | *1916* | *1920* | *1924* | | *1928* |
| *1896* | .82 | .53 | .67 | .53 | .74 | .59 | .48 | (.70) | .47 |
| *1900* | | .87 | .93 | .88 | .93 | .89 | .83 | (.88) | .77 |
| *1904* | | | .94 | .95 | .89 | .95 | .96 | (.81) | .81 |
| *1908* | | | | .94 | .93 | .92 | .91 | (.88) | .79 |
| *1912* | | | | | .92 | .93 | .93 | (.88) | .79 |
| *1916* | | | | | | .91 | .85 | (.90) | .80 |
| *1920* | | | | | | | .97 | (.83) | .76 |
| *1924* | | | | | | | | | .77 |

*Figures in parentheses in 1924 column refer to the combined Democratic and Progressive vote

## TABLE 10.3
### Correlation of Democratic Vote in Presidential Elections, 1856–1896*

| | Election Years | | | | | | | | | |
|---|---|---|---|---|---|---|---|---|---|---|
| | *1860* | *1864* | *1868* | *1872* | *1876* | *1880* | *1884* | *1888* | *1892* | *1896* |
| *1856* | .89 | .60 | .53 | .71 | .80 | .82 | .84 | .73 | .61 | .79 |
| *1860* | | .55 | .63 | .68 | .78 | .83 | .86 | .79 | .54 | .84 |
| | | (–.06) | (–.26) | (.03) | (–.19) | (–.30) | (–.16) | (–.24) | (–.31) | (–.27) |
| *1864* | | | .85 | .55 | .65 | .62 | .60 | .67 | .17 | .09 |
| *1868* | | | | .62 | .64 | .68 | .57 | .56 | .38 | .33 |
| *1872* | | | | | .75 | .58 | .47 | .33 | .29 | .22 |
| *1876* | | | | | | .88 | .80 | .70 | .49 | .47 |
| *1880* | | | | | | | .90 | .87 | .68 | .63 |
| *1884* | | | | | | | | .93 | .61 | .61 |
| *1888* | | | | | | | | | .71 | .64 |
| *1892* | | | | | | | | | | .54 |
| | (.80) | (.31) | (.41) | (.30) | (.58) | (.75) | (.74) | (.80) | (.70) | (.75) |

*Row figures in parentheses refer to the Douglas vote alone in 1860 and the combined Democratic and Populist vote in 1892.

**TABLE 10.4**
**Correlation of Democratic Vote in Presidential Elections, 1828–1864***

| | Election Years | | | | | | | | | |
|---|---|---|---|---|---|---|---|---|---|---|
| | *1832* | *1836* | *1840* | *1844* | *1848* | *1852* | *1856* | *1860* | | *1864* |
| *1828* | .93 | .05 | .38 | .68 | .60 | .67 | .82 | .79 | (−.37) | .39 |
| *1832* | | .22 | .50 | .77 | .65 | .74 | .77 | .77 | (−.25) | .08 |
| *1836* | | | .71 | .62 | .46 | .48 | .24 | .17 | ( .25) | .06 |
| *1840* | | | | .84 | .63 | .61 | .45 | .36 | ( .14) | −.02 |
| *1844* | | | | | .79 | .80 | .74 | .70 | (−.09) | .27 |
| *1848* | | | | | | .78 | .79 | .69 | ( .15) | .31 |
| *1852* | | | | | | | .81 | .84 | ( .12) | .46 |
| *1856* | | | | | | | | .89 | (−.24) | .60 |
| *1860* | | | | | | | | | | .55 |

*Figures in parentheses in 1860 column refer to Douglas vote alone.

The standard deviation provides a means of further distinguishing these two types of elections, by measuring the dispersal of state differences around the national mean. A Deviating election is the result of largely temporary factors, the effect of which is felt generally in the electorate. The shifts of the individual states will therefore tend to be within a relatively narrow range. A low standard deviation will result.[24]

In an election in which cleavages are significantly altered, voters are not equally affected, nor do they tend to be attracted only toward one party. Rather, there are movements of unequal degree and in both partisan directions. The shifts of the individual states will therefore vary considerably, and the standard deviation will be relatively high.

Figure 10.5 represents the standard deviation around the national mean of state differences over time. The pattern is pleasantly regular, and there are few anomalies. The standard deviation for 1916, for example, is a low 5.39, substantiating our earlier belief that this was a Deviating rather than a critical election.

Conveniently, the pattern corroborates many of our earlier conclusions. There are peaks in 1836, 1864, 1896, 1924, and 1964, indicating the movement of voters between the parties in these years. However, we find not only isolated critical elections, but periods of assimilation after a decisive vote, indicated by the gradually declining standard deviations, and periods of development before a vital election, with increasing standard deviations. The 1964 increase, for example, was preceded by changes in the four earlier contests.

**FIGURE 10.4**
**Means of Differences from Average State Votes, Presidential Elections, 1832–1964**

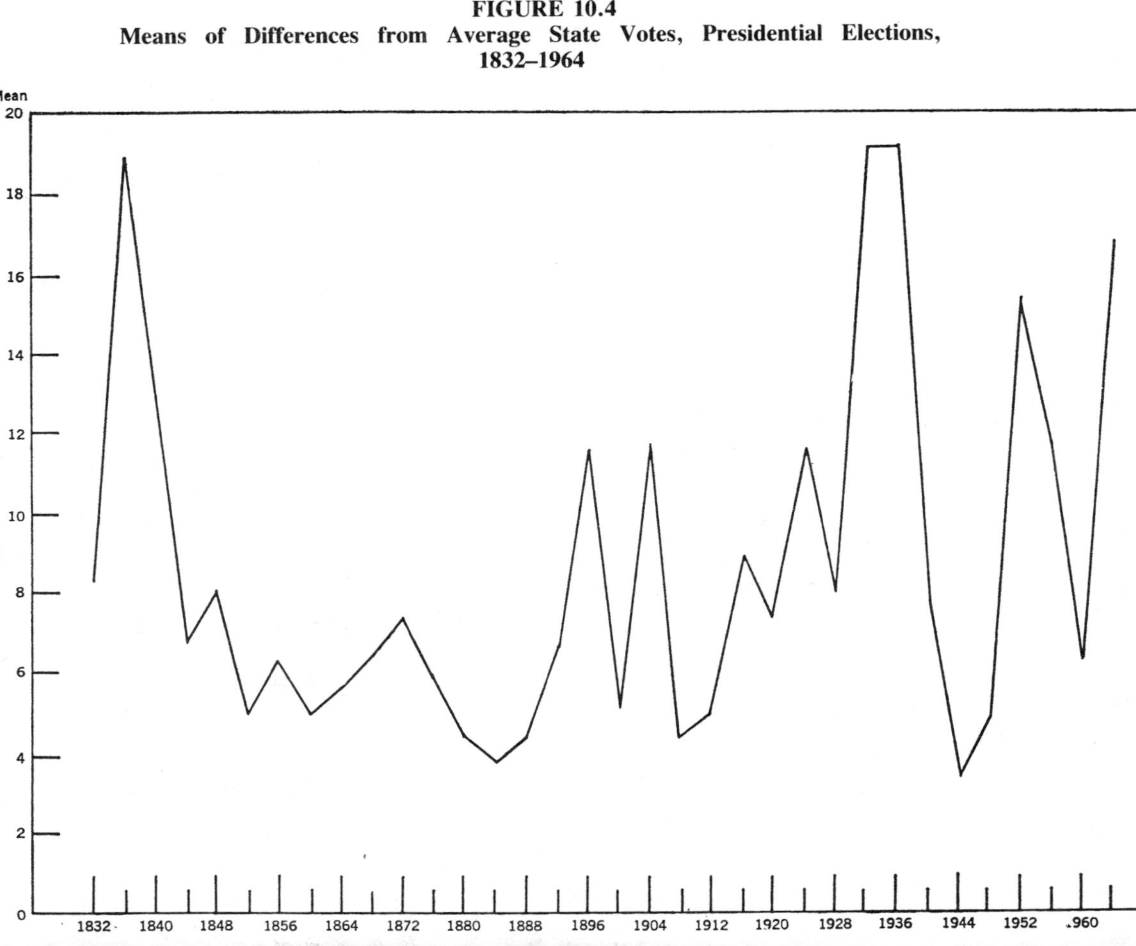

**FIGURE 10.5**
**Standard Deviation of Differences from Average State Votes, Presidential Elections, 1832–1964**

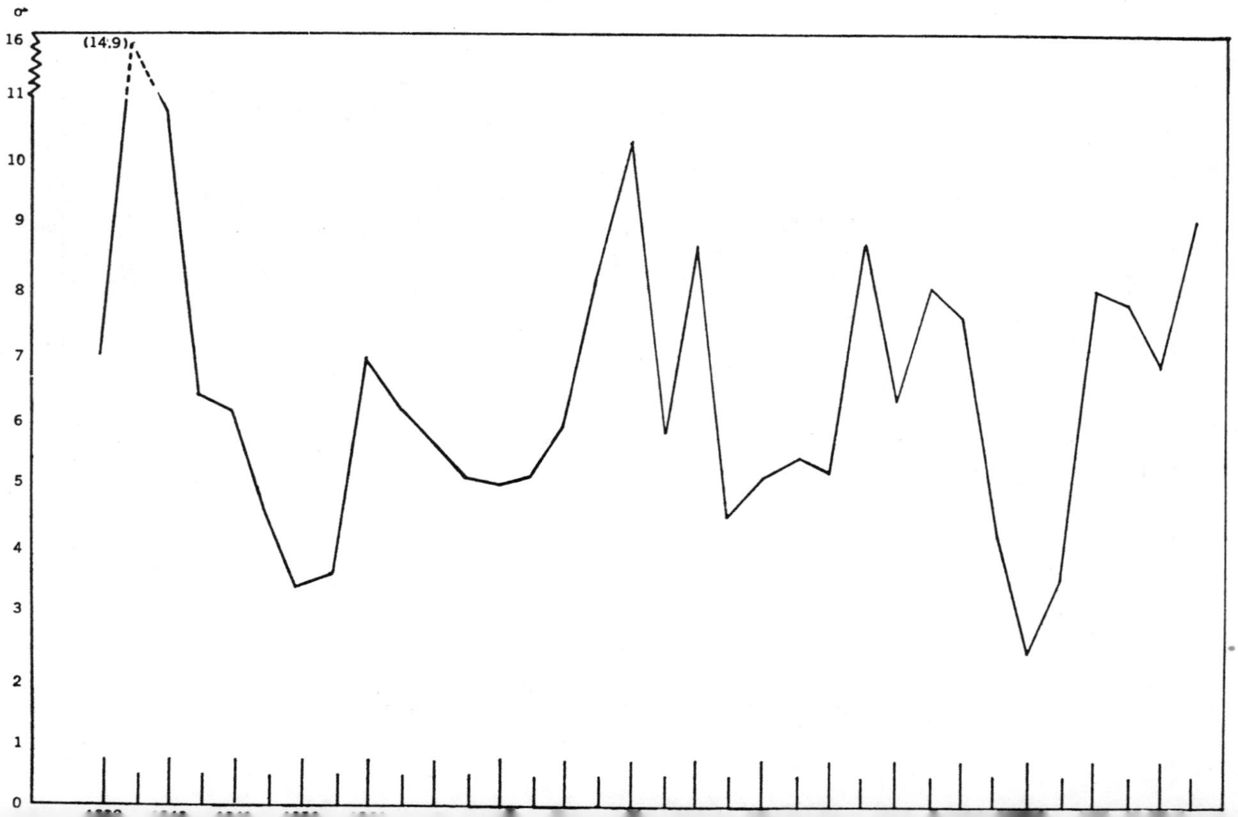

## A Survey of Presidential Elections

We now have five statistical measures available with which to classify elections. To summarize, an ideal Converting or Realigning election would be likely to show a low correlation to the immediately preceding election, to the average of four preceding elections and to the series of individual elections which both precede and follow it. The mean of state differences from the "normal" state votes and the standard deviation would tend to be high. In a Converting election, the majority party would retain its status; in a Realigning contest, the former minority would become dominant. In the model Maintaining or Deviating election, the opposite statistical results would be evident. The majority party would win the White House in the Maintaining case, but would be temporarily displaced in a Deviating contest. (Detailed statistical results are presented in the Appendix.)

By all indications, the victory of Martin Van Buren in 1836 was a Converting election. There is a low correlation to the 1828 and 1832 votes, and sharp increases in the mean of state differences and the standard deviation. Historical evidence indicates a considerable change in the leadership of both parties, the center of gravity of the Democratic party moving away from the South toward the Middle Atlantic states. In the balloting, the basis of party support shifted strongly in the same direction. The Democrats gained 10 or more percentage points in the six New England states, and lost a similar proportion in 10 states, 7 of them slave areas. As McCormick writes of the South in particular, "Although the new alignments did not become firm in some states until after 1837, the basic outlines of what were to be the Democratic and Whig parties had been delineated."[25] By 1844, a period of electoral continuity is evident, relatively undisturbed by the plethora of third parties, the admission of new states, and the substitution of the Republicans as the principal opposition party in 1856.

The second break in electoral continuity resulted from the Civil War. The 1860 vote, in the face of the contemporary upheavals, bears a strong resemblance to the past. If we combine the Douglas and Breckinridge percentages, the total shows a correlation of .89 with the 1856 results. The party did not change its geographical support, in other words, but this support had divided into two opposing factions.

During the Civil War and Reconstruction, changes in party loyalty became evident. The correlation coefficients tend to be low, whatever figure is used to represent the Democratic vote of 1860, and the same conclusion results if we compare later elections or use four-election averages. The net import of these statistics is a definite break in traditional bases of support. The Republican party became dominant in the nation, making 1864 a Realigning election. The degree of Republican victory in this year is exaggerated by the absence of the

Confederate states, but the signs of change are evident in the Northern states alone, as the Republicans assimilated former Whigs, Know-Nothings, Constitutional Unionists and even Democrats. The party bore the new name of Union in 1864, and "it is a much debated question," writes Dennis Brogan, whether it had much "in common with the agglomeration of 'Anti-Nebraska' men of 1854, or even with the Republican Party of 1856 or 1860."[26] Readjustments in the electorate continued for some time after 1864. Stability returned in 1876, when a considerable return to ante-bellum loyalties is evident.[27]

The post-Reconstruction system was not long-lived. Whatever measurement is used, a transformation of the political order is evident with the Populist movement of 1892 and the Bryan-McKinley presidential contest of 1896. The change is evident in both of these years, not only in 1896, which is often classified as the single crucial election of the period.[28] Transformations in party support were geographically widespread. Nineteen states changed more than 10 percentage points from their "normal" Democratic vote in 1896. Ten states showing Democratic losses were all located in the Northeast. Nine states with large Democratic gains were all in the South and West. Extensive changes also occurred within states and in the leadership of the parties, as evidenced in the splintering of each party and in the campaign appeals to social class.[29]

The Populist Party was a crucial element in the change. In 1892, Populist votes appear to have come largely from former Democrats; in 1896, many Populists then supported Bryan.[30] The decisive break of 1892–96, however, did not immediately result in the establishment of a new electoral coalition. Future years saw additional changes, and Republican dominance was sealed more firmly in 1900 than in the more-noticed first contest of McKinley and Bryan. Thus, 1896 was a great watershed, but it did not by itself fix the future contours of American politics.

Another change in the party system took place, as is well known, in the period 1924–36. The discontinuity is evident in the measures used here, but it is less dramatic than the revisions of earlier periods. Unlike previous changes, those associated with the time of the Depression and New Deal were not principally sectional in character. Realignment occurred in most states, along lines of social class, residence, and ethnicity.[31] Measurements of state-wide voting can capture some of these changes, but not in the fine detail of sample surveys.

To the extent that aggregate figures are useful, they point to 1924 as a transitional year, and the Progressive party as a "halfway house" for those leaving their traditional party. Changes in this election are signified by the high mean of differences from "normal" state votes and high standard deviations. The Progressive vote probably came from former adherents of both major parties, but there is some indication that it tended to be more from Republican loyalists.[32]

The transition to a Democratic majority extended over a number of elections, but the most critical appears to be 1928. The correlation coefficients for this election are the lowest for any twentieth century contest before 1960. Al Smith lost 10 percentage points or more from the average Democratic vote in seven states, all of them southern or border. He gained strongly in seven other states, four of them urban and Catholic, the rest largely rural and Progressive. There was sufficient change in 1928 to constitute it a Realigning election, although the new Democratic majority did not become evident until 1932.[33] The new pattern was then continued for the next four contests.[34]

By the methods employed here, the four most recent presidential contests constitute another critical period, culminating in the 1964 Conversion of the dominant Democratic majority. Strains in the New Deal coalition were already evident in 1948, when the Dixiecrats temporarily split the party. There was no fundamental alteration in that year, but greater change is evident in 1952, when all of our measures indicate discontinuity from the past. Shifts toward the Republicans occurred in all social groups and in all parts of the nation. Geographical variations were evident within the general trend. Differences from the four-election averages were greatest in sixteen states, all in the South or Mountain regions.[35]

The 1964 election represents a radical break from past results, and the statistics strongly suggest that it was a Converting election, retaining the same Democratic party as the majority, but on a new basis of popular support. The correlation coefficients for this election are astoundingly low, given the generally moderate to high figures, even in the case of arbitrarily paired elections. The 1964 Democratic vote is positively related to that of only two years other than 1960, both involving third parties. Johnson's vote is related to Truman's vote alone in 1948 ($r = .65$), and to Douglas's vote alone in 1860 ($r = .40$). In all of these cases, the Democratic vote was highly sectional in character, and severely depressed in the South.

There was large variation from traditional Democratic levels in most states. Of course, the Democratic vote increased substantially, as Johnson gained the largest percentage of the total vote ever achieved by a Democrat. The important point is that the gains were not relatively equal in all states, as would tend to be the case if all areas were reacting only to the temporary oddities of Goldwaterism. The party vote decreased from its four-election average in the five Black Belt states of the South, while it increased over 18 percentage points in eleven states of the Northeast and five of the Midwest.

The final test of a critical election must remain persistence. In the final analysis, 1968 and 1972 will tell if the pattern of 1964 did constitute a true Converting election. It is possible that the great transfer of voters between the parties was only a temporary reaction to the admittedly unusual circumstances of the time. It would be quite remarkable if such were the case. The events of 1964 left their mark in the control of state legislatures by the Democrats, the passage of "great society" legislation, intensification of the civil rights movement, organizational changes and conflicts in both parties, and the memories of the voters. Republican strength in the South continued to grow in the 1966 elections. Democrats lost considerably last November, but these losses were not simply a return to pre-1964 voting patterns. Democrats were elected in areas of former party weakness, such as Maine and Iowa, but were defeated in traditional bastions such as Illinois and Minnesota. The future impact of "black power" and other developments is now uncertain, but clearly significant. Change, not simple continuity, seems evident.

*Limits and Problems*

The apparent Conversion of the electorate in recent years is generally contrary to the conclusions of sample surveys on the persistence of party identification. After the 1964 election, Stokes found "almost no perceptible shift in the single most important type of response disposition, the electorate's enduring party loyalties."[36] His conclusion both points to the limitations of the methods employed here, and offers an opportunity for discussion of some general problems of electoral analysis.

Geographical units are used here for analysis. We examine the voting patterns of states, not that of individuals, whose behavior must be inferred, rather than directly examined. Evidence of continuity or change in political cleavages is therefore evidence about the persistence of geographical bases of party support, not conclusions about the loyalties of demographic or psychological reference groups.

The use of areal units is partially the simple result of necessity: only these data are historically available. This form of analysis has intellectual validity as well. For much of American history, the important social conflicts have also been geographical, i.e., sectional, conflicts. Party loyalties have been grounded on areal issues, traditions, and leadership. Examination of aggregate voting returns can therefore provide insight into individual behavior. Conclusions based on this data will be made even more confidently as smaller geographical units are analyzed, and as social characteristics are correlated with political material.[37] Moreover, in dealing with the presidency, we are dealing with a geographical system of selection, the Electoral College. Since national parties are centered around the presidential contest, analysis of their support in geographical terms is legitimate.

Areal data are nevertheless subject to certain distortions. As the reapportionment controversy has reminded us, acres or political units are not people. There can be considerable discrepancy between the voting of states, as units, and of the particular voters within them. The likelihood of such discrepancy would appear to be increased when, as above, all states are counted equally regardless of population. To deal with this possibility, a second analysis was performed, using the same techniques, but weighting the vote of each state by its population. Details are provided in the Appendix. The striking conclusion is that there is very little effect on the results: the same elections are located as critical, and the statistics derived do not differ greatly from those obtained previously.

Another possible distortion is the masking of voter changes within a state. Apparent stability in the total state returns might disguise considerable, but countervailing, party shifts by individual voters.[38] More relevant to the present discussion is the opposite distortion. When vote shifts are geographically concentrated, the methods employed here will tend to exaggerate the degree of change. In 1948, exclusion or inclusion of the Dixiecrat vote in Truman's total immensely affects all of our statistical indicators, even though the Dixiecrats received less than 3% of the national popular vote. The same factor accounts for the extremity of the shifts evidenced in 1960 and 1964, since vote changes have tended to be geographically concentrated, particularly in the South.

Results obtained using aggregate returns will therefore differ from those of surveys of an approximate random sample of individuals. Other differences are to be expected because this study focuses only on presidential voting, while surveys deal with other offices as well. Furthermore, we have been concerned with actual voting, while surveys emphasize "party identification," the voter's basic loyalty to a particular party. These identifications will show considerably less variation than the vote, and a vote for the opposition party will usually precede a change in identification. As Campbell himself suggests, the critical election provides a party with the opportunity, by its actions in office, permanently to win those voters who have given it power, or to regain its lost adherents.[39] Republicans for Johnson and Democrats for Goldwater may have made 1964 a Converting election, but the evidence in changed party identifications will not be fully apparent until later surveys.

These methodological differences are partially responsible for different conclusions about the meaning of recent elections. This analysis of aggregate election returns indicates a shift in electoral cleavages, with the 1964 election altering the geographical basis of support of the majority Democratic Party. Reported survey results indicate the continuity of past loyalties. Both conclusions can be right, since they deal with different aspects of the political system.

Even the surveys, however, provide some indications that meaningful change is taking place, although it has not been highlighted by scholarly analysis. Even where identifications have not yet altered, "party images" have been modified. In the South, where the vote change has been greatest, Matthews and Prothro find significant revisions in what the voters "like" and "dislike" about the Democrats and Republicans. Such alterations of traditional images may be the prelude to the further step of changing identifications.[40] Outside the South, results both from the Michigan surveys and from other sources also indicate substantial change in voter perceptions of the parties. Some of the variation may be due to purely temporary factors, but "party images" also include tenacious elements, which directly affect the basic identification.[41]

Most importantly, there is evidence that there has been change in party identifications as well. Belief in their immobility has been an unquestioned, but perhaps unjustified, article of faith. The evidence that party identification has been stable is largely based on aggregate figures from the surveys, not on analysis of individual behavior. We find, for example, that the proportion of Republicans from 1952 to 1964 always remained in the range of 24–32% of the total electorate.[42] It is therefore assumed that a given 24% of the voters were always Republicans, that 68% never identified with the G.O.P., and that only 8% ever changed their loyalties. This is a vital error, the same error which is often made in the analysis of aggregate voting data. In both cases, the net change between parties is assumed to be the total change.

The case for stability in party identification is largely based on limited net change. In examining identifications in 1956 and 1960, for example, Converse's data show that 14% of Southerners and 26% of non-Southerners changed their loyalties to some degree. Yet, because there is no strong trend in one direction, he devotes little attention to these conversions.[43]

In theory, virtually all voters could have changed their party identifications from 1952 to 1964, even while the percentage supporting each party remained relatively stable. This is an unlikely situation, but it is also unlikely that the net change and the gross change are the same. Moreover, even marginal shifts can be decisive. An 8 percent change in the vote would usually create a landslide. Similarly, even an 8% change in identifications might be indicative of a Converting or Realigning election. In reality, the shifts in party identification are even higher.

The pattern of party loyalties is like a square dance—the important element in the dance is the movement and change of positions. We do not understand the dance by statically noticing that the number of sides to the square is always four or that there are equal numbers of men and women. The action comes when each dancer leaves one partner and takes another. To measure stability in party identifications, it is necessary to examine the behavior of individuals, as the Michigan surveys have indeed done. Ideally, respondents to a previous survey should be reinterviewed, as in the 1960 study. Alternately, persons can be asked to recall past identifications, as was done in the 1956 and 1964 surveys.

The results are interesting. Of the 1956 sample, 18 percent indicated that they had changed their party loyalty at some time in the past. Compare this finding to that obtained upon reinterviewing in 1960. In the intervening four years, using the same categories as in 1956, 11 percent of the total group had changed their identifications. (Changes from Independent *to* either Democratic or Republican, or from strong to weak partisanship, are not included, only changes *from* the two parties.) In other words, there was more than half as much change in party loyalty in the four-year period from 1956 to 1960 as in all of the years (perhaps twenty for the average respondent) in which the interviewees had been politically active before 1956.

In 1964, a different sample was interviewed, of which 22 percent indicated some change in party identification in the past. Changes at all elections, not only in the previous four years, are included here. It seems significant that, eight years further away from the realignments induced by the Depression and New Deal, stability in party loyalty had actually decreased in comparison to 1956.[44] Fuller analysis of these responses are necessary before any final conclusions are reached, but there does seem sufficient evidence, in the survey results themselves, to support a suspicion that party identification has not been unchanging, but rather that significant numbers of voters have been altering traditional loyalties.[45]

In recent elections, therefore, statistical analysis of state voting indicates considerable shifts in the geographical bases of party support. The extent of change found in sample surveys is less, but there are numerous clues in that material to justify a tentative belief that the 1964 presidential contest was indeed a Converting election.

## Conclusion

It is now possible to summarize our findings and to attempt a classification of presidential elections. It is obvious that categorization is not a simple matter, for elections are not always of one type or another. Some convenient simplifications are lacking. For example, change in voter loyalties does not fit any neat cyclical pattern, with change occurring after a fixed number of years.[46] There is a tendency, it is true, for critical elections to occur approximately once in every generation, but the length of time between these contests varies considerably. The party system which became stabilized in 1876 lasted only until 1888, while the different party system which began to appear in 1924 still greatly affects politics today. Electoral change is periodic, but the periods are irregular.

Difficulties also exist in isolating the turning points in these periods, the critical elections. It is apparent that electoral change is neither unheralded nor precipitate. In most cases, there is not a single critical election, sandwiched between two periods of great stability. Rather, there are times of unease preceding the most crucial year, and a period of assimilation after it. Typically, the critical election represents a break in electoral continuity, but does not result in the immediate establishment of a new and persistent voter coalition. Thus, the elections identified as critical here do not show high correlations with later ballots, but following contests do demonstrate this stability. Persistence comes after the critical election, and partially as a reaction to its upheavals.

This conclusion is at variance with Key's original definition of a critical election. The disagreement is partially attributable to a difference in method. Key identifies critical elections by focusing on the extreme cases, the areas showing the most change toward or away from the new majority party. The methods used here are based on examination of all areas, and therefore include changes in the middle ranges as well. MacRae and Meldrum, who also include all areas, show similar results—less precipitous changes coming in the total critical period, rather than in a single election.[47] Key himself recognized the point in his later writings.[48]

Despite the many pitfalls, it may be suggestive to position elections within the categories offered in figure 10.1. The horizontal dimension clearly represents a nominal classification—the left and right sides are exclusive and exhaustive. The vertical dimension is more in the nature of a continuum—particular elections may not be clearly stable or critical, but may tend to an intermediate position. Therefore, the distinction between a Deviating and Realigning contest, or a Maintaining and Converting election, is somewhat subjective and arbitrary. The change which exists in every election is disguised, as is the existence of critical periods, rather than single crucial ballotings.

On the basis of the data developed here (listed in detail in the Appendix), the elections of 1836, 1896, and 1960–64 are classified as Converting, and those of 1864 and 1928–32 as Realigning. The victories of the first Harrison, Taylor, Lincoln in 1860, Cleveland, Wilson, and Eisenhower are considered Deviating, and the others are classified as Maintaining.[49] In order to isolate a small number of critical elections, fairly strict standards have been applied in making this classification. Modified standards would obviously change the designation of individual elections.

The most accurate characterization of our political history would be one of electoral eras. The life cycle of an electoral era typically begins with, or soon follows, a third-party election. The first such era began with the contest of 1836, in which the Democrats faced three opposition Whig candidates. The period came to an end in 1860 with the division of the Democratic party, and the nation. The next period ended with the emergence of the Populists in 1892, and the Republican dominance that began with the victories of

McKinley began to disappear with the 1924 appearance of the LaFollette Progressives. The end of the New Deal era was heralded by the Democratic split of 1948.

Third parties arise when traditional loyalty seems inadequate to many voters. Often, the rise of third parties accompanies or precedes change in these loyalties sufficient to constitute a critical election. This election may continue the same party in power, on the basis of a realigned majority, or result in an overthrow of its power. The changes in the critical year itself, as we have seen, will not necessarily be permanent. Further readjustments are likely in succeeding contests.

After a time, stability is achieved. Stable periods tend to resemble earlier eras. Thus, after the adjustments which result from the critical election, correlations between paired elections of different periods are fairly high. For example, the correlation of the vote in 1876 and 1860 is .78; that in 1900 and 1888, .85; and that in 1932 and 1920, .80. Part of the process of readjustment is an apparent return by the voters in some states to past voting traditions. Even with the transformation of the electoral coalition, a strong degree of continuity is present.

The transition from one electoral era to another, resulting from considerable partisan movement by the voters, is an impressive manifestation of democratic control. Voters intervene decisively to change the political terms of reference. Party support and party programs become more congruent. Old policies and slogans are replaced by new, possibly more appropriate, appeals. The confusions of a waning order give way to the battle cries of an emergent party division. The Eisenhower elections did little to change the content of American politics from the dated themes of the New Deal. The Kennedy-Johnson administration, and the 1960–64 elections, did present new issues and conflicts. If 1964 did indeed constitute a Converting election, it may have provided the electoral foundation for the governmental resolution of longstanding issues.

## Appendix

Since this study is basically one of geographical distribution of party support, no special effort was made to compensate for differences among the state in population or votes. Moreover, past work on this subject, from Key onward, has used unweighted data. A number of readers, however, have suggested the desirability of weighting. To investigate the question, the procedures used were adapted for use with weighted data, leading to a new set of statistics, corresponding to those of figures 10.3, 10.4, and 10.5.

The weight for each state was its number of representatives in Congress in

## TABLE 10.5
## Data for Classification of Presidential Elections[a]

| [b]Year, Category | r: Last Election | r: Four Elections | Mean State Difference | Standard Deviation | Associated Elections Before | Associated Elections After |
|---|---|---|---|---|---|---|
| 1832-M | .93 | .93, .93 | 8.34, 5.90 | 6.83, 5.11 | 1 | 0 |
| 1836-C | .22 | .14, .05 | 18.81. 15.73 | 14.89, 14.92 | 0 | 1 |
| 1840-D | .71 | .54, .38 | 13.27 12.37 | 10.56, 10.19 | 1 | 1 |
| 1844-M | .84 | .79, .81 | 6.82, 6.69 | 6.22, 6.08 | 1 | 4 |
| 1848-D | .79 | .75, .57 | 8.12, 10.04 | 6.02, 8.13 | 1 | 3 |
| 1852-M | .78 | .74, .74 | 5.02, 4.22 | 4.53, 3.60 | 2 | 2 |
| 1856-M | .81 | .78, .79 | 6.33, 6.39 | 3.35, 3.53 | 3 | 1 |
| 1860-D | .89 | .86, .77 | 5.06, 5.25 | 3.55, 3.35 | 4 | 0 |
|  | (–.24) | (.02,–.29) | (24.33, 23.80) | (18.58, 18.43) | (0 | 0) |
| 1864-R | .55 | .51, .34 | 5.70, 5.98 | 6.78, 6.97 | 0 | 1 |
|  | (–.06) | (.31, .19) | ( 6.99, 7.43) | ( 7.69, 7.40) | (0 | 1) |
| 1868-M | .84 | .67, .63 | 6.43, 5.61 | 6.09, 5.93 | 1 | 0 |
| 1872-M | .62 | .69, .61 | 7.41, 6.57 | 5.58, 5.19 | 0 | 1 |
| 1876-M | .75 | .80, .78 | 5.94, 5.76 | 4.99, 4.69 | 1 | 3 |
| 1880-M | .88 | .80, .78 | 4.50, 3.69 | 4.89, 4.34 | 1 | 2 |
| 1884-D | .90 | .78, .77 | 3.88, 3.45 | 5.08, 4.79 | 2 | 1 |
| 1888-M | .93 | .80, .79 | 4.38, 3.63 | 5.81, 5.38 | 3 | 1 |
| 1892-D | .71 | .66, .73 | 6.55, 5.67 | 8.05, 5.67 | 1 | 0 |
|  | (.80) | (.76, .83) | ( 9.15, 6.87) | ( 9.95, 7.86) | (3 | 6) |
| 1896-C | .54 | .53, .70 | 11.53, 7.62 | 10.21, 6.85 | 0 | 1 |
|  | (.75) | (.71, .80) | ( 9.21, 7.02) | ( 8.49, 5.97) | (1 | 1) |
| 1900-M | .82 | .84, .94 | 5.16, 3.80 | 5.59, 3.30 | 1 | 6 |
| 1904-M | .87 | .81, .91 | 11.68, 9.50 | 8.70, 6.17 | 1 | 5 |
| 1908-M | .95 | .91, .96 | 4.47, 3.27 | 4.48, 3.19 | 2 | 4 |

**TABLE 10.5**
***Continued***

| | | | | | |
|---|---|---|---|---|---|
| 1912-D | .94 | .90, .95 | 5.02, 3.50 | 5.04, 3.77 | 3 | 3 |
| 1916-D | .92 | .94, .95 | 8.96, 7.17 | 5.34, 4.49 | 4 | 2 |
| 1920-M | .91 | .95, .95 | 7.30, 8.51 | 5.15, 5.19 | 5 | 1 |
| 1924-M | .97 | .94, .96 | 11.69, 10.96 | 8.81, 8.04 | 6 | 0 |
| | (.83) | (.89, .92) | ( 6.78, 5.48) | ( 5.71, 5.41) | (4 | 0) |
| 1928-R | .77 | .80, .77 | 7.94, 9.02 | 6.19, 6.18 | 0 | 0 |
| | (.79) | (.81, .78) | ( 7.80, 7.97) | ( 6.12, 6.48) | (0 | 0) |
| 1932-R | .77 | .85, .89 | 19.21, 18.98 | 8.02, 6.86 | 0 | 4 |
| 1936-M | .93 | .87, .89 | 19.20, 19.92 | 7.50, 6.97 | 1 | 3 |
| 1940-M | .92 | .94, .94 | 7.78, 7.89 | 4.16, 4.27 | 2 | 2 |
| 1944-M | .98 | .94, .96 | 3.35, 2.61 | 2.38, 2.06 | 3 | 1 |
| 1948-M | .94 | .95, .95 | 5.01, 5.18 | 3.45, 3.26 | 4 | 0 |
| | (–.33) | (–.35,–.24) | (12.86, 12.21) | (19.68, 18.15) | (0 | 0) |
| 1952-D | .77 | .77, .73 | 15.31, 13.62 | 7.98, 8.21 | 0 | 1 |
| | (–.16) | (.76, .68) | (13.36, 11.93) | ( 5.72, 6.18) | (0 | 1) |
| 1956-D | .83 | .73, .71 | 11.77, 11.44 | 7.73, 7.31 | 1 | 0 |
| 1960-C | .37 | .36, .28 | 6.05, 6.05 | 6.78, 5.83 | 0 | 0 |
| 1964-C | .31 | –.44,–.55 | 16.82, 16.37 | 9.00, 7.91 | 0 | |

[a]The second figure listed in columns 3, 4 and 5 are the statistics derived from state election results weighted by the number of Congressional Representatives.

[b]The data in parentheses refer: in 1860 and 1864, to the Douglas vote alone in 1860; in 1892 and 1896, to the combined Democratic and Populist vote in 1892; in 1924 and 1928, to the combined Democratic and Progressive vote in 1924; in 1948 and 1952, to the Truman vote alone in 1948. The categories are: M– Maintaining; D– Deviating; C– Converting; and R– Realigning.

the designated election year, or in the later of paired years. Although apportionment is not perfectly proportional to population, it is accurate, simple, and a reliable indicator of relative population. The electoral vote, a suggested alternative, was rejected because it is biased toward smaller states. The total vote for each state, another alternative, is more difficult to obtain accurately for distant elections, and harder to use statistically. Weighting by representatives changes the number of cases for each variable, or election. For 1964, illustratively, the number of cases is no longer the 50 states, but is the 435 representatives. Nevada and New York are no longer each a case. Delaware is still one case, but New York is 41.

No extended analysis of these results will be offered here; the data are included in the table below. In regard to the location of critical elections, weighted data tend to reinforce the original conclusions. Change in 1836, 1864, 1928, and 1960–64 is even more marked, although the differences are not great. Weighted data reduce the degree of change evident in 1892–96, but do not require any modification of these years' designation as a critical period. The general conclusion one would reach is that the additional computational problems occasioned by weighted data do not seem to bring proportionately increased insights. Indeed, in an unusual case, weighted data can cause new problems. The election of 1848, for example, becomes sharply distinguished by this method. The reason does not appear to be that 1848 was a critical election. Rather, the cause is the concentration of votes for the Free Soil party in New York. Van Buren's personal appeal in a state with nearly a sixth of the nation's representatives seriously distorts the weighted results, but his local attraction is not decisive if unweighted votes are used.

Table 10.5 summarizes all of the data obtained. Included for each year are coefficients of correlation with the previous election and the average of the previous four elections, the mean of state differences, and the standard deviation. The last three statistics for weighted data are also included in the appropriate columns. The number of "associated elections" denotes the number of consecutive elections before and after the given year which are highly correlated with the results of that year. (A high level is defined as a coefficient of .69 or better for the nineteenth century, and .82 for 1900 and later elections.) Each election is also provisionally classified as Maintaining, Deviating, Converting, or Realigning.

## Notes

1. The most notable works are those of the Survey Research Center, particularly Angus Campbell *et al.*, *The American Voter* (New York: Wiley, 1960) and *Elections and the Political Order* (New York: Wiley, 1966). A recent important work is V. O. Key, Jr., *The Responsible Electorate* (Cambridge: Harvard University Press, 1966).

2. *Journal of Politics* 17 (February 1955):4. Key also suggested that critical elections evidenced deep concern and high involvement by voters. However, these characteristics are difficult to establish historically and are not vital to the concept. Further work on the subject includes Key, "Secular Realignment and the Party System," *Journal of Politics* 21 (May 1959):198–210; Duncan MacRae, Jr. and James A. Meldrum, "Critical Elections in Illinois: 1888–1958," *American Political Science Review* LIV (September 1960):669–83; and Charles Sellers, "The Equilibrium Cycle in Two-Party Politics," *Public Opinion Quarterly* XXIX (Spring 1965):16–38.
3. *The American Voter*, pp. 531–38. The additional category, Reinstating, is best understood as a sub-category of Maintaining. Cf. Philip Converse *et al.*, "Stability and Change in 1960: A Reinstating Election," *American Political Science Review* LV (June 1961):269–80.
4. Further work by the same authors on this subject is included in chapters 4, 7, and 10 of *Elections and the Political Order*.
5. The Michigan researchers have resorted to this data when attempting to analyze the more distant past. For imaginative use of this material, see Lee Benson, *The Concept of Jacksonian Democracy* (Princeton: Princeton University Press, 1961). A general discussion of the uses and limits of electoral data is found in Austin Ranney, *Essays on the Behavioral Study of Politics* (Urbana: University of Illinois Press, 1962), chap 2.
6. Marian Irish and James Prothro. *The Politics of American Democracy*, 3rd. ed. (Englewood Cliffs, N.J.: Prentice-Hall, 1965), pp. 300–01.
7. *The American Voter, p. 534; Elections and the Political Order*, p. 74.
8. *The American Voter*, p. 531, places Republican victories from the Civil War to the 1920s in the Maintaining category, but on p. 536, the authors write of "the realignment accompanying the election of 1896." In *Elections and the Political Order*, p. 74, the existence of a Republican majority prior to 1896 seems to exclude this election as Realigning, but on p. 76, McKinley is grouped with Lincoln and Franklin Roosevelt as victors in Realigning contests.
9. The "normal" majority party must be assumed at some point in time from historical evidence. For example, we can make the rather safe assumption that the Democrats were the majority party after 1936. After the initial assumption, the election results will indicate when this majority status began and when other changes have occurred. Emphasizing the success or failure of a given party, rather than change as such, avoids the need for a sub-category such as the SRC's Reinstating election. It also avoids the problems, inherent in Irish and Prothro's scheme, of dealing with two consecutive Deviating elections, as in 1912–16.
10. The percentages are from Svend Petersen, *A Statistical History of the American Presidential Elections* (New York: Ungar, 1963); *Congressional Quarterly Weekly Report*, Vol. 21 (March 26, 1965), p. 466.
11. The third-party elections are those of 1848, 1860, 1892, 1904 to 1924, and 1948. It should be noted that the number of states (N for a given variable, or election) is not constant. It increased over time as new states were admitted to the Union and as states began to choose electors by popular vote. It decreased temporarily during the Civil War and Reconstruction, when Confederate states were excluded from the balloting. The correlation of any pair of elections, therefore, is only of those states participating by popular vote in both elections.
12. For uses of this method using county data, cf. V. O. Key, Jr., and Frank Munger, "Social Determinism and Electoral Decision: The Case of Indiana," in Eugene Burdick and Arthur Brodbeck, *American Voting Behavior* (Glencoe: The Free

Press, 1959), pp. 281–99; and Thomas A. Flinn, "Continuity and Change in Ohio Politics," *Journal of Politics* 24 (August 1964):521–44.

13. This assumption could prove false if voter realignment occurred within the states, but the net effect of countervailing movements was masked by state-wide returns. The Democratic percentage in a given state might then remain stable, but the party's votes would be quite different from those of the past. Political developments affecting social groups differentially should be reflected, however, by unequal vote changes from one state to another. While the divergences of states have lessened greatly in recent decades, considerable diversity remains.
14. The Democratic percentage of the total vote is used for all years, except 1860, where the Douglas and Breckinridge percentages are combined, and 1948, where the Truman and Thurmond percentages are combined. If the Douglas vote alone is used for 1860, the correlation coefficient drops to −.24. If the Truman vote alone is used, the coefficient decreases to −.41. Since both elections saw a short-lived division of the Democrats, not a real break, it seems appropriate to statistically reunite the factions.
15. *Op. cit.*, figure 1, p. 671.
16. If a state had not participated in all of the four previous elections, its "normal" vote was assumed to be the mean for as many of the four in which it had voted—1, 2, or 3. The "normal" vote figure is therefore less reliable for the period immediately after a state has joined the Union. New states are not included at all for the first election in which they participated. Confederate states are included immediately upon rejoining the Union, their "normal" vote being the prewar Democratic percentage.
17. This procedure is suggested by MacRae and Meldrum, p. 670, although they only correlate successive elections. Cf. Benson's discussion. pp. 125–31, of "stable phases" and "fluctuation phases."
18. I have adopted this method from David B. Truman, *The Congressional Party* (New York: Wiley, 1959).
19. Of the total of 595 correlations of the 47 variables, relating elections over 140 years, the mean coefficient of correlation is a reasonably high .54, while the mode and median are .65.
20. Between 1864 and 1896, the number of states participating in the Presidential election increased from 25 to 45. During the stable period of 1876–88, only Colorado entered the Electoral College. In 1844–60, however, coefficients were high even though the number of states increased from 25 to 32. Results for the 1824 election are not included because the data are unreliable and because few states then employed popular votes to choose the President.
21. It is to highlight such changes that absolute differences are used. If signed arithmetical differences were used, negative and positive variations would tend to cancel one another. This method is different from that of MacRae and Meldrum, who measure changes only from one election to the next, p. 670, and also different from that of Sellers, p. 33ff., who concentrates on the differences in the two parties' votes.
22. It should be noted that this graph and the next are to be interpreted differently from figures 10.2 and 10.3. Change in the earlier graphs was evidenced by a decline in the curve; in the present cases, change is evidenced by an increase in the vertical values.
23. Cf. Arthur S. Link, *Wilson: Campaigns for Progressivism and Peace* (Princeton: Princeton University Press, 1965), esp. chap. 4.

24. The cleavages remain, although the partisan breaking point may change. For a similar analysis of class voting, cf. Robert Alford, *Party and Society* (Chicago: Rand-McNally, 1963).
25. Cf. Richard P. McCormick, *The Second American Party System* (Chapel Hill: University of North Carolina Press, 1966), for an excellent account of the changes in the party system. The quotation is from p. 339.
26. *Politics in America* (New York: Harper and Row, 1954), p. 55. Cf. David Donald, *The Politics of Reconstruction* (Baton Rouge: Louisiana State University Press, 1965).
27. Correlation of the 1876 vote with that of Douglas in 1860 is −.19, but it is a high .78 with the combined Douglas and Breckinridge tallies.
28. Cf. MacRae and Meldrum, pp. 678–81. The change in 1892 did not come only in western, silver states. Indeed, six of these "radical" states were excluded from the 1892 calculations here, since they were not in the Union in earlier elections.
29. Cf. Stanley L. Jones, *The Presidential Election of 1896* (Madison: University of Wisconsin Press, 1964).
30. A statistical indication of the source of Populist votes is the higher correlation of the 1892 vote with that of 1888 (.81) when Populist and Democratic votes are added together than when Democratic votes alone are considered (.71). The correlation of the combined 1892 vote with that of 1896 is .75, higher than the coefficient achieved if comparison is made to the Democratic vote alone, .54.
31. Cf. *The American Voter*, pp. 153–60; Samuel J. Eldersveld, "The Influence of Metropolitan Party Pluralities in Presidential Elections since 1920," *American Political Science Review* XLIII (December 1949):1189–1205; Samuel Lubell, *The Future of American Politics* (Garden City: Doubleday Anchor, 1956); Ruth C. Silva, *Rum, Religion and Votes* (University Park: Pennsylvania State University Press, 1962).
32. The coefficient for the Democratic vote alone in 1920 and 1924 is extremely high, .97. If the Progressive vote is added to the Democrats' for 1924, however, the correlation falls to .83.
33. Key, "A Theory of Critical Elections." and MacRae and Meldrum, also find 1928 to be critical. Smith gained votes in Massachusetts, Rhode Island, New York, Illinois, Wisconsin, Minnesota, and North Dakota.
34. When change takes place over a number of years, classification of individual elections becomes awkward. It might be more precise to classify the 1928 election as a Converting or Deviating election to explain Hoover's victory, but it then becomes even more complicated to correctly appraise the 1932 results.
35. For indication of change within the South, cf. Donald S. Strong, "The Presidential Election in the South, 1952," *Journal of Politics* 17 (August 1955):343–89.
36. Donald E. Stokes, "Some Dynamic Elements of Contests for the Presidency," *American Political Science Review* LX (March 1966):27.
37. The Inter-University Consortium for Political Research is still in the process of obtaining and preparing county electoral data and Census material. When this immense task is completed, fuller national analysis will be possible.
38. See H. Daudt. *Floating Voters and the Floating Vote* (Leiden: Stenfert Kroese, 1961), chap. 2, and the discussion of the New Deal period, pp. 553–34 above.
39. *The American Voter*. pp. 554–55.
40. Donald Matthews and James Prothro, *Negroes and the New Southern Politics* (New York: Harcourt, Brace and World, 1966), chap. 13.
41. "Some Dynamic Elements of Contests for the Presidency," pp. 19–28; *The*

*Harris Survey*, January 11, 1965; Thomas W. Benham, *Public Opinion Trends: Their Meaning for the Republican Party* (Princeton: Opinion Research Corporation, 1965).

42. *Elections and the Political Order*, p. 13.
43. *Ibid.*, pp. 224–26.
44. Percentages are calculated from the data in *The American Voter*, table 7-2, p. 148; *Elections and the Political Order*, table 12-2, p. 225; and Inter-University Consortium for Political Research, *1964 Election Study Codebook*, Question 51, Deck 6, col. 11-12. SRC is now preparing further materials on this subject.
45. In a more recent publication, Angus Campbell writes, "The question which the 1964 vote raises is whether we are entering a period of party realignment. . . . There are indications in our survey data of a movement of this kind." However, this conclusion is also based on analysis of the distribution of party identifications, not on changes in these loyalties. Cf. "Interpreting the Presidential Victory," in Milton C. Cummings, Jr., *The National Election of 1964* (Washington: The Brookings Institution, 1966), esp. pp. 275–81.
46. Cyclical explanations are advanced in Louis Bean, *How to Predict Elections* (New York: Knopf, 1948).
47. MacRae and Meldrum, pp. 681–82.
48. V. O. Key, Jr., *Politics, Parties, and Pressure Groups*, 5th ed. (New York: Crowell, 1964), p. 537.
49. Two tests define a critical election: correlation to the last election and to the four-election average of less than .70 (in the nineteenth century) or .80 (twentieth century); and a coefficient of variation greater than 75. The latter measure is the standard deviation divided by the mean, with the result then multiplied by 100. Alternately, low correlation to the previous election alone, combined with a high mean (15 or greater) and high standard deviation (8 or greater), would define a critical election.

# 11

# Future Southern Congressional Politics

## I

Southern alienation from the national Democratic party has been evident since the 1928 presidential election.[1] The 1960 contest showed increased disaffection: the Republican party won thirty-three electoral votes in Virginia, Tennessee, and Florida, while fourteen electors from Alabama and Mississippi used their legal discretion to cast ballots for Senator Harry F. Byrd. In the other states of the former Confederacy, the Democratic margin was comfortable only in Georgia.

At the present time, however, Republican strength is largely confined to the presidential level. Even after the great effort made in the 1962 elections, the GOP holds only one Senate and eleven House seats in the eleven southern states. While flirting with "free elector" plans and presidential Republicanism, southern leaders have not attempted to destroy one-party control in other elections.

Through the one-party system, a variety of interests have been served. Officeholders generally have been grateful for the absence of competition. Conservative economic groups have been able to dissipate the energies that might become organized through a competitive political system. "A loose factional system lacks the power to carry out sustained programs of action, which almost always are thought by the better element to be contrary to its immediate interests,"[2] Segregationists have been able to prevent, at least until now, the full participation of the Negro in the political battle and the egalitarian demands that would follow. Even some Republican leaders have been wary of two-party politics, fearing a loss of the scraps of patronage and prestige which they have long monopolized.[3]

The long-term trend is certainly toward a two-party South. As elaborated by Alexander Heard, competition is being stirred by major changes in the southern economy and society. They include the immigration of Northerners and the emigration of Negroes, the abolition of racial restrictions on voting, industrialization, and urbanization. They are leading to "a clearer identification of economic interest with political action."[4] As economic and social issues claim priority over racial questions, the Republican appeal will grow.

The specific timing of party competition depends on the perceptions of dominant southern groups. They will become Republican when forced or persuaded to see this as in their interests. That time may now be near. The pressures against the one-party system can be seen in the case of Congressional elections, which probably are the most crucial for the national political system.

## II

The southern one-party system is now sustained chiefly by the advantages accruing to the region in Congress. The rules of seniority give "the occupants of safe southern seats an outpost on the Potomac for sniping and breaking up incipient attacks."[5] Aside from relatively infrequent primary challenges,[6] these senators and congressmen are virtually guaranteed tenure at the Capitol. From their positions of power, they can benefit their particular constituencies,[7] while also defending the region against attacks on segregation.

The usefulness of congressional seniority depends on the absence of a Republican threat to Democratic officeholders. There is considerable evidence that southern congressmen will not long enjoy this political immunity. In the last three presidential elections, there has been a tendency for the number of districts uncontested by the Republicans to decrease and for the Republican congressional vote to increase. This is shown in Table 11.1, in which the five

**TABLE 11.1**
**Southern Republican Congressional Vote**

| | Number of Districts* | | | | | |
|---|---|---|---|---|---|---|
| | Rim South | | | All South | | |
| Republican Vote | 1952 | 1956 | 1960 | 1952 | 1956 | 1960 |
| 0% [Uncontested] | 36 | 27 | 30 | 72 | 61 | 62 |
| Below 20% | 3 | 5 | 5 | 9 | 9 | 13 |
| 20%–33.2% | 7 | 7 | 8 | 8 | 10 | 13 |
| 33.3%–49.9% | 9 | 15 | 11 | 11 | 19 | 11 |
| 50% and over | 6 | 7 | 7 | 6 | 7 | 7 |

* In 1952 and 1956, the 8th and 22nd districts of Texas were combined. For purposes of comparison, they are considered as separate districts in all computations.

rim states are listed separately.[8] By contrast, the party vote in these elections generally decreased in the previous thirty years.[9]

It is evident that the increase in Republican strength was considerable from 1952 to 1956 and that a slight decline followed in 1960. The latter is to be expected, given the general Democratic upswing. However, it is apparent that there is a significant Republican residue from the elections and events of 1952 to 1960, and that the previous declining trend has been reversed. As was to be expected, Republican strength is concentrated in the rim South.

Another tabulation indicates more thorough Republican growth. If attachment to the GOP is reaching below the presidential level, there should be increasing correspondence between the votes for President and the votes for congressmen. A truly converted Southerner will vote for the entire ticket, not just for its leader. As shown by table 11.2, the trend in fact is toward a closer relationship, and it is particularly marked in the five rim states.

There appears to be some definite long-term growth in the Republicans' strength below the presidential level. This would be even clearer except for the large number of uncontested congressional districts. Obviously, the GOP congressional vote cannot increase, either in absolute numbers or in relation to the presidential vote, unless there are Republicans actually running for the House of Representatives. In many states, the progress of the party has been slowed by the inability or reluctance of the local parties consistently to present congressional candidates.[10] Where such men are offered, however, there is an undoubted and uniform tendency for the congressional vote to increase in total numbers and to approach the presidential vote. This is shown in table 11.3.[11]

In every temporal comparison, the later Republican congressional vote more closely approximates the presidential vote. The rise in Republican strength in the South is not merely the growth of "presidential Republicanism." It is being accompanied, indeed led, by the development of firm party strength. Thus, in districts contested in all elections, the congressional GOP vote increased 20% from 1952 to 1956 and another fifth from 1956 to 1960. In the same period, the presidential vote rose by only 12% and 15%.

Table 11.3 also indicates the payoff for persistence. The deepening of Republican loyalties occurs after a number of elections in which party candidates for Congress have been available. If nominees are continuously advanced, the local organization gradually gains practice, knowledge, and funds. At the same time, the voters become accustomed to the existence of a Republican ticket, rather than a Republican presidential candidate alone. Analysis of districts contested in 1960, as in table 11.4, shows the results. The closest ticket voting exists in those districts in which competition has been most frequent and most persistent. Lack of these qualities results in a loss of Republican votes.

Of course, the increase in Republican votes is not due to changes in voter

**TABLE 11.2**
**Republican Congressional and Presidential Vote**

| | Rim South | | | All South | | |
|---|---|---|---|---|---|---|
| | **1952** | **1956** | **1960** | **1952** | **1956** | **1960** |
| (A) Congressional Vote (1,000s) | 790 | 1458 | 1601 | 909 | 1672 | 1769 |
| (B) Presidential Vote (1,000s) | 2987 | 3148 | 3533 | 4090 | 4213 | 4724 |
| Relationship of (A) and (B) | .26 | .46 | .45 | .22 | .40 | .37 |

**TABLE 11.3**
**Southern Republican Vote in Contested Districts**

| | Relationship of Republican Congressional and Presidential Vote | | |
|---|---|---|---|
| **Districts Contested:** | **1952 (N=28)** | **1956 (N=42)** | **1960 (N=41)** |
| In Given Years | .67 (28) | .69 (42) | .74 (41) |
| In All Three Elections | .73 (15) | .79 (15) | .83 (15) |
| In 1956 and 1960 | --- | .72 (28) | .78 (28) |
| In 1952 and 1960 | .70 (22) | --- | .80 (22) |
| In 1952 and 1956 | .69 (20) | .76 (20) | --- |
| Only in 1956 and 1960 | --- | .63 (13) | .69 (13) |
| Only in 1952 and 1960 | .58 ( 7) | --- | .66 ( 7) |
| Only in 1952 and 1956 | .50 ( 5) | .65 ( 5) | --- |

**TABLE 11.4**
**Southern Republican Vote in Contested Districts, 1960**

| **Types of Districts** | **Relationship of Congressional and Presidential Vote, 1960** |
|---|---|
| Newly Contested in 1960 (N=6) | .45 |
| Only Contested in 1952 and 1960 (7) | .66 |
| Only Contested in 1956 and 1960 (13) | .69 |
| Contested in Three Elections (15) | .83 |
| All Contested in 1960 (41) | .74 |

habits alone. Congressional candidates are generally being named only in those districts in which the party believes it has some fundamental strength. The point is still valid, however, that there are such areas and that the GOP has a substantial and increasing number of followers in those districts.

This recent strength appears to be substantially based. Transient causes, such as Eisenhower's personal popularity in 1952 and 1956, and anti-Catholic feeling in 1960, have had some effect, to be sure. However, these factors cannot explain the steady and significant increase in the GOP congressional vote. Neither do temporary rebellions by frustrated segregationists account for the changes in voting patterns.

The new and permanent strength of the Republicans is in the rim South and in urban areas, in which a GOP vote is based on economic rather than racial issues. Included in the districts showing strong support for the party are Arlington and Richmond in Virginia, Houston and Dallas in Texas, Tampa and Cape Canaveral in Florida. In 1960, of thirty-one districts showing a high correlation between the Republican presidential and congressional vote, sixteen were wholly or partially composed of major cities.[12]

Republican progress in southern congressional contests is slow but apparently secure. Increasingly, southern Democratic congressmen will be forced to make a choice. If they wish to remain Democrats in office, they will find themselves in need of support from the national party and its presidential ticket. They will no longer be able to be completely independent, secure against any electoral threat. The result of these needs is likely to be increased cooperation and policy agreement with the national leaders. If they refuse cooperation, they must face a rising Republican challenge without significant support from the national party.

At the same time, there is less reason for the national Democratic party to accept southern defiance and defection. It can now actually bargain with the southern congressman. He is no longer politically invulnerable. Failing in party loyalty, he may find himself facing, unaided, a formidable Republican opposition and, possibly, bearing the additional burden of attacks by loyal Democrats in his own constituency.[13] The choice increasingly will be between Democratic loyalty, with a degree of acceptance of party policy and candidates, or outright and consistent support of the Republican party.

The national Republican party too is likely to demand a clear choice of loyalty. In the past, the GOP could present no real threat to southern legislators. Making a virtue of necessity, the party accepted the nominal Democratic allegiance of the South and hoped for no more than a Dixiecrat revolt in support of the Republican presidential candidate and for policy agreements in Congress. Now the Republicans can and must attempt to win congressional seats in the South in their own name.

In order to win control of Congress, the party has no alternative but to honestly contest southern elections. In recent years, Democrats have invaded many traditionally Republican areas, from Maine to Hawaii. Outside of the South, the two-party vote has been closely divided, yet the GOP has won control of Congress only once since 1946, and then only by the narrowest margin and with the aid of a presidential landslide. For its own self-interest, the Republican party will be putting increased pressure on the Southerners, either by inviting them to change parties or by challenging them at the polls.

In state politics, it has been noted that even small opposition parties promote "a degree of cohesion and responsibility that is almost completely lacking in the dominant parties of the one-party systems, and thus clarify the choice that the voter must make."[14] The Republican party is clearly growing in the South. As it becomes organized more extensively, the outcome is likely to be increased Democratic party unity and, consequently, more persistent and meaningful two-party competition in the region.

## III

The choice between support of the Democratic or Republican party must be made by individual congressmen, present and future. Each will consider a number of factors, including the electoral division of his district, party traditions, and the public policies of the national groups. Some will be most interested in the preservation of segregation. Insofar as this is their objective, it will not be served by continued membership in the Democratic party.

This is not just because of the commitment of the "presidential wing" of the party to civil rights. Southerners in Congress have often shown ability to block the programs of a Democratic president. Rather, the cause of future segregationist alienation is to be found in Congress itself, particularly in the increasing numbers and influence of Negro legislators.

Among Democrats in Congress, there are really two large groups from one-party areas: legislators from the South and legislators from the core areas of the large nonsouthern cities. Although, unlike most Southerners, big-city Democrats usually face Republican opposition, they are easily elected and re-elected. Like their fellow partisans from the South, they are able to accumulate seniority and status.[15]

Democratic dominance of big-city elections is significant for the South because this party control is becoming, or can become, Negro control. In recent years, the metropolitan centers have come to include a large and increasing percentage of Negroes, who now comprise a fifth of the population of the twenty-five largest cities,[16] and often a majority of the population in at least one congressional district.

The city cores have long been Democratic. They are now becoming Negro as well, while remaining Democratic. Table 11.5 below indicates two things.

**TABLE 11.5**
**Democratic Vote in Nonsouthern Districts, by Negro Population***

| Negro Percentage of Population | Number of Districts | Democratic Vote (%) 1952 | 1956 | 1960 |
|---|---|---|---|---|
| 20%–25.0% | 5 | 53 | 53 | 63 |
| 25.1%–29.9% | 5 | 57 | 57 | 66 |
| 30.0%–39.9% | 6 | 64 | 65 | 70 |
| 40.0%–49.9% | 5 | 70 | 73 | 77 |
| 50% and over | 5 | 65 | 65 | 74 |

* Not included in this table are three California districts in the 30% range and one with 23% Negro population. All of these districts were technically non-contested in 1952 because of the cross-filing primary system. Comparisons with the 1956 and 1960 elections are therefore impossible.

The areas with large Negro concentrations are increasingly Democratic, on the average giving some two-thirds of their vote to the party. Secondly, the Democratic percentage generally increases as the Negro proportion in the areas increases.[17]

It is likely that the congressmen elected from these areas will be both Negro and Democratic. All but one of the five districts now containing an absolute majority of nonwhites do, in fact, have Negro congressmen. A fifth Negro was elected in 1962 from a new Los Angeles district. Legislators elected from these districts will probably be relatively safe from primary challenges, since the most efficient urban machines now in existence are those in the Negro wards.[18]

The influence of Negro voting in big-city districts is already apparent. Of only four Negroes in the 87th Congress, two were committee chairmen—William Dawson of Government Operations and Adam Powell of Education and Labor. In the not-distant future, more Negroes will be congressmen and some will survive long enough to become chairmen. In 1960, Negroes constituted a majority of the population in two districts in Chicago and one each in Detroit, New York, and Philadelphia. They represented over 40 percent of the population in five additional districts in Baltimore, Detroit, New York, and Cleveland. It would not be too difficult for Negroes to win and retain these ten seats.[19] Proper placement on committees, combined with continued local victories and Democratic congressional majorities, would result in substantial influence. For the longer future, there are an additional nine districts with a 30 percent or more Negro population, and eleven with a 20 to 30 percent Negro population. Given nonwhite population growth, and the natural political strength of a unified minority, these districts too might have Negro legislators within a foreseeable time.

As the Negro population in the core cities increases, the result will be that more Negroes will be elected to Congress and will serve for longer periods. They will rise, through the seniority system, to positions of influence and to committee chairmanships when the Democrats are in control of Congress. The institution of seniority, long noted for its conservative and prosegregationist effects, may well come to serve opposite objectives. Democratic majorities in Congress now result in increased influence for those opposed to integration and civil-rights legislation. By helping to elect Democrats in the North, Negroes are in the anomalous position of advancing Howard Smith to chairman of the House Rules Committee.

Ironically, the opposite may soon be true: southern Democratic votes will help to elevate Negroes to positions of power. Indeed, the situation has already occurred. Despite southern unhappiness, the inexorable workings of seniority have enabled Congressman Powell to investigate and attack segregation in education, employment, and labor unions. When this occurs, the value of the one-party system to Southerners, or at least to segregationist Southerners, has become questionable, if not totally illusory. In addition to civil-rights action, liberal legislation in general is likely to be advanced by Negro Congressmen. Elected by low-income and disadvantaged voters, they will usually endorse programs of governmental welfare and economic regulation.

It should be noted that the Senate represents a different situation. Negroes are not likely soon to be elected, and continuously re-elected, to the upper chamber and obviously cannot gain seniority there. This can provide only limited comfort to the South. The Republican threat is probably greater in the Senate, because it is simpler to challenge 22 seats there than 106 in the House. Moreover, since Negroes cannot yet rise from the House to the Senate, their seniority in the lower chamber will accumulate more rapidly. In any case, the close battles between liberals and conservatives today occur in the House. Thus, increased Negro strength there is most significant.

In the past, conservative Democratic Southerners enjoyed the best of two possible worlds. In a Democratic Congress, they held influential positions which could be used to block or delay measures they considered obnoxious, such as civil-rights legislation. In a Republican Congress, they lost their positions, but could usually remain assured that no legislation repugnant to them would be passed.

In the future, Southerners may find both their positions and their policies endangered in a Democratic Congress. Continued support of the party would subject Southerners to increased competition by the Republicans at home, and to increased pressure to support the legislative program of the national Democratic party. Continued allegiance would also require them to support northern Negroes for seniority posts.

Because it would overcome some of these disadvantages, membership in the Republican party will be more attractive to Southerners than in the past. By joining the GOP, the southern representative would be able to ride the rising political tide. Insofar as he favors more conservative domestic policies, he would find substantial support among Republicans.[20] While he would not be assured of any privileged consideration on seniority, he would not be required to vote for Negroes as committee chairmen, since none are likely to be elected continuously as Republicans.

It is not likely that all southern Democrats will become Republicans. Many are too committed, by tradition, belief, and political necessity, to change their party label. Others will find the defense of segregation too unimportant to justify a metamorphosis, or will regard the Republican party as inadequate to its defense. Some will remain Democrats while relying on remaining devices, such as the Senate filibuster, to defend their interests. In the long run, the South will lose some of its power in Congress and in the nation.

In any case, Southerners cannot expect to defend segregation permanently. Neither of the national parties is likely to adopt a segregationist position as the price of southern adherence in Congress. Instead, the choice of party must be made on other grounds. Many southern representatives will be attracted to the GOP by its relative conservatism and by its increasing political strength in the region. Others will be urged on this course by the rising Negro strength in the Democratic party and in Congress.

The full realization of these trends will probably require the removal of the integration issue from national politics. Now that a Democratic, as well as Republican, administration has used military force to support school desegregation, the way may be open for the full development of two-party politics in the South. This trend in turn may lay the basis for a party system with limited but distinct differences between the parties and for increased central authority within the parties. Contrary to some views, these effects do not require "changes in current institutions and procedures which would deprive nominal southern Democrats of those advantages that make them loathe to shed their Democratic label."[21] These shifts will come about through the continuation of political trends now evident and likely to continue for a considerable period. One hundred years after the Civil War, the outlook is for a truly national political system.

## Notes

1. See V. O. Key, Jr., "Hoovercrats and Dixiecrats," in *Southern Politics* (New York: Alfred A. Knopf, Inc., 1949), pp. 317–44, and Allan P. Sindler, "The Unsolid South: A Challenge to the Democratic National Party," in Alan F. Westin, ed., *The Uses of Power: 7 Cases in American Politics* (New York: Harcourt, Brace and World, 1962), p. 239.
2. Key, p. 308. See Duane Lockard, *New England State Politics* (Princeton: Prince-

ton University Press, 1958), chap. 12, for a discussion of the effect of party competition on social policy.

3. See William Buchanan, "Cracks in Southern Solidarity," *Antioch Review* 15 (September 1956):351–64, and V. O. Key, Jr., "The Erosion of Sectionalism," *Virginia Quarterly Review* 31 (Spring 1955), especially pp. 170–74.
4. Alexander Heard, *A Two-Party South?* (Chapel Hill: University of North Carolina Press, 1952), pp. 144–56. See also Harry Ashmore, *An Epitaph to Dixie* (New York: W. W. Norton & Company, Inc., 1957).
5. Buchanan, pp. 351–52.
6. It is estimated that nearly half of Southern Congressmen face neither primary nor general election contests. See Julius Turner, "Primary Elections as the Alternative to Party Competition in Safe Districts," *Journal of Politics*, 15 (May, 1953), p. 201.
7. It is not coincidental that the major share of the space agency's expenditures will be made in southern states. See *The National Observer*, February 4, 1962.
8. The data for all tables is from U.S. Bureau of the Census, *Congressional District Data Book (Districts of the 87th Congress)* (Washington: Government Printing Office, 1961), tables, I, III. The "rim South" includes Florida, North Carolina, Tennessee, Texas, and Virginia. Contrary to tradition, I have included Arkansas in the Deep South, on the basis of resistance to school integration, along with Alabama, Georgia, Louisiana, Mississippi, and South Carolina.
9. Heard, chap. 4, especially pp. 70–73.
10. Local "deals" are one reason. In Tennessee, "trading across party lines has been notorious. . . . The state's political sophisticates take it for granted that agreement exists between Democratic and Republican leaders to minimize political strife—to create, in effect, two one-party systems." See Heard, p. 108.
11. To avoid distorted percentages resulting from very small numbers, a contested district is here considered one in which the Republicans get at least 10% of the congressional vote. However, the Mississippi third district is counted as contested in 1960, although the Republican vote was below this figure. This is because the district did meet the criterion in 1952, and a valid comparison requires its inclusion.
12. Analyzing the 1952 election, Donald S. Strong concluded that urban, and particularly higher-income, endorsement of the GOP was "the most consistent and persuasive finding." He predicted correctly that segregationist support of the Republicans would decline, but that the vote of higher-income urban dwellers would become more definitely Republican. See "The Presidential Election in the South, 1952," *Journal of Politics* 17 (August 1955):343–89.
13. In Texas, loyal Democrats in 1961 were reported to support Republican John Tower for the Senate rather than a conservative and anti-Kennedy Democrat, William Blakely, who was subsequently defeated. See *Wall Street Journal*, May 25, 1961.
14. Austin Ranney and Willmore Kendall, *Democracy and the American Party System* (New York: Harcourt, Brace and Company, 1956), p. 197.
15. Turner, *loc. cit.*, indicates that primary challenges in "safe" districts in the Northeast occur in only 29.7% of elections, compared to 57.5% in the South.
16. *The New York Times*, April 15, 1962.
17. These two trends are related. The districts are classified here by the percentage of Negro population in the 1960 census. It is likely that the proportion of nonwhites increased in each of these areas during the three presidential elections involved. As this change in population occurred, the areas became more firmly Democratic.

18. See James Q. Wilson, *Negro Politics* (Glencoe, Illinois: The Free Press, 1960), particularly chaps. 2, 3, and David Hapgood, *The Purge That Failed: Tammany v. Powell* (New Brunswick: Eagleton Institute, 1959).
19. A Negro candidate for Congress from Cleveland was defeated in 1962, in part because of the Republican sweep in that state. It is likely that a Negro will soon represent the district, however.
20. See Austin Ranney, ''Republicans and Democrats: Principles and Perversities,'' in Alfred Junz, ed., *Present Trends in American National Government* (New York: Frederick A. Praeger, 1961), p. 52.
21. Sindler, p. 280.

# 12

# Nixon and the End of Presidential Politics

After George McGovern's massive defeat, I am reminded of the apocryphal question asked of Mrs. Lincoln at Ford's Theatre, ''But aside from that, Madam, how did you enjoy the show?'' Is there any cause for Democrats to cheer after the historic burial of the erstwhile leader of a ''new coalition''?

In fact, if they can forget the inconvenient reality of Richard Nixon in the White House, there is cause for long-term cheer by the Democrats. Although Nixon even surpassed Franklin Roosevelt's 1936 performance, his party actually fell back. Democrats gained Senate seats, lost only a handful in the House (the same handful they had gained in 1970), and now hold 31 statehouses. By contrast, F.D.R. reduced the Republicans in 1936 to a small band of 17 senators and 89 representatives.

There are other indications of deep Democratic strength in the nation. The party continues to hold a wide edge in voter identifications, and this edge has been increased by the large influx of young voters. When the new voters have selected a party, they have preferred the Democrats by margins of over 2 to 1, and the under-25s actually gave a majority of their vote to McGovern. Through the reforms of the past four years, the party has revitalized itself, becoming a semi-mass party, open to the emerging politically conscious groups of feminists, blacks, Chicanos and other non whites, as well as youth. By contrast, the Republicans have remained stagnant and have explicitly rejected internal reforms.

And, yet, there is the overwhelming fact of the Nixon triumph. Can anyone but a partisan Dr. Pangloss speak of basic Democratic strength when the party nominee carries but one state in the electoral college? Perhaps we are actually witnessing the coming of a major new alignment of the political parties, comparable to that of the New Deal period. Perhaps, as Mr. Nixon and publicists such as Kevin Phillips hope, there is a ''new majority'' under construction, conservative in ideology, socially composed of suburbanites, white ethnics, and middle-income workers, and regionally centered in the South and West.

The first data available on the election do not support this interpretation (or hope). In fact, the astonishing fact is the great stability in voting patterns which is revealed. The areas and groups of relative party strength remain the same as in the past. The Democratic core remains the cities, union workers, minorities, the East, and the Midwest. Across all socioeconomic divisions, ethnic groups, and geographical areas, there is a close correspondence between the 1968 vote for Humphrey and the 1972 vote for McGovern. Of course, the latter did far worse, but the relative position of groups remains quite similar. For example, Italians are reported to have given Humphrey 50 percent of their vote, and McGovern 33 percent, a 17 percent decline, while Jews declined from 84 percent Democratic to 69 percent, a 15 percent drop. Nixon gained 17 percent between the two elections, and this is approximately the margin he gained universally. Nor can we find basic conservatism among the voters in the nationwide approval of strong government action on behalf of ecology measures, such as the passage of bond issues in New York and Florida, the imposition of controls on seashore use in California, and the rejection of the winter Olympics in Colorado and a highway bond issue in New Jersey. Conservatism does exist on such issues as law and order and life styles, but not on basic spending questions.

An incipient realignment, then, does not appear to explain the unusual combination of presidential and other election results. I believe this disjunction is part of a larger fission in which the presidency is being separated effectively from partisan politics. Nixon can win re-election as president while his party continues to decline because voters no longer consider the office in partisan terms. This perception goes beyond the act of splitting the ticket. Rather, in the voter's mind, there is no ticket. He has one ballot for president and another ballot for everything else—as is literally true in Georgia and some other states. Party is relevant only to his latter choice, while the presidency is becoming a plebiscitary office. Parties serve mechanically to fill the office, but they have little organic connection with it.

The isolation of the presidential office has been the subject of complaint by professional politicians. President Nixon was noticeably absent from this year's campaign, much to the chagrin of Republicans hoping to be carried into office on his alleged coattails. Nixon took almost no action to help such ideological colleagues as Tower in Texas or Powell in New Hampshire, and appears unaffected by the lost opportunity to win control of Congress. These actions cannot be dismissed simply as a short-term strategy to win the 1972 campaign, because complaints about Nixon's ineffective party leadership have been heard since he first entered the White House. Moreover, the same complaints were heard earlier in regard to Lyndon Johnson. Yet Nixon and Johnson were both partisan figures, who owed their prominence to their party histories. Not personality, but office, accounts for their neglect of party duties.

The causes of this development can be located first in the evolution of campaign techniques. Political parties developed as organizations to elect a president. When Madison and Jefferson began their partisan correspondence, when Jackson initiated the first national convention, when the spoils system was expanded, the purpose was always the same—capture of the White House. In periods of indirect communication between presidential nominees and the voter, and when individual canvassing was the major campaign method, parties were organizationally suited to this electoral goal. They registered voters, persuaded or bribed them, and brought them to the polls. It was therefore in a president's self-interest to lead and strengthen his party. In turn, the electorate relied primarily on party loyalty in making its decisions.

In the modern period, a presidential candidate does not need much more than a party label as a means of securing access to the ballot (and George Wallace even did without that). He appeals directly to the voters through the mass media, prerecorded telephone messages, direct mail, and so forth. Individual canvassers cannot, and do not try, to reach 140 million voters sprawled across a continent. Instead, the candidate himself presents his personality, style, and issue positions to an electorate conditioned to choose "the best man," not the best party. It is no longer in the self-interest of the president to identify himself with other persons sharing his Republican or Democratic label. As George Reedy has observed, the result is the increasing isolation of the chief executive.

Organizational developments strengthen this trend. Little direct patronage is left to the president, with the severing of the post office and other extensions of civil service. Revenue sharing will probably reduce the discretionary spending power of the national executive, even as it increases the opportunities for local boodle. Of course, there is still much discretion left in the granting of such favors as defense contracts, but these matters promote direct contributions to a president's individual campaign, not to a party. Rather little of the Nixon "secret funds" was distributed to the senatorial, congressional, and gubernatorial candidates.

Even the nomination of a president may soon become a non-party matter, at least among Democrats. The import of the McGovern-Fraser reforms and of the proposed party charter is that the mass base of the party (or its enthusiastic members, at least) should choose the national ticket without intervention by the organized party leaders. In fact, one of the 1972 guidelines specifically prohibited ex officio delegates at the convention. This is the pure plebiscitary ideal—the direct choice of a presidential candidate by self-styled party members and the exclusion of the "machine." Nominees chosen in this manner will have only a random relationship with the organized party. Indeed, when McGovern attempted to strengthen that relationship after his nomination, many of his supporters became suspicious that he was somehow violating the mandate of the convention.

More than any other factor, the isolation of the presidency is being forced by the predominance of foreign affairs in the conduct of the office. Not only are foreign policy decisions more obviously critical than those of domestic policy, they are also more glamorous to a president. The ritual of foreign visits or the thrill of disposing of megatons is more attractive than filling the pork barrel. And it is easier, in the sense that the president can make his decisions with less opposition from competing politicians and less need to win domestic consent from Congress or the mass public.

But foreign policy is not well suited to partisan debate. Until recently, these issues have not been organized along party lines, and the tradition of bipartisanship is likely to be reinstituted after Vietnam. Even when such questions do become partisan, they cannot be easily argued and subject to the constant tests of domestic issues. The inability of Congress effectively to direct an end to the Vietnam war underscored this difficulty. Ultimately, foreign policy questions become, for the electorate, questions of personality. Which man can be trusted with the nuclear trigger? Which candidate can negotiate better or stand up to the Russians? The nature of the issues therefore furthers the movement toward making presidential elections a choice of individuals, not a choice of parties. They thereby bring us closer to an end to true politics in the choice and conduct of the presidency.

This development of the presidency bodes ill for the future of American society. If not in campaigns for president, where will Americans hear and debate the domestic problems of their nation? If not from the president, where will the energy and leadership come for resolution of problems of race, poverty, and the quality of life? There is no present alternative in the American system. The accumulation of domestic ills over the past 20 years is not because there wasn't enough money for both guns and butter or because a definite priority was given to guns, but because presidents could not devote effort to both foreign and domestic programs. The limited resources are not taxes or will, but the president's time and political strength. Nixon's relative success in foreign policy and negligible domestic record are not personal idiosyncrasies, but of the essence of the foreign-oriented presidency in a government without alternative leadership. It is only the latest replication of the decline of Johnson's Great Society with the escalation of Vietnam, and of F.D.R.'s replacement of Dr. New Deal by Dr. Win-the-War.

To deal with this problem will require more than a Democratic victory in 1976. Even if the Democrats re-establish themselves as the majority party, the institutional problems will remain. Party reconstruction is not enough. The presidency must be reconstructed if the nation is to be rebuilt.

# 13

# The Presidential Election of 1984

*I can call spirits from the vasty deep.*
*Why so can I, or so can any man,*
*But will they come when you do call for them?*
—Henry IV, Part 1

Ronald Reagan did evoke some spirit, whether friendly sprite or fearsome demon.

Winning the presidential election against Walter Mondale, Reagan gained 59 percent of the popular vote. He achieved a record high of 525 electoral votes, losing only those of Minnesota and the District of Columbia. Supported by nearly 55 million Americans, the incumbent president accumulated majorities in virtually every group in the population. In so doing, he obtained more votes for his Republican candidacy than had ever been cast for a U.S. politician.[1]

While the results of the election are clear, their meaning is more clouded. What genie has been released from that bottle? Will it bring war and social disharmony, or national strength and prosperity? Is it only a pleasant phantom bearing the likeness of the reelected president? Or does it also carry political flesh and blood?

Ronald Reagan may have achieved no more than a great personal triumph over an ineffective opponent. Or he may have won, more substantively, an endorsement of his policy proposals. Perhaps the voters, looking backward, simply judged the Reagan record and found it good. Or, looking forward, they may have moved the nation toward a new conservative and Republican alignment. All of these explanations have some validity, but we see the election of 1984 as neither a triumph of personality nor a policy referendum. Rather, in approving the conduct of the Reagan administration, the voters prepared the way to a new American politics.

## The Results

### *Geography*

The Reagan victory was both broad and deep. Even in Minnesota, the one state he lost, he fell short by only 4,000 votes, a fraction of a percentage point. The national results were certainly a landslide, but in some states they were more like a political earthquake. The president won by margins of nearly 2 to 1 in such diverse areas as Yankee New Hampshire, Sunbelt Florida, the hard plains of Nebraska, and the soaring mountains of Utah.

Beneath the nearly unanimous victory, however, there are significant variations. Although the rain of presidential defeat fell on the Democrats throughout the nation, they could find some silver linings in the unfriendly clouds. They did relatively well in two areas of the country. The first was the Northeast, where they had a traditional base of support among city residents, factory workers, and members of minority and ethnic groups. Of the 13 areas in this region, including the District of Columbia, seven gave Mondale relatively large proportions of their vote, and only New Hampshire provided a large margin for Reagan. (These variations can be seen in Figure 13.1.)

The second source of Democratic consolation could be found in an unusual location. Mondale, contrary to tradition, did well in areas originally settled by New England Yankees, which had long supported liberal Republicans. These included states such as Wisconsin and Iowa in the Midwest, Oregon and Washington on the Pacific Coast, as well as southern New England. These tended to be the places where John Anderson had done best in the 1980 election, adding to poll evidence that much of his support, once Republican, had been converted to the Democratic cause over four years. It is one indication, although limited, that the 1984 balloting registered partisan change.

On the Republican side, there were also significant geographical variations, and two notable regions of strength. Most prominent on the map was the party's strength west of the Mississippi. In all but two of the 14 states from the Great Plains to the western slopes of the Rockies, from the Texas empire to the wilderness of Idaho, Reagan won at least five votes out of eight. Mondale had no notable support in any state in this region.

Reagan's other geographical base was in the more advanced economies of the South, particularly Virginia, Florida, and, again, Texas. His large pluralities in these states were, in part, simply expansions of the Republicans' past bases in Dixie. They also showed the party's particular appeal to areas that combined high technology, recent industrial growth, and a low proportion of

**FIGURE 13.1**
**The National Vote in 1984**

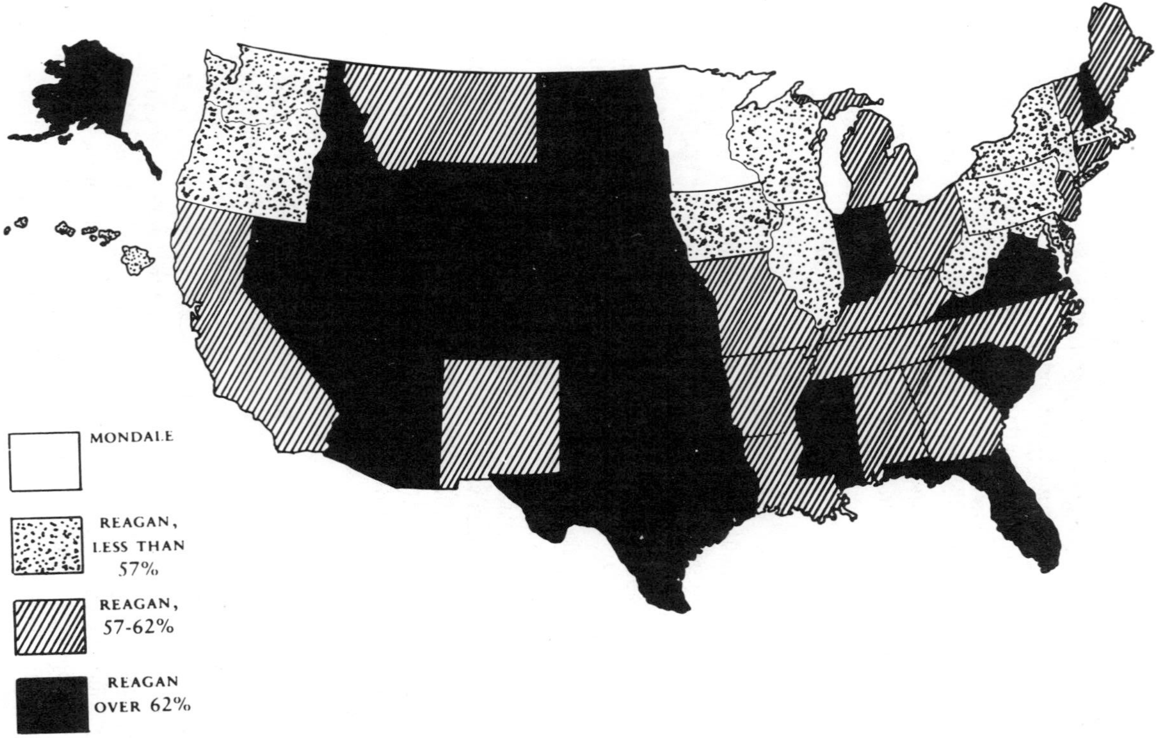

MONDALE

REAGAN, LESS THAN 57%

REAGAN, 57-62%

REAGAN OVER 62%

black voters. (The same favorable combination for Republicans could be found in New Hampshire, their redoubt in the Northeast.)

The remaining 19 states were quite similar in their vote, coming within three percentage points of the national average. Despite the significant regional differences we have noted, the election was more striking for this relative uniformity. The states close to the national average were quite diverse, including old Yankee Republican strongholds such as Maine, as well as the Democrats' former industrial heartland in the Midwest. Perhaps most significantly, most of the former Confederacy, the once-solid South, reflected the general mood of the nation, although the overall Dixie results masked severe internal racial divisions in the region.

Between Reagan's two elections, the nation had become more unified—at least electorally, if not ideologically. Individual states shifted in opposite directions, but toward a common Republican majority. Compared to 1980, Reagan actually lost proportionate support in 12 states, almost all in places where he had done extremely well in the earlier contest. In contrast, he gained particularly in 10 states. Seven of these were in the South, where 1980's close contests had been converted to 1984's large victories.

The geographical results of the election, in summary, show that there is a distinct regional cast to each major party's support. Not only is the Republican coalition obviously the larger one in 1984, but it also shows signs of being a stable and widespread coalition.[2] The regional pattern of the Reagan vote persisted over the four-year period, indicating that the Republican support has some depth.* At the same time, voter reactions were more similar from state to state in 1984 than in 1980, indicating that the Republican party had achieved some breadth as well.†

### *Demography*

The social bases of the Reagan victory are both self-evident and hidden. The president won majorities among virtually every population group—the landslide contained rocks of almost every description. Of the demographic groups listed in table 13.1, Mondale won only among blacks, Hispanics,‡

‡Because of their small numbers, it is difficult accurately to estimate the vote of Hispanics. Other polls reported that Reagan had won as much as 47 percent of this group.

*The linear correlation of the results in the two elections is .87, a historically high figure, indicating stability in party coalitions.

†The standard deviation of the vote measures the similarity of votes among the states. In 1984, it was 8.8 percentage points, compared to 9.9 in 1980, again suggesting greater political similarity across the nation.

TABLE 13.1
The Presidential Vote in Social Groups, 1984 and 1980

| Percent of 1984 total | | 1984 Reagan | 1984 Mondale | 1980 Reagan | 1980 Carter | 1980 Anderson |
|---|---|---|---|---|---|---|
| | Party | | | | | |
| 38 | Democrats | 26 | 73 | 26 | 67 | 6 |
| 26 | Independents | 63 | 35 | 55 | 30 | 12 |
| 35 | Republicans | 92 | 7 | 86 | 9 | 4 |
| | Sex and marital status | | | | | |
| 47 | Men | 61 | 37 | 55 | 36 | 7 |
| 53 | Women | 57 | 42 | 47 | 45 | 7 |
| 68 | Married | 63 | 37 | Not available | | |
| 32 | Not married | 51 | 47 | Not available | | |
| | Age | | | | | |
| 24 | 18-29 | 58 | 41 | 43 | 44 | 11 |
| 34 | 30-44 | 58 | 42 | 54 | 36 | 8 |
| 23 | 45-59 | 60 | 39 | 55 | 39 | 5 |
| 19 | 60 and older | 63 | 36 | 54 | 41 | 4 |
| 8 | First-time voter | 60 | 39 | Not available | | |
| | Occupation | | | | | |
| 30 | Professional/manager | 62 | 37 | 57 | 32 | 9 |
| 13 | White-collar | 59 | 40 | 50 | 41 | 8 |
| 14 | Blue-collar | 53 | 46 | 47 | 46 | 5 |
| 3 | Unemployed | 31 | 68 | 39 | 51 | 8 |
| 21 | Use computer home/job | 62 | 37 | Not available | | |
| 26 | Union household | 45 | 53 | 43 | 48 | 6 |
| | Income* | | | | | |
| 15 | Under $12,500 | 46 | 53 | 42 | 51 | 6 |
| 27 | $12,500-$24,999 | 57 | 42 | 44 | 46 | 8 |
| 21 | $25,000-$34,999 | 59 | 40 | 52 | 39 | 7 |
| 18 | $35,000-$50,000 | 67 | 32 | 59 | 32 | 8 |
| 13 | Over $50,000 | 68 | 31 | 63 | 26 | 9 |
| | Education | | | | | |
| 8 | Less than high school | 50 | 49 | 46 | 51 | 2 |
| 30 | High school graduate | 60 | 39 | 51 | 43 | 4 |
| 30 | Some college | 60 | 38 | 55 | 35 | 7 |
| 29 | College graduate | 59 | 40 | 52 | 35 | 11 |
| | Race and ethnic group | | | | | |
| 86 | White | 66 | 34 | 55 | 36 | 7 |
| 10 | Black | 9 | 90 | 11 | 85 | 3 |
| 3 | Hispanic | 33 | 65 | 33 | 59 | 6 |

**TABLE 13.1**
*Continued*

| Percent of 1984 total | | 1984 Reagan | 1984 Mondale | 1980 Reagan | 1980 Carter | 1980 Anderson |
|---|---|---|---|---|---|---|
| | Religion | | | | | |
| 51 | White Protestant | 73 | 26 | 63 | 31 | 6 |
| 26 | Catholic | 55 | 44 | 49 | 42 | 7 |
| 3 | Jewish | 32 | 66 | 39 | 45 | 15 |
| 15 | White Born-again Christian | 80 | 20 | 63 | 33 | 3 |
| | Region | | | | | |
| 24 | East | 52 | 47 | 47 | 42 | 9 |
| 28 | Midwest | 61 | 38 | 51 | 40 | 7 |
| 29 | South | 63 | 36 | 52 | 44 | 3 |
| 18 | West | 59 | 40 | 53 | 34 | 10 |
| | Community size | | | | | |
| 12 | Large cities | 36 | 62 | 35 | 54 | 8 |
| 55 | Suburbs-small cities | 57 | 42 | 53 | 37 | 8 |
| 33 | Rural and towns | 69 | 29 | 54 | 39 | 5 |

*Family income categories in 1980: under $10,000, $10,000-$14,999, $15,000-$24,999, $25,000-$50,000, and over $50,000.

SOURCES: The New York Times/CBS News poll; *New York Times*, 8 November 1984.

Jews, members of union households, residents of large cities, and persons either unemployed or with the lowest family incomes. These were not only minorities in an ethnic or political sense; even when added together, they constituted only a minority of the total population. However strongly Mondale won their support, he could not—and did not—win the presidency through their loyalty alone.

While Reagan won majorities in most groups, he did not show the same depth of support in all elements of the population. These relative differences are more significant for the long run, for they reveal the character of the 1984 Republican majority and provide hints about its durability and policy directions. Three points are important: the continuity of a shrunken New Deal coalition; the particular strengths of the newer Reagan coalition; and the significant shifts of some groups over the four-year period between his two national victories.

The New Deal coalition developed 50 years ago in the era of Franklin D. Roosevelt. Democrats won enduring support from a number of overlapping groups: ethnic minorities, particularly Catholics, blacks, and Jews; blue-collar workers, especially those in unions; urban residents; and white southerners. First forged in the political heat of the Great Depression, the alliance was solidified as new voters entered the electorate with strong Democratic loyalties, and strengthened through the policy actions of the party's leaders. Even in 1965, two decades after the death of Roosevelt, Democrats held a lead over Republicans of almost 2 to 1 in basic party loyalties, and had lost the presidency only twice in nine contests.[3]

The outlines of that coalition are still evident in the 1984 results, if we focus on the relative position of groups. Racial minorities and Jews voted Democratic. Catholics did support Reagan, but in much lower proportions than Protestants, maintaining the established religious division. Union members and their families stayed with the Democrats, and blue-collar workers provided only a thin Republican plurality.

The most dramatic change from the past is among white southerners. Previously, Democratic loyalty was as traditional in Dixie as fried chicken. By 1984, tastes had changed, and the white vote in the South was more solidly for Reagan (at 72 percent) than in any region. Among the other New Deal groups, the Democratic problem was not dramatic losses but drift—the slow erosion of numbers and loyalty. There are now fewer blue-collar workers, urban residents, union members, and therefore a smaller obvious base of support. Other groups, such as Catholics, maintained their numbers but lessened their loyalty. Economic growth and the Democratic programs of the welfare state enabled many of the party's faithful to achieve security and prosperity, and to turn their attention to new political appeals.[4]

This weakening of the Democrats is evident in two other long-term trends. The first is the gradual decline of party loyalty itself, as Independents become a larger part of the population. Until recently, this trend did not affect the Democrats alone, as they were able to maintain a rough 3 to 2 advantage among those who stayed loyal to either major party. Nevertheless, they were more likely to suffer from this tendency. As the majority party, they were more subject to defection. Furthermore, the Democrats have been less adept at using advertising and the campaign technology that is critical in appealing to an independent electorate. They have relied more on party loyalty and mass organization to win their votes, and were therefore more vulnerable to declines in these influences.

Young voters have been a second problem for the party. As the children of the "baby boom" and the succeeding "baby bust" entered adulthood, they did not simply take on their parents' partisanship, but frequently declared themselves Independents.[5] By 1984, they held enormous potential for change in national politics. Comprising two of every five voters, but without firmly established loyalties, they were readily susceptible to new strategies and arguments. Until 1984, Democrats had renewed their strength each year by doing relatively well among political neophytes. In this election, youth turned toward the Republicans, as three of every five new voters chose Reagan.

Furthermore, this group was more likely to identify with the Republican party (by a 39 to 34 margin) and to vote for the Republican party in House elections (by a 50 to 41 edge). These results are a dark portent for the Democratic future. The party might be able to dig out after Mondale's landslide defeat, but it could not easily sustain a continuing hail of rocks.[6]

The Reagan coalition in 1984, while broad, was not simply a cross-section of the nation. In part, it was the reverse image of the remaining elements of the New Deal coalition, with particular strength among whites, Protestants, persons of higher income, and those in higher-status jobs. It also comprised more novel elements. The best way to see this characteristic is not to look at the voting in 1984 alone, but to compare this election to others, by focusing on shifts among some groups from their voting in 1980 and 1976.

In table 13.2, we have isolated those demographic groups that increased their Republican vote by over 10 percentage points, either between the two Reagan victories or over the longer period from 1976 to 1984. Clearly, the Republicans have become a more defined conservative party over the past four years, relying strongly on an ideological appeal and on groups responsive to such appeals. However, elections cannot be won in the United States by such narrow coalitions. More significant may be the longer, eight-year drift to the party of ''middle America''—blue-collar workers, high school graduates, and persons of moderate income.

**TABLE 13.2**
**Major Changes in Republican Vote—1976, 1980, 1984**

| | Change 1980 to 1984 | Change 1976 to 1980 |
|---|---|---|
| Men | +4 | +9 |
| Conservatives | +9 | +2 |
| White Protestants | +10 | +6 |
| Born-again Christians | +17 | NA |
| Catholics | +6 | +5 |
| High-school graduates | +9 | +6 |
| Blue-collar workers | +6 | +6 |
| Moderate income* | +10 | +1 |
| White southerners | +11 | +9 |
| Independents | +8 | +2 |
| Age 18-29 | +15 | −4 |
| Age 60 and older | +9 | +2 |
| White (non-Hispanic) | +11 | +3 |
| Rural and town residents | +15 | +1 |

*In 1976-80, 44 percent of population, earning $10,000-$25,000. In 1980 and 1984, 48 percent of population, earning $12,500-$35,000.

There have been few trends over this period in the Democratic direction. Blacks, Jews, and the unemployed have increased their support, but they have no other companions on their lonesome partisan road. While Hispanics remain Democratic, their loyalties have become less intense. In comparison to men, women voted relatively Democratic, but the "gender gap" fell below the party's expectations. Another unfavorable straw in the wind was the large Republican plurality (62–37) among computer users.[7]

These data do not in themselves demonstrate that there was fundamental political change in the 1984 election, but they do raise the possibility. We have considered only the presidential election, and a full analysis must also take into account the congressional results and other trends. We will reconsider the meaning of the election results after describing the course of the presidential campaign.

## The Campaign

For all the difference it made, America could have skipped the 1984 campaign. Whether the election had been held in the preprimary winter, after the summer conventions, or in November's fall, Ronald Reagan would have won an overwhelming victory.

Almost half the voters had made their decision at the beginning of the year, and only a fourth even waited for the televised debates.[8] As a result, as seen in figure 13.2, there was little change in sentiment over the course of the year. There were some variations, particularly rallies toward Mondale after the Democratic convention in San Francisco and after the first debate. The dominant trend, however, was simple consolidation, as the electorate crystallized its sentiments into a rock-hard majority for Reagan.

### *The Republican Mood*

Generally, campaigns can be waged on issues or personalities. The Reagan effort used both. The president was credited with achieving prosperity for the nation, with the economy registering an astonishing growth of over 10 percent early in 1984, along with low inflation. In foreign policy, Reagan boasted that "America is back, standing tall," citing the successful American intervention in Grenada and increased military capability. Even setbacks such as the lost lives of marines in Lebanon were presented as honorable deaths.

Beyond his record, Reagan was personally attractive. In the government of the United States, the president is not only the head of the government but the head of state. In the latter role, Reagan was a superb "cheerleader," using his ceremonial position to enhance the nation's congenital optimism and to underline its beliefs. He was "America as it imagined itself to be—the bearer of the

**FIGURE 13.2**
**The 1984 Campaign in Opinion Polls**

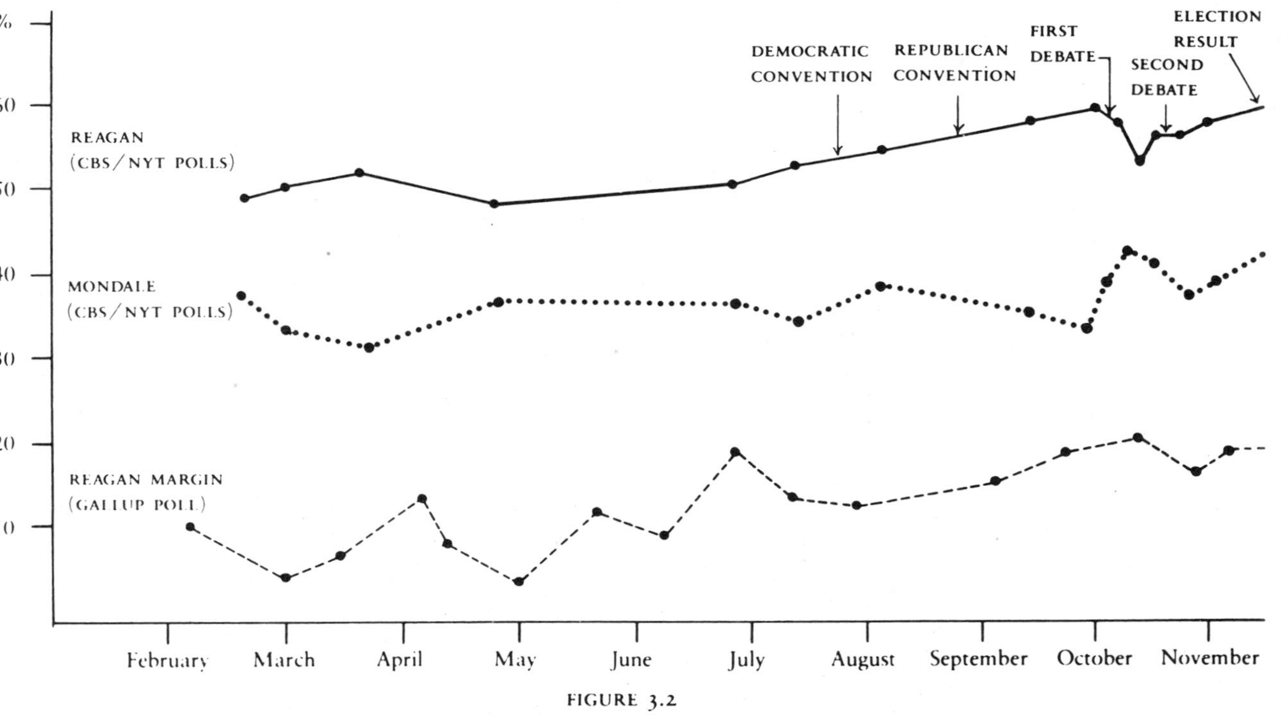


SOURCE: CBS News/New York Times poll and the Gallup poll.

traditional Main Street values of family and neighborhood, of thrift, industry, and charity instead of government intervention where self-reliance failed.''[9]

Reagan did not rely on charm alone. The considerable resources of an incumbent administration were used to make appeals to various groups and to rebut the opposition. Mondale criticized Reagan's failure to meet with Soviet leaders. Reagan countered by inviting the Soviet foreign minister to the White House. Democrats attacked his environmental record. He responded by signing wilderness legislation at the bird sanctuary on the Potomac. The president was berated as callous toward the needy. He replied by opening a housing project for the elderly in New York. Farm complaints were met by a new loan guarantee program, and industrial unemployment by a promise to reduce steel imports.

The president made conspicuous use of his formal powers. The executive rose garden became a telegenic background for the appointment of Hispanics and the visit of the Israeli prime minister. The administration tried to gain credit for encouraging news, such as a national increase in college board scores or a decrease in crime rates. It avoided potential bad news until after the election, such as its tax program or the expected size of the budget deficit. Even a wary press could do little more than report ''the news'' as defined by the White House.[10]

The Republican campaign artfully promoted both the record and the man, equating all the positive aspects of American life with the president individually and with administration programs generally. Advertisers who had previously produced upbeat commercials for Pepsi-Cola now filmed ''scenes from a sunlit land in which no one was sick, sad, fat, infirm, or afflicted by ring around the collar.'' As the president spoke of a ''springtime of hope,'' the television spots proclaimed, ''It's morning again in America,'' showing a wedding, a family moving into a new home, fertile fields, and rugged construction workers.[11] Literally wrapping Reagan in the American flag, the longest advertisement concluded with a virile policeman raising the star-spangled banner to a new patriotic anthem:

> I'm proud to be an American, where at least I know I'm free,
> And I won't forget the men who died who gave that flag to me;
> And I'll gladly stand up—next to you—
> And defend her still today,
> 'Cause there ain't no doubt I love this land;
> God Bless the U.S.A.

### *The Democratic Messages*

In their search for an upset, the Democrats changed strategies a number of times. These revisions made the Mondale campaign appear to be uncertain and mismanaged. There were embarrassingly bad decisions, such as opening the formal campaign at a New York Labor Day rally hours before the parade began. The fundamental problem, however, was not so much the defects of the Democrats but the advantages of the Republicans. Each effort by Mondale and Geraldine Ferraro was met by the frustrating polls, which continued to show a steady Reagan lead.

The first Democratic problem was a self-inflicted wound. As was usual for national candidates, Ferraro had promised to make her income tax returns public, as well as those of her husband, John Zaccaro, a wealthy real estate broker. A week before the statements were due, however, she announced that her husband had refused to release his personal returns, leading the press and public to assume that the couple had something to hide. Eventually, Ferraro achieved a press victory from the controversy. In a 100-minute televised conference, she disclosed all of her finances, showed that she and Zaccaro had paid large income taxes, and won the open admiration of her questioners. Nevertheless, the campaign was damaged, costing the Democrats time they needed to maintain their postconvention momentum.

More fundamentally, the financial disclosures tarnished the luster of Ferraro, who was being held to particularly high standards as the first woman running nationally. Democrats and feminists could legitimately complain that financial disclosure rules were written on the sexist assumption that men were the chief wage-earners in a family. Still, most voters probably shared that assumption, and they became permanently suspicious of the Democratic running mate. Before the controversy, the congresswoman was relatively unknown but favorably regarded by a 2 to 1 margin. From that point, she became familiar to the public, but 35 percent regarded her critically, almost as many as were favorable. Ultimately, Ferraro may have gained a few votes for the Democratic ticket, but what had once seemed to be an asset became little more than a balance of gains and losses.[12]

The campaign then turned back toward issues, or, at least, jogged in that direction. Mondale's challenge on taxes and the federal deficit had originally upset the Reagan camp. Contradictory statements were made by Republican leaders, continuing the division evident at the party convention. To counter Mondale, the president said he would increase taxes only as a "last resort" and promised that individual income tax rates would not increase. To correct the deficit, he left open the possibility of increasing revenues through "tax simplification." Reagan then dismissed the problem, optimistically quipping, "To our opponents every day is April 15; to us, every day is the Fourth of July."

Governmental finance was one of the many issues Mondale attempted to address. Because polls showed that Reagan policies were less popular than the president himself, the Mondale organization believed that a continued "issues strategy" would eventually lead to a national day of revelation. Voters would come to understand that only Mondale would do what a majority wanted in regard to deficits, or a nuclear freeze, or environmental controls, or civil rights. The flawed premise of this strategy was that it viewed a presidential election as a gigantic public opinion poll on an accumulation of issues. A presidential election does involve issues, but it is most simply a choice of leadership to deal with recognized societal needs by acceptable means. While voters did recognize the problems cited by Mondale, they continued to see Reagan as the better leader to revolve these problems.[13]

Tax increases were hardly likely to win the election for Mondale. Not only are they unpopular, they are technical and unemotional. Religion, the second major issue of the campaign, was more evocative. Reagan, appearing at a prayer breakfast after the Republican convention, condemned opponents of compulsory school prayer as ''intolerant,'' and argued that ''religion and politics are necessarily related,'' raising fears of a mingling of church and state. Mondale attacked evangelist Jerry Falwell, arguing that the fundamentalist minister would influence the choice of Supreme Court justices. Opponents of abortion shadowed Ferraro on the campaign trail, vehemently presenting their right-to-life position against her advocacy of women's right-to-choice. As a devout Catholic woman, Ferraro was particularly vulnerable to these attacks.

In these controversies, the Democratic candidates again were on the popular side. Strong majorities opposed Falwell's Moral Majority and the absolutist right-to-life position. However, few votes were cast on this basis, so the issue of religion did not aid the ticket. The larger effect was to distract attention, preventing the Democrats from making a coherent attack on the strong Reagan fortress. As one Republican leader put it, ''You don't win many votes by raising taxes and arguing with archbishops.''[14]

A third Democratic emphasis was on the danger of nuclear war. A television ad inspired by rock videos showed the ''red alert'' telephone at the White House ringing, foretelling an imminent foreign attack. Reagan's program for a ''Star Wars'' missile defense, it warned, would mean that computers, not the president, would be in charge, making a nuclear holocaust more likely. While the nuclear freeze movement had shown strong popular support in the past, foreign and defense policy was not stressed consistently by the Democrats. In the conflict with Reagan's patriotic themes, Mondale was unable to gain any advantage.

In the last weeks of the campaign, although still unable to make substantial gains, the Democrats recovered the enthusiasm and the message of their national convention. Mondale found an appealing theme, speaking now of his philosophy instead of his programs, emphasizing fairness instead of finances, displaying emotion instead of expertise, invoking values instead of advertisements. To larger and more enthusiastic crowds, he declared, ''I would rather lose a race about decency than win one about self-interest.'' In his closing effort, wrote David Broder, Mondale rested his case "on the best of the Democratic tradition which he embodies," while showing himself to be "an effective, attractive and decent politician."[15]

## *The Television Debates*

The Democrats' only true opportunity to gain victory against the overwhelming odds was in the televised debates, which were actually joint press conferences. To win Reagan's consent to the debates, the Democrats had to accept limitations on their number, timing, and format. Still, they had gained an equal forum. Now national television audiences of more than 100 million people would see Reagan and Mondale (twice, on 7 and 21 October) or George Bush and Ferraro (only once, on 11 October) answering the same questions, on the same austere platform, before the same nonpartisan audience of the League of Women Voters.

Simultaneously, the debates sent two kinds of messages. The manifest message was the positions of the candidates on the issues, as posed by news reporters. The contenders informed viewers of their stands on matters as diverse as the likelihood of Armageddon and the control of illegal immigration, while questioning each other's records. Previous research has shown that voters do learn from these discussions, and this effect probably occurred in 1984 as well.[16]

More dramatic was the latent message. Most viewers would find it difficult to sort out the claims, statistics, and refutations of the debaters. They could more easily judge their competence, trustworthiness, and abilities. This meant more than the candidates' images, or personalities; it meant their character, their leadership and vision, their basic fitness for the highest offices the electorate cold confer. Voters could sense these qualities with their own eyes and ears—and the news media were more than willing to help the audience by providing instant analyses of "Who Won?"

On these grounds, the debates provided surprises. In the first, Mondale made a strong impression by combining courtesy toward the president with a pointed attack on his policies and, even more, his competence. Mondale's theme was, "There's a difference between being a quarterback and a cheerleader." He gibed at the president, "It's not what he doesn't know that bothers me, it's what he knows for sure [that] just ain't so." In closing, Reagan added to his problems, by admitting that he was "confused," and by giving a rambling statement, cluttered with statistics, as if he were a college student who had crammed too much for a final exam.

In the most dramatic moment of the debate, made more dramatic by later television editing, Mondale responded to Reagan's use of a line from the 1980 debate with Jimmy Carter:

> *Reagan:* You know, I wasn't going to say this at all, but I can't help it: there you go again. . . .
>
> *Mondale:* Now, Mr. President, you said: "There you go again." Right. Remember the last time you said that?
>
> *Reagan:* Um hmm.
>
> *Mondale:* You said it when President Carter said that you were going to cut Medicare. And you said: "Oh, no, there you go again, Mr. President." And what did you do right after the election? You went out and tried to cut $20 billion out of Medicare.[17]

The harmful effects of the president's mediocre performance were exaggerated by adverse press commentaries. As the week went on, the public came to believe not simply that Mondale had won one contest but that there had been no contest. The *Wall Street Journal*, usually a bastion of conservatism, then further worsened the Republican situation by printing a long-prepared article that raised the question of the president's age. Was his mediocre performance in the debate an indication that the nation's oldest chief executive was unable to continue?

The Republicans took a number of steps to limit the damage from the first debate. Reagan campaigned more vigorously to demonstrate his health. Mondale's criticisms on Social Security were rebutted by a firm pledge to maintain present and future benefits. Negative advertising against Mondale began to appear on television. Particular attention was directed toward the next debates.

The Bush-Ferraro confrontation became a preliminary bout before the rematch of the presidential candidates. The incumbent took an aggressive stance, to emphasize his experience in office. To undo the Reagan losses, he tried to stress the president's command of the government. In enthusiastic, even sycophantic tones, he told of Reagan meeting the Soviet foreign minister: "I wish everybody could have seen that one—the president, giving the facts to Gromyko in all of these nuclear meetings—excellent, right on top of that subject matter."

Ferraro's purpose was to prove her competence, and to dispel doubts raised by her sex and relative inexperience. She presented herself more as a lawyer and a Mondale advocate, rather than the feisty campaigner she was on the road. Only once did she allow herself to display anger. Responding to Bush's position on U.S. policy in Lebanon, she shot back, "Let me just say, first of all, that I almost resent, Vice-President Bush, your patronizing attitude that you have to teach me about foreign policy."

The second presidential debate centered on foreign policy. Mondale again stressed Reagan's competence, repeatedly insisting that he did not meet the basic standards of the presidential office, "to be in charge of facts and run our government and strengthen our nation." On this occasion, however, Reagan was more than equal to the challenge. Presenting himself as an advocate of nuclear disarmament, he stated a simple credo, "A nuclear war cannot be won and must never be fought." On the critical issue of his age, he ended all discussion with the best one-liner of the campaign: "I will not make age an issue in this campaign. I am not going to exploit for political purposes my opponent's youth and inexperience."

The overall effect of the debates was to assure Reagan's victory. At the first confrontation, Mondale had changed the tone of the campaign. He was now taken seriously by the public and press, and party leaders, once reluctant supporters, became open backers. While he performed less strongly in the second trail, he still showed his competence and knowledge. Among those voters who relied on these shows to decide their vote, the Democratic candidate gained three out of four votes. His problem was that less than a tenth of the electorate used the debates to determine their choice.[18]

By the time of the second debate, expectations had changed. Mondale was like a pole-vaulter, facing a higher challenge with each success. He now needed a spectacular second performance to make further gains. Particularly important was the question, raised for a brief moment after the first debate, of the aging president's competence. Reagan no longer had to meet high standards. He needed only to reassure the electorate that he was of sound mind. Ultimately, these forums served only to bring the campaign back to the central focus, the Reagan record. "By revealing more of both men," wrote one journalist, "the debates cut down to size some of the issues that [had] been dominating the campaign: Mondale's image as a wimp, Reagan's as an unparalleled communicator. . . . But by pruning back these personal issues, the debates suggested how secondary they may be."[19]

Polls underlined the debates' limited impact. Mondale gained both a more favorable personal evaluation and higher standing in the expected vote. Nevertheless, Reagan still won personal approval from two-thirds of the voters, and his expected vote barely changed. Rather than changing minds, the debates helped people to settle their minds. The first debate brought Mondale the voters who were likely to mobilize behind him eventually, just as the second debate reinforced the support Reagan already had. Television provided the stage for a drama whose ending was already foreshadowed.[20]

## *The Campaign's Meaning*

Despite its limited impact on the final vote, the campaign was more than sound and fury. The mood and messages of the candidates signified something, the future direction of American public policy.

As they campaigned, Reagan and Mondale sometimes followed the established signposts of American politics as they moved toward the center of the political road. Both camps tried to depict the opposition as extremist, yet both imitated each other's proven appeals. With the fervor of a New Dealer, Reagan made heroes of Roosevelt and Truman. The president defended the Social Security System, praised the former Shah of Iran for his low-income housing projects, and deplored the exploitation of Mexican immigrants. Mondale often adopted the language of traditional conservatism. He treated federal budget deficits as a mortal sin, ridiculed the possibility of sharing antimissile defense systems with the Soviet Union, and enshrined the independence of the Supreme Court.

These movements toward the center still left the candidates far apart on different sides of the political road. William Safire correctly advised the voters the day before the balloting: "Do not be misled: The persuasive leaning-center-ward during the campaign is all a lie, while the phony-sounding professions about different 'visions of America' is the truth."[21] In his presidency, Reagan had provided ample evidence of his beliefs in limited government and assertive foreign policy. In a constant public life, Mondale had faithfully shown his commitment to social welfare and diplomatic accommodation.

The candidates spoke, and the citizenry responded decisively. But what was its reply?

## Meanings and Theories

Interpreting a presidential election is different from scientific explanation. We cannot design a controlled experiment, or repeat the campaign while varying the candidates, the issues, or the environment. Politics is not physics. It is more like meteorology, where we try to understand the causes of hurricanes while recognizing that winds are sometimes inexplicable. In reviewing the 1984 election, we will deal with four interpretations.

### *A Triumph of Personality*

The most common explanation of Reagan's victory is Reagan himself. The president's success is not due to his record or his philosophy, but to his "image." In this interpretation, tens of millions of Americans voted for a likable individual, who successfully combined stirring if vague rhetoric, a confident personality, an actor's communication skills, and a verbal commitment to religion and family.

The personal emphasis was evident in Reagan's campaign. A film biography of the president, the keynote of his effort, pictured him as an attractive individual, ceremoniously and dramatically representing the nation. Reagan was shown meeting American troops in Korea, walking toward the sunset with his wife, commemorating the Normandy invasion of World War II, cheerfully surviving the 1981 assassination attempt, and celebrating the American Olympic victories. Almost nothing in the film dealt with specific programs and objectives.

Reagan's critics often share this personal interpretation. Indeed, it is comforting to Democrats to believe that they lost only to a "great communicator," who will soon be gone from politics. His success is denigrated by these critics as indicating that Americans have abandoned their judgment to a "kindly grandfather." Walter Mondale himself felt compelled to profess his personal liking for the president, even as he attacked Reagan's policies and his inattention to the duties of the chief executive.

In an extension of this emphasis on personality, Mondale gets the personal blame for the Democrats' defeat. As a campaign joke had it, when Reagan met with the Cabinet, the president fell asleep, but in a Mondale administration, the Cabinet would fall asleep. The former Vice-President was seen as dull "Norwegian wood," a poor performer on television, beset by inefficient campaign organization, and harmed by inchoate advertising. The problem for the Democrats was not the message, but the messenger.

Certainly this interpretation has some validity. The Reagan effort did focus on his personal attributes, as summarized in the repeated slogan, "Leadership That's Working." The president's campaign stops featured ceremony, flags, and good feelings, while avoiding issues and drowning reporters' questions in the noise of helicopter engines. The Mondale organization's deficiencies were also evident, in poor scheduling and in its handling of the Ferraro financial issue. The Democratic slogan, "They're Fighting for Our Future," was neither memorable nor effective, since it conveyed no symbolic meaning and defined no difference between the major parties. (Did voters need to be assured that Mondale and Ferraro were in favor of the future? Would anyone believe that Reagan and Bush were against it?)

All this can be granted without seeing the election as decided on personal grounds. In the glow of election victory, Reagan appears greatly loved, but the evidence is not consistent. During the depths of the 1982 recession, his popularity in the Gallup poll fell below that of all recent chief executives. Even when he recovered his popular standing, he stood little better at the beginning of the election year than Jimmy Carter at a comparable point in 1980, and below Richard Nixon's level in 1972. Moreover, the president also had high levels of *dis*approval, and some of these antipathies showed in the election vote. A universally admired person would not have 91 percent of a major voting bloc (blacks) in opposition. Reagan did arouse passion, but also division.[22]

Reagan's popularity, while substantial by election day, was also substantive. His vaunted communication skills would have done him little good if unemployment had remained at the painful levels of 1982, or if the United States were involved in a Vietnam-like war in Central America, or if the Social Security System had gone bankrupt. To show the limited impact of simple imagery, Amitai Etzioni suggested, "One need simply imagine that instead of talking about God, family and country, the president was extolling Zen Buddhism, unilateral disarmament and sexual license. His rating would of course crash within a week."[23] Reagan was, to be sure, a good salesman, and his product may have been wrapped attractively, even deceptively, but there still was a product.

Criticism of Mondale also seems exaggerated. Within his party, the Minnesotan was not an extremist candidate, who might be expected to alienate mainstream Democrats. Rather, Mondale was a very appropriate Democratic candidate, personifying the party's philosophy and recent history. His nomination was not a personal coup but the choice both of the leadership and a plurality of the rank and file. His legitimacy was further validated in the election, when he won the votes of 73 percent of identified Democrats, more than Carter, even in the face of Reagan's swollen vote.

Despite complaints after the election, Mondale was not regarded by the public as a poor candidate—except in comparison to his opponent. Even at the nadir of his campaign, in September, pluralities thought the Democrat more caring and less reckless than Reagan. Although the president was considered better on other qualities, Mondale still was rated better than either Jimmy Carter or the 1980 version of Ronald Reagan on five of six other qualities, such as competence, judgment, and understanding of problems.[24]

Postelection complaints about the Mondale organization conflict with earlier descriptions of its awesome efficiency. Blaming it later for the election defeat is a search for scapegoats rather than a discovery of causation. The basic feature of the campaign, after all, was that very little changed after the conventions, and that a Reagan victory was almost preordained. To the extent that there was change, particularly in the last month, the trend benefited the Democrats. Mondale could claim the credit for these limited gains because of his performance in the debates and his vigorous closing efforts. The election was a victory for Reagan, but not a personal defeat for Mondale.

### *A Policy Choice*

A second interpretation of the 1984 balloting pictures it as a "mandate" for the president's program. After the 1980 elections, Reagan used this argument to gain his legislative program, even though most observers saw the result more of a repudiation of Jimmy Carter than an endorsement of the Republican platform.[25] Victorious politicians prefer such explanations, for they provide the legitimacy of popular approval for their programs.

Policy choices in elections are difficult to accomplish. They require, at least, that candidates take definable positions, that the voters correctly perceive these positions, and that the voters then cast their ballots on the basis of these positions. Even when all of these conditions are met, an election may still not be clearly the result of issue voting.[26]

In 1984, Reagan's campaign gave little attention to future policy directions. Proclaiming in victory that "you ain't seen nothing yet," Reagan left the electorate to wonder what would follow, other than "four more years" in the same direction. Even at the general level of philosophy, it is difficult to interpret the election as a mandate. Only a fraction of Reagan's voters defended their vote as the choice of a "real conservative," even fewer than in 1980. Furthermore, compared to the previous contest, both the congressional elections and voting on state referendums evidenced less of an ideological character.

When voters dealt with specific policies for the future, they made little connection between their vote for Reagan and their issue preferences. Table 13.3 demonstrates the point by summarizing the results of two polls. On five significant issues, Reagan's position was backed only by minorities, usually small, of the voters. Nevertheless, the president was endorsed by a majority of these respondents. The Republican campaign successfully evaded an election based on future policy decisions. The focus became the president's ability to drive the engine of national government, perhaps in reverse gear, rather than the particular road he would travel.

Tax policy provides an important specific example. Voters agreed that taxes would go up, but also blamed the Democrats for the budget deficit. On election day, government spending and the deficit had become the most im-

**TABLE 13.3**
**Policy Positions and the Vote in 1984**

| | Favor Reagan, favor position | Favor Reagan, oppose position | Oppose Reagan, oppose position |
|---|---|---|---|
| Equal Rights Amendment | 32% | 27% | 34% |
| Pollution controls | 10 | 42 | 39 |
| Nuclear freeze | 23 | 29 | 37 |
| Aid to the poor | 34 | 14 | 46 |
| Abortion | 28 | 31 | 32 |

SOURCES: Harris poll of 24 July 1984, as reported in *National Journal* 16 (11 August 1984): 1542; for abortion issue, the *New York Times*, 19 August 1984, A1.

portant issues, stressed by a fourth of the electorate. By then, however, some of these citizens had apparently become convinced that Reagan would find a way to restrain taxes, others were expressing such hopes rather than convictions, and still others wanted Reagan even if it meant higher taxes. Whatever the motives, even these fiscal worrywarts gave Reagan 59 percent of their votes.[27]

On other issues as well, the Reagan coalition included substantial proportions that disagreed with the president on the issues. Overall, two-thirds of his backers agreed with him on an issue they considered of major importance, but a fifth disagreed with their chosen leader on some vital question. For example, 13 percent of the president's own backers stressed defense policy and also favored a nuclear freeze; another tenth both emphasized poverty as a national problem and wanted to increase aid to the poor.[28]

These patterns make it difficult for the president to claim a prospective mandate from the voters for any policy innovations. He did not present the electorate with a new agenda, and it, therefore, could not endorse an innovative program. Columnist Mark Shields correctly concluded, "In Reagan's last campaign he once again ran against the past, making the 1984 vote a referendum on the 1980 results." In so doing, he achieved "a landslide without a mandate." The landslide itself still needs an explanation.[29]

### *A Retrospective Judgment*

Theoretical explanations of voting behavior emphasize that voters are likely to vote retrospectively rather than prospectively. They judge the past records of candidates and parties rather than look toward the future. This makes sense for an electorate that has relatively little time or inclination to devote to political thought, and that inevitably cannot know the future. Of course, voters do worry about what will happen in the next four years, but they use past performance as a means to choose future leadership. If unforeseen problems arise—as they surely will—it is better to have a trusted executive dealing with these problems.[30]

The electoral situation in 1984 was particularly appropriate for this kind of judgment. An incumbent president was running, so his performance and programs could be taken as a good indication of his later course—especially in the case of Reagan, who had a consistent public record and ideology. His opponent, Walter Mondale, has been vice-president in the previous administration, so a direct comparison could be made between the two parties' achievements. Furthermore, using the immense control of the White House over the news, the Republicans resolutely focused attention on a matching of the records of the Reagan and "Carter-Mondale" administrations.

The retrospective quality of the election is evident throughout the results and can be documented in four ways. The first is the significance of the economic situation. Reagan's victory was directly correlated to the voters' belief that their own financial situation, and that of the nation, had improved in his term. If the vote had been confined to those who saw the economy as stable or declining, Mondale would have been elected. The effect was the same, but in the opposite direction from 1980, when the perceived decline in the economy was a strong cause of the Carter-Mondale defeat.

A second demonstration of a retrospective vote is found in the stability of the vote from 1980 to 1984. There was relatively little switching between the two elections. As voters were focusing on the past, they reaffirmed their past ballots. Only a tenth of all voters in 1984 changed their electoral choice. However, Reagan got the better of these changes, by 6 to 4. By holding his previous support, and adding new voters, he was able to increase his vote to landslide proportions.*

The third indication is the way voters dealt with policy issues. There was no clear electoral mandate on policy directions. However, there was considerable coherence in evaluations of the ability of the two candidates and the two parties to deal with these issues. Voters might not know *what* to do about a particular policy problem, but they showed far more agreement on *who* they believed more trustworthy and competent in handling the problem. In mid-October, by a 4 to 3 margin, the electorate was more inclined "to trust the future of this country" to the Republicans. The voters considered Reagan and Bush better able to handle the economy, control inflation and the federal budget deficit, keep the nation out of war, stand up to Russia, maintain strong military defenses, and deal with prayers in schools. Democrats were preferred in regard to providing fairness, aid to the poor, and Social Security, but these were not the dominant concerns as the electorate judged the record of the past four years.[31]

Finally, the voters themselves acknowledged the retrospective basis of their judgment. Three out of five cited "strong leadership" and "experience" as major reasons for their decisions, and heavily supported Reagan, who was the only experienced presidential leader in the race. In assessing Reagan's qualifications, the voters were far more favorable in 1984 than in 1980, as actual performance in office led them to give him higher ratings for intelligence, a command of the issues, ability to maintain peace, and even, despite his advancing years, physical capability. As William Schneider wrote, "Vot-

*Of Reagan's 59 percent of the total ballots, 41 percent came from his 1980 supporters, 6 percent from 1980 Carter backers, 10 percent from previous nonvoters, and 2 percent from Anderson voters. Mondale's 41 percent total included 25 percent who had supported Carter, 4 percent who switched away from Reagan, 9 percent previous nonvoters, and 3 percent recruited from Anderson. See *National Journal* 16 (November 10, 1984) :2131.

ers acknowledge that Reagan has done the two things he was elected to do: curb inflation and restore the nation's sense of military security,'' and the electorate then followed ''its traditional inclination—'You don't quarrel with success.' ''[32]

*A Party Realignment*

All elections are significant, but some are more significant, for they may be ''realigning'' votes, in which ''new and durable electoral groupings are formed.''[33] We have already reviewed the shifts in the geographical and demographic bases of the 1984 vote that suggest a new Republican majority coalition in presidential elections. The durability of this majority remains uncertain until future ballots are counted, but there are some indications of relative permanence.

There have been to presidential elections since the death of Franklin Roosevelt and the end of the Second World War. Strikingly, the Democrats have won only one of these contests convincingly, the Johnson landslide of 1964. While the party has managed three other narrow victories, it has lost the remaining six contests, including all but one election since Johnson. This is hardly the record expected of a national majority party. Moreover, the Democrats' losses cannot be laid simply to the faults of individual candidates, even if these men could be separated from the party that nominated them. Overwhelming defeat has been the common fate of Democrats from the party's left (McGovern), right (Carter), and center (Mondale).

Despite this electoral record, Democrats have still ranked as the majority party because of their strength in nonpresidential elections and their lead in the underlying partisan identifications of the voters. Despite its weakened effect in recent years, partisan loyalty remains the single best predictor of vote. The 1984 results, however, point to cracks even in this foundation of the Democratic monolith. After the election, as many citizens considered themselves Republicans as Democrats (32 percent for each party). When those who ''lean'' to a party are added in, Republicans actually commanded a plurality, 47–44. Although the figures were unreliable, because of the immediate effects of the Reagan landslide, they still made much better news for Republicans than Democrats.[34]

When realignments do occur, they are particularly evident among the young and other new voters. The Republicans therefore had special reason to cheer in their advantage (50–42) among the most impressionable younger group, aged under 30. New registrations in 1984 showed the same trend. Although the Democratic efforts got the most publicity, Republicans actually enrolled more new voters, particularly in the party's southern and western strongholds. Nationally, the new 1984 registrants gave Reagan a 61 to 39 majority. While the total vote was barely higher than in 1980 (52.9 percent of the voting age population, a slight increase of 0.3 percent), the Democrats found even less favor among the nonvoters.[35]

A final hint—not proof—of realignment can be found in the closer relationship between the voters' partisanship and their ideological positions, as specified in table 13.4. The entries in the table show the vote for Mondale for various combinations of party loyalty and self-declared ideology. The numbers in parentheses show the percentage received by Carter in 1980 among the same group. Thus, among liberal Democrats—the first entry—Mondale won 88 percent, compared to Carter's 70 percent.

Reading through the figures, we can see that Mondale's support was affected by both factors. Compared to 1980, ideology has become more important—although still less of an influence than party. Mondale consolidated the liberal vote, especially among Democrats and Independents, yet he did worse than Carter among the growing ranks of conservatives. Increasingly, the parties on the presidential level seem to be not only historical labels but coalitions of like-minded men and women.**

These indications of a turn toward the Republicans should not be exaggerated, since the Reagan sweep was not accompanied by a general Republican victory or a clear policy direction. It is possible that the presidency has now become completely nonpartisan, individualized and distinct from the general political system, so that elections for the chief executive have no larger

**TABLE 13.4**
**Party and Ideology in the Presidential Vote, 1984**
**(in percent voting for Mondale)**

| | Partisanship | | | |
|---|---|---|---|---|
| | Democrats | Independents | Republicans | Total |
| Ideology | | | | |
| Liberals | 88 (70) | 60 (50) | 11 (25) | 70 (68) |
| Moderates | 76 (66) | 41 (31) | 7 (11) | 46 (45) |
| Conservatives | 56 (53) | 13 (22) | 4 ( 6) | 18 (24) |
| TOTALS | 73 (72) | 35 (34) | 7 (10) | |

**Another indicator is the ideological composition of the voter coalitions of each candidate. Fully half of Reagan's vote in 1984 came from self-declared conservatives, and only 8 percent from liberals. These figures compared to 42 percent and 10 percent, respectively, in 1980. Mondale received 30 percent of his vote from liberals, and 17 percent from conservatives, compared to 27 percent and 18 percent, respectively, for Carter. The remaining voters are "moderates."

import. Evidence for this view includes Reagan's lack of coattails to aid other Republicans, widespread ticket-splitting, and the victories of Democrats and incumbents for other offices.

In the long run, however, the presidency cannot be totally isolated from the rest of American politics. In his second term, Reagan's actions are likely to strengthen the Republican position. In economic policy, the party's constituency will be reinforced by 1988 through tax laws likely to give even more emphasis to business incentives and less to redistributing income to the poor. Reagan is likely to appoint two to four Supreme Court justices, providing a long-term bulwark for conservative values. The reallocation of electoral votes after the 1990 census will probably show a further shift toward the Sunbelt strongholds of the Republicans. With a skilled political leader and efficient organization, the party will have the opportunity to extend its gains beyond the White House, toward control of the state governments, and, after 1990, the redistricting and capture of Congress.

## Parties and Philosophy

Controversies over ideas will be at the foundation of future party struggles. In 1984, these philosophical differences were unusually evident, even if they weren't always clear in the personal arguments between Mondale and Reagan. The differences between Democrats and Republicans were captured in two different pictures, or images, used by party leaders.

The Republican philosophy could be painted as the 1984 Olympic Games—an event that President Reagan, in fact, did glorify in his acceptance speech. America's athletes gave splendid individual performances, matching the Republican emphasis on individual economic enterprise. The Los Angeles spectacle was turned over by the local and federal governments to private entrepreneurs. Its financial and artistic success seemed to support Reagan's desire to shift programs away from government. Nor did complaints about discrimination or demands for affirmative action intrude on the Olympic celebration. The path to Olympic success was the same as that suggested by Republicans in the broader society. Women competed fully and well, but totally separated, posing no threat to men. Blacks were offered the role model of Carl Lewis, combining natural talent, intense work, and family support to gain four victories, national recognition, and personal wealth.

The Games allowed us to bask in national glory, stirred by repeated raising of the flag, much as the president tried to do in the campaign. For two weeks, because of the Soviet boycott, communism simply disappeared from the world. The president seemed to wish it could happen in reality. The Olympic image of the athlete's lonely struggle to master the physical world was matched by the campaign image of the president's solitary battle to master the political world. Even the Olympic slogan, "Higher, Faster, Stronger," was adapted by the Republicans.

The contrasting Democratic philosophy was pictured well by Governor Mario Cuomo's image, in his Democratic convention keynote speech, of a covered wagon moving toward a new frontier. He identified the occupants of the wagon, not by individual names, but as members of groups—Catholics, minorities, women, the disabled. The wagon's journey, he suggested, in keeping with Democratic party philosophy, requires more than individual effort. Even reaching the frontier involves a common defense against the "red" menace (of Indians, if not communists), and the need for cooperation continues after reaching the promised land.

The world of the frontier is a harsh world. Resources are scarce, so mutual aid is required, to reap crops, raise barns and build schools, pave roads and care for the poor. For Democrats, these activities require government and sacrifice. Taxes will be collected, and sometimes raised. Social standards of "fairness" will be applied, meaning that some people's income will be reduced, and other people will receive benefits. Women and men both work hard on the frontier. With this picture in mind, Democrats see equal rights legislation not as a theoretical issue but as a recognition of reality.

These two pictures, although somewhat exaggerated, do resemble the different portraits drawn by the parties. Republicans stress individualism, optimism, the virtues of economic accumulation, a national melting pot. Democrats stress communalism, the need for sacrifice, social concern, and ethnic diversity. Both are patriotic; both quote Jefferson, Lincoln, and the two Roosevelts; and both champion "family values"; but they speak from different traditions, and offer different visions of the future.

At present, Republican ideas also seem more congenial to the American people. Polls show more people willing to call themselves conservatives, and fewer concerned with promoting social welfare and minority rights. A return to traditional values stressed by Republicans is evident outside of politics, in earlier marriages, an increase in the birthrate, higher enlistments in the military, and nostalgia for the more quiet music of the 1950s. Individuals stress material gain, not social concern, as the themes of the 1970s "me generation" replace those of 1960s activists. Nationalistic pride is evident, from cheers of "U.S.A." at the Olympics to widespread approval of American intervention in Grenada.

Democratic opportunities remain. A new generation of leaders will take over the party by 1988, building on its successes in state and congressional campaigns. Problems of organization and adaptation to the new technology of politics are remediable. The party can also find encouragement in population trends: More women are working and accepting feminist ideas; more minority youth will enter the electorate; more workers are feeling economic constraints.

The basic need for the Democrats, however, is not leadership, organization, or demographic advantage—it is intellectual. Imitating Republican calls for fiscal restraint or rapid armament would make the party little more than a "me too" party, a pale moon in the political solar system, reflecting the light of the opposition's dominant sun. Democrats need not be extremist, or the apparent captive of "special interests," but they do need to be different to obtain different results at the ballot box.[36]

"Fairness" may be the last Democratic answer to the Republican slogan of "opportunity." The electorate responded well to the theme at the Democratic convention and during the campaign, and even Reagan voters acknowledged Mondale's and his party's superiority on this standard. It symbolizes the party's tradition, and resonates in the American tradition. Like the patriotic optimism of Reagan, the cause of fairness can capture the idealism of youth and the imagination of Americans. It means more, however, than dealing with the valid grievances of racial groups, feminists, and other organized groups. A party of fairness also must consider the needs of blue-collar workers barely meeting mortgage payments, white southerners tentatively meeting the demands of a changing society, and women intentionally meeting their schoolchildren at home.

The data of the 1984 election, and the trends they reveal, do still show a likely Republican dominance in presidential elections. But future events are not fully predictable, and leadership and ideas can change politics. Geraldine Ferraro offered the party a theme to combine its ideals with traditional values: "When we find jobs for . . . the unemployed in this country, you know we'll make our economy stronger and that will be a patriotic act. When we reduce the deficits and we cut interest rates, . . . young people can buy houses, that's pro-family and that will be a patriotic act. . . . When we stop the arms race, we make this a safer, saner world, and that's a patriotic act."[37]

Ferraro is emblematic of the Democrats' possibilities. Her nomination extended opportunities for women and a white ethnic group. Her words may suggest the best way for the party to counter a new Republican majority.

## Notes

1. Walter Mondale's defeat in the Electoral College was not quite as severe as that of Alfred E. Landon, who won only the eight electoral votes of Maine and Vermont in 1936. Since that time, however, seven electoral votes had been added, with the admission of Alaska, Hawaii, and the District of Columbia, enabling Reagan to surpass Franklin Roosevelt's total of 523.
2. See Gerald Pomper, "Classification of Presidential Elections," *Journal of Politics* 29 (August 1967): 535–66; Walter Dean Burnham, *Critical Elections and the Mainsprings of American Politics* (New York: Norton, 1970).
3. Kristi Andersen, *The Creation of a Democratic Majority* (Chicago: University of

Chicago Press, 1979); Aage Clausen et al., "Electoral Myth and Reality: The 1964 Election," *American Political Science Review* 59 (June 1965): 321–36.

4. These changes could be clearly seen in the 1970s, and were noted in Norman Nie et al., *The Changing American Voter* (Cambridge: Harvard University Press, 1976), chap. 13. The theoretical basis is provided by V. O. Key, "Secular Realignment and the Party System," *Journal of Politics* 21 (May 1959): 198–210.
5. See Pomper, *Voters' Choice* (New York: Harper, 1975), chap. 5; Helmut Norpoth and Jerrold Rusk, "Partisan Dealignment in the American Electorate," *American Political Science Review* 76 (September 1982): 522–37; Martin Wattenberg, *Decline of American Political Parties* (Cambridge: Harvard University Press, 1984), chaps. 3, 4.
6. The New York Times/CBS News poll, as reported by Adam Clymer in the *New York Times*, November 11, 1984, p. 30.
7. All data not otherwise cited are from the CBS News/New York Times poll, either derived from the original data made available by CBS News or as reported in the *New York Times*, November 8, 1984, p. A19.
8. Los Angeles Times exit poll, reported in *National Journal* 16 (November 10, 1984): 2131.
9. "Campaign '84: The Inside Story," *Newsweek*, November/December 1984, p. 38.
10. Hedrick Smith, *New York Times*, September 19, 1984, p. A1.
11. The Republican television campaign is described in "Campaign '84," pp. 87–90.
12. CBS News/New York Times polls of August, September, and twice in October. In the election day exit poll, a tenth of the voters said that the vice-presidential candidates were a major factor in their vote. Of these, the Democrats won six of ten votes. In the *Los Angeles Times* exit poll, however, only 4 percent cited the vice-presidential candidates. Of these, 56 percent preferred Bush.
13. See Jeffrey Smith, *American Presidential Elections: Trust and the Rational Voter* (New York: Praeger, 1980).
14. The opinion data are from William Schneider, in *National Journal* 16 (September 8, 1984): 1690–91, and Adam Clymer, *New York Times*, November 25, 1984, Section *IV*, p. 2E. The quotation is from Frank Holman, New Jersey Republican state chairman.
15. *Washington Post*, October 31, 1984.
16. Alan Abramowitz, "The Impact of a Presidential Debate on Voter Rationality," *American Journal of Political Science* 22 (August 1978): 680–90; Douglas Rose, "Citizen Uses of the Ford-Carter Debates," *Journal of Politics* 41 (February 1980): 214–21.
17. Texts of the debates may be found in the *New York Times*, October 9, 1984, pp. A26–A29; October 12, 1984, pp. B4–B6; 23 October 1984, B27–B29.
18. Los Angeles Times exit poll, November 7, 1984.
19. R. Brownstein, "Raising the Stakes," *National Journal* 16 (October 27, 1984): 2040.
20. Los Angeles Times poll, October 11, 1984; CBS News/New York Times poll, October 23–25, 1984. The effect of the televised debates is strikingly similar to that reported for radio broadcasts in the first scientific study of voting: Paul Lazarsfeld et al., *The People's Choice* (New York: Columbia University Press, 1944).
21. William Safire, "Nobody's Perfect," *New York Times*, November 5, 1984, p. A19.

22. *National Journal* 16 (August 11, 1984): 1542.
23. "The Democrats Need a Unifying Theme," *New York Times*, October 5, 1984, p. A31. V. O. Key made a similar point in refuting the earlier argument that Franklin Roosevelt's election victories were based on personality rather than policy performance. See *The Responsible Electorate* (Cambridge: Harvard University Press, 1966), p. 56.
24. CBS News/The New York Times poll, September 12–16, 1984, p. 3.
25. For example, see Gregory Markus, "Political Attitudes during an Election Year," *American Political Science Review* 76 (September 1982): 538–60.
26. The theoretical problems are discussed by Richard Brody and Benjamin Page, "Comment: The Assessment of Issue Voting," *American Political Science Review* 66 (June 1972): 450–58; and in Nie et al., chaps. 7–10.
27. Los Angeles Times exit poll, *National Journal* 16 (November 10, 1984): 2131.
28. Adam Clymer, *New York Times*, November 11, 1984, p. 30. See Stanley Kelley, Jr., *Interpreting Elections* (Princeton: Princeton University Press, 1984), for an incisive discussion of the theory and methods employed in analyzing election mandates.
29. "Where's His Mandate?" *Washington Post*, November 2, 1984, p. A23.
30. This position is persuasively argued in the major work of Morris Fiorina, *Retrospective Voting in American National Elections* (New Haven: Yale University Press, 1981). Also see Anthony Downs, *An Economic Theory of Democracy* (New York: Harper, 1957).
31. CBS News/New York Times poll, October 14, 1984; Los Angeles Times poll, October 16, 1984.
32. William Schneider, "Performance Is the Big Campaign Issue, and That Gives Reagan a Big Edge," *National Journal* 16 (October 6, 1984): 1894–95.
33. V. O. Key, "Theory of Critical Elections," *Journal of Politics* 17 (February 1955): 3–18.
34. *New York Times*, November 19, 1984, p. B10.
35. *Washington Post*, November 2, 1984, p. A1; *National Journal* 16 (November 10, 1984): p. 2132; Committee for Study of the American Electorate, *Non-Voter Study '84–'85*, November 12, 1984.
36. The metaphor is from Samuel Lubell, *The Future of American Politics* (Garden City, N.Y.: Doubleday, 1956).
37. Closing statement at the vice-presidential candidates' debate, reported in the *New York Times*, October 12, 1984, p. B6.

# PART III
# Parties

# *Part III: Parties*

Academic analysis distinguishes between facts and values, but scholars' values inevitably affect both what they study and what they seek. This mingling of fact and value has been notably evident in the scholarship on political parties, where analysts have been advocates of these institutions, not purely dispassionate observers.[1]

Without apology, my own endorsement of strong political parties is unconcealed in the essays in this section. Parties make sense of voters' choices and elections' outcomes, translating the inevitably garbled messages of the millions into the understandable speech of the powerful. Parties organize the political system, invest leaders with the legitimacy of popular approval, promote collective action, and link leaders and followers in common efforts toward the achievement of popular goals. The basic thesis here is that "political parties created democracy and that modern democracy is unthinkable save in terms of the parties."[2]

Despite their importance to democracy, parties have never held a secure place in political theory, especially in the United States. The difficulty is that parties are so different from the usual subject matter of political theory. Their leaders' frequent vulgarity comports ill with the philosophers' search for ideal statesmen. Their evident self-interest in power and privilege does not match the utopians' goal of the general good. Even as organizations, parties are a strange hybrid of private groups involved in public affairs, which fail to fit the usual models.[3] The following essays are, in part, efforts to illustrate the many contributions, even if indirect and unintended, that parties do make to democracy.

Commitment to political parties involves a concern for their health and survival. In this section, a continuing focus is the ways in which parties are changing, whether change comes through the parties' own response to the political environment or as the result of deliberate efforts by outsiders. I am skeptical or critical of those outside efforts that are heralded as "reform," for these actions often have meant the weakening of the parties and therefore, in my view, have also meant the weakening of democracy. Instead, I repeatedly urge actions toward party "renewal," a strengthening of the parties and, consequently, of the democratic system.

Change in the political parties is persistent during the period in which these essays were written, but the direction of change is not consistent. As a result, the tone evident in these writings is also inconsistent, varying from despair engendered by observed trends of party decline to guarded optimism stimulated by observed trends of party improvement.

Innovations I regard as negative, such as the domination of presidential nominating conventions by individualist campaigners, are offset by developments I regard as positive, such as the institutionalization of national party organizations. Unable to reach any final conclusion about the future, I share the uncertainty of the discipline.

These arguments are developed more fully in the first essay, which was originally prepared for a Rutgers University conference on democratic thought. The essay begins with an analysis of the parties' contributions to American governmental institutions, to voters, and to civil society.[4] Despite these contributions, parties are held in low repute, because they implicitly challenge American beliefs in individualism, privatism, consensus, equality, and classlessness. To improve the standing and effectiveness of the parties, I argue for a deliberate program of party renewal, a public policy toward politics itself.

Strengthening of the parties was first championed by political scientists in a 1950 report of a committee of the American Political Science Association.[5] The next essay is a favorable examination of that report, upon the twentieth anniversary of its publication. Most of the recommendations of the report have not been achieved but, the argument runs, its authors correctly predicted the future development of American politics. Even more relevant today than in 1950 are their concerns over policy incoherence, an inflated presidency, voter alienation, and the potential development of extremist politics.[6]

These threats could be averted, according to the essay below, by the emerging development of new voter alignments within the parties and clearer policy differences between the parties. Although cautious, the conclusion pointed toward the possible emergence of a new era of responsible parties. That prediction was overstated, but not completely wrong. One source of error was the expectation that the recent enfranchisement of eighteen year olds might provide the popular support for basic political change. In the event, the new political generations contributed disproportionately to partisan dealignment, rather than party revival.[7]

A less optimistic view is evident in the next essay, "The Decline of Partisan Politics." Centering on the presidential nominating system, the essay finds that parties have lost their central place in selecting candidates. At the same time, the parties are showing new organizational strength. The apparent paradox is resolved by reconceptualizing the parties as merely private associations that seek power within a general system of interest-group competition.

The change in the parties' position is detailed in two studies of national nominations. The first describes the nomination of Hubert Humphrey as the Democratic nominee for vice-president. I was fortunate to serve as a minor aide to Humphrey during the 1964 national convention, and to brief him on convention history (while he had his hair cut). The article was intended to be purely descriptive but now records a bygone era, when national nominations were made through internal party processes, rather than external and individualist campaigns.

On the presidential level, the next chapter analyzes the new nominating system that had developed by 1976. New rules had increased the number of primaries, altered the methods of selecting convention delegates in these primaries, and changed the apportionment of delegates among the states.[8] By reconstructing the convention vote under different and plausible rules, I present alternative scenarios under which neither Jimmy Carter nor Gerald Ford would have won his party's leadership. More generally, I argue, the new rules have weakened the capacity of the traditional state parties, while not yet leading to their replacement by strong national organizations.

The scene shifts to Great Britain in the next essay, a previously unpublished paper co-authored by Patricia Sykes in the course of her research on the Social Democratic Party. Britain is the home of both modern democratic theory and of modern strong parties, providing a good empirical base for examining the relationship between theory and practice. For this task, we attempt to exemplify four different theories of democracy by describing local party organizations of the four significant British political parties. The article relies principally on individual interviews, but is supported by a mail questionnaire to local party activists in the two constituencies we examined.

The four models (and their British exemplars) present democracy as, respectively: the competition of elites (Conservatives); policy choice (Labour); individual participation (Liberals); and Madisonian pluralism (Social Democrats). Each of these theories has practical problems in implementation, suggesting the limitations of any single interpretation of democracy. Empirically, subsequent visits convinced us that the models do indeed fit British parties. This conclusion is true even in the most surprising case, the application of pluralism to the transient Social Democratic Party. Indeed, Dr. Sykes later interviewed a framer of the party constitution, who stated that he had been consciously influenced by Madison's theories.[9]

''Party Politics in 1984,'' written during the presidential campaign of that year, returns to the general problems of American parties as mass coalitions, as organizations, and as governmental institutions. Ever optimistic, I find some signs of party renewal in the endorsements of prestigious national committees, improved party capabilities, and deepened voter support. These modest trends have continued in the past three years, as evidenced by recommendations of the Commission on National Elections, the organizational development of the national Republican and Democratic party committees, and higher levels of party attachment by the electorate.[10]

Party renewal remains uncertain and arduous. The volume concludes with the program of the Committee on Party Renewal, which I have co-chaired for a number of years. This program remains as the uncompleted agenda for the reconstruction of our political parties. As such, it is also the agenda for the continued viability of American democracy.

## Notes

1. Leon Epstein demonstrates this point, in *Political Parties in the American Mold* (Madison: University of Wisconsin Press, 1986), chap. 2.
2. E. E. Schattschneider, *Party Government* (New York: Holt, Rinehart and Winston, 1942), p. 1.
3. Joseph Schlesinger brilliantly solves this problem in "On the Theory of Party Organization," *Journal of Politics* 46 (May 1984): 369–400.
4. Especially on the last point, I have learned much from Wilson Carey McWilliams, as in his essay, "Parties as Civic Associations," in *Party Renewal in America* (New York: Praeger, 1980), chap. 4.
5. Committee on Political Parties, "Toward a More Responsible Two-party System," *American Political Science Review* 44 (September 1950): Supplement.
6. The original article included data analysis on changed voter perceptions of the parties. These data were elaborated in a later article, "From Confusion to Clarity," which is included earlier in this volume. My positive evaluation originally was presented as a paper at the 1970 meetings of the American Political Science Association. It was countered before the same audience by Evron Kirkpatrick, whose negative evaluation was published as: "Toward a More Responsible Two-Party System: Political Science, Policy Science, or Pseudo-Science?," *American Political Science Review* 65 (September 1971): 965–90.
7. Helmut Norpoth and Jerrold G. Rusk, "Partisan Dealignment in the American Electorate," *American Political Science Review* 76 (September 1982): 522–37.
8. Byron Shafer has analyzed the effect of rules changes more extensively in *The Quiet Revolution* (New York: Russell Sage, 1985). Nelson Polsby criticizes the rules changes in *Consequences of Party Reform* (New York: Oxford University Press, 1983).
9. Patricia Sykes, *Party Leaders: Private Goods and Public Good* (Ph.D. diss., Yale University, 1985), p. 1ff. For fuller analysis, see Sykes, *Losing from the Inside* (New Brunswick: Transaction Books, 1988).
10. See Commission on National Elections, *Electing the President: A Program for Reform* (Washington, 1986), and Martin Wattenberg, *The Decline of American Parties, 1952–1984* Cambridge: Harvard University Press, 1986), chap. 9.

# 14

# The Contribution of Political Parties to American Democracy

Americans do not like political parties.

This basic attitude can be traced in the intellectual history of the nation, in legislation, and in current public opinion and alleged "reforms." To those who see political parties as vital agents in a functioning U.S. democracy, the depth of the antiparty sentiment is a challenge and a frustration.

We find antiparty attitudes expressed even in the most unlikely places. Annually, to celebrate Washington's birthday, the Senate of the United States engages in the ritual of hearing a reading of the first president's farewell address. This body of 100 politicians, every one elected as a partisan Democrat or Republican, attend a denunciation of parties as agents that "render alien to each other those who ought to be bound together by fraternal affection" and which "make the public administration the mirror of the ill-concerted and incongruous projects of faction, rather than the organ of consistent and wholesome plans digested by common councils, and modified by mutual interests."[1]

Although Washington's farewell warning was particularly directed against the rising challenge of the new Republican Party, that group's leaders shared many of his beliefs. James Madison had written similar sentiments in *The Federalist*, the basic exposition and defense of the Constitution. The central problem Madison addressed was "that our governments are too unstable, that the public good is disregarded in the conflicts of rival parties, and that measures are too often decided, not according to the rules of justice and the rights of the minor party, but by the superior force of an interested and overbearing majority." The virtue of the Constitution, he argued, was its ability "to break and control the violence of faction," that is, of groups and parties, "whether amounting to a majority or minority of the whole, who are united and actuated by some common impulse of passion, or of interest, adverse to the rights of other citizens, or to the permanent and aggregate interests of the community."[2]

Like many political theorists and politicians, Madison found it necessary to modify his principles when confronted with the realities of government. Unhappy with the administration of the government under Washington and Alexander Hamilton, he organized a national coalition, which brought Thomas Jefferson to the presidency. Yet Jefferson, too, although owing his triumph to party politics, would not accept its desirability. He sought not the continuance of partisanship but its dissolution. "We have called by different names brethren of the same principle. We are all Republicans; we are all Federalists," he urged in his first inaugural address.[3] In thus minimizing the differences of the past decade, he was being conciliatory toward his opponents, but he also hoped to eliminate them peacefully. Shortly after taking office, he clarified his meaning: "Nothing shall be spared on my part to obliterate the traces of party and consolidate the nation, if it can be done without abandonment of principle."[4]

After Jefferson, others also did their part "to obliterate the traces of party." Attempts to deal with U.S. parties through legislation and extralegal enactments have occurred in three major periods in U.S. history.[5] They are alike in basic characteristics. Each period has witnessed an attempt by would-be reformers to weaken the power of party officials, to reduce the hierarchical components of party organization, and to increase at least nominal participation within the parties. Most fundamentally, in each period, the philosophical basis of these reforms has been the replacement of organized political coalitions by the direct, unmediated intervention of the individual citizen.

These tendencies could only be partially seen in the first period of reform, 1820–40, when national nominating conventions and national mass parties replaced the congressional caucus. These changes broadened the nomination of the president beyond the capital and enabled state and local politicians and some party members to participate. Creating a national party structure and platform transformed the parties from elite cadres to elite organizers of an expanding electorate. Democracy was surely served, but at some cost to the cohesion and national perspective provided by the congressional caucus. With the new system, moreover, "whatever chances the nation might have had to develop a form of parliamentary or cabinet government were gone forever."[6] Parties lost some of their capability to build a ladder of advancement from Congress to the presidency. Instead, from Andrew Jackson to Jimmy Carter, the White House became more accessible to those antagonistic to the parties' legislative delegations.

It is not until the twentieth century, however, that the fullest attack on institutionalized political parties becomes evident. The second great period of party change came in the Progressive movement at the beginning of this century; the final era is our own, beginning in the mid-1960s. In these latter two periods, the challenge to parties has been open, obvious, and successful in most respects. Legislators, activists, and impersonal social forces have combined to weaken, circumvent, restrain, and degrade the formal party organizations.

Without disputing the desirability of any particular change, the total result can be seen as bringing us close to the full dissolution of the parties as effective political contestants. Let us briefly note some of the major results of these antiparty actions. Local and state nominations are now decided by direct primaries open to almost all voters, regardless of past loyalty, rather than negotiated within the parties. Presidential nominations are effectively determined in a series of state primaries and in the mass media and are only formally ratified in national conventions. Political financing is provided by the government or private interest groups directly to candidates, while party treasuries are empty. The very structure of the ballot encourages voting for persons of different parties, and elections are scheduled to reduce the likelihood of party trends across national, state, and local levels. Municipal officials are largely chosen on a nonpartisan basis, with parties prevented from using these positions as sources of training and future recruitment to higher offices. Most government workers are selected on the basis of anonymous examinations and then barred from political activity, while even the highest administrators are increasingly recruited from within the bureaucracy or professional associations rather than on the basis of political service. Thus, the parties have lost their former dominance in a number of functions: nominations, recruitment, electioneering, and government staffing.

The position evidenced in this legislation is present as well in public attitudes toward the parties. Even before the upheavals of the 1960s led to a general decline of trust in our institutions, Americans were skeptical about the worth of political parties. A majority believed, repeating the thought of Washington, that "our system of government would work a lot more efficiently if we could get rid of conflicts between the parties altogether," and nearly two-thirds complained that "the parties more often that not create conflicts where none really exists."[7]

More recently, political parties have received even less support. Once, only a quarter of the voters disclaimed loyalty to the major parties, but now, nearly two-fifths assert their independence. While seven out of ten voters once had something good to say about at least one party, now, a majority cannot find anything positive about either Republicans or Democrats.[8] The decline in attitudes toward the party system is equally stark. By 1974, the proportion of voters supporting the placement of party labels on ballots was down to a minority 38 percent, and parties had the least public confidence among major political institutions.[9]

In brief, then, Americans have denounced parties in theory, restricted them in legislation, almost eliminated them in reform, and scorned them in opinion polls. Nevertheless, we have continued to employ them, and even to cherish them, in practice. Americans—like other peoples—are often ambivalent. This is the nation, after all, which constitutionally abolished the use of intoxicating liquors and then vastly increased its consumption of alcohol. We resent as well our dependence on political parties but continue to imbibe in partisan politics. But—unlike the alcoholic—this dependence is not from weakness and not a debilitating illness. Our political parties are strengths in our governing processes and free the nation for constructive activity.

The American fondness for parties is evident throughout our history. Washington denounced narrow factionalism but became the instrument of the Federalists. Madison proceeded from his penetrating analysis of the evils of factions to the organization of the first popular-based party in the world. Jefferson was elected president through his organization and then created an effective executive-legislative bridge in the Republican congressional caucus. So it has gone for nearly 200 years. The great innovations in public policy have been dependent on organized political action through the political parties. Abraham Lincoln maintained the Union by mobilizing his new Republican Party in Congress and the border states. Franklin Roosevelt created the welfare state through enactment of a party program of social legislation. John Kennedy and Lyndon Johnson established a new agenda for the nation by their party leadership. Conversely, our most recent presidents have provided negative proofs of the importance of parties. Unable to mobilize their weakened factions, Richard Nixon resorted to corruption, while Jimmy Carter has floundered in frustration.

Citizens, too, show support for political parties despite their expressed reservations. Loyalty to parties has often been almost an article of religious faith, exemplified by the solid Republican patricians of Dutchess County, New York, who never voted for their good neighbor, Franklin Roosevelt, and by the Boston Irish clan, which was solidly Democratic except for the "family disgrace," the one Republican. Still today, when party loyalty is denigrated, more than three-fifths of the voters will assert their identification with the Democrats or Republicans. Even in the 1960s, over two-thirds agreed that "democracy works best where competition between parties is strong" and that "people who work for parties during political campaigns do our nation a great service"; there has been a regular increase since then in individual financial contributions to election campaigns.[10]

The work of parties has drawn praise as well as blame from scholars and practitioners. Martin Van Buren set the tone for a long tradition of party approbation: when "the principles of contending parties are supported with candor, fairness, and moderation, the very discord which is thus produced may in a government like ours, be conducive to the public good."[11] In the nineteenth century, the place of parties was honored in thought, and devotion to party was observed in practice. The most pointed defense was offered by George Washington Plunkitt, a Tammany ward leader at the beginning of this century. The nation depended on the parties, Plunkitt argued tersely:

> I ain't up on sillygisms, but I can give you some arguments that nobody can answer.
>
> First, this great and glorious country was built up by political parties; second, parties can't hold together if their workers don't get offices when they win; third, if the parties go to pieces, the government they built up must go to pieces, too; fourth, then there'll be hell to pay.[12]

Some defend political parties, then, and many Americans depend on them. These attitudes and this behavior should be seen not as defects but as necessary and desirable attributes of an effective large-scale republic. We often neglect these attributes because we are not always willing to accept a fully democratic system. In the coming years, however, we must either acknowledge the mutual reliance of our parties and our democracy—or lose both.

The benefits of political parties are threefold: to institutions, to voters, and to civil society. Institutionally, the chief benefit of political parties is captured in the political scientists' phrase "the aggregation of interests." Conflicting interests are evident in every society. Indeed, they can be found even in the family; one famous commentator suggested that an investigation of the origins of parties "would have to be carried back to the garden of Eden, where the first caucus was held by Eve and the serpent."[13] Madison found the causes of faction "sown in the nature of man" and listed their bases as including "a zeal for different opinions concerning religion, concerning government and many other points . . . an attachment to different leaders ambitiously contending for pre-eminence and power" and, most importantly, "the various and unequal distribution of property. Those who hold and those who are without property have ever formed distinct interests in society."[14]

Parties are the means by which these various interests can be reconciled and by which they can be compromised to provide at least partial satisfactions to all contenders. The aggregation of interests by the parties is evident throughout our politics; three brief examples can denote a large range of activities. First, consider the variety of ethnic groups in the United States, each group having legitimate claims to a share of power. Without unifying mechanisms, campaigns could become, as in nonpartisan elections, divisive controversies between Catholics and Protestants, blacks and whites, Irish and Italians. When they are functioning well, parties submerge these communal clashes in a joint search for electoral victory. Their means is the "balanced ticket," by which all groups receive some recognition in return for mutual ballot support.

Anti-Catholic Democrats will still vote for a Catholic candidate so long as he or she is a Democrat, and some of the same whites who oppose school integration will vote for a black candidate for school superintendent running under their party label.

A second example of interest aggregation is the party platforms, often attacked as meaningless quadrennial rhetoric. Detailed examination of these documents shows, however, that they are surprisingly specific and frequently implemented.[15] They are important as means by which different interests establish a claim on the government while adjusting to the demands of other groups. In 1976, to illustrate this point, Republicans favoring a hard-line foreign policy could be reconciled to the candidacy of Gerald Ford by praise of Alexander Solzynitzhen; among Democrats, feminists could be enlisted in the Carter coalition by support of the Equal Rights Amendment.

Third, parties aggregate interests in their legislative decisions. Their cooperative behavior is exhibited even in the terms we use, such as *horsetrading*, *logrolling*, and *backscratching*. Urban representatives will vote for high farm price supports and will expect rural legislators in turn to approve public housing subsidies; national parks in the Rockies are traded for national seashores on the coasts.[16] This cooperation is inevitable and necessary in governing a continental nation. It becomes feasible, as well as somewhat coherent ideologically, when included in a total party program.

These three examples are deliberately chosen to illustrate the realities of parties in the United States. Balanced tickets, platform compromises, and legislative trading are not philosophical enterprises, and our parties are not intellectual societies. They are groupings of generally honorable but relatively ordinary people who are interested in power more than in principles. Like other men and women, they are typically self-interested, occasionally devious, and only rarely altruistic. The important point is not the motives of politicians but their institutional functions. In order to win office, politicians must heed expressed public demands. By aggregating these interests, parties do not, to be sure, guarantee that all interests will be heard—and even less that they will be heard at the same volume. However, they do provide a means by which some demands can be combined and made effective.

Aggregation of interests is particularly necessary, given the formal governmental structure of the United States. The Constitution has served us well, but only because we have not adhered to its provisions rigorously. A literal implementation of the original document would have given us two legislative chambers with only formal relations, an executive branch completely distinct in its base of authority, and a severe demarcation between the national and state governments. Amendment of the Constitution, in practice rather than by law, has enabled the parties to bridge its gaps through such integrative institutions as the national nominating conventions, the joint meetings of the president and congressional party leadership, the House and Senate party caucuses, the governors' conferences, and the intergovernmental political career.[17]

The more important benefits of parties, however, are not to institutions but to voters, our second category. These contributions depend on competition between the parties, that is, on a party system. Aggregation of interests and constitutional bridging, after all, are achieved by authoritarian parties, yet few advocate the Soviet Communist Party as a model for the United States. Because U.S. parties provide a choice, they enable the voters to exercise at least an indirect influence over the course of government.

Admittedly, that choice is limited and, often, clouded. It is difficult to find advocates of either free market capitalism or a socialized economy among major party candidates, while both Republicans and Democrats simultaneously urge an increase in social security benefits and restraints on governmental spending. Nevertheless, voters do see some significant difference between the parties. In 1976, for example, 70 percent of the nation found a conservative-liberal distinction between them: the Democrats were chosen as the more liberal party by a three to one margin:[18] What the voters saw reflected the reality of the parties. Democratic economic policy has been markedly different from that of the Republicans, their platforms and actions reflecting a definite concern with problems of unemployment, while Republicans have devoted considerably greater attention to inflation. Illustratively, in 1976, the Democratic platform spoke of unemployment 48 times, the Republican only once.[19] Floor voting in Congress also shows a distinct party split, with northern Democrats supporting liberal policies three times more frequently than Republicans.[20]

More significantly, it is possible for the parties to promote popular influence over government even if there are not marked policy differences between them. This effect is achieved because one party can be held responsible for governmental action, so that it provides a convenient target for the electorate's praise and blame. Voters have too many pressing tasks, from making money to making love, to follow the arcane procedures of government and to understand all the issues and outcomes. Instead, they can rely on the convenience of party labels and simply vote for the "ins" when times are good and for the "outs" when dissatisfied. Many Americans follow this simple and not unreasonable rule to achieve a rough political justice. Democrats, therefore, suffered defeat when their leader, Lyndon Johnson, conducted an unpopular war in Vietnam, and Republicans were replaced when Nixon attempted to subvert the laws. "By virtue of the combination of the electorate's retrospective judgment and the custom of party accountability, the electorate can exert a prospective influence if not control,'' as Key argued: therefore, ''governments must worry, not about the meaning of past elections, but about their fate at future elections.''[21]

Worried about elections, parties are responsive. They respond particularly to demands voiced by large numbers of people. This characteristic has made parties the special agency of the poor and disadvantaged. Those who have wealth, education, and other privileges can often make their own way politically and, in any case, have less need for governmental aid. The poor have only one real advantage, their numbers, in the enduring contest, underlined by Madison, over ''the various and unequal distribution of property.'' But numbers are also the most basic resource in a democratic system and the resource of most interest to the parties.

The close association between the interests of parties and those of the lower classes has been repeatedly exemplified. As Aaron Burr registered craftsmen to promote Jefferson's election, so radical Republicans after the Civil War forced the enrollment of emancipated slaves. In state politics, there is a definite association between the degree of party competition and the level of redistributive public policy.[22] On the municipal level, cities without partisan elections devote less attention to the problems of the poor such as low-income housing, social welfare service, urban redevelopment, and employment.[23]

The classic example of the service parties provide for the disadvantaged was the urban machine. Corrupt and inefficient, the machine also showed a genuine concern for its constituents. As one leader put it: ''I think . . . that there's got to be in every ward somebody that any bloke can come to—no matter what's he's done—and get help. Help you understand; none of your law and your justice, but help.''[24] The machine did meet the needs of its poor supporters, providing jobs; emergency aid; desired illegal services, such as gambling; entertainment; opportunities for social mobility; and intervention with the law. At the same time, it promoted the economic development of the cities and even engaged in some imaginative urban planning, as in the development of New York City's subway and parks systems.

Today, the urban machine has virtually disappeared, its functions assumed by nonpartisan bureaucracies and ombudsmen. Welfare needs are supplied better, surely, for food stamps are far more plentiful and regular than Christmas turkeys. But something also has been lost, for the machine did not provide charity. It supplied a service in exchange for votes. This implicit bargain was more dignified to the poor surely than the largesse of government. The welfare state is, necessarily, an impersonal organization; the machine was an expression of neighborly concern and of the interdependence of leaders and led. The party machine, therefore, helped to bring the poor into politics, first as objects and then as participants; the welfare state only considers the poor as ''clients,'' not as equals. The machine was egalitarian in its basic attitudes.

This nonelitist character of the machine is nicely described by Plunkitt's advice to the aspiring politician:

> Get a followin', if it's only one man, and then go to the district leader. . . . The leader won't laugh at your one-man followin'. He'll shake your hand warmly, offer to propose you for membership in his club, take you down to the corner for a drink and ask you to call again. But go to him and say: "I took first prize at college in Aristotle; I can recite all Shakespeare forwards and backwards" [and] he'll probably say: "I guess you are not to blame for your misfortune, but we have no use for you here."[25]

The machine illustrates the third kind of contribution made by parties, the promotion of a democratic life-style. Parties are democratic in the most basic egalitarian sense, for in the voting booth, each person counts as one and only one. Parties seek votes and ultimately do not care if the hands that move the levers are black or white, male or female, or rich or poor. Parties, more than any other U.S. institution, accept our national premise, namely, that "all men are created equal."

A democratic life-style means widespread public participation in the affairs of the community. Competing parties promote participation, at least in general elections. It is hardly coincidental that voting rates are highest in those areas with the most vigorous two-party competition, that parties have spearheaded the successive extensions of the franchise, that electoral turnout was greatest in those periods of U.S. history when party loyalty was strongest, and that the contemporary decline in turnout closely parallels the decline in party strength.

Yet, political parties are more than collections of voters. They are communities in themselves, which function to promote broader involvement in the larger community. They provide training, an awareness of others' needs and interests, and a personal understanding of democratic manners. Parties promote intimacy among their members, respect for the opinions of their constituents, and possible future leadership for the nation.

The communitarian aspect of party organizations is particularly notable in the selection of future leadership. Like members of other small groups, partisans get to learn one another's strengths and weaknesses in great depth. Party members watch each other, test each other, and gossip about each other. They learn through long and repeated experience whose word can be trusted, who will follow through on assignments, who is informed on public questions, and who disguises selfish interests in the cloak of the general interest. Relying on their personal experience, they are uniquely knowledgeable in the selection of public officials.

A democratic life-style involves more than participation in periodic elections. It also involves a commitment to public questions, an extension of the individual beyond his or her private concerns. Parties promote this maturation. Voters generally, and properly, are concerned with advancing their individual interests; party activists must take note of the interests of others. Voters act in isolation or in alliance with their close associates; campaigners must coordinate their activities with others in the common enterprise. Voters discharge their duty in a brief occasional act; partisans immerse themselves in the ongoing public world. For members of the parties, Tocqueville's description of the American is still accurate: "He takes a lesson in the form of government from governing. The great work of society is ever going on before his eyes and, as it were, under his hands."[26] Parties serve to make citizens out of voters.

By previous reckoning, parties are evaluated as immensely important to U.S. institutions, voters, and society: to recapitulate, they aggregate interests, as illustrated by ticket balancing, platform writing, and legislative trading; bridge the separation of governmental agencies; offer a choice to the electorate; enforce responsibility for policy on the governing party; respond to the needs of large groups, particularly the disadvantaged; provide welfare aid to the poor; stimulate participation; promote community life; foster a democratic life-style; and enlarge the political views of citizens. These merits surely account for the continued use we make of the parties. But if parties are that desirable, why do Americans have such unfavorable attitudes toward them? Why do we continue to reform them, even to the present point of almost eliminating them?

Certainly, one source of antipathy toward parties is a valid criticism of their faults. Their theoretical merits are often lost in their negative practices. Parties can degenerate from public agencies to private factions. Instead of pursuing a coalitional program, they may become instruments only for personal ambitions. Rather than offering the voters instruments for collective choice, they may obscure their policy objectives or serve the interests of the wealthy and the privileged. Rather than fostering community participation, they can become closed elites.

Political parties are based on private motives and therefore always present the possibility that these private interests will come to predominate over the public functions of parties. Party organizations are bureaucracies to some extent and, as in other bureaucracies, the interests of the organization may receive more emphasis than the needs of its clientele. The urban machine, even with its virtues, was also the fullest institutional expression of these defects of parties. It ignored fundamental social issues, dampened but left unsolved the grievances of the poor, concentrated political power in a few, usually corrupt, hands, and debased the quality of political discourse. These deficiencies were a major stimulus of the movement to reform parties.

There is also a deeper source of the antipathy toward parties. Unfavorable attitudes toward parties also derive from conflicts among American values, as well as from the inherent challenge that the very existence of parties presents to our most esteemed beliefs. We hold conflicting values, and parties emphasize the conflicts. We need parties, but we resent them, because they remind us of our confusions and inability to resolve some of the problems of our society. Mistaking effect for cause, we believe that by eliminating parties, we can remove the confusion and inability to resolve the problems. Let me briefly cite five illustrations.

One favored U.S. belief is individualism. Part of American mythology is captured by such figures as the rugged frontiersman, the lonely inventor, and the self-reliant Horatio Alger character, who overcomes problems by his or her own efforts. The political analogue of the rugged individualist is the independent voter, who studies all issues and then makes his or her own personal, rational decision. But parties are collective bodies. They exist in order to organize men and women to reach shared goals, and their existence underlines the incapacity of individuals to achieve their goals without mutual aid. In the individualistic ideology, political independence is the highest estate. To the parties, loyalists are the best citizens and independents are only fence-straddling "mugwumps," who have their mug on one side of the fence and the wump on the other.

A related U.S. value, and one increasingly evident in social and political life, is privatism. Automobiles are preferred over public transportation, detached homes over apartments, individually owned condominiums over cooperatives, personal television over motion picture theaters, individualistic psychological therapy over social movements, isolated recreation (such as running) over participatory team sports, and the nuclear family or the singles scene over the kin group. In politics, we find the substitution of the televised commercial for the public address, the selling of personalities for the discussion of issues, and the ideal of the private voting decision for that of partisan loyalty. However, parties are public, not private, bodies. Party politicians are gregarious people who love to mingle with others, talk, laugh, and physically touch one another. Private politics suggests an image of the lonely voter at home, pondering decisions; party politics suggests an image of a crowded three-ring circus.

Consensus is a third value that is highly esteemed in the United States. Programs are inevitably rationalized in terms of their contribution to the public good, and the general welfare and a commitment to these philosophical abstractions is particularly evident in the antiparty literature. Thus, Madison could defend the Constitution as ensuring that "a coalition of a majority of the whole society could seldom take place on any other principle than those of justice and the general good."[27] The U.S. search for consensus is evident in ecumenical religion, mass culture, and even car styles. In politics, it is evidenced in bipartisan foreign policies, the reverence often paid to the presidential office, and the explicit disavowal of appeals to economic classes or other specific interests. But parties are by nature, even etymology, expressions of particular groups, efforts to win advantages for some interests even at the expense of others, as well as vehicles for personal ambition and selfishness. Parties are institutional expressions of conflict, recognitions that "the passions of men will not conform to the dictates or reason and justice without constraint," as Hamilton said, and that "ambition must be made to counteract ambition," as Madison agreed.[28] An emphasis on consensus presumes that disputes can be resolved—that the lion and the lamb can lie down together. By contrast, the development of parties presumes that coercion is at least implicit in political settlements and that the lamb had better watch its chops.

Parties even challenge the basic U.S. belief in equality. We assert that each man and woman is equal to every other, certainly in regard to politics. As Tocqueville has long made us aware, equality is the basic U.S. value, affecting all aspects of our lives, from commerce to dress. "Equality is their idol," he wrote; "Nothing can satisfy them without equality, and they would rather perish than lose it."[29]

Parties, too, share this value and aid considerably in its achievement. But in another sense, parties challenge the reality of equality. If citizens were truly equal in their knowledge, access, participation, and interests, parties would not be necessary. Parties exist because of a division of labor. They are specialized enterprises, providing information to less aware voters, evidencing greater political participation by their activists, and promoting the interests of some groups over others. We necessarily rely on the parties to structure our political communications, just as we necessarily rely on the telephone company to structure our voice communications. Yet, who loves Ma Bell?

Finally, parties challenge the U.S. ideal of a classless society. Public opinion polls inform us that most people place themselves in the amorphous category of the middle class; status differences are carefully disguised, so that it is difficult to tell a Cadillac from a Ford; unions and management lobby together to ease governmental regulation of their industries; and television creates a common mass culture, in which class differences are rarely noted—and never argued. The absence of class consciousness has been repeatedly underlined, occasioning satisfaction by liberals and despair by socialists. However, even our non-Marxian parties make us aware of the uncomfortable fact of status differences: their historical appeals are to the working class and the classical bourgeoisie, and their programs and legislative voting are most distinct on issues related to relative group advantages. To the limited extent we have been willing to acknowledge that politics involves economic conflict, the parties have embodied this consciousness.

One can—and I probably do—exaggerate the degree to which Americans hold fast to these values. There are other contrasting American commitments—to community, public involvement, competition, differentiation, and even class conflict.[30] The persistence of parties evidences these other beliefs, and parties themselves share in both sets of values. We are, ultimately, ambivalent, but the parties more fully embody one side of the internal quarrel of the American mind.

The conflict between parties and these specified values culminates in the dispute over direct democracy, exemplified in progressive legislation, and in such mechanisms as the direct primary, initiative, referendum, and recall. The advocates of direct democracy expect intense individualistic activity to achieve the common good. No intermediate organizations, such as parties, are desirable, because such organizations will limit the equal power of autonomous individuals. No class movements are necessary, because the common good will harmonize the interests of all particular interests. Democracy to the Progressives and their modern heirs is an organism that needs no care and feeding, in which, without any special mechanisms, "accountability is always to the composite citizen—individual unknown—always permanent, never changing, the necessitated result being that the public servant must serve the composite citizen who represents general welfare."[31]

The Progressive ideology has largely carried the day. After all, how can one argue against such clichés as, "Vote for the man (or woman) not the party," or, "There's no Democratic or Republican way to clean the streets"? Our schools spread the nonpartisan message, and parties are virtually absent from textbooks except as historical references.[32] Even candidates, sensing public sentiment, emphasize their personality over their political heritage, attack their opponents as "bosses," and avoid both party labels and the other members of their tickets.

In recent years, as already noted, social forces and alleged reforms in the spirit of the Progressive ideology have brought the parties to their present weakened state. These changes are neither accidental nor conspiratorial. They are, rather, the latest manifestations of those U.S. values hostile to parties. Individualism is evident in the revision of nominating procedures, especially in the Democratic party. The new rules of the party stimulate the choice of convention delegates by direct primaries rather than by party processes; they provide for proportional representation of the primary vote and thus restrict the building of coalitions; they give no assured representation in the highest party councils to its officials or those persons elected in its name; they minimize the states as political organizations; and they emphasize not party service in the choice of delegates but demographic characteristics of age, sex, and race. The basic unspoken premise of these changes is that the only important political relationship is that between the individual voter and the presidential nominee. The plebiscite among atomized individuals is replacing political organization.

Privatism, the complement of individualism, is also evident, particularly in campaigning, which is no longer conducted in public places, such as the streets or county fairs. Electoral messages are received in the isolation of television dens, and their meaning is not discussed among the voters, but only by strangers, the commentators of the press. Financing of elections through party committees has been replaced by contributions from wealthy individuals, anonymous checkoffs through the income tax system, or interest groups. Candidates emphasize their personalities or their activities in sports or entertainment rather than their political service. We no longer vote for persons who represent the historical heritage and identifiable program of a political party but for persons whose faces we see but whose souls we cannot touch.

We continue as well to disregard the issue of class in our politics. This neglect is most evident in our attempted reform of election finance. Watergate demonstrated the corruptibility of the existing electoral system, but in the process of responding to those evils, we created new dangers. Now, wealthy individuals are free to spend as much money as they want on their own campaigns or on behalf of others. We now legally permit, indeed encourage, corporations to contribute to campaigns. In the last congressional campaign, specialized "political action committees" provided the majority of funding for congressional chairpersons, an average of $45,000 for each.[33] In total, some 2,000 groups spent $35 million advocating the special interests of corporations, as well as unions and other groups.[34] At the same time, contributions of individuals and spending by parties have been restricted considerably. At one time, we understood the danger of direct corporate involvement in elections and precisely labeled business contributions as *corrupt practices*. Today, we do no more than require that the contributions go through a separate political action committee rather than come directly from the corporate treasurer's office.

To be sure, corporations and other groups have interests that they should legitimately promote in elections. But only parties can aggregate these interests into a program that gives some recognition to a variety of demands. To be sure, candidates should make us aware of their personal qualifications, but only a team of partisan officials, sharing a historical record and some common responsibility, can readily be held to account by the electorate. To be sure, individual voters should exercise their best judgment in casting ballots, but only parties dependent on votes are likely to champion the cause of the disadvantaged and to promote a participatory, egalitarian life-style. If we value these qualities and if we value democracy, we must take action to renew our political party system.

We need a new period of reform, a time in which to develop a public policy toward politics itself and in which to center our efforts on the reconstruction of the political parties. This call has been made before, and usually futilely. A distinguished group of political scientists published a program for constructive party reform as long ago as 1950. They warned that the consequences of inaction would be incoherence in public policies, a dangerous enlargement of presidential power, public cynicism, and the growth of extremist movements.[35] Their recommendations for action were not heeded, but their predictions have proven accurate. We find ourselves unable as a nation to design a coherent policy to meet the energy shortage, to regulate the economy, or to control our foreign policy. We alternate between presidents who are too strong for our liberties or too weak for our security. We find fewer than a fifth of the voters expressing confidence in the three branches of the national government. We see loyalties attached not to known, accountable parties but to single-interest groups, such as antiabortionists, or single men, such as George Wallace.

There is still hope and time available. The need for stronger parties is becoming evident. The Democrats are developing a broadly participatory national party, and the Republicans are forging strong organizational links from the state to the federal level. State parties are being rebuilt by concerned citizens, who have written a new party charter in Massachusetts, organized open party caucuses in Minnesota, and increased local participation in California. Awareness of the problem is becoming apparent in the mass media, and there are nascent movements toward party rebuilding in Congress.

There are many steps to be taken, among which the three following institutional steps merit particular discussion. First, we need to revise the election finance laws, so that funds are provided to parties for their continuing organization, research, and training and so that campaign funds are channeled through the parties rather than independently to candidates. Second, we must reverse the trend toward presidential selection through a series of distracting, hyperbolic, and expensive primaries and enable the state party organizations more fully to exercise their experienced judgment in the choice of the chief executive. Third, we should encourage the trend to midterm party conventions and any other devices that will make the president more responsible to his colleagues in Congress and to the members of his party.

Neither these reforms nor any other will in themselves rebuild the parties. Ultimately, democracy depends more on an active citizenry than on institutions and leaders. It depends on widespread participation in those intermediate organizations and voluntary groups that stand between the individual and the overarching national state. Watergate should have made us aware again of the dangers of concentrated power, as American life should remind us daily of the need for more intimate communities. Party renewal is also a renewal of U.S. democracy. As Tocqueville warned, "There are no countries in which associations are more needed to prevent the despotism of faction or the arbitrary power of a prince than those which are democratically constituted."[36] We would do well to heed that warning.

## Notes

1. James Richardson, ed., *Messages and Papers of the Presidents* (Washington, D.C.: Government Printing Office, 1897), pp. 209–11.
2. James Madison, *The Federalist, No. 10* (New York: Modern Library, 1941), pp. 53–54.
3. George Biche Huszar, *Basic American Documents* (Ames, Iowa: Littlefield, Adams, 1953), p. 115.
4. Cited in Richard Hofstadter, *The Idea of a Party System* (Berkeley: University of California Press, 1970), p. 151.
5. Austin Ranney, *Curing the Mischiefs of Faction* (Berkeley: University of California Press, 1975), pp. 1–21.
6. Ibid., p. 15.
7. Jack Dennis, "Support for the Party System by the Mass Public," *American Political Science Review* 60 (September 1966): 605.
8. Norman Nie et al., *The Changing American Voter* (Cambridge: Harvard University Press, 1976), p. 58.
9. Jack Dennis, "Trends in Public Support for the American Party System," *British Journal of Political Science* 5 (April 1975): 200–08.
10. Dennis, "Support for the Party System," p. 606, and Dennis, "Trends in Public Support," p. 211.
11. Martin Van Buren, *Autobiography*, p. 50, edited by Hofstadter, *The Idea of a Party System*, pp. 251–52.
12. William L. Riordan, *Plunkitt of Tammany Hall* (New York: Dutton, 1963), p. 13.
13. M. Ostrogorski, "The Rise and Fall of the Nominating Caucus, Legislative and Congressional," *American Historical Review* 5 (December 1899): 254.
14. *The Federalist, No. 10*, pp. 55–56.
15. Gerald Pomper, *Elections in America* (New York: Dodd Mead, 1968), pp. 149–203.
16. David Mayhew, *Party Loyalty Among Congressmen* (Cambridge: Harvard University Press, 1966).
17. See Joseph Schlesinger, *Ambition in Politics* (Chicago: Rand McNally, 1966).
18. Data from the University of Michigan, Center for Political Studies, 1976 Election Study, variable 3194.
19. Edward Tuffe, *Political Control of the Economy* (Princeton: Princeton University Press, 1978), pp. 76–77.
20. "Conservative Coalition Loses Strength," *Congressional Quarterly Weekly Report* 36 (December 18, 1978): 3442.
21. V. O. Key, Jr., *The Responsible Electorate* (Cambridge: Harvard University Press, 1966), p. 76ff.
22. Brian Fry and Richard Winters, "The Politics of Redistribution," *American Political Science Review* 64 (June 1970): 508–22.
23. Willis Hawley, *Nonpartisan Elections and the Case for Party Politics* (New York: Wiley, 1973), chap. 6.
24. *The Autobiography of Lincoln Steffens* (New York: Harcourt Brace, 1931), p. 618.
25. Riordan, *Plunkitt of Tammany Hall*, p. 10.
26. Alexis de Tocqueville, *Democracy in America* (1835), ed. Phillips Bradley (New York: Vintage, 1954), vol. 1, p. 330.
27. Alexander Hamilton, *The Federalist, No. 51* (New York: Modern Library, 1941), p. 341.

28. James Madison, *The Federalist, No. 15* (New York: Modern Library, 1941), p. 92, and Madison, *The Federalist, No. 51*, p. 337.
29. Tocqueville, vol. 1, p. 56.
30. See Wilson Carey McWilliams, *The Idea of Fraternity in America* (Berkeley: University of California Press, 1973).
31. Oregon Senator Brown, arguing for direct election of U.S. senators, in *Congressional Record*, 61st Cong., 3rd sess., 1911, 46, p. 2595–96.
32. See Sue Tolleson Rinehart, "The Mischief of Factions: Political Parties in School Textbooks" (paper delivered at annual meeting of American Political Science Association, Washington, D.C., September 1979).
33. *New York Times*, December 25, 1978, p. 1
34. *Congressional Quarterly Weekly Report* 27 (June 2, 1979): 1043.
35. American Political Science Association, Committee on Political Parties, "Toward a More Responsible Two-Party System," *American Political Science Review* 44 (September 1950): 91–96 (supp.).
36. Tocqueville, vol. 1, p. 202.

# 15

# Toward a More Responsible Two-Party System?

In 1950, a quixotic committee of the American Political Science Association proposed reforms looking "toward a more responsible two-party system."[1] Its proposals were widely read and commented on, and the Committee became a favorite target for academic attack.[2] Eventually, political scientists became bored with the topic and abandoned discussion of responsible parties. In practical politics, moreover, the reform proposals were largely ignored.

A generation later, however, political conditions in the United States may make these proposals more useful and feasible than they were when originally published. The deficiencies of the 1950 *Report* remain, and will not be reargued here.[3] It is more useful to dispute the criticisms made at the time, and to remember the correct predictions made by the Committee on Political Parties. We can then turn to empirical voting data which suggest that the times are appropriate for basic changes in American politics in the directions suggested in 1950.

## The Critics

A review of criticisms of the *Report* reveals as much about the state of political science in 1950 as it demonstrates about the failings of the Committee. Particularly notable among the critics was their relative satisfaction with the state of the nation, a satisfaction derived from their pluralist bias. Many critics were not only analysts but champions of American parties; they believed the parties had promoted a pluralist system that had achieved a high measure of stability and decency. Perhaps Clinton Rossiter spoke for this group when he hoped that readers of his book who might come to it "with a skeptical attitude to party politics will go away with a better understanding of the logic of our political system, and thus perhaps with more pride in it."[4]

This satisfaction with American politics led to a stress on stability as the primary virtue of a political system. The critics of the *Report* posited a causal relation between "non-responsible" parties and government stability. Basic consensus was presumed to be necessary for democratic government. In the United States, a nation of "high civil-war potential" because of its multiplicity of classes, races, sections and interests, the achievement of consensus was particularly difficult. The great accomplishment of the American party system had been that it created agreement in the face of great diversity. By their cross-sectional and non ideological character, the parties were able to encompass all groups, or at least some of every group. They "give everyone the feeling that the rest of society is concerned about the welfare and prestige of people in his stratum. . . . No group, in other words, has reason to feel that the rest of the society is a kind of giant conspiracy to keep it out of its legitimate 'place in the sun.' "[5]

The defense of the parties was often buttressed by historical analysis of the Civil War. This ultimate case in political instability was attributed to the breakdown of the parties, and was held to exemplify the virtues of non-ideological parties.

> The lesson which America learned was useful: in a large federal nation, when a problem is passionately felt, and is discussed in terms of morals, each party may divide within itself, against itself. And if the parties divide, the nation may divide; for the parties, with their enjoyable pursuit of power, are a unifying influence. Wise men, therefore, may seek to dodge such problems as long as possible. And the easiest way to dodge them is for both parties to take both sides.[6]

This case for the parties was plausible but unscientific. There was virtually no theoretical specification or empirical verification of the social, economic, and psychological sources of stability. Such concepts as cross-cutting cleavages, relative deprivation, and diffuse support were unknown or unused.[7] Lacking such conceptions, students of American politics noted that there had been stability (i.e., the absence of general political violence) for nearly a century and that the parties had been "non-responsible" during that period, and they drew an unproven causal connection between the two observations.

Defenders of the American parties believed that the party system had achieved not only stability, but also some measure of justice through the "invisible hand" of pluralist politics. That all groups gained something in the bargaining process was demonstrated through analyses of interest-group conflict over legislation or the diverse appeals and constituencies of the electoral party. Some strange conclusions followed from occasional "academic studies which, derived from the premise of pluralism, proceed compulsively to vindicate it."[8] Peter Drucker, for example, cited the Taft-Hartley Act as evidence of the countervailing power of labor unions, although the unions themselves considered it a "slave-labor act."[9] Goodman saw the diversity of American parties as a means whereby "our system, whether intentionally or not, protects those who are unaware and inactive by placing checks on those who are aware and active."[10] Fuller research was to show that the incoherent party system adversely affected precisely the inactive and unaware—the poor and the blacks—by simply excluding them from voting.[11]

Pluralist studies and defenses did often note the unequal power of different groups, but observation of inequalities rarely led to a basic questioning of the fairness of the entire model.[12] When the unequal distribution of power was considered, it was often defended as protection of "minority rights." The minorities being protected were generally numerically small but economically or regionally powerful groups, such as businessmen or segregationists. There was rather less concern with those minorities presumably needing the most support—Negroes, the isolated poor, the unorganized, or those unpopular minorities that the Supreme Court had already recognized as having disproportionate burdens to bear in the political fray.[13] In this unusual pluralist world, more concern was expressed for the protection of socially advantaged than of deprived groups.

The deficiency of the pluralist defense of American parties is illustrated, ironically, by an example given by two critics of responsible parties. Writing approvingly in 1956 of gradual racial integration of the schools, the authors conclude:

> Thus the anti-segregationists and the pro-segregationists each get part—but not all—of what they want; no interracial or intersectional civil war breaks out; and a situation is preserved in which the gradual erosion of southern-white attitudes toward the Negroes that has been taking place during the past quarter-century or more—and, in which, in the present writers' opinion, lies the best hope for the ultimate solution of this difficult problem—can continue its work. Certainly this is not the "swift, purposive, and vigorous" national government action demanded by the advocates of more "responsible" parties; but it *is* a kind of action which, whatever else can be said about it, preserves our consensus and yet does not permanently fix the status of Negro schoolchildren at its present level.[14]

The failure of "all deliberate speed" and consensual politics to deal with the racial question is now apparent. Inattention to the race issue and confidence in its early resolution were widespread at the time, but this example shows the general defects of pluralist theory and pluralist critiques of responsible parties. Pluralism tends toward complacency, toward a neglect of institutional inequalities, and toward unconcern with social policy.[15] The APSA *Report* did not have these particular defects.

The reviewers of the *Report* also exhibited an inattention to empirical evidence which is strange to recall in this post behavioral era. One far-ranging critique included the following assertions without apology or supporting data:

—"The real choice is between a relatively weak two-party system with many outside interest groups or a very strong multi-party system with few nonpartisan interest groups."

—In Europe, "the splitting of the electorate into a mulitiplicity of parties which occurred through the increasing radicalization of party programs, in turn was the logical result of what we might call competitive program specificness."

—"The present system of constituent-representative relationships is one of remarkable closeness considering the size of the country and of the electoral districts."

—In foreign policy, "the basis of consensus is broad enough to allow for compromise and thus, among other things, plays down any process of aggrandizement by the President at the expense of Congress."[16]

Armchair speculation of this sort is what led to the insistence on empirical testing of hypotheses. Terms are undefined, classifications are unjustified, and data are generally lacking. The best purpose served by these criticisms was to demonstrate the importance of the *Report's* suggestion for further research on American politics.

One notable critic of the *Report* did employ empirical evidence. Julius Turner disputed the assumption of the Committee that American parties did not exhibit any policy differences. Examining congressional roll calls, he found that the parties could be distinguished on 407 of 455 tallies in eight selected Congresses. While his test was the blunderbuss of chi-square, he was noteworthy for his appeal to the data, rather than for his desire simply to attack the *Report*.[17]

In the same article, Turner went on to criticize the *Report* on empirically weaker grounds. Coherent parties, he argued, would result in one-party domination of most areas.

> To the extent that segments of the population can identify their political desires with the program of one party or the other, competition at the polls will be reduced in the United States except in those fortunate constituencies where opposed groups are equally balanced. . . . Regardless of the organization provided, you cannot give Hubert Humphrey a banjo and expect him to carry Kansas. Only a Democrat who rejects at least a part of the Fair Deal can carry Kansas, and only a Republican who moderates the Republican platform can carry Massachusetts.[18]

The proposition seems reasonable, but it was neither theoretically nor empirically demonstrated. It is possible to argue that more programmatic parties would actually encourage greater competition, as various interests aligned themselves with one party or the other until each was within distance of electoral victory. Such movement would be consistent both with coalition theory and with spatial theories of party competition.[19]

In relation to the empirical data, Turner himself acknowledged that most congressional districts were politically noncompetitive in 1950, even in the absence of responsible parties. Later developments would show that programmatic parties were not inevitably incompatible with partisan competition. Detailed investigations of midwestern and southern politics failed to substantiate Turner's thesis.[20] Apparently party responsibility and party competition were independent of each other. The *Report*'s desire to achieve both conditions was not inherently contradictory.

## The Predictions

With the advantage of more than 20 years of hindsight, we can see the inadequacy of some criticisms of the APSA *Report*. Confidence in the adaptability of American institutions, pluralist assumptions, and limited empirical data blunted these attacks. Moreover, we are now more aware of the foresight of the original Committee. In many respects, American politics has developed in the directions it forecast in 1950.

A change critical to the development of responsible parties has been the decline of sectionalism, particularly the growth of party competition in the South. Since 1952, not a single state of the old Confederacy has voted Democratic in all presidential elections. The Republicans have recently held as many as 5 of 22 Senate seats, 4 of 11 governorships, 26 of 106 House seats, and at least a tenth of the state legislative seats in six southern states. The vote for U.S. representatives, perhaps the best single indication of popular support for the party, showed the Republicans winning a third of the southern vote in 1968.[21]

The decline of sectionalism is also evident in the spread of Democratic strength to previously unknown territory in New England and the Plains states. The net result of these countervailing tendencies is that states resemble one another more closely in national politics. The dispersion of the presidential vote has decreased considerably, which indicates that all states are reflecting more nearly the same distribution of political forces and responding to the same national issues. Thus, the standard deviation of the Democratic presidential vote, by states, stood at a median of 8.6 for the five presidential elections following the publication of the 1950 *Report*, compared with a median of 12.7 for the five contests preceding 1950. The changes in this measure are evident in table 15.1. The existence of competitive parties in all sections makes voter choice more meaningful. Alternative programs become a real possibility.

**TABLE 15.1**
**Democratic Presidential Vote, by States, 1932–1968**

| Year | Mean | Standard Deviation |
|---|---|---|
| 1932 | 62.8 | 14.1 |
| 1936 | 64.8 | 12.7 |
| 1940 | 59.2 | 13.6 |
| 1944 | 56.6 | 12.1 |
| 1948 | 48.3 | 11.7 |
| 1952 | 43.9 | 8.6 |
| 1956 | 42.3 | 7.0 |
| 1960 | 48.5 | 5.5 |
| 1964 | 58.8 | 11.1 |
| 1968 | 40.5 | 9.6 |

The Committee also foresaw the increased involvement of interest groups in electoral politics, and the development of de facto alliances with the major parties. Significant labor-union activity had already begun by 1950. Since that time, the unions' involvement has increased, and other interested groups have become politicized as well. Even the tendentious figures on campaign spending reveal the trend. Labor-union campaign spending on a national level rose from $1.8 million in 1950 to $7.6 million in 1968. This represented a rise in labor involvement from 8.1% of total national spending to 12.2%. Even more significant was the fact that the unions' spending grew from 22% of the combined Democrat-labor expenditures in 1956 to 36% in 1968.[22] Other groups such as the American Medical Association have also become involved, although on a less massive or less publicized scale.

A third change that the Committee predicted—the wish being father to the thought—was a closer alignment between party identification and policy preferences. While Key demonstrated a certain historical correspondence between party vote and policy choice, the relation has not been extremely close. Moreover, it could be argued that issue preferences were the effect, rather than the cause, of partisan preference.[23] Whatever the causal sequence, any increase in the correlation of party and issue preferences would indicate a greater ideological coherence in party politics. Party differences would then correspond more closely to policy differences in the electorate. Our previous analysis shows that party coherence has apparently increased in the past 20 years (see data in table 2.1, chapter 2).

The Committee on Political Parties foresaw not only trends but dangers as well. In the complacent mood of 1950, these warnings were largely disregarded. In the more apprehensive mood of 1971, we can more fully appreciate the Committee's foresight. Without responsible parties, four deleterious consequences were predicted.[24] First, the Committee warned, programs would not be coherent, for "the political foundation of appropriate government programs is very unstable when it is not supplied by responsible party action." Without quarreling over the meaning of "appropriate" policy, one can agree that there has been a lack of persistent support for many programs. Policies on foreign aid, military intervention, civil rights, or social welfare depend on volatile constituencies and ad hoc, bipartisan coalitions. The deficiencies of this process have become increasingly apparent as national attention has centered on problems requiring long and continuing effort, such as international development, racial integration, and environmental protection. Sustained action has been possible only on policies that have been removed entirely from partisan discussion, such as the Marshall plan, the landing on the moon, or, temporarily, legal equality for black southerners. Other programs—notably the anti poverty effort—have suffered from uncertainty and erratic changes.[25]

From the lack of coherent parties arises a second danger forecast by the *Report*, the overextension of presidential power. A "nonresponsible" party system "favors the President who exploits skillfully the arts of demagoguery, who uses the whole country as his political backyard, and who does not mind turning into the embodiment of personal government." The existence of inflated presidential power is widely acknowledged today. It is revealed in the failure of Congress to override a single presidential veto for ten years, in increasing delegation of legislative power, in presidential manipulation of opinion through the mass media, and, too tragically, in the conduct by three presidents of America's longest war without formal congressional action. It would be naive to believe that the existence of responsible parties would have prevented Vietnam, but it is clear that their absence increased the discretionary power of the executive.

The *Report* further warned of the possible disintegration of the two parties. Even in 1950, it believed that "a sizable body of the electorate has shifted from hopeful interest in the parties to the opposite attitude." These political Cassandras were not heeded then, for their statements seemed egregiously incorrect, in the face of survey data indicating that an overwhelming number of voters did identify with the major parties. By 1968, however, independents had become the second largest grouping in the electorate, while among college students, a clear majority did not identify with either the Democrats or Republicans.[26]

In addition to the decline in party loyalty, the Committee feared the development of "an unbridgeable political cleavage," for "if the two parties do not develop alternative programs that can be executed, the voter's frustration and the mounting ambiguities of national policy might also set in motion more extreme tendencies to the political left and the political right." In 1950 this warning was surely incredible. Twenty-one years later it seems most prescient. The development of political polarization is now a cliché, empirically demonstrated by the ten million votes for George Wallace and the far smaller numbers but equally obtrusive threats of Black Panthers, Weathermen, and other "revolutionaries." The development of extremist movements has been attributed to many causes, from permissive child-rearing to institutionalized racism, but surely one cause is strictly political—the perceived inability of our institutions to respond to intense demands for governmental action. As the *Report* warned, the absence of effective institutions has undermined the legitimacy and strength of the entire constitutional structure.

## The Perceptive Electorate

The trends and dangers of American politics have developed in many ways forecast by the Committee on Political Parties. At the same time, the electorate has come closer to fulfilling the requirements of a responsible party system.

A critical link between voter preferences and electoral choice was missing at the time of the *Report*. To effectuate his policy views, a voter must be able to support an appropriate party. Voters then, however, did not see the parties as representing policy differences. Only a minority believed that the parties differed on any of 16 detailed issues. Twenty years after the New Deal, for example, less than a third of the most informed voters believed there was a difference between the parties on the issue of government guarantees of full employment. Moreover, the electors did not have a clear view of the issue stances of Democrats and Republicans. Even among interested voters, consensus on the policy positions of the parties (i.e., agreement by 75% of the respondents) was achieved on only one issue. In such cases, "where there is a babel of perceptions about positions on a prominent issue, the significance of the public mandate becomes inscrutable."[27]

The American electorate of the 1950s thus could not sustain a system of responsible parties. There has been a striking shift in voter awareness. The evidence indicates that contemporary voters are far more likely to see a difference between the parties and to agree on the relative ideological positions of the parties. They more often believe that the parties are different, and that the

Democrats are liberal and the Republicans conservative. The changes are not total or complete, and the data are limited, but they do indicate that the potential for responsible parties is slowly emerging (see the data in tables 2.2 to 2.6, chapter 2).

There is no obvious demographic explanation for the electorate's increased awareness of differences between the parties. Neither the passing of generations, nor improved education, nor regional and racial difference provides a simple explanation. Yet in recent years, considerable political learning (or misperception, depending on one's view of the "real" character of the parties) took place. The explanation may be directly political. The events of the 1960s possibly served to make politics more relevant and more dramatic to the mass electorate. In the process, party differences were developed and/or perceived. Democrats diverged from Republicans, Democrats became liberal, and voters became more aware. The publicized battles over medicare and federal aid to education, the identification of a Democratic administration with programs of social welfare and civil rights, and its involvement in the dramas of Birmingham and Selma, made these issues appear to be particular concerns of the Democratic party. In the development of mass consciousness, a crucial event may have been the election of 1964, in which Barry Goldwater sought to clarify and widen the ideological differences between the parties.[28] Whatever the causes, the electorate now more fully satisfies one of the basic conditions for a responsible party system.

Other trends further increase the possibility—but by no means the certainty—of responsible parties. Some barriers to such change have been reduced. The power of congressional enclaves is being slowly decreased through the spread of party competition, the accidents of individual replacement (as in the passing of southern Democratic hegemony in the Senate), and deliberate reform actions such as the 1970 legislative reorganization act. Tentative steps toward party discipline have been taken in such actions as the exclusion of John Bell Williams from the House Democratic caucus and the purge of Charles Goddell from the national Republican party.

Moreover, state and local parties no longer have firm control over their own decisions. Out-of-state candidates now seek local nominations. New York and Connecticut last year held their first state-wide primaries, bringing to final fruition—for good or ill—the reform movement's challenge to the party organization's control over state nominations. Federal patronage available at local levels has been virtually eliminated with the establishment of an independent postal service. The traditional urban machine continues to weaken under the combined assaults of the old reform movements and the new thrust toward black control of urban areas. The national conventions, once the most prominent locale for bargaining between sovereign state parties, have come increasingly under the influence of unifying forces, such as television and nationwide campaigning. The power of the state parties will be further reduced by the reforms of the McGovern Commission.[29] The decline of local party power is fulfilling an essential precondition for more responsible parties.[30]

These developments toward a stronger national politics are a product of the incompetence of the traditional parties in dealing with national problems of economic management, race, and foreign policy. These trends also follow from the parties' inability to represent an electorate of 120 million that is transient, greatly affected by electronic means of communication, and of decreasing inherited loyalty. The decline of localized parties in turn reflects the establishment of a centralized nation-state—economically centralized by mature capitalist industry, governmentally centralized by an articulated national bureaucracy, and socially centralized by technology and a mobile population.

The nation is more ready for responsible parties today than in 1950. The possibility of their development is increased by the availability of mass energy for reform. Michael Rappeport finds an increasing correspondence of party and ideological position, which parallels the congruence we have found between partisanship and issue positions.[31] This correspondence is particularly notable among young voters whom we have also found to be more cognizant of party differences. The recent enfranchisement of eleven million voters under 21 may therefore create a new base of mass support for coherent parties. The new votes and new consciousness of blacks may also be turned in this direction. Differences between the parties are recognized more by blacks than by whites, and their needs for effective party action are greater. The narrowing of educational disparities in party perceptions is another indication of greater political consciousness. The increased independence of all voters also creates a potential for reform.

Other factors work in the opposite direction. The national parties have become less cohesive in the last generation, as many of their functions have been assumed by groups such as wealthy contributors, pollsters, the media, and campaign consultants. Politicians increasingly adopt stances of partisan independence. The weakening of state and local organizations has not meant a compensating strengthening of the national party. Rather, the addition of new primaries and other convention reforms is likely to disperse power still further. Moreover, many persons in the American electorate remain unconcerned with policy questions and unaware of party positions. And finally, the institutional obstacles to party government in the United States are enduring and deep, as the critics of the 1950 *Report* stressed.

There is no guarantee that the new political energies evident in the United States will be turned in the direction of responsible parties. Trends are not certainties. Other possibilities are drift, disaster, patchwork solutions, luck, and repression. The appeals of George Wallace, of black nationalism, of radical "thrashing," and of mindless patriotism are certainly more dramatic than the limited attractions of party reform. The era of pluralist consensus has clearly ended. The potential for a new era of responsible parties does exist. Whether the potential is developed may be the critical question for the future of American politics.

## Notes

1. "Toward a More Responsible Two-Party System," *American Political Science Review*, 44 (September 1950), Supplement. The *Report* was also separately published by Rinehart in 1950.
2. Major critical articles were Julius Turner, "Responsible Parties: A Dissent from the Floor," *American Political Science Review* 45 (March 1951), 143–52; Austin Ranney, "Toward a More Responsible Two-Party System: A Commentary," *American Political Science Review* 45 (June 1951), 488–99; Murray S. Stedman and Herbert Sonthoff, "Party Responsibility: A Critical Inquiry," *Western Political Quarterly* 4 (September 1951), 454–68; T. William Goodman, "How Much Political Party Centralization Do We Want?" *Journal of Politics* 13 (November 1951), 536–61. One prominent work can be viewed without great exaggeration as an extended refutation of the recommendations of the APSA Committee: Austin Ranney and Willmore Kendall, *Democracy and the American Party System* (New York: Harcourt, Brace, 1956).
3. Extended discussion of the subject continued in textbooks. See Hugh A. Bone, *American Politics and the Party System*, 2nd ed. (New York: McGraw-Hill, 1955), pp. 612–23; William Goodman, *The Two-Party System in the United States* (Princeton: Van Nostrand, 1960), p. 25; Clinton Rossiter, *Parties and Politics in America* (Ithaca: Cornell University Press, 1960), pp. 173–86; Frank Sorauf, *Party Politics in America* (Boston: Little, Brown, 1968), p. 16.
4. Rossiter, *Parties and Politics*, p. 1.
5. Ranney and Kendall, *American Party System*, p. 508.
6. Herbert Agar, *The Price of Union* (Boston: Houghton Mifflin, 1950), p. 689.
7. See Seymour Lipset and Stein Rokkan, *Party Systems and Voter Alignments* (New York: Free Press, 1967), pp. 1–64; E. G. Runciman, *Relative Deprivation and Social Justice* (Berkeley: University of California Press, 1966); David Easton and Jack Dennis, *Children and the Political System* (New York: McGraw-Hill, 1969), p. 3.
8. Henry Kariel, *The Decline of American Pluralism* (Palo Alto: Stanford University Press, 1961), p. 3.
9. Peter Drucker, "A Key to American Politics: Calhoun's Pluralism," *Review of Politics* 10 (October 1948): 412–46.
10. Goodman, *The Two-Party System*, p. 659.
11. Walter Dean Burnham, "The Changing Shape of the American Political Universe," *American Political Science Review* 59 (March 1965): 7–28.
12. Important critiques were presented by Kariel, Grant McConnell, *The Decline of Agrarian Democracy* (Berkeley: University of California Press, 1953), and E. E. Schattschneider, *The Semi-Sovereign People* (New York: Holt, Rinehart and Winston, 1960).
13. See Justice Harlan F. Stone's famous fourth footnote in U.S. v. Carolene Products Co., 304 U.S. 144 (1938).
14. Ranney and Kendall, *American Party System*, p. 532.

15. For an incisive general critique, see Theodore Lowi, *The End of Liberalism* (New York: Norton, 1969).
16. Stedman and Sonthoff, "Party Responsibility," pp. 459, 462, 465, 466.
17. Turner, "Responsible Parties," pp. 144–49. See also Turner, *Party and Constituency: Pressures on Congress* (Baltimore: The Johns Hopkins Press, 1950).
18. Turner, "Responsible Parties," pp. 150–51.
19. See William Riker, *The Theory of Political Coalitions* (New Haven: Yale University Press, 1962), pp. 2, 3. Sven Groennings *et al.*, eds., *The Study of Coalition Behavior* (New York: Holt, Rinehart and Winston, 1970), Part II; Anthony Downs, *An Economic Theory of Democracy* (New York: Harper, 1957), pp. 7, 8.
20. John Fenton, *Midwest Politics* (New York: Holt, Rinehart and Winston, 1966); Bernard Cosman, *Five States for Goldwater* (Tuscaloosa: University of Alabama Press, 1966).
21. Republican National Committee, *The 1968 Elections* (1969).
22. "1968 Campaign Financing," *Congressional Quarterly Weekly Report* 27 (December 5, 1969): 2435.
23. V. O. Key, Jr., *The Responsible Electorate* (Cambridge: Harvard University Press, 1966). See the review by Angus Campbell in the *American Political Science Review* 60 (December 1966): 1007–08.
24. *Report*, pp. 93–95.
25. See Lowi, *End of Liberalism*, pp. 6–9; and Daniel P. Moynihan, *Maximum Feasible Misunderstanding* (New York: Free Press, 1969).
26. The Gallup Poll, reported in *The New York Times*, of July 20, 1969, p. 25, and December 14, 1969, p. 55. Contrast Angus Campbell *et al.*, *The American Voter* (New York: Wiley, 1960), p. 124.
27. Campbell *et al.*, *American Voter*, pp. 182–84.
28. For a contrary view, see Philip Converse, "Electoral Myth and Reality: The 1964 Election," *American Political Science Review* 59 (June 1965): 330–35.
29. Democratic National Committee, Commission on Party Structure and Delegate Selection, *Mandate for Reform* (1970). While the McGovern Commission reports only to the Democratic convention, its proposals have obvious relevance to the Republican party as well.
30. See E. E. Schattschneider, *Party Government* (New York: Holt, 1942), pp. 6, 7.
31. "Trends in American Political Behavior" (paper presented at conference of the American Association for Public Opinion Research, Lake Placid, N.Y., May 22, 1970). Dr. Rappeport's paper is based on data collected since 1959 by the Opinion Research Corporation.

# 16

# The Decline of Partisan Politics

Political parties, along with mass elections, have been the hallmarks of modern popular democracy. The relationship between elections and democracy is obvious, even tautological. We do not properly speak of American democracy until the achievement of white male suffrage in the Jacksonian period, or of British democracy until the enfranchisement of the working class in 1867. It is also true that the development of competitive political parties has paralleled, and often preceded, growth in popular participation. Thus, the end of one-party Republican rule in 1824 stimulated America's expansion of the suffrage, as the competition of the parliamentary Liberal and Conservative parties promoted the extension of voting rights to English labor.

The historical union of parties and mass politics continues in modern times. National independence movements are typically led by a political party which sponsors and then employs mass suffrage to further freedom from colonial rule. The Congress party of India, the Mapai in Israel, and the Neo-Destour in Tunisia, are among the many examples provided by the twentieth century. Moreover, it is precisely these exemplary movements that have combined their own institutionalization with popular expansion and, thereby, have provided the most stable governments.[1]

## Parties, Elections, and Democracy

The joining of parties and democracy is not only historical but also often viewed as logically necessary. The principles of democracy—popular sovereignty, political equality, popular consultation, and majority rule—require partisan institutions for their realization. James succinctly points to their crucial role in democratic practice:

> The problem is how to organize and structure the relationship of the people to their agent, the government. Only if people control the government are they citizens. If the government can manipulate their responses, the people are only subjects. Classical democratic theorists did not pay a great deal of attention to the problems of staffing and operating the governmental institutions they pre-

scribed. In doing so, they virtually ignored politics, the activities and processes by which governmental policies are developed, influenced, decided, and enforced.[2]

Parties are found to fill this deficiency in prescriptive democratic theory. Once they were regarded as unhealthy challengers of national unity or, at best, tolerated as an undesirable but inevitable product of political freedom. Only recently have they become accepted as an accurate index of the existence of democracy itself, as much a part of its definition as mass suffrage.[3] Indeed, Duverger concludes, "liberty and the party system coincide. . . . The rise of parties and especially of working-class parties has alone made possible any real and active cooperation by the whole people in political affairs."[4]

In the acknowledged close relationship of parties and elections and democracy, the focus has been on the effect of parties on elections. Parties have been analyzed as fulfilling basic functions for a democratic system. Thus, Ranney and Kendall make "organizing elections" the first of four roles performed by the American party system. "A community, we have learned, needs *some* agency or agencies (a) to define the alternatives open to it, (b) to make clear to the voters what actually is involved in the choice among those alternatives, and (c) to encourage them to use their sovereign power to make the choice for themselves. . . . In the United States, as in the other democracies, the *parties* have taken on these tasks."[5]

Like others, these authors also mention other roles and functions of the parties, such as organizing government, promoting democracy, and nurturing consensus. Some writers have stressed a "constituent" role for parties[6] or urged a greater influence on public policy.[7] In most of the literature on American politics, however, the stress has been on the electoral functions of the parties—the recruitment and nomination of candidates, the writing of platforms, however vague, and the consequent framing of policy directions, the conduct of campaigns, and the staffing of electoral machinery. "In a word, the parties make the electoral process *work*"[8] and this has been the major function performed by the parties.

There is abundant evidence of—and commentary upon—the impact of the parties on the electoral process. More unique is the impact of the electoral process upon the parties. A political feedback loop has become evident recently, in which the nature and outcomes of elections affect the parties, leading to new influences upon succeeding elections, and further consequences for the parties themselves.

The net result of this process is the decline of partisan politics, most evidently in the choice of the president. The process has now reached the point at which the American political party is little more than one of many groups, not greatly disparate in their influence, which participate in elections. The party has been reduced from a quasi-public agency to a private association. Once a source of power, it has become another contestant for power in the pluralistic system.

## *The Party Past*

This decline can be easily noticed if we briefly review the position parties held in the electoral process through most of American history, even as recently as the end of World War II. Parties then typically possessed either legal or practical monopolies of three vital factors: legitimacy, resources, and recruitment.

The legitimacy of parties was evident in the loyalties expressed by the voters. Americans were fiercely loyal to the two major parties, whatever their labels in any particular historical era. Most voters retained the same party attachments throughout life. Although periodically disrupted at times of critical realignment,[9] even these realignments could be explained more by generational change than individual conversion.[10]

The depth of affection could be located in political humor, which abounds in stories such as that of the Irish family in Boston in which all the children developed well, except for the black sheep who became a Republican. It can be found in the accounts of the "militaristic" period of the nineteenth century, in which partisans were as devoted to the Republican and Democratic standards as their fathers in the Civil War had been loyal to the Union and Confederacy.[11] It can be found in the aggregate election statistics, in which communities returned virtually the same vote for each faction year after year, and ticket splitting or "drop off" in the vote at one end of the very long ballot was almost undetectable.[12] It can be found in modern survey data, in which up to 90 percent of the national samples of the 1950s identified consistently and openly with the major parties.[13]

Parties classically possessed not only legitimacy, but resources. One resource was access to the ballot itself, as the formal rules (written by party-dominated state legislatures) essentially eliminated nonparty candidates, even after adoption of the Australian ballot. Campaigning resources were also controlled by the parties, most evidently when precinct canvassing and turnout were the principal means of winning votes. The financing needed for elections was another party resource, with money raised and spent by party committees or individuals closely associated with these organizations, and independent organizations existed largely as means to evade unrealistic and unenforceable spending ceilings.[14] Patronage provided a means of supplying and multiplying these resources. Spoilsmen reinforced the party monopoly of governmental positions, campaigned for the organization, and contributed to its coffers.

The channels of political recruitment were also dominated by the parties. For most governmental offices in the United States, distinct ladders of political advancement could be located, with the rungs of the ladder held together by the party organizations.[15] Distinct regional patterns could be found as well, such as the apprenticeship system practiced by the Chicago Democratic organization.[16] In the Senate, in the ten-year period after the World War II, only 9 percent came to the body without previous political office.[17] Party domination of recruitment was evident in the highest office, the presidency, as well. Except for victorious generals, every national candidate advanced through a number of party positions before receiving his nomination. Precise rules of "availability" existed and served to explain "why great men are not elected president."[18]

Party domination of the presidential electoral process was based on these monopolies of legitimacy, resources, and recruitment. It can be illustrated by the nominations of 1932, the last year before the modern period of presidential races. In the incumbent Republican party, President Herbert Hoover was easily renominated despite his ineffectiveness in coping with the Great Depression. In control of executive patronage, he was able to keep the state parties in line and to ignore the signs of popular discontent evident in the few, and ineffective, state primaries.[19]

In the Democratic party, Franklin D. Roosevelt used the traditional base of the governorship of New York to win friends in party organizations throughout the nation, while largely ignoring primary contests. A contentious convention was capped by an explicit deal for the vice-presidency, bringing Roosevelt the nomination on the fourth ballot.[20] The campaign was conducted through the party organizations, with funds raised by them or closely allied committees, and with the issues largely confined to the conduct of the incumbent Hoover administration. Even though the election would ultimately be seen as one stage in a process of critical realignment, voting patterns showed significant continuity with the recent past: the ecological correlation of the vote, using states as units, reached the considerable level of .85, indicating the persistence of past loyalties even in this period of change.[21]

## The Modern Electoral Process

The contrast of this historical sketch with the modern election of the president is so great that we are really dealing not simply with a changed system, but an essentially different process. The differences are evident in five aspects: recruitment, strategies of nomination, campaign finance, national conventions, and electoral behavior. In each, considerable change has already occurred, and the effect of these changes is likely to be further deterioration of the parties in the future.

*Presidential Recruitment*

Presidential recruitment has changed in both its character and its sources. Campaigns for the White House now begin essentially through a process of self-selection and depend for their success on the development of organizations personally bound to the candidate. In what is perhaps the archetype of the modern campaign, that of John Kennedy in 1960, nine persons were critical: three members of the family, four personal friends and staff members, a public opinion analyst, and only one professional politician, John Bailey.[22] These persons had not been chosen because of their party positions. They were persons personally selected by the candidate to advance his personal career. As White summarized the process:

> John F. Kennedy in his fourteen years in politics has had many servants, many aides, many helpers. As he has outgrown each level of operation, he has gently stripped off his earlier helpers and retained only those who could go with him effectively to the next level. These men here assembled were those who had survived a decade of Kennedy selection.[23]

Since 1960, the importance of these personal organizations has become even more evident. Their character has evolved even further from coalitions such as John Kennedy's, based on personal loyalties. Increasingly they are based on relatively formal and contractual relationships, in which the candidate receives the services of strategists, media experts, pollsters, and other experts in exchange for a commercial fee or the opportunity of power. There is "a new kind of loyalty very much like 'bastard feudalism.' No longer does a clever and idealistic young man gravitate automatically into the sphere of a local leader. . . . He can join 'the Kennedys,' or he can attach himself to the retinue of some other 'good lord' who can promise high adventure and reward."[24]

The sources of presidential recruitment have changed as well. The traditional national candidates, such as Roosevelt, were the governors of large states. Their success in obtaining nominations had many sources, including their ability to evade the difficult decisions of national policy. A more important reason, however, may have been their command of the crucial resources of delegate votes at the national conventions. When state parties controlled their own means of delegate selection, the governor of a large state such as New York could be assured from the beginning of at least 15 percent of the number needed for victory.

The situation has altered dramatically. In the period since Roosevelt's first nomination, the most important base for presidential candidates has become the vice-presidency, once deprecated as "not worth a bucket of warm spit." Every vice-president in this period has become a presidential possibility, and a third of all nominations for the White House have gone to members of the group. In further contrast to the past, senators are more likely than governors to receive consideration, and they are almost as common as presidential nominees.[25]

In the past quarter of a century, only two governors have received their party's nomination, and both are exceptions that underline the loss of the traditional power of state parties. Adlai Stevenson was not selected because of his influence as governor of Illinois, but because he fit the needs of national party factions and interest groups for a unifying candidate. In 1976, the candidacy of Jimmy Carter is even firmer evidence of the decline of traditional bases of power. He surrendered state power long before the national convention. Although he received home state support, this support was due to a primary victory, rather than to party organization. He essentially lacked a local base of power, while he developed a transcending national constituency. Governors may still be nominated for president, but not because they are governors. To the contrary, they must demonstrate that they are national, not state, figures.

### *Nomination Strategies*

The Carter example leads to discussion of the second general change in the presidential electoral process, the new strategies of nomination. The basic change has been from strategies in which coalitions were based on geography, i.e., state parties, to those in which the coalitions are constructed from interest groups, demographic elements of the population, and issue publics. Candidates pursuing a purely geographical strategy have been remarkably unsuccessful, as illustrated by the universal failure of "favorite sons" in 1976. These candidates were unable to carry their home states if they were not viewed as serious national candidates as well. Thus Lloyd Bentsen was shut out in his native Texas and George Wallace seriously challenged in his Alabama domain. Conversely, even serious candidates cannot be assured that they will control their home states, as illustrated by the challenges to Wallace and to Californian Edmund G. Brown, Jr.

Even less successful are governors who seek to maintain control of their state delegations simply for bargaining purposes. Many observers had predicted a bargained Democratic convention in 1976 because of the assumed power of Democratic governors. In the event, no governor was able to maintain this control, as would-be kingmakers such as Hugh Carey in New York or

Milton Schapp in Pennsylvania found themselves overwhelmed by the national tides flowing over their personal turfs. Only in the case of California could the governor exercise some control, even while losing a quarter of the delegation, but this relative success required a candidate with more than a parochial home-state appeal.

The presidential nominating campaign has been nationalized. No longer is it true that there are no national parties, only fifty state parties, as the old textbook cliché read. At least for the presidency it would be more accurate to say that there are no state parties, and perhaps no national parties as well. The state parties have largely and deliberately written themselves out of the presidential nomination. Beset by new and complex rules for the selection of delegates, many state organizations have simply left the choice and mandate of convention delegates to state primaries.

The parties' place has been taken by candidate organizations. As campaigners, these candidate organizations are far different from the locally centered groups of the traditional state parties. By the 1976 campaign, canvassing itself was being handled by out-of-staters. Hundreds of Georgians went to New Hampshire to campaign for Jimmy Carter, while large numbers of Michiganders rang Florida doorbells for President Gerald Ford. That this "carpetbagging" drew little attention and no criticsm is quietly impressive evidence of the nationalization of the nominating process, and of its separation from local influences.

Other large national forces are affecting the nominiations. A principal means of campaigning is through the mass media. The standing of candidates is now certified not by their support among party leaders or their particular office but by a small group of reporters and commentators for newspapers, magazines, and television. "They are acknowledged experts, well connected in political circles throughout the land. Their reports appear in the nation's most prestigious newspapers and respected news broadcasts. . . . Collectively they are what columnist Russell Baker has called 'the Great Mentioniser,' the source of self-fulfilling stories that a person has been 'mentioned' as a possible presidential nominee."[26]

The national strategies of candidates are directed toward winning the notice of "the Great Mentioniser" and of the press generally, and then gaining more widespread public attention. Various tactics will be used to win this attention, since public opinion, and its measurement in the national polls, is usually decisive. Vital issues may be emphasized, as McGovern stressed Vietnam in 1972; or primary victories may be employed to demonstrate an attractive personality, as Carter did in 1976. Whatever the tactics employed, however, their common feature is that they depend little for their success on the support of party organizations.

Standing in the public opinion polls has become decisive in winning presidential nominations. With conspicuous exceptions, such as McGovern and Carter, the leader in the national polls before the primaries almost always goes on to win designation. Furthermore, it is virtually certain that the preconvention poll leader, even an insurgent such as McGovern or Carter, will be victorious in his party. To be sure, poll standings are affected by primaries and by direct support of the state parties, "but the strongest relations are the long-run effects in the opposite direction—the effects of national opinion on winning both the state primary elections and the presidential nomination."[27]

Candidates appeal to geographically diffuse constituencies, not to areal coalitions. The constituencies may be McGovern's opponents of the Vietnam War, or Ronald Reagan's ideological conservatives, or Carter's seekers for governmental purity, or Henry Jackon's laborites. Their common feature is their lack of local coloring. The diminishing impact of geography can also be seen in the convention decisions themselves. Until recently, there was a stable voting structure in both parties, in which the states could be consistently ordered along a single dimension.[28] In the Republican party, factions could be arrayed geographically and ideologically, from conservative to liberal, as in table 16.1. Conservative candidates such as Robert Taft or Barry Goldwater received their support from the same end of this spectrum (largely southern

**TABLE 16.1**
**Convention Candidates: Distribution of Votes for Selected Candidates (As Percentages of Their Total Votes*)**

| | Conservative | | | | Liberal | |
|---|---|---|---|---|---|---|
| *Republican Candidates* | *I* | *II* | *III* | *IV* | *V* | *N* |
| Eisenhower for president (1952) | 8.3% | 6.7% | 8.3% | 16.8% | 59.9% | 590 |
| Goldwater for president (1964) | 28.0 | 17.1 | 25.0 | 22.4 | 7.5 | 879 |
| Nixon for president (1968) | 27.0 | 17.2 | 25.3 | 12.6 | 17.9 | 673 |
| Ford for president (1976) | 20.3 | 6.8 | 13.9 | 8.4 | 50.6 | 1122 |

| | Liberal | | | | Conservative | | |
|---|---|---|---|---|---|---|---|
| *Democratic Candidates* | *I* | *II* | *III* | *IV* | *V* | *VI* | *N* |
| Kennedy for president (1960) | 28.9% | 24.5% | 19.3% | 25.4% | 0.5% | 1.4% | 685 |
| Johnson for president (1964) | 3.0 | 3.2 | 5.0 | 2.5 | 16.3 | 70.0 | 402 |
| Humphrey for president (1968) | 15.1 | 14.7 | 12.3 | 18.9 | 12.9 | 26.1 | 1689 |
| McGovern for president (1972) | 30.8 | 12.0 | 8.0 | 33.3 | 8.3 | 7.6 | 1676 |

*All votes are calculated before shifts. Alaska, Hawaii, and the territories are excluded.

and midwestern) and liberals from the other end (largely eastern). In the Democratic party, with the direction reversed, liberals received most support from the Midwest and Far West, conservatives from the South.

This structure has not been evident since 1964. There is limited correlation between the 1968 and earlier results.[29] Furthermore, in the 1972 Democratic and 1976 Republican conventions, the break from past patterns persists. Previous correlations of convention votes over time reached .95. However, the reproductibility of convention results is only .73 for the Democrats in 1972 and but .60 for the Republicans in 1976.[30] Thus, we find such anomalies as midwestern opposition to the liberal McGovern and support for the more moderate Carter, California support of Reagan, and southern and midwestern endorsement of Ford.

### *Political Money*

The decline of established partisan politics is further promoted by developments in campaign finance, most particularly the post-Watergate reform acts of 1974 and 1976. The full effects of the laws will not be known for some time, and they will certainly be different from both the intentions of Congress and the expectations of academic observers. The general effect, however, is already apparent. It is to shift money, the most vital resource of politics, from the parties to the control of individual candidates and to nonparty individuals and groups.

The new law, supplemented by the Supreme Court's interpretive decision of 1976, takes money away from the parties, while it provides finances for individuals and outside agencies. The parties are deprived of money by the limitations on individual contributors who may not give more than $1,000 to any single recipient. The total amount of spending by a candidate or party is also limited. While the national party may spend $3 million, its presidential candidate is limited to $20 million, plus adjustments and fund-raising expenses. While these restrictions are easily justified as means of preventing corruption, their effect is to limit politicians rather than to restrict electoral spending generally.

In fact, the law and the Supreme Court do not limit the influence of money in elections—but rather only the influence of party money. Four aspects of the legislation are particularly important. Existing provisions provide for federal subsidies for campaigning, but these subsidies are paid to candidates, not to parties. With the candidates provided seven times the capital that is permitted parties, this provision promotes the increasing separation of national candidates from the parties. Furthermore, subsidies are paid only to presidential candidates, leaving the rest of the party from Congress to local office fiscally unrelated to the head of the ticket. As interpreted by the Supreme Court, moreover, even the limitations on spending may be ignored by a candidate who declines federal subsidies and raises his own funds. Therefore, candidates of personal wealth or with close connections to such wealth—e.g., a Rockefeller or Kennedy—can still spend unlimited sums. Finally, there is no limitation on contributions or expenditures "independent" of the candidates and parties. Therefore individuals or groups are free to raise and spend whatever they wish, so long as they do not become allied to the political parties. It now becomes ever more to the advantage of political interests to ignore established politicians.

This legislation may become the classic illustration of the dominance of latent over manifest functions. We may doubt that Congress intended to subvert the political parties, but this is the cumulative impact of the finance law. It provides a sufficient explanation of the astounding Republican contest of 1976. The conventional wisdom of politics—and political science—cannot explain the near-success of Ronald Reagan. An incumbent president, however chosen, should easily win renomination. In the beginning of the election year, President Ford had achieved a measure of personal popularity; the Vietnam War had ended; there were signs of economic expansion; and the president had the support of almost all important party officials. Compared to Herbert Hoover's position in 1932, there was no reason to doubt his convention sucess. Nevertheless, Reagan persevered, and the availability of money must be considered a major reason for his persistence. Regardless of party pressure or early primary defeats, Reagan could continue to count on personal contributions, which were doubled in value by federal subsidies. He further benefited from independent expenditures by his sympathizers. The national government thus subsidized insurgency against its own chief executive.

In the Democratic party, with no incumbent leader, the law promoted factionalism, providing support for all comers, regardless of their standing in the party or chances of success. George Wallace, who split the party in 1968, gained proportionately the most federal subsidies, while even Ellen McCormack, running in opposition to the platform, became eligible for federal grants. The Supreme Court's suspension of the law during the vital primary period also affected the race, leaving Morris Udall in debt while allowing Carter, a relatively wealthy candidate, to raise funds privately.

The finance laws reinforce the other developments we have noted. They provide support for the personal, candidate-oriented organizations which now dominate presidential politics. They demand a national constituency, since funds must be raised in at least twenty states to be eligible for federal matching. By ignoring and slighting parties, they promote the general tendencies to emphasize other means of campaigning. They stimulate appeals to ideological and interest groups. Together, surely, these changes do not promote anything resembling a "responsible two-party system." Rather, they foster the turn toward "antiparty government."

### *The Decline of Conventions*

New finance laws have accelerated another trend, the elimination of the party nominating convention as a significant decision-making body. No convention since 1952 has taken more than a single ballot to nominate its presidential candidate. Throughout this period, moreover, with the exception of the 1976 Republican confrontation, the winner of the nomination has been determined before the convention actually convened. Only large blunders could have prevented the nominations of such front-runners as Kennedy in 1960 or Nixon in 1968, even though there was a spurious excitement to these meetings.

Once described as "a chess game disguised as a circus," the convention now resembles more a newspaper chess column in which amateurs replay the moves of past masters. Among the reasons for this decline of the convention is the loss of political expertise. The participants at these conclaves never acquired the skill to conduct grand negotiations, or have lost this ability through disuse. Like all talents, that of striking political deals requires practice, but contemporary convention delegates and their leaders have no experience upon which to draw. Even the few survivors of a bygone age, such as the late Mayor Richard J. Daley, find their skills atrophied through disuse. Surely the Deomcratic conventions of 1968 and 1972 were ideal occasions for the emergence of a compromise or dark-horse candidate, such as Edward Kennedy. Yet, in both years, the party's leaders fumbled away the opportunity to choose this likely winner.

The incapacity for negotiation was further demonstrated in 1976. Before the succession of Carter primary victories, there were widespread predictions of a negotiated nomination at the convention. A massive number of primaries, a bevy of candidates, and new rules for proportional division of delegates appeared certain to prevent any one candidate from winning the nomination by storm. Despite all of these favorable institutional factors, however, the party could not forestall the personal drive of one of the least known, and least well-connected, candidates. The likely result of a negotiated convention is further testament to the politicians' lack of control. A brokered convention, it appeared, would quickly turn to Hubert Humphrey, one of its oldest campaigners, who already had been defeated for the presidency. After decades of growth into the dominant party of the nation, with thirty-five governors and sixty-two senators available, the party would be so unresourceful as to turn to a proven loser. This hypothetical outcome is surely testament to the limited abilities of the pretended "bosses."

Largely without design, the Democrats in 1976 did nominate a candidate with personal appeal, supported by a skilled organization, who could unite the party. This result, however, is more a credit to Carter than the party. The situation among the Republicans provides still fuller evidence of party decline. With an incumbent president avid for nomination, with virtually all of their elected governors and national officials supporting him, the Republicans still could not prevent the insurgency of Ronald Reagan, nor control their own convention. While the Kansas City conclave did evidence real decision-making power, it also demonstrated the absence of party decisiveness.

The critical agencies in presidential nominations have changed. One of the most vital is the mass media, which appraise candidates, their abilities, and their chances of success. Candidates use the media to appeal directly to vital constituencies, rather than bargaining with party representatives. The media's particular interest in news results in the exaggeration of the importance of discrete events, and their interpretation of these events defines reality. Thus, the New Hampshire primary has been transformed from a minor test of popularity in a minor state to the event which gives a candidate "momentum." Television has further contributed to the decline of the convention by making classic negotiations virtually impossible, for "open covenants openly arrived at" are as difficult to achieve domestically as internationally. Parties do not want to present a messy picture of bargaining to their costless television audience. Instead they seek to present an image of unity and concord, and the result is dullness and impotence.

Party power over nominations has also been displaced by the spread of state primaries which mandate delegate votes. As recently as the 1960s, primaries elected fewer than one-third of the delegates and were useful largely as confirmations of the candidates' popular standing and electoral appeal. By 1976, nearly three-fourths of the delegates were chosen in these contests, and they had become decisive. A candidate carrying most, not necessarily all, of the primaries, would win the nomination as did McGovern and Carter. The convention could retain some power of decision only if the voters were clearly divided, as in the Reagan-Ford confrontation. The odds surely are against recurrence of this latter pattern. By removing the party organizations from the nominations, state presidential primaries sever the head of the political party's body—a dangerous condition.

### *Voters and Parties*

Electoral behavior provides the final evidence of the decline of the parties. The organized parties have less influence because they have less value to candidates. To win a presidential nomination once brought an aspirant not only ballot position, funding, and campaign workers. Most importantly, it assured him of a substantial share of the vote simply on the basis of the Democratic or

Republican label he had won. This label is less helpful today, and candidates therefore need pay less to its manufacturers.

The decreased impact of partisanship is abundantly clear. In answers to standard questions on self-identification, one-third to two-fifths of the American electorate now disclaim affective ties to the parties, and the proportion reaches a majority among the youngest voters.[31] There is a general disdain for parties, reflected in the large proportions who see them as contributing little to the maintenance of democratic government.[32]

Beyond identification, there are multiple indicators in actual behavior of disaffection from the parties. Nearly one of seven 1968 voters cast ballots for the third-party candidacy of George Wallace, and polls during that campaign placed his strength as high as one-fifth of the electorate. Electoral instability is evident as well in ticket splitting, in defection from the party of self-identification, and in vote switching from one election to the next.

The limited appeal of party loyalty is demonstrated in table 16.2, which partitions the electorate of 1972 on various dimensions to reach the core, partisan voter. We first separate the new voters in 1972, since they have not yet been able to develop a history of loyalty. We then successively locate the self-identified independents, those self-identified Democrats or Republicans who voted against their party's presidential nominee, those (of the remainder) who switched votes from 1968 to 1972, and finally those who split their tickets in the congressional race. Of all voters, only about one-third passed all of these tests.[33]

These aggregate figures may underestimate the electoral effect of partisanship. More complicated procedures, however, lead to the same conclusion, evidencing an increased effect of issue preferences and candidate appeals. One estimate is that party loyalty, even under favorable statistical assumptions, cannot explain more than half of the variance in the vote.[34] Another is

**TABLE 16.2**
**Composition of the 1972 Electorate**

| *Group* | *Percent of Total* | *(N)* |
|---|---|---|
| New voters of 1972 | 15.8 | (192) |
| Self-identified independents (excluding new voters) | 23.4 | (285) |
| Defectors from party identification (excluding new voters) | 16.0 | (195) |
| Switchers from 1968 vote (excluding previous groups) | 4.4 | (54) |
| Ticket splitters in 1972 (excluding previous groups) | 5.2 | (63) |
| Consistent partisan voters | 35.2 | (429) |
| Total | 100.0 | (1218) |

SOURCE: 1972 Election Study of the Center for Political Studies, University of Michigan.

31 G. Pomper, *Voter's Choice* (New York, 1975), p. 23.

32 J. Dennis, "Support for the Party System by the Mass Public," *American Political Science Review*, 60 (1966), 600–615; J. Dennis, "Trends in Public Support for the American Party System." Paper presented to the annual meeting of the American Political Science Association, Chicago, 1974.

that the percentage of pure partisan, issueless voters has declined drastically, from 42 percent in 1960 to 23 percent in 1972.[35] Other analysts place more emphasis on the appeals of candidates, rather than issues.[36] The common area of agreement is that party loyalty alone cannot be relied upon to win votes.

Candidates will be successful in this situation when they are, or can be made to appear, independent of the parties. Surely part of the success of Jimmy Carter must be explained by the opposition of the very party leaders whose favor was once needed to assure nomination. Similarly, the Repulican party designation was crucially affected by crossover votes, Democrats who felt no hesitancy in voting in Republican primaries. Thus, although Ford was the consistent choice of his own party's rank-and-file, he was threatened by these invaders who felt neither loyalty to their "own" party nor repugnance at formally entering the opposition. As strategies outside the parties show success and as voters become uncommitted to maintaining their past loyalties, we can expect further waning of party vigor.

## The Effect on the Parties

The state of the parties appears rather pitiful, when sketched at the present time. However, the important point is a dynamic one: the contemporary electoral process stimulates further decline of the parties. The lessons learned in one election become part of the influences in the postelectoral period and in the next contest, leading to acceleration of these trends.

One effect will be on candidate strategies. The success of Carter and Reagan's near nomination will encourage future candidates to emphasize their asserted independence of the party leaders. Indeed, this development was already evident in 1976 when California Governor Brown belatedly entered the presidential primaries, emphasizing his novelty and independence. Insurgency is no longer the crusade of political Don Quixotes; it is the likely path to the political kingdom.

### *Loss of Party Functions*

More generally, we can say that the electoral success of insurgents demonstrates that the political parties have lost their monopoly over recruitment. This loss is evident beyond the presidential level. The last areas to nominate state candidates through party processes were Connecticut and Indiana, but these bastions have fallen, and nomination through the direct primary is now universal. Even attempts by the party leaders to endorse candidates in the primary are now limited. Where attempted, such efforts are likely to be self-defeating, as in New York, where the party endorsement brings a candidate not votes but the burden of charges of "bossism." Nor are party careers necessary to advancement. The ambitious can switch parties, as did Donald

Riegle and John Lindsay, or be elected as pure independents, as did Governor James Longley of Maine, or seek high office without previous political experience, as did John Glenn and James Buckley.

Additionally, the party has lost its monopoly over vital resources. Presidential funds, as we have noted, are now independently provided through the federal government, and the 1976 Democratic platform promises similar support for congressional candidates. George Wallace was able to secure a place on the ballot in all of the fifty states, despite the opposition of both major parties, and the Supreme Court has facilitated access by other independent candidates, such as Eugene McCarthy in 1976. Campaigning is now accomplished not by party canvassers, but through the mass media or, locally, by unions and public employees organizations protected from party patronage demands by civil service laws. Delegates to national conventions are elected on the basis of their candidate preference, not as rewards for their loyalty and service to the organization.

As the parties become less able to control these vital resources of the electoral process, the voters respond less to their weakening appeals. The parties then lose their most vital strength, their very legitimacy. Slogans such as "vote for the man, not the party" come to be descriptions of behavior, not only advertising rhetoric. The data of table 16.3 point to a nonpartisan electoral future. Five political generations are defined, on the basis of the time they first voted: before the New Deal, during the Roosevelt elections, in the postwar period of 1948 to 1956, the 1960s, and 1972. These generations are then traced over the last four presidential elections. The data show that the proportion of Independents has risen considerably and that strength of partisanship has declined.[37] They also reveal that this increase has occurred in all political generations and that it is greatest among the rising generations in the electorate. It is therefore quite likely that Independents will soon constitute a plurality of the nation. The parties are disfavored by the voters. In this situation, they are likely to be ignored by ambitious office seekers and to be neglected in such public policies as campaign financing.

### *The New Party Strength*

At the same time as the parties have been weakened by these many tendencies, there has been another, apparently countervailing trend. This is the development of strong national party organizations, evident particularly among the Democrats. The party has created a coherent set of national institutions and binding rules which sharply contrast with the traditional portrait of the parties as decentralized and incoherent. It is simply no longer true, as Schattschneider wrote in his classic description, that incoherence "constitutes the most important single fact concerning the American parties."[38] Coherence

**TABLE 16.3**
**Partisan Identification by Political Generations***

| | *Strong Democrat* | *Weak Democrat* | *Inde-pendent* | *Weak Republican* | *Strong Republican* | *(N)* |
|---|---|---|---|---|---|---|
| Pre-New Deal | | | | | | |
| 1960 | 22.9% | 23.1% | 16.6% | 16.8% | 20.6% | (637) |
| 1964 | 30.7 | 20.7 | 14.6 | 15.4 | 18.5 | (410) |
| 1968 | 26.5 | 25.9 | 16.9 | 13.1 | 17.5 | (343) |
| 1972 | 20.5 | 24.8 | 19.6 | 15.8 | 19.3 | (419) |
| New Deal | | | | | | |
| 1960 | 20.3 | 25.3 | 26.8 | 13.9 | 13.6 | (679) |
| 1964 | 27.8 | 26.8 | 22.5 | 13.1 | 9.9 | (497) |
| 1968 | 20.2 | 26.2 | 26.4 | 18.0 | 9.3 | (451) |
| 1972 | 20.5 | 26.9 | 25.3 | 15.3 | 11.9 | (620) |
| Postwar | | | | | | |
| 1960 | 20.9 | 27.3 | 26.9 | 11.2 | 13.7 | (498) |
| 1964 | 25.1 | 27.5 | 25.9 | 13.6 | 8.0 | (375) |
| 1968 | 23.3 | 25.7 | 31.5 | 13.0 | 6.6 | (378) |
| 1972 | 15.7 | 25.9 | 35.3 | 13.1 | 10.1 | (567) |
| The 1960s | | | | | | |
| 1960 | 3.7 | 40.7 | 29.6 | 11.1 | 14.8 | (54) |
| 1964 | 22.9 | 25.7 | 32.9 | 12.0 | 6.4 | (249) |
| 1968 | 11.6 | 24.9 | 43.2 | 14.4 | 5.9 | (354) |
| 1972 | 8.9 | 24.8 | 46.0 | 13.4 | 6.9 | (642) |
| New voters | | | | | | |
| 1972 | 8.7 | 27.1 | 50.9 | 7.0 | 5.4 | (391) |

SOURCE: G. Pomper, *Voters' Choice* (New York, 1975).
*Cell entries are percentages adding horizontally by rows to 100 percent, except for rounding errors.

is evident in such indexes as congressional voting, where party unity has recently increased. It is even more evident in party organization.

Over the past twenty years, the national Democratic party has placed a number of restrictions on its once-sovereign state units. Beginning in 1956, state delegations to the national conventions were required to pledge loyalty to the national ticket—a relatively modest requirement. After 1964, racial discrimination in the selection of delegates was banned and was enforced by the exclusion of segregated state units. The most complete changes came as a result of the reform efforts of the McGovern-Fraser commission before the 1972 convention and of its sucessor, the Mikulski commission. The national party mandated increased and relatively proportional participation in party affairs at all levels by designated demographic groups (particularly racial minorities, women, and persons under thirty years of age). By 1980, the party will actively seek equal numbers of women and men. Further, it required changes in the means of selecting delegates, even when in conflict with state law or party practice, and has now established a complete system of proportional representation in every electoral unit. Delegate fees, early meetings, and irregular practices have been effectively abolished.

The party has also created itself as a national body, rather than as a collection of state units. Membership in the national convention is no longer based principally on electoral votes, a reflection of the states as constituent elements, but now equally weights the contribution of these states to a national Democratic vote. Similarly, the national committee once acknowledged state sovereignty by giving equal representation to all states, but now is weighted by the size of states and includes representatives from all branches of federal, state, and local government.

For the first time in American political history, the Democrats in 1974 adopted a national party charter, which gave permanent existence to the party, and provided for mid-term conferences of the party, giving it a visible existence other than during the four days of a presidential nominating convention. New organs of party government were created, including a national finance council, a national education and training council, and a judicial council to settle disputes and interpret party rules. The rudiments of a full governing structure are now in place, including the traditional legislative, executive, and judicial branches.

The national party is able to exercise these powers in the absence of legal constraints. In the 1972 Democratic convention, important credentials disputes turned on the right of the convention to exclude delegates from Illinois and California duly elected under state law. In both instances, these delegates were barred because the credentials committee ruled that they failed to meet some of the new reform rules. A critical decision of the Supreme Court upheld the right of the party to self-government because of the "the large public interest in allowing the political processes to function free from judicial supervision."[39]

The independence of political parties was further acknowledged in a later case involving the Republicans. A challenge brought against the national party disputed the allocation of convention delegates, arguing for application of the "one man, one vote" principle, in the same fashion as the apportionment of state or congressional representatives. The Circuit Court of Appeals, later upheld by the Supreme Court, declined to intervene, declaring the party free to organize "in the way that will make it the most effective organization . . . without interference from the courts."[40]

These decisions are important in themselves for they seem to conflict partially with the earlier position of the Supreme Court which recognized political parties as virtually a formal part of government. It was for this reason that the "white primary" was abolished, even when no state law was involved.[41] In these recent cases, however, the parties are permitted actions which are contrary to state law or which are different from principles of representation applied to formal governmental institutions. The result is to make the parties, at least on the national level, autonomous and potentially strong institutions. At the same time, the parties, as we have argued, are becoming weak influences in the political process. There is a seeming contradiction in the existence of strong institutions of little effectiveness.

### *The Party as Private Association*

The apparent contradiction can be resolved if we recognize that we are witnessing the transformation of American political parties. One element of the transformation is structural, an internal shift of power from state to national parties. While state parties are losing their functions, national parties are developing as coherent organizations. While state parties are not able to control national decisions such as the presidential nomination, national parties are more able to control state decisions such as the selection of convention delegates.

A more basic transformation is occurring as well, altering the place of parties generally in American politics. In the scholarly literature, and even in practice, parties held a special place among the many contestants for power, being recognized as the major intermediate associations between the citizen and the government. While multitudes of interest groups attempted to influence government, the political party was unique as an aggregator of interests, for "no interest group or alliance of such groups has supplanted the party as a device for mobilizing majorities."[42]

In contemporary America, it seems more accurate to describe the political party as little more than another private association or interest group. Like other associations, such as the American Medical Association, it attempts to influence elections, but both groups have only marginal effects. Like other associations of a nominally "private" character, it successfully claims independence from governmental regulation. The courts have long been hesitant to interfere with the internal organization of churches or unions. Now the courts have extended similar freedom, based on the same First Amendment principles, to the parties. This reluctance to prescribe party rules suggests that the organization of the Democrats and Republicans is no more politically relevant than the structure of the Episcopal Church or the United Mineworkers.

In elections, the parties are becoming only one of many actors, not the chief contestants. Parties are wooed by ambitious candidates, but so are the mass media. Parties contribute funds to these candidates, but so do private individuals and interest groups. Parties campaign for their nominees, but so do labor unions, and often more widely and more effectively. Parties sponsor candidates, but so do conservationists, business groups, and ideologues of various persuasions.

Even in their most characteristic functions, nominations, the formal party organizations lack an exclusive position. Delegates to the national conventions are successfully sponsored by these organizations in some places, such as Cook County, Illinois. Success is also achieved by interest groups, such as the 1976 Labor Coalition Clearinghouse, which chose over 400 Democratic delegates, by ideological groups such as New York liberals, and, most decisively, by candidate factions acting outside of or in opposition to the established parties. Once won, a party nomination must be supplemented by endorsements of interest groups, the media, and factional leaders. Eventually, with the increase in electoral instability, a party label on a candidate may come to have no more effect than a union label on clothing.

The nonpreferred position of the parties has now been partially incorporated into federal law. When Congress adopted a revised finance law following the Supreme Court's 1976 decision, a vigorous effort was needed to allow parties to receive contributions in the same manner as other political committees. The final statute does give some particular recognition to the parties, since individuals may contribute up to $20,000 to the parties, while they are limited to $5,000 in gifts to other committees. Nevertheless, the law still places the parties in the same juridical position as other private groups, even if it is more well-endowed for purposes of electioneering. However, parties are limited in their spending—giving them a less advantageous position than other committees, which may spend freely.

More generally, the political parties are being incorporated into the overall American system of "interest group liberalism."[43] The liberal model sees politics as a struggle of competing interests. Government is neither to grant privileges nor to handicap any group in this struggle. Government is to be an arbiter, to maintain the competition itself. Its role "is one of ensuring access particularly to the most effectively organized, and of ratifying the agreements and adjustments worked out among the competing leaders and their claims."[44]

This model explains many actions of American legislatures and bureaucracies and the character of policy outputs. We now see its application to the electoral process itself. Parties are permitted access, but so are other groups. Government encourages this access through financial subsidies, but no distinction is made among those seeking funds on the basis of their adherence to party principle or discipline. The goal becomes particpation for its own sake. Individual participation is encouraged through widespread primaries easily subject to crossovers and insurgencies. Candidate participation is encouraged by easy access to campaign subsidies and "equal time" on the mass media. Group participation is encouraged by permitting independent committees to solicit funds and spread propaganda. New social movements are encouraged through easy placement on the ballot and postelection subsidies. Government does not limit access to the political competition, nor regulate the organization of the competitors, but rather seeks only to stimulate more activity.

The defect of interest group liberalism as a general mode of government is its neglect of policy outcomes. Its application to electoral politics evidences the same defect, for it deprives the parties of a continuing, substantive meaning. Party programs then vary with the character of the particular activists and candidates of a specific time, rather than providing a persisting opportunity for voter judgment. To be sure, the national parties are more organizationally coherent and better able to enforce a measure of internal discipline. What the parties increasingly lack is a palpable reason for coherence and discipline. "There is therefore no substance. Neither is there procedure. There is only process."[45]

Many social trends have promoted the decline of partisan politics in the United States. At root, however, the decline can be traced to a theoretical failure, the placement of the parties within the ideology of interest group liberalism. The place of parties has not been fully considered, even by those most concerned with party reform. These advocates have championed the liberal solution of greater popular involvement in party decisions, while also seeking strengthened national organizations.[46] No contradiction between these aims was seen, as even the notable Schattschneider committee called for both centralized and open parties, arguing, "Clearly such a degree of unity within the parties cannot be brought about without party procedures that give a large body of people an opportunity to share in the development of the party program."[47] Today, the contradictions between these two goals are increasingly apparent. Parties can be both hierarchical and participatory only if they are also irrelevant.

The special place of parties must be rethought—and reclaimed. Ultimately, this revival of partisan organizations is properly the concern of advocates of representative government itself. The parties have provided the basic means of aggregating social interests, of simplifying choices for a mass electorate, and of permitting responsibility to be fixed for governmental achievements and failures. They have permitted the voters to make at least a retrospective judgment on public policy and occasionally to provide direction for the future.[48] In the context of the 1976 elections, it is difficult to see these functions being fulfilled. While a Jimmy Carter may enforce unity on the Democrats, this is a personal triumph, implying no permanent responsibility of the party. Among Republicans, the most basic agreement between Ford and Reagan was that neither had any responsibility for the actions of a twice-elected president of their party. Can elections without parties then be anything but short-term choices of particular candidates and their idiosyncratic policies?

The ultimate cost of the decline of parties is the loss of popular control over public policies and the consequent inability of less privileged elements to affect their social fate. "Political parties, with all their well-known human and structural shortcomings, are the only devices thus far invented by the wit of Western man which with some effectiveness can generate countervailing collective power on behalf of the many individually powerless against the relatively few who are individually—or organizationally—powerful."[49] The policy result of party decline will be a fundamental conservatism, with no alternate agency available to generate the political power of a popular majority.

Elections will surely continue, for they have demonstrated their social utility in investing rulers with legitimacy. Social movements will periodically express the discontents of neglected and disadvantaged groups. Grievances will be heard and responded to from time to time by sensitive individual leaders and by legislators concerned over their personal or their constituents' futures. The republican form will persist, even while alienation further develops.

Yet, if the decline of partisan politics continues, if parties become only one among many participants in elections, much will be lost. We may identify the losses as choice, as clarity, as diffuse support, or as the effective aggregation of political interests. But, in a single word, the loss will be that of democracy.

## Notes

1. Samuel P. Huntington, *Political Order in Changing Societies* (New Haven, Conn., 1968), chap. 7.
2. J. James, *American Political Parties in Transition* (New York, 1974), p. 7.
3. R. Hofstadter, *The Idea of a Party System* (Berkeley, Calif., 1969).
4. M. Duverger, *Political Parties* (New York, 1954), p. 424ff.
5. A. Ranney and W. Kendall, *Democracy and the American Party System* (New York, 1956), p. 505.
6. T. Lowi, "Party, Policy and Constitution in America," in W. N. Chambers and W. D. Burnham (eds.), *The American Party Systems* (New York, 1967).
7. American Political Science Association, Committee on Political Parties, "Toward a More Responsible Two-Party System," *American Political Science Review* 44, (1950): supplement.
8. Ranney and Kendall, *Democracy and the American Party System*, p. 505.
9. V. O. Key, "A Theory of Critical Elections," *Journal of Politics* 17 (1955): 3–18.
10. P. Beck, "A Socialization Theory of Partisan Realignment" in R. G. Niemi (ed.), *The Politics of Future Citizens* (San Francisco, 1974), pp. 199–219.
11. R. Jensen, *The Winning of the Midwest* (Chicago, 1974).
12. W. D. Burnham, "The Changing Shape of the American Political Universe," *American Political Science Review* 59 (1965): 7–28.
13. A. Campbell, P. Converse, W. Miller, and D. Stokes, *The American Voter* (New York, 1960), p. 124.
14. A. Heard, *The Costs of Democracy* (Garden City, N. Y., 1962).
15. J. A. Schlesinger, *Ambition and Politics* (Chicago, 1966).

16. M. Snowiss, "Congressional Recruitment and Representation," *American Political Science Review* 60 (1966): 627–39.
17. D. Matthews, *U. S. Senators and Their World* (Chapel Hill, N. C., 1960), p. 51.
18. J. Bryce, *The American Commonwealth*, 3d ed. (New York, 1914), Vol. 1 , p. 80.
19. R. Bain, *Convention Decisions and Voting Records* (Washington, D. C., 1960), p. 234ff.
20. J. A. Farley, *Behind the Ballots* (New York, 1937), pp. 132–53.
21. G. Pomper, "Classification of Presidential Elections," *Journal of Politics* 29 (1967): 566.
22. T. H. White, *The Making of the President 1960* (New York, 1961), pp. 59–63.
23. Ibid., p. 63.
24. L. Chester, G. Hodgson, and B. Page, *An American Melodrama* (New York, 1969), p. 233.
25. W. Keech and D. Matthews, *The Party's Choice* (Washington, D. C., 1976), p. 218ff.
26. Ibid., p. 13.
27. J. R. Beninger, "Winning the Presidential Nomination: National Polls and State Primary Elections, 1936–1972," *Public Opinion Quarterly* 40 (1976): 37.
28. F. Munger and J. Blackhurst, "Factionalism in the National Conventions, 1940–1964," *Journal of Politics* 27 (1965): 375–94.
29. G. Pomper, "Factionalism in the 1968 National Conventions," *Journal of Politics* 33 (1971): 826–30.
30. The correlation is calculated as a Democratic comparison of McGovern's support, by states, with that of the combined Kennedy, Humphrey, and Stevenson vote in 1960, and a Republican comparison of Ford's support with that of Eisenhower in 1952. These were judged the most comparable previous convention alignments. The 1976 roll call is found in *Congressional Quarterly Weekly Report* 34 (August 21, 1976): 2313.
31. G. Pomper, *Voter's Choice* (New York, 1975), p. 23.
32. J. Dennis, "Support for the Party System by the Mass Public," *American Political Science Review* 60 (1966): 600–15; J. Dennis, "Trends in Public Support for the American Party System," (paper presented to the annual meeting of the American Political Science Association, Chicago, 1974).
33. The figures in table 16.2 were calculated to eliminate overlapping of the various categories, so that the ticket splitters, for example, are only those voters who otherwise meet all tests of party loyalty. In the total sample, however, many persons do manifest more than one of these behaviors. Overall, independents constituted 30 percent of the 1972 sample: 27.1 percent defected from their self-identified party; 27.3 percent were party switchers from 1968 to 1972; and 29.5 percent split their presidential-congressional tickets.
34. Pomper, *Voter's Choice*, p. 163.
35. N. H. Nie, S. Verba, and J. Petrocik, *The Changing American Voter* (Cambridge, Mass., 1976), p. 302.
36. S. Kirkpatrick, "Candidates, Parties and Issues in the American Electorate," *American Politics Quarterly* 3 (1975): 268.
37. Pomper, *Voter's Choice*, p. 23.
38. E. E. Schattschneider, *Party Government* (New York, 1942), p. 32ff.
39. *O'Brien* v. *Brown*, 409 U.S. 1 (1972).
40. *Ripon Society* v. *National Republican Party*, 525 F.2d 567 (1975), cert. denied 96 S.Ct. 1147 (1976).

41. *Smith* v. *Allwright*, 321 U.S. 649 (1944); *Rice* v. *Elmore*, 165 F.2d 387 (1947).
42. D. B. Truman, *The Governmental Process* (New York, 1951), p. 272.
43. T. Lowi, *The End of Liberalism* (New York, 1969), chap. 3.
44. Ibid., p. 71.
45. Ibid., p. 97.
46. A. Ranney, *Curing the Mischiefs of Faction* (Berkeley, Calif., 1975).
47. American Political Science Association, "Toward a More Responsible Two-Party System," p. 18.
48. V. O. Key, *The Responsible Electorate* (Cambridge, Mass., 1966).
49. W. D. Burnham, *Critical Elections and the Mainsprings of American Politics* (New York, 1970), p. 133.

# 17

# The Nomination of Hubert Humphrey for Vice-President

The nomination of Hubert Humphrey as the 1964 Democratic candidate for vice-president constituted one of the most unusual incidents in recent political history. It was achieved through an active campaign, but one of limited public involvement. Humphrey's designation was achieved ostensibly through the deliberate choice of one individual, Lyndon Johnson, but only after an extensive effort to direct his choice to the Minnesota senator. All of the participants in the decision were greatly influenced by the presence of Robert Kennedy, who was not even a candidate by the time of the Atlantic City convention.

Moreover, the vice-presidential nominating contest was remarkable in that it existed at all. The office involved is one which has been the object of ridicule for almost all of American history. The common evaluation of the "second counsel" was most bitingly expressed by the famous Mr. Dooley:

> Th' prisidincy is th' highest office in th' gift iv th' people. Th' vice-prisidincy is th' next highest and th' lowest. It isn't a crime exactly. Ye can't be sint to jail f'r it, but it's a kind iv a disgrace. It's like writin' anonymous letters. At a convintion nearly all th' dillygates lave as soon as they've nommynated th' prisidint f'r fear wan iv thim will be nommynated f'r vice-prisidint. . . . If ye say about a man that he's good prisidintial timber he'll buy ye a dhrink. If ye say he's good vice-prisidintial timber ye mane that he isn't good enough to be cut up into shingles, an' y'd betther be careful.[1]

More recently, the office has been paid greater respect. Increasing governmental responsibilities have been placed upon the vice-president, particularly since the passage of the National Security Act.[2] The political importance of the office has increased as well, as demonstrated most strikingly by Richard Nixon's successful bid for his party's presidential designation in 1960. Above all, the assassination of John Kennedy has made politicians and voters aware of the significance of the vice-presidency.

## The Outlook in 1964

Until November 22, 1963, no serious controversy existed in regard to the future national leadership of the Democratic party. Renomination of the successful 1960 ticket was certain. Senator Humphrey, for his part, seemed to have reached the culmination of his career. After unsuccessful attempts to win a national nomination in the past, he had become Senate party whip, and might expect eventually to be majority leader. The road to the White House, however, appeared blocked. John Kennedy, if re-elected, would be president until 1969. The principal alternative inheritors of his leadership appeared to be Attorney-General Robert Kennedy or Vice-President Lyndon Johnson. Certainly Humphrey had little reason to expect to be the center of activity in Atlantic City. Free of other commitments, he agreed to do a twice-daily commentary for the American Broadcasting Company during the convention.

The Dallas assassination necessarily brought great political changes. Johnson's accession to the presidency carried with it the leadership of the party. His nomination for a full term was rapidly assured, but the question of a vice-presidential candidate was thrown completely open. The most obvious possibility was the attorney general. It is doubtful if Johnson ever wanted Robert Kennedy on the ticket with him. There were many differences of temperament and policy between them. A proud man, the new president naturally wanted to win the forthcoming election without debt to the name of his martyred predecessor. Moreover, the two men had been rivals in the past, and Johnson had suffered defeat in 1960 after a campaign directed by Robert Kennedy.[3]

Despite his own feelings, however, Johnson had to take account of the great political strength of the attorney general. After the assassination, Robert Kennedy became the object of deep emotional support. In the three years that his brother had been president, moreover, the national party machinery had become dominated by those close to their family. Indeed, a movement to place the attorney general on the ticket began in earnest early in 1964. In the New Hampshire primary, through write-in votes, 25,000 Democrats indicated their preference for him as the vice-presidential candidate.

Johnson played a waiting game, expecting the emotional reaction to the assassination to subside, while he preserved his freedom of choice. To maintain that freedom, he began to create an extensive public list of possible running mates. Inclusion of Sargent Shriver served to decrease the concentration on Robert Kennedy as the political heir of the late president. Addition of other names served to prevent a concentration of support or opposition on any other single possibility.[4]

Hubert Humphrey had been mentioned as a possible candidate from the first. He had the advantages of a widespread and generally favorable public reputation, accumulated governmental experience and demonstrated ability in a wide range of subject areas. His political strength was equally important. The Minnesota senator was an active participant at the four previous Democratic conventions. He led the successful fight for a stronger civil rights plank in the 1948 convention, and was a favorite son candidate in 1952. Four years later, he actively sought the vice-presidential nomination and in 1960 he fought John Kennedy in the presidential primaries. Through such experiences, he developed a wide acquaintanceship in the party, which he strengthened by a heavy schedule of attendance and speeches at the great variety of American political functions.

Humphrey's political assets were well suited to the campaign he was about to enter. He had the broad party support and personal friendships—including that with Johnson—that were to prove vital in 1964. In previous national campaigns, he failed because he lacked the resources necessary to win mass support—money, or "charisma," or professional advice.[5] In this campaign, these deficiencies, where they still existed, were of less importance.

The senator was also able to make good use of the unique position held by President Johnson. By the time the Democratic convention met, the delegates had accepted, almost as self-evident truth, the proposition that "the presidential candidate selects his own running mate." An unbounded prerogative was assumed to exist. Historically, this was certainly not the case. Open contests for the vice-presidential nomination have been frequent, and internal party conflict over the choice has been common. Perhaps the only presidential candidate who actually dictated the selection of a running mate was Franklin Roosevelt in 1940.[6] His preference for Henry Wallace aroused such antipathy within the party, however, that it was not a happy precedent for Johnson.

The freedom granted the president was historically unique. In part, it can be explained by the fact that he was still enjoying the "honeymoon" accorded a new president—a "honeymoon," moreover, occurring immediately before the expected consummation of the November election. The Kennedy assassination, too, had left its mark. Democrats remembered, in keynoter John Pastore's words, "that day four years ago in Los Angeles when John F. Kennedy said, "I need you, Lyndon Johnson.' "[7] They believed that the choice had been made by Kennedy alone and, as proven by the transfer of power after the assassination, that it had proven a wise choice. It therefore followed, in party logic, that the best choice would always be made by the presidential candidate acting independently.

The president's freedom, however, while greater than in most conventions, was not unlimited. Other elements of the party at least retained the prerogatives Bagehot had accorded to the British Crown: the rights to be consulted, to encourage, and to warn. Johnson might have succeeded in forcing the convention to ratify even some outrageous choice, but it would have been very costly in political support, a cost he was not likely to assume.

For Humphrey, the limits on the president served to increase his own chances for the vice-presidential nomination. These limits brought Johnson's attention to focus on prominent political figures, such as the Minnesota senator, and decreased his consideration of obscure "dark horses." At the same time, Humphrey had the favor of the president. Coming to the Senate in the same year, 1948, the two had always been friendly. They shared the intense experience of defeat by John Kennedy in 1960. After the assassination, the Minnesotan became virtual leader of the Senate Democratic party. Humphrey was particularly prominent during the three-month filibuster on civil rights legislation, which occupied the Senate during the very time the vice-presidential campaign was conducted.

Unlike Robert Kennedy, then, Humphrey did not have to pressure the president into making a choice he personally opposed. Instead, his task was to persuade Johnson to make a selection he found satisfactory, at least, or actually favored personally. The strategy decided upon, more by his staff than the senator himself, was that of "the next best man." All efforts were directed toward convincing significant persons and groups that the running mate should be selected strictly on grounds of ability, rather than narrow electoral appeal. A short document was distributed, usually without comment, to the press, prominent individuals, party personnel, and others who might be able to influence the "attentive public" or the president himself. The theme of the document was simple:

> The sudden death of President Kennedy, the subsequent succession of President Johnson, the present vacancy in the office of the Vice-Presidency, have all underlined the necessity for the Vice-President to be the man next-best-qualified for the Presidency itself. . . . [Other] factors—in the nuclear age—are overshadowed by the necessity of guaranteeing that, should tragedy befall the President, the nation would be under the most experienced and capable leadership available.[8]

A small staff of the senator's close friends and assistants was assembled to spread this message. Fewer than two dozen persons were continuously involved in this campaign.

## Pre-Convention Campaigning

The actual conduct of the campaign cannot be portrayed as following a logical and pre-established plan. Like most political efforts, it was marked by considerable innovation, intuition, and improvisation. Chronology does not help greatly to order events, either, for several efforts were being conducted simultaneously. The organized campaign for Humphrey began in January 1964. Commenting on a poll of Democratic county chairmen which showed him the leading candidate, the Minnesota senator carefully showed his interest and deference: "It is, of course, an honor to be associated with President Johnson," he replied, "and it would be a singular honor to be with him on the Democratic ticket. . . . The decision for vice-president, however will be made by the Democratic convention, which I am confident will respect the wishes in this matter of President Johnson."[9]

In the weeks following, there was only one date of crucial importance. This was July 30, the day on which President Johnson formally excluded Robert Kennedy from consideration for the vice-presidency. Without further explanation, the president told the press he had decided against any "member of the Cabinet or those who meet regularly with the Cabinet."[10] This criterion also ruled out of consideration Secretaries Dean Rusk, Robert McNamara, and Orville Freeman, as well as Sargent Shriver and Adlai Stevenson. Until this time, Humphrey was only one of several possible candidates. After July 30, his backers shifted their emphasis toward building a consensus on behalf of the senator.

The pre-convention campaign can be best analyzed by observing the efforts made to win support from three important elements: the major constituent interests of the Democratic party, the delegates and leaders of the national convention, and the general public. For purposes of analysis, the latter group is considered to include the president, although he was obviously the object of the other efforts as well.

As Will Rogers once quipped, the Democrats constitute "no organized party." Rather, they are a heterogeneous assembly of divergent interests. Humphrey attempted to win support from all of these various groups. Labor backing was vital. In March, Walter Reuther blocked a movement at the annual convention of the United Automobile Workers to endorse Robert Kennedy for vice-president. He then campaigned among his union colleagues for Humphrey. By July, all members of the AFL-CIO Executive Council had indicated their support of the Minnesotan, and George Meany, president of the labor federation, was particularly emphatic in his support.[11] These endorsements were important not only as a direct aid to the senator. They also indicated that Robert Kennedy lacked some of the support his brother held in 1960. Polls of labor leaders, taken at the behest of the Humphrey staff, also indicated strong labor endorsement of the senator. Similarly, polls among Democratic farm leaders indicated wide backing for the Minnesotan, and this preference was reinforced by that of party leaders from farm areas.

The senator had the early support of civil rights groups, because of his long championing of their cause and his current leadership of the Senate floor fight. When cloture was invoked and a strong civil rights act passed under

Humphrey's leadership, his standing with these groups was further strengthened. This demonstration of legislative skill also caused Humphrey to exult that "an albatross has now become my greatest asset."

Humphrey strength was notable within the party organization. A June Gallup poll of 3,000 county chairmen showed him ahead of all other contenders as the personal preference of the chairmen. Leading Robert Kennedy, the runner-up in the poll, by nearly a 2 to 1 margin, Humphrey headed the field in all regions but the South. In that area, he trailed Stevenson and Senator William Fulbright. With these exceptions, the Minnesotan led all other possibilities by a 2 to 1 margin in southern chairmen's preferences.

Opposition to Humphrey existed, but was restricted. As shown in the poll of chairmen, he was relatively weak in the South, where his liberalism alienated many, but not all, voters and leaders. Thus, most southern senators favored other candidates, but the majority whip did win the endorsement of some southern colleagues. This support was rendered even as the protracted civil rights filibuster continued.

The Minnesotan also lacked support from the bulk of the remaining big city "machines," such as those of Chicago, New York, and Philadelphia. In part, this position was based on loyalty to Robert Kennedy and the desire to have a Catholic on the national ticket. Moreover, Humphrey's liberalism, intellectualism, and effusiveness, as well as his rural, Protestant heritage, were alien and suspect. These groups, however, were neither sufficiently concerned nor sufficiently powerful to attempt to block Humphrey. Significantly, they were not united. In New York, for example, while older "bosses," such as Charles Buckley of the Bronx, personally opposed Humphrey, younger "reform" elements supported the senator.

The only other element of the party potentially opposed to Humphrey was the business community. Normally, a Democratic ticket expects and seeks only limited support from industry. In 1964, however, the Republican party's nomination of Barry Goldwater and President Johnson's personal stress on national unity indicated increased importance for this group within the party. To gain its endorsement, Humphrey attended a series of private receptions for business leaders in July, seeking to allay suspicions that he was unfriendly to their interests, and accepted invitations to address groups such as the American Management Association.

No direct solicitations were made of those present at the business receptions, but volunteers were asked to let the president know their opinion of Humphrey. Others offered financial help or spoke to other businessmen on his behalf. Although all of them did not later support Humphrey, those attending the meetings included President Eisenhower's treasury secretary, the president of the New York Stock Exchange, and executives of such firms as Sears Roebuck, Metropolitan Life Insurance, General Dynamics, the New York

Central Railroad, Anaconda, and Inland Steel. Members of both parties and leaders of corporations of various sizes were included. The emphasis was toward proportionately greater representation of Democrats and middle-sized firms.

These various efforts were directed in part at gaining the support of the president. They were undertaken, however, in recognition of the fact that the president would be influenced by the opinions of the many elements in the Democratic coalition. That Johnson did not have a completely free choice was indicated by the elimination of Defense Secretary McNamara. This occurred well before the July 30 announcement. Labor leaders strongly objected to the inclusion of a former corporation president on the national ticket, particularly one associated with the Ford Motor Company, a traditional opponent of Walter Reuther's Automobile Workers. McNamara's rejection of a 1961 AFL-CIO nomination for a Defense Department position had also roused resentment. Party organization leaders, particularly the Michigan state party and National Chairman John Bailey, also were severely critical of the possible nomination of a non political figure and one, moreover, who had voted for and contributed large sums to the Republican party. Faced with these objections, the president recognized the political limits on his freedom of choice and rejected the Defense head.

The second major effort in the pre-convention campaign was directed toward the party convention delegates. This effort was carefully discreet. No "pressure" was applied, and the Humphrey group was extremely cautious to avoid any action which might seem to be an attempt to force the hand of the president. The basic purpose was defensive, to be prepared for any change in the situation.

Many of the actions in this period were directed toward preparing for a possible floor fight. In part, this preparation was due to memories of the 1956 convention, when Adlai Stevenson had allowed the convention a free choice of his running mate. Surprised on that occasion, and conditioned by their past experience, Humphrey backers did not want to be caught off guard again should Johnson allow the delegates to make the decision. Few, however, expected the president to permit this freedom. Far more likely, it was thought, was an attempt to stampede the convention into the nomination of Robert Kennedy by an emotional invocation of the late president's memory. Such an attempt was feared even after the July 30 statement.

To prepare for any open contest, the Humphrey group began to canvass delegates. Although similar in many respects to a presidential campaign, the effort was far more reserved. The friendships, contacts, and knowledge gained in four previous conventions were put to use. The senator's supporters had learned, in Theodore White's words, "The root question of American politics is always: Who's the Man to See? To understand American politics is, simply, to know people, to know the relative weight of names—who are heroes, who are straw men, who controls and who does not."[12]

Delegates were won without primary election contests or open attempts to win commitments from state parties. In a few cases, known supporters of the senator were contacted and asked, if possible, to win designation as convention delegates. Since no contests were expected at the national convention, party leaders of moderate influence were able to win places without controversy. In order to judge the strength of the various candidates, a letter containing an informal poll was sent to pro-Humphrey leaders in each state. Dated July 30, the letter asked for the preferences of each delegate among four vice-presidential possibilities: Robert Kennedy, Humphrey, Shriver, and Stevenson. Space was left for indications of the past convention status of the delegates and remarks. Copies of the poll results were to be sent to a designated "local coordinator" and to the unnamed "resident" at a suburban Washington address. The anonymity of the poll indicates how careful the Humphrey group was to avoid an open campaign and to respect the freedom of the president. The date of the letter, and its list of names, indicate that the senator's backers were not informed any considerable time before the president eliminated the major rivals of the Minnesotan.

In reply to the poll, varying assessments were received. A majority of the delegates were prepared to accept Johnson's vice-presidential preference, but among the contenders, Humphrey had the most support. With this information, his backers were reasonably well informed as to the sources of support for each possible candidate. Robert Kennedy, in this informal poll, was shown to be the second-strongest contender. However, his support was less broadly based than that of Humphrey, being centered in the Northeast. Almost all southern delegations were strongly opposed to Kennedy's nomination. Significantly, while not enthusiastic about Humphrey, they were willing to accept his designation. Some delegates favorable to Humphrey not only answered the poll, but also announced their preference to the local press or wrote to the president on Humphrey's behalf.

Even the best of plans might go astray. Some preliminary thought was given to a convention organization, but these tentative plans ultimately were abandoned. Many in the Humphrey group feared that the convention would become "an emotional bath" in memory of John Kennedy, and that this would lead to the nomination of the attorney general for vice-president. In news interviews and in a trip to Poland and Germany, Robert Kennedy seemed to be publicizing his qualifications. A poll taken by this writer indicated that he was the choice of a plurality of New Jersey delegates, and similar support in other states had been found by the Humphrey group. Rumors were current that Mrs. Jacqueline Kennedy would attend the convention to arouse emotional support for her brother-in-law.

To avert a Kennedy bandwagon, Humphrey backers hoped for public support of the senator by President Johnson before the opening of the convention, and these wishes were partially met by the public disapproval of Robert Kennedy on July 30. The anxieties were further relieved when the Democratic National Committee changed the convention program, deferring a special memorial tribute to President Kennedy, introduced by his brother, until after the nominations were made. The postponement was also announced on July 30, reportedly after a personal decision by the president.[13] In the event, the memorial did become the occasion for a spontaneous emotional demonstration. Delay helped Humphrey.

The president's actions left the Humphrey staff free to concentrate on building support for their own candidate, rather than defending against any other possibility. After the July 30 statement, the White House, probably upon the personal direction of President Johnson, encouraged Humphrey to develop support in his own cause.[14] The senator and his staff then expanded the third phase of the campaign, seeking the support of the more general public. Best characterized by one aide as "a campaign not of silence, but of restraint," it was oriented toward gaining the endorsement of influential officials, public spokesmen, and the press, without stimulating a mass movement which might offend the president.

One means of maintaining this delicate balance was to isolate Senator Humphrey himself from most of the overt activity. The sampling of delegate sentiment and other sensitive tasks were left to the staff and friends. The senator kept himself before the public by his activities in the Senate. He accepted a number of invitations for television interviews, speeches, and press conferences. Though non political in inspiration and content, a half-hour television program on "My Childhood" was particularly effective.

Humphrey also continued his contract for television commentaries during the convention with ABC. The Minnesotan had many personal reasons, including financial need, for adhering to his earlier commitment. Politically, it would have been difficult to withdraw from the agreement without appearing to pressure the president. For similar reasons, Humphrey continued as a delegate to the convention and even appeared on the floor before his own nomination.

While the senator remained available, discreet public support was stimulated. At this time, all politically important visitors to the White House were being asked their opinions on the ticket. Even Senator Humphrey was asked about his rivals. As he described the situation later to a reporter, "It's like a guy calling the girl next door—who he knows is madly in love with him—to ask the phone number of the newest broad in town."[15] When friends of the senator expressed a desire to aid his nomination efforts, they were provided with basic information. A diagram was prepared, comparing the biographies of the leading potential nominees. Without comment, it demonstrated the greater variety of experience and longer political services of the senator. One could note, for example, that in 1948 Humphrey had been a leader in the Democratic convention and had been elected to the Senate. In the same year, Robert Kennedy had entered law school, McNamara had held a middle-level management position, and Eugene McCarthy had been elected to his first term in the lower house of Congress.

The senator ultimately won the endorsement of a large number of opinion leaders, including some 40 Democratic senators and, according to a White House survey, "nearly all significant party figures in 26 states and the District of Columbia, and a clear majority in six additional states."[16] The mass media were also contacted discreetly, and some columnists and editorial writers virtually endorsed the Minnesotan. The *New York Times*, for example, while making the customary acknowledgment that "the power to choose his running mate lies, as it always has, with President Johnson," also pointedly described Humphrey as "a man with experience, broad interests and demonstrated integrity and capacity . . . a man of presidential quality."[17]

Through most of their campaign, the Humphrey group had emphasized the argument of "the next best man." As their campaign widened, they attempted to prove the electoral appeal of the senator as well. At first, this was a purely defensive maneuver. Great suspicion was voiced about the members and staff of the Democratic National Committee, and their possible support of the attorney general. Members of the senator's staff, in some cases, felt that the president might receive incorrect reports, warning him of possible defeat in November unless he ran with Robert Kennedy.

More positively, the Humphrey group attempted to demonstrate the political strength the Minnesotan would bring to the ticket. A poll taken by the White House showed that Robert Kennedy was indeed the most popular of the vice-presidential possibilities, but that Adlai Stevenson was considered the most qualified. Significantly, Humphrey placed second in both categories, indicating that he might be the best over all choice. In late May, a national sample was questioned on the standing of a possible Republican ticket of Goldwater and William Scranton in opposition to Democratic tickets of Johnson and Humphrey and Johnson and Robert Kennedy. In these matchings, the Johnson-Humphrey ticket received 2.1% more of the "vote" than the Johnson-Kennedy slate. The senator's advantage held in all subdivisions of the sample except among Catholics but, still, a Johnson-Humphrey ticket received 84.9% of that group's support.

The nomination of Goldwater was also turned to Humphrey's advantage. Geographically, the nomination made the Mid west, where the Minnesotan was strongest, the crucial area for November. The Republican choice also centered the contest for marginal gubernatorial, senatorial, and congressional seats on this area. The Democrats could now regard the East as relatively safe, making it unnecessary to nominate a candidate from that area, such as Robert Kennedy. Analyzing probable patterns of group voting, a number of political scientists found reasons to support Humphrey's candidacy. Seen as crucial to the party were a large increase in the number of Negro voters, a consolidation of union members behind the ticket and an appeal to farmers of the Mid west and the Plains.

To win this support, it was argued, would require an intensive campaign by a well-known, popular, and effective candidate. Since such an effort could not be mounted by an incumbent president, it would fall to the running mate. Humphrey, it was said, did have the stamina and popularity to win new Negro support, curtail the "white backlash" among union members, encourage a defection among Republican farmers, and assume much of the campaign's duties for the president.[18]

To be sure, Humphrey still represented some political liabilities. He was relatively weak in the South and among businessmen and Catholics. The importance of each of these groups was indicated, respectively, by Goldwater's "southern strategy," his conservative ideology, and his Catholic running mate, William Miller. However, the long pre-convention campaign had lessened the opposition to Humphrey's nomination among all these groups. As the Democrats prepared to open their convention, the Minnesota senator was clearly in a leading, if not yet dominant, position.

## At the Convention

In Atlantic City, the attitude of the senator and his staff was a combination of hope and anxiety. All were sure that Humphrey was the choice of the various elements of the party and that he was accepted by the delegates and the public as "the next best man." They believed, too, that he was the president's own personal preference. It was now clear that Robert Kennedy would not challenge his elimination from the contest, but was instead preparing to run for United States Senator from New York. Nevertheless, problems remained.

The first of these was keeping Humphrey activities within bounds. By the time of the convention, the support of the Minnesotan had become so obvious that it was dangerous. The senator's group feared that the president would feel himself pressured and, in order to reassert his own power, would recommend another candidate. To avoid offending and alienating the president, plans for the convention were drastically revised. Humphrey's headquarters at the Shelburne Hotel became instead the Minnesota delegation's headquarters (and therefore available for use by Senator McCarthy as well). Reservations for large numbers of rooms were canceled or forfeited. The staff, including

Humphrey's administrative assistant, was scattered through many hotels in Atlantic City, with many listed as attached to ABC, rather than to the senator.

Many efforts were made to dampen any overt campaign. A reception on the convention eve was sponsored by the Minnesota state delegation, rather than by the senator. Staff members were told not to discuss the vice-presidential nomination in public. If asked, they were to reply that the president was free to make his own decision, and that all persons should support that decision. Humphrey took this position himself on the innumerable occasions he was asked for personal comments. In this atmosphere of uncertainty, rumor and anxiety flourished.[19]

A second and more serious threat to Humphrey was the contest over the seating of the Mississippi delegation. The regular and all-white delegation was challenged by the "Mississippi Freedom Democratic Party." This integrated group had little legal claim to convention seats, based on state law and past practice. It did have a strong moral claim, however, considering the deliberate exclusion of Negroes from political participation in Mississippi, the spate of segregationist terrorism in the state during the summer, and the likelihood of disloyalty to the national ticket by the regular organization.

In terms of convention politics, the Mississippi contest did not really center on that state. Whatever the decision, it seemed unlikely that Negroes would be permitted political participation in the state, that the regular party would support the national ticket, or that Johnson would carry the state in the November election. The real concern of the party leadership, including Johnson and Humphrey, was to avoid a floor fight. They wished to present an image of unity and rationality to the national television audience, in contrast to the emotionalism and divisiveness of the Republican convention at San Francisco. They wanted also to prevent a walkout of other southern delegations, and a consequent weakening of the party's strength in the region of Senator Goldwater's greatest appeal.

It fell to Humphrey, by dint of the president's request and his own prominence at the convention, to seek a formula which would satisfy these demands. The senator was in a delicate position. Since he was relatively weak in the South, he had to conciliate that section. A walkout by southern delegates, moreover, might convince the president and the party that the ticket required a more moderate candidate for vice-president. Even if he had wanted to, however, Humphrey could not consider the southern position alone. A floor fight could be obtained if eleven delegations on the Credentials Committee signed a minority report and if eight delegations requested a roll call vote. The senator, therefore, had to find a settlement which would represent an overwhelming consensus, not merely a majority position.

At first, the senator argued for a three-point proposal known as the "Wyoming plan." The regular Mississippi delegation would be seated, if it took a loyalty oath to the party. The Freedom party would be welcomed as non voting guests of the convention. Finally, in the future, state parties would "assure that voters in the state, regardless of race, color, creed, or national origin, will have the opportunity to participate fully in party affairs." The proposal was presented to a subcommittee headed by Walter Mondale, attorney general of Minnesota and a Humphrey supporter. It won endorsement there by a 4 to 1 vote, but failed to win the necessary consensus in the full committee.

To leave time for more bargaining, the report of the committee was delayed for 24 hours. In this period, one change was made. "In recognition of the unusual circumstances presented at the hearing, and without setting any precedent for the future," two members of the Freedom Democratic party would be seated as voting "delegates-at-large." The Humphrey communications network was activated, every state delegation was contacted, and the influence of the White House was brought to bear. The new plan won the support of sufficient delegations to prevent an open convention conflict. The compromise was rejected by both Mississippi factions, but Humphrey's objectives had been fully met. The party had recognized the moral claims involved and had taken at least a token action against discrimination in party affairs. Party unity had been preserved and all but the intransigent Alabama and Mississippi delegations had remained loyal.

For the senator, the result was a personal success. Dealing with an emotional issue in the frenetic atmosphere of the convention, he had solidified a broad coalition within the party. He had demonstrated his leadership without severely antagonizing any element. The solution of the credentials contest removed the last potentially serious obstacle to his nomination.

It was still conceivable that the president would indicate a different choice, and accomplish his selection. At this point, however, there would be an extremely high price to pay in disaffection and resentment. The president had preserved his freedom of action to meet any new development, but no such development had occurred. The Minnesotan had come to the convention as the leading candidate. While there he had retained, even strengthened, his position.

The remaining period was one of waiting on the part of the senator and of managed drama by the president. By Tuesday, the day before the nomination, the senator was informally notified of his selection. Buttons, signs, and hats with "Johnson and Humphrey" designations—in preparation for a week—were ordered for final delivery to a private home. Aides began writing an acceptance speech. Johnson, in Washington, continued to suggest names, to fence with reporters, and to build tension. Finally, on Wednesday, hours before the nomination itself was scheduled, he called Humphrey to the White House.

The final dramatic moment came that evening immediately after Johnson had been nominated by acclamation. In an unprecedented action, he appeared to announce his choice of a running mate. His speech indicated the success of the Humphrey group's basic strategy. The president argued their thesis, that the vice-president should be "a man best qualified to assume the office of President of the United States, should that day come. . . . This is not a sectional choice; this is not merely just a way to balance the ticket; this is simply the best man in America for this job." He indicated as well the success of the campaign to win public support for the senator, when he noted that the choice was reached "after discussions with outstanding Americans in every area of our national life" and represented "the enthusiastic conviction of the great majority of the Democratic party."[20] Humphrey's nomination by acclamation followed.

The political value of the long selection process was indicated the following week when the Harris survey asked voters their opinions of the vice-presidential nominees. Humphrey led the Republican candidate by a 7 to 3 margin. Moreover, he was preferred over Miller more than the president was preferred over Goldwater in every area of the country and among virtually every social group. Significantly, the major reason for Humphrey's support was that he was considered "better qualified, [more] experienced" than his opponent.[21] The public, too, had accepted the thesis of the "next best man." The final test of this choice came on November 3, when Hubert Humphrey was elected Vice-President of the United States.

## Conclusions

The nomination of Senator Humphrey points the way to the future of the vice-presidency. In the past, whatever attention was given to the office centered on its governmental, rather than political, aspects. This focus was evident among politicians as well as academicians.[22] The recent history of the vice-presidency should serve both to increase attention to the office in general and to foster particular interest in its political character.

It seems likely that we will find more campaigning for the office of "second counsel" in forthcoming elections. The presidential nomination itself has gradually become the object of public and vigorous campaigning. As some candidates adopt these practices for the running-mate position as well, others will be required to follow their example.[23] Such efforts will certainly be evident when an incumbent president is a candidate for renomination. With the top position on the ticket thereby foreclosed, ambitions will be directed toward the second slot. Campaigning is unlikely, however, to attain fully the intensive, openly competitive and mass character of a presidential effort. The influence of the president and other party leaders will remain too great to enable a candidate to win nomination largely on the basis of popular backing.[24]

The attempt, rather, will be to gain the support of important factions and to use evidence of voter appeal to win such backing.

The campaigns for the two nominations will be alike in one other respect. They will be exercises in the building of coalitions. The entire nominating process is one of building a majority coalition. In the past, the vice-presidential nomination has been one of the prizes used to build a consensus in support of the ticket-leader. If the Humphrey case is indicative, the second spot will no longer be simply a trading device. There will be efforts to build a consensus behind this choice separately or, more likely, the same coalition will be evident in the selections of both candidates. We are less likely to see "balanced" tickets, in which the two running mates represent distinctively different positions. In both parties in 1964, there was an ideological consistency to the tickets that is startling when compared to such combinations of the recent past as Dewey and Bricker or Stevenson and Sparkman.

The choice of a coalition, by definition, is different from the choice of a single individual, even one with the responsibilities and political acumen of the president. The common belief, constantly reiterated in 1964, is that the presidential nominee selects his own running mate. This view, albeit with guarded qualifications, is also frequent in the scholarly literature. "The Presidential nominee ordinarily can, in fact, make the choice, although the range of his discretion may differ with circumstances,"[25] wrote V. O. Key. "When a presidential nominee is named, he and other party leaders sit around in a room and select the vice-presidential candidate,"[26] declared an experienced politician. "The opinion of the presidential nominee is always the most important influence,"[27] according to others.

A closer look at the record of vice-presidential nominations, however, results in a different conclusion. Paul David examined the four conventions since 1896 in which an incumbent president sought renomination when the vice-presidency was vacant. In all four cases, "the President was able to exercise only limited influence on the situation. . . . Seemingly the choice tended to be made by the convention, with other leaders exercising as much influence as the President."[28] Even in 1964, there were limits on the president, though they were less constrictive than in the past.

Not only is this contention incorrect; it is wrong as a matter of principle. In a free society, there is nothing inherently objectionable in the nomination being "an instrument of compromise—compromise between factions, between sections, between interests and even perhaps between back room political bargainers."[29] No democratic system can easily accept the proposition that the vital choice of future leadership is the prerogative of any single individual. In 1964, the president did endorse the individual who was the clear choice of the majority of delegates and of party factions. The outcome, then, did not violate fundamental democratic beliefs. The proposition of unlimited presidential discretion, however, does violate these beliefs.

The emotions aroused by the assassination of John Kennedy permitted the unusual freedom accorded the new president. It was felt that he was entitled, in effect, to name a successor to his now-vacant office, and that Kennedy's successful choice of Johnson indicated the desirability of unlimited freedom. However, Kennedy did not act alone—he stated his preference and then worked among the leaders of his party to win agreement. This is far different from leaders passively accepting a designation. The Dallas tragedy should remind us of the significance of the vice-presidency and of the importance of the choice of a man to that office. In a democracy, important choices must be made through widespread participation, not through the personal preferences of a few leaders.

The nomination of Hubert Humphrey was accomplished in part through such participation, but it offends a democrat's sense of decency that any one individual should be accorded even the theoretical right to deny the popular choice. Whatever our reaction to the specific selection made in 1964, we should reject the premise. Consent, not dictation, is the basic process of free government.

## Notes

1. Finley Peter Dunne, *The World of Mr. Dooley*, ed. Louis Filler (New York: Collier Books, 1962), pp. 50–51.
2. See Irving G. Williams, *The Rise of the Vice-Presidency* (Washington: Public Affairs Press, 1956), pp. 231–258.
3. The best account of the vice-presidential nomination at the 1960 convention is in Arthur M. Schlesinger, Jr., *A Thousand Days* (Boston: Houghton Mifflin, 1965), pp. 39–58. Strains between Johnson and Robert Kennedy probably began at this time.
4. For an account of the vice-presidential nomination in 1964, as seen from the perspective of Lyndon Johnson, see "The Choice of Humphrey, Step by Step," *The New York Times*, August 28, 1964, p. 1.
5. Humphrey's difficulties are chronicled by Theodore H. White, *The Making of the President 1960* (New York: Atheneum, 1961), pp. 29–36, 109–14.
6. See James M. Burns, *Roosevelt: The Lion and the Fox* (New York: Harcourt, Brace, 1956), pp. 428–30.
7. *The New York Times*, August 25, 1964, p. 22.
8. This quotation, and all other material not specifically documented, is from papers by or interviews with supporters or members of the staff of Senator Humphrey. I have withheld specific titles or names because pledges of anonymity were made at the time of research.
9. *The New York Times*, January 3, 1964, p. 10.
10. *Ibid.*, July 31, 1964, p. 1.
11. See *ibid.*, March 23, 1964, p. 21, for an account of the UAW convention. The labor endorsements of Humphrey are confirmed by Theodore H. White, *The Making of the President 1964* (New York: Atheneum, 1965), p. 273.
12. White (1961), p. 136.
13. *The New York Times*, July 31, 1964, p. 9.

14. White (1965), p. 273, confirms this statement and names James Rowe as the source of encouragement. It seems unlikely that Rowe acted without prompting in so vital a matter.
15. The Making of HHH," *Newsweek* (September 7, 1964), p. 19.
16. *The New York Times*, August 17, 1964, p. 1.
17. *Ibid.*, August 18, 1964, p. 30.
18. The report was prepared by Donald G. Herzberg, director of the Eagleton Institute of Politics at Rutgers University, after consulting various associates, including the present author.
19. The influence of rumor at a national convention is vividly described by Aaron Wildavsky in "What Can I Do?: Ohio Delegates View the Democratic Convention," in Paul Tillett, (ed.), *Inside Politics: The National Conventions 1960* (New Brunswick: Rutgers—The State University, 1962), pp. 112–19.
20. *The New York Times*, August 27, 1964, p. 23.
21. *The Harris Survey*, in *The Philadelphia Inquirer*, September 4, 1964, p. 3.
22. Most of the literature is concerned either with the duties—or lack of them—of the vice-president or the problems of presidential succession. Aside from the works cited above and below, see John D. Feerick, *From Falling Hands* (New York: Fordham University Press, 1965); Louis C. Hatch and Earl R. Shoup, *A History of the Vice-Presidency of the United States* (New York: American Historical Society, 1934); Clinton L. Rossiter, "The Reform of the Vice-Presidency," *Political Science Quarterly* 63 (September 1948): 383–403; Ruth C. Silva, *Presidential Succession* (Ann Arbor: University of Michigan Press, 1951); Irving G. Williams, *The American Vice-Presidency: New Look* (New York: Doubleday, 1954); Lucius Wilmerding, "The Vice-Presidency," *Political Science Quarterly* 68 (March 1953): 17–41.
23. See Gerald Pomper, *Nominating the President* (Evanston: Northwestern University Press, 1963), chaps. 5, 7, 8.
24. As Donald Young suggests, "Most campaigns for the second office will continue to be conducted under cover, since in most cases the Presidential candidate will make the choice, and he will not likely react favorably to efforts to bring public pressure to bear in behalf of a particular candidate." See *American Roulette* (New York: Holt, Rinehart and Winston, 1965), p. 313.
25. V. O. Key, Jr., *Politics, Parties and Pressure Groups*, 5th ed. (New York: Crowell, 1964), p. 429.
26. Charles Halleck, cited by Hugh A. Bone, *American Politics and the Party System*, 3rd ed. (New York: McGraw-Hill, 1965), p. 333.
27. Malcolm Moos and Stephen Hess, *Hats in the Ring* (New York: Random House, 1960), p. 157. See also William Goodman, *The Two-Party System in the United States*, 2nd. ed. (Princeton: D. Van Nostrand, 1960), p. 213—"The presidential nominee by well-established custom is considered to be entitled to a major voice in the selection of his running mate and in some cases designates him outright."
28. Paul T. David, Ralph M. Goldman, and Richard C. Bain, *The Politics of National Party Conventions* (Washington: The Brookings Institution, 1960), p. 59.
29. Edgar W. Waugh, *Second Counsel* (*Indianapolis:* Bobbs-Merrill, 1956), p. 198. Waugh's own preference is uncertain. He seems to disapprove of bargaining for the vice-presidential nomination and even abstractly to favor an appointive vice-president. His final conclusion, however, is: "It is good to have competition for the nomination. But the competition should be among those whom the Presidential candidate has indicated as highly acceptable to him." In practical terms, such a method might be no more than a disguise for dictation by the presidential nominee. See *Ibid.*, pp. 198–208.

# 18

# New Rules and New Games in Presidential Nominations

Politics resembles sport in many ways. We each have our favorite players whose performance we watch and rate. Political statistics such as the number of delegates won are examined as avidly as batting percentages. As baseball buffs recall the great games of the past, so political historians recall the great conventions of 1860 or 1952.

One of the basic features of both sports and politics is the formal rules within which the game is played. The rules prescribe the behavior of the players and lead to standards for judging performance. When the rules are changed, the outcome of the contest is also likely to change. Understanding this basic fact, football teams with weak kickers favor restrictions on field goals, and baseball teams with strong pinch hitters favor the use of designated hitters. For similar reasons, advocates of strong national government in 1787 changed the constitutional rules of the United States.[1]

In recent nominating politics, the rule book has been rewritten. From one of the most significant reform periods in American history[2] has come a new game, bringing changes as extensive as those that followed the legalization of the forward pass in football. Although there were other causes, these rules changes are important explanations of the surprising features of the 1976 major party conventions, particularly the victory of Jimmy Carter, and the close race of Ronald Reagan.

## New Rules

We will examine the effects of three kinds of rules changes on the 1976 contests: increased use of primaries, changes in primary election rules, and reapportionment of delegates. Most obvious has been the growth of primaries as means of selecting delegates to the national conventions.[3] This latest surge in primaries came after the raucous Democratic convention of 1968 and the subsequent initiation of party reform. By 1976, primaries or preference polls were involved in the selection of 76.9 percent of the Democratic delegates and 71.5 percent of the Republicans. (The figure is a slight exaggeration, for it includes delegates from states holding purely advisory preference polls, such as Vermont and Montana, as well as all delegates from states using mixed systems. The territories are excluded from all calculations.)

A number of related explanations may be offered for the increase in primaries. One factor—both cause and effect—is the decline of the convention as an arena for bargaining. The purpose of the party conclave is no longer to select a nominee, but to legitimize the individual who has proved his mettle and his popularity in the long pre convention period. Primaries, rather than floor votes, now provide critical information about the relative strength of the contenders and the likely winner of the nomination. "Politicians who are uncertain about who the nominee will be, which of the contenders is most electable, and therefore which of the competing proto-coalitions to join, appear to use publicly available and reliable indicators of relative candidate strength in making their calculations."[4]

The expansion of the primaries has been abetted by the development of the mass media. Politics has become more open with the development of peering electronic journalism. Television, with its need for a continuing supply of confrontations and excitement, gives great weight to primary results and indeed has made the New Hampshire primary, first in the nation, into a major source of state tourist revenue. After each primary, television and other commentators determine the standing of each candidate, counting their delegates, labeling them as front-runners or also-rans, and thereby significantly affecting their chances in future primaries. Indeed, "The media's picture of the world matters more than reality."[5]

In 1976, the federal government provided another cause, money. By providing matching funds for virtually any candidate, more extensive campaigns were facilitated. In the past, restricted finances were an important means of limiting entry into the presidential race. The federal political finance laws which followed Watergate partially removed this restriction. Candidates could at least begin their campaigns relatively easily, as demonstrated by the early proliferation of Democratic candidates, who included not only such obvious hopefuls as Henry Jackson, but also such single issue aspirants as Ellen McCormack.

Increased significance for the primaries is apparently in keeping with the long-term trends of American politics toward more public involvement in the parties. Opinion polls consistently show the general public supporting a national presidential primary, and the proliferation of state contests is in keeping with this preference. The arguments against primaries are subtle at best, elitist at worst. It is much simpler to leave the nominating decision to an apparent expression of direct democracy.

A second major change in the rules has been revision of the primaries themselves. Basically, the change has been one from an emphasis on the representation of state parties, as cohesive and relatively monolithic political units, to the representation of party voters, acting as individuals. This change parallels the shift from the convention as the site of bargaining between state parties to the convention as simply the formal expression of the preferences of the activist electorate.

Primaries come in three basic varieties. In the "winner-take-all," or plurality system, all of the state's delegates are awarded to the candidate who receives the most votes, whether or not a numerical majority. If there is a strong party organization, this system magnifies the influence of those leaders who can deliver a sizable bloc of delegates to their preferred candidate. Even if no strong organization exists, the larger states still become valuable prizes and candidates therefore are likely to give greater weight to the demands of their citizens. In 1976, only California Republicans used this system.

The winner-take-all system in nominations is based on an analogy to the Electoral College, emphasizing the federal character of the political system and giving power to large and cohesive units. Philosophically and politically opposed to this scheme are those which emphasize the representation of the individual voter, seeking to give each person, or at least each substantial minority, some voice in the relevant political decision. In the election of the president, the conclusion follows that electoral votes should either be divided proportionally in each state or that the chief executive should be chosen directly.

Proposals for proportional representation are based on the similar premise that individuals or minority groups within the states should have some measurable effect. The premise led to the Democratic mandate of 1976 that delegates from each state should be "chosen in a manner which fairly reflects the division of preferences expressed by those who participate in the presidential nominating process in each state."[6] States would no longer be treated as units, and state parties would not be allowed to bargain as monolithic units.

But the Democrats went one step further, providing not only for proportionality, but for localism. A system for proportional representation can be applied to districts of varying size. Smaller districts reward insular groups with limited general appeal. In 1976, the Democrats went in this direction, by requiring that at least three-fourths of the delegates of any state be chosen below the state-wide level. Overall, proportional representation was the most common system employed.

In the final rules, however, the Democrats avoided complete local proportionality by making two reservations to the general principle. Delegates could be chosen from areas as large as congressional districts, so that the plurality winner in such a district could win all of the delegates. Second, candidates would be entitled to delegates only if they won at least 15 percent of the votes in the relevant district. These two rules provided some means of limiting the fractionalization of preferences by eliminating very small minorities and by providing for a degree of cumulation up to the congressional district level. This "loophole" system was almost as common in 1976 as proportional division.[7]

A third change in recent years has been the reapportionment of delegates among the states, shifting the basic resources of the conventions, delegate votes, among the states and therefore increasing the opportunities of some candidates and detracting from the opportunities of others.

Until the 1912 convention, the basis of convention apportionment was clear and unchallenged. Delegates were distributed among the states in accord with electoral votes, usually a simple multiple of this figure. The result in the 1912 Republican convention was that William Howard Taft gained many delegates from the southern states which had sufficient population to have large numbers of delegates but which had few Republican voters. It was these controlled southern delegations which enabled Taft to beat off the Progressive challenge of Theodore Roosevelt.

The Republican party maintained this traditional system largely intact throughout 1976, while adding "bonus" delegates to each state which voted for the party's candidate for president, or governor, or senator in the last election. For the 1976 convention, the effect of this system was to provide a bonus reward to virtually every state, since the Republicans had won all but Massachusetts in the previous presidential election. The G.O.P. system emphasized only victory, not the number of Republican members or votes for the party in a state. Its result therefore was to strengthen the one-party states, rather than the competitive ones, and the less liberal states.

The Democratics after 1968 shifted to a new basis for apportionment. For the electoral college basis and the bonus votes, they substituted a formula which provided essential equal weight to a state's population and to its past Democratic vote. The obvious effect of this system was to give more votes to the larger, more competitive and more liberal states. Because electoral victory as such was not rewarded, there was very little change in apportionment after the disastrous defeat of McGovern in 1972.

The changes in apportionment, like those in the primary election rules, represent a shift in the total political system. Apportionment on the basis of the electoral college was a recognition of the states as political units. Providing bonus votes for successful state parties still treats them as separate groups, but adds a national element, for they are relatively advantaged or disadvantaged as they contribute to overall national success. The Democratic shift disregards the state parties as other than convenient units. Individual citizens or individual Democratic voters are the basis of apportionment. The rules formally recognize only voters and a national party; there are no intermediary institutions, the state parties. The same implication runs through the requirement of proportional representation. It is the closest approach any major American party has made to populist democracy.

## New Games

I will seek to discern the effects of the rules changes by examining the differential success of the candidates in different structural situations. We will assumes that the effects seen in states using a particular set of rules would apply to all states if they all adopted the same rules. Admittedly, this assumption of uniform effects is an over simplification, and other causes of political change must be acknowledged.

### *Effects of Primaries*

Table 18.1 indicates the effect of the first major change, the spread of primaries. The first row comprises those states adopting this system after 1968. The broadening of the direct electoral system was clearly of benefit to Carter and to Reagan. The Georgian won nearly two-thirds of the delegates from these thirteen new primary states and the Californian won close to 60 percent of their votes. Without the aid of these supporters, it is conceivable that Carter would have been denied the Democratic nomination. (In this analysis, we are trying to isolate the effects of the primaries from post primary bandwagons and the conventions. The figures reported for the Democrats thus are the best estimates after the primaries or caucuses themselves, including uncommitted votes. In the actual convention balloting, Carter received far more votes, as his opponents dropped out and the uncommitted came over to his side. In the Republican case, the uncommitted are counted as they actually voted in the convention, since these delegates were essentially in one camp or the other from the beginning, despite their nominal status. Delegates required to vote for a particular candidate, even if personally opposed, are also held to that legal requirement in this analysis. The territories are excluded.) Carter was far weaker in the states with longer histories of primary participation or which still chose delegates in caucuses. In these two areas, where state parties presumably had greater influence, he won only about a third of the delegates.

The same point is made in the bottom part of the table, which shows, in vertical columns, the distribution of each candidate's strength. Carter received a disproportionate share of his convention delegates from these new primary states. He fell below a random distribution in both the states with older primaries and those which relied on more traditional methods of caucuses and conventions. If the parties had been stronger, and better able to control the nominating procedures, Carter might have been stopped.

**TABLE 18.1**
**Sources of Candidate Strength in 1976 Primaries**

| | Democrats | | | | | | | Republicans | | |
|---|---|---|---|---|---|---|---|---|---|---|
| State Category | Carter | Udall | Jackson | Wallace | Brown | Others | (*N*) | Ford | Reagan | (*N*) |
| | Distribution of Delegates by Areas[a] | | | | | | | | | |
| New Primary States | 65.8 | 11.2 | 1.8 | 6.4 | 2.4 | 12.4 | (623) | 41.2 | 58.8 | (532) |
| Old Primary States | 32.7 | 10.8 | 11.1 | 6.5 | 13.0 | 25.9 | (1665) | 67.3 | 32.7 | (1072) |
| Pure Caucus States | 31.8 | 12.4 | 6.3 | 4.2 | 1.0 | 44.3 | (686) | 43.3 | 56.7 | (639) |
| | Distribution of Delegates by Candidate[b] | | | | | | (Total) | | | (Total) |
| New Primary States | 35.0 | 21.0 | 4.6 | 22.5 | 6.3 | 9.5 | (20.9%) | 18.0 | 30.5 | (23.7%) |
| Old Primary States | 46.4 | 53.6 | 77.4 | 61.2 | 90.8 | 53.1 | (56.0%) | 59.2 | 34.2 | (47.8%) |
| Pure Caucus States | 18.6 | 25.4 | 18.0 | 16.3 | 2.9 | 37.4 | (23.1%) | 22.8 | 35.3 | (28.5%) |
| (*N*) | (1172) | (334) | (239) | (178) | (238) | (813) | (2974) | (1217) | (1026) | (2243) |

[a] Entries are percentages which add horizontally by rows.
[b] Entries are percentages which add vertically by collumns.

The other Democrats were quite different. Jackson's support came overwhelmingly from the areas which had not changed the rules greatly from the past. He did best in the older primary states, specifically Massachusetts and New York, and the bulk of his votes came from these areas. The most statistically normal candidates were the ideologically diverse pair, Udall and Wallace. They did about as well in each of the three categories of states and their delegates were gathered in proportion to the total distribution of delegates.

Carter's victory can be attributed, in part, to the opportunity provided by the extension of the primaries to new states. To be sure, the opportunity needed to be exploited skillfully. Moreover, we cannot know how Carter would have done under the old rules. It is certainly possible that he would have won as many delegates from the southern delegations of Arkansas, Georgia, Kentucky, North Carolina, and Tennessee. It is more doubtful that he could have overcome the favorite son candidacy of Lloyd Bentsen in Texas without a direct primary. In Michigan, it is also possible that many delegates would have been withheld if the process had been controlled by the state party, as in the past.

In the Republican case, Reagan ran best in the new primary states, and might have won the Republican designation if the primary system had been extended to more states in 1976. He also did well in the caucus areas where the zeal of his ideological supporters could be brought to bear. Reagan's weakness was in the older primary states, in which nearly half of the delegates were chosen, but where Reagan won only a third. Ford won his nomination in these areas, but it was not a personal victory. The margin of the former president in these states came almost entirely from New York and Pennsylvania where delegates were elected as formally uncommitted. The strong party organizations in these states eventually brought the bulk of these delegates to Ford, and they are included in his totals. In contrast to Carter, who circumvented the state parties, Ford owed his victory to these organizations. His was the victory of an older politics, in which strong state parties had real influence on the nominations.

### *Effects of Proportionality*

The second major change was the shift toward proportional representation in the primaries. It is possible to estimate the results which would have followed if any of the three systems in use had been universally applied. As Lengle and Shafer have shown, the results can differ significantly, depending on the system employed. In 1972, they argue, "The beneficiary of the power hidden in the rules of the game was Senator George McGovern." The South Dakotan benefited from the prevalence of district systems, according to their calculations, but he would have trailed Humphrey if winner-take-all systems had been universally applied.[8]

Their analysis is flawed by the exclusion of California, in which McGovern actually did best under the very system they advocate.[9] However, despite the empirical error, it remains true that "the ground rules often did as much as the vote in establishing who 'won' and by how much." On the basis of the actual results, and a considerable number of speculative operationalizations, we can reconstruct the 1976 primaries *as if* there were consistent rules in all states. Table 18.2 summarizes these results.[10]

In the actual primaries, Carter won over 40 percent of the delegates. This proportion is strikingly close to that which has been previously calculated as the convention roll call percentage which leads to victorious bandwagons.[11] In nominating history, candidates achieving over 40 percent commonly have been able to move on quickly to victory. Carter's bandwagon rolled in the states rather than on the convention floor, but the process was similar. As victory seemed likely, opponents left the race, uncommitted delegates joined the front-runner, and a voting majority was secured.

But the result was not inevitable. If delegates had been distributed in accord with strict principles of proportional representation, applied state-wide and

**TABLE 18.2**
**Hypothetical Outcomes of 1976 Primary Contests**

| Candidate | Actual | P.R. | Winner-Take-All | Districted |
|---|---|---|---|---|
| | | Democrats | | |
| Carter | 954 (41.7%) | 828 (36.2%) | 1278 (55.8%) | 1107 (48.4%) |
| Udall | 249 (10.9) | 293 (12.8) | 0 ( 0.0) | 195 ( 8.5) |
| Jackson | 196 ( 8.6) | 213 ( 9.3) | 378 (16.5) | 196 ( 8.6) |
| Wallace | 149 ( 6.5) | 254 (11.1) | 35 ( 1.5) | 65 ( 2.8) |
| Brown | 231 (10.1) | 212 ( 9.3) | 366 (16.0) | 348 (15.2) |
| Others | 509 (22.2) | 488 (21.3) | 231 (10.1) | 377 (16.5) |
| Totals | 2288 (100%) | 2288 (100%) | 2288 (99.9%) | 2288 (100%) |
| | | Republicans | | |
| Ford | 634 (39.5%) | 675 (42.1%) | 756 (47.1%) | 685 (42.7%) |
| Reagan | 669 (41.7) | 672 (41.9) | 591 (36.8) | 662 (41.3) |
| Other | 301 (18.8) | 257 (16.0) | 257 (16.0) | 257 (16.0) |
| Ford, with N.Y., Pa. | 940 (58.6) | 902 (56.2) | 1013 (63.2) | 912 (56.8) |
| Reagan, with N.Y., Pa. | 664 (41.4) | 702 (43.8) | 591 (36.8) | 692 (43.1) |

with no minimum quota, Carter would still have led, but in this case with only 36 percent of the delegates. As the leader, but still distant from victory, he would have been the obvious target for a coalition of minorities. Moreover, proportional representation would have diminished Carter's impact in precisely those earlier primaries in which his strength was exaggerated by the legal structure and by the mass media. Through February and March, Carter would have gained but 86 delegates in the primaries under this alternative, rather than the 104 he actually won, excluding the special case of Illinois. The numbers are small in either case compared to the total number of delegates, but it is possible that the Carter drive, short of money and attention in its early stages, would have been halted if different rules had been in existence.

More generally, Carter almost always got better than a proportionate share of the delegates. Electoral systems of any kind tend to exaggerate the share of seats won by the leading faction, and this same tendency was evident in the Democratic front-runner's drive. In the seven largest states, for example, Carter got large bonuses in Texas, Michigan, Ohio, and California, received his fair share in Pennsylvania and New York and was disadvantaged only in Illinois, where the preference poll he led was unrelated to the selection of delegates dominated by the Daley organization.

As Carter was advantaged, his rivals lost votes they would have won under proportional representation. Jackson, Udall, and Wallace together would then have had a third of the delegates, rather than the quarter they actually secured. The strategic situation would have been altered as well. With more delegates in hand, these—and other—candidates would have found fundraising easier, would have been better able to resist Carter pressures in state caucuses and other primary states, and would have been more likely to remain in the race and accumulate delegates who eventually were won by Carter.

The opposite system would be that of a winner-take-all. From the cumulative results, it would appear that Carter would have been the biggest gainer under this system. He would have won a decisive majority of all primary delegates, and presumably would have secured the nomination even earlier than occurred in fact. Senator Henry Jackson and Governor Jerry Brown still would have lost the nomination but their delegate totals would have been higher than they actually achieved. The general effect of this system would be quickly to eliminate minor candidates and to focus the race on two or three contenders, just as plurality systems tend to eliminate minor parties and to reduce elections to contests between two major parties. An example of this likely tendency in 1976 is provided by Morris Udall, who never came in first in a primary, but was able to sustain his campaign because he did accumulate delegates even while he repeatedly, often narrowly, missed victory.

If the rules were different, strategies would also change. If the plurality system were widespread, Brown, being fairly confident of a late sweep of the

California delegation, might have entered the campaign more vigorously and earlier. Jackson's fortunes would certainly have improved. The Washington senator actually won both of the two largest primaries in the earliest stage, those of Massachusetts and New York. If these had been winner-take-all elections, he would have come up to the critical Pennsylvania contest with 378 delegates, while Carter would have had but 239 (assuming that he could not win Illinois in an open contest with an organization candidate). Jackson would then have had the media title of front-runner and would not have suffered the burden of appearing to be but a stand-in for a reluctant Hubert Humphrey. A Carter defeat in Pennsylvania would severely damage his campaign under these rules and would most likely prevent the future sweeps which inflate his final total under the hypothetical winner-take-all system. George Wallace would have been most severely damaged.

The district system, as might be expected, shares some of the effect of the plurality system, but to a lesser degree. Carter's share of the delegates would be exaggerated beyond proportional representation and sufficiently to assure his victory. It would have deflated the support of Udall and Wallace and of minor challengers. Realizing these effects, Carter forces at the convention in 1976 unsuccessfully sought to maintain the loophole in the future as a means to limit any challenge to Carter for a second term.

Speculations cannot prove a case, and we cannot actually rerun history, either statistically or in reality. We can be assured that if the rules had been different, the strategies of the candidates, and the interpretations of results, would have been different. Contrary to some observers, I conclude that the change in the Democratic rules did have an effect,[12] and that Carter's effort would have been handicapped, although not necessarily repulsed, by a pure system of proportional representation.[13] A pure system of plurality elections might have further sped the Carter bandwagon, but it can also be argued that it would have made Jackson the early front-runner.

The rules' effects are different in the Republican party. They are also more difficult to estimate, because there was no state-wide ballot in New York and Reagan did not enter the Pennsylvania preference poll, making unavailable an index of relative popularity in that state. Two early analyses differed on these effects. Ronald Reagan for one believed that he would have won the nomination if a pure system of proportional representation had been in effect.[14] Using more precise analysis, Gerston and Cohen find that Ford benefited from the district system employed in New York, Pennsylvania, New Jersey, and West Virginia, and furthermore, "If Republicans had uniformly used either a pure proportion or plurality system, Ford would have increased his delegate totals at Reagan's expense."[15]

Our more detailed analysis generally supports the latter conclusions. A winner-take-all system certainly would have benefited Ford. In reality, the only pure plurality system existed in California and worked to Reagan's advantage. If universal, this system would have widened the margin between the two Republicans by more than a hundred delegates, even excluding New York and Pennsylvania. If Ford also had won these states on a plurality basis—the most likely outcome—he would have virtually won the nomination on the basis of primary victories alone.

The other two systems, universally applied, would not in themselves have aided Ford. In the primary elections as held, Ford won nearly 40 percent of the delegates, actually trailing Reagan in committed delegates. On a pure proportional system, he would have won 42.1 percent and, under the pure district system, 42.7 percent, gaining a thin margin in both cases. Reagan too would have gained under either of these systems, but only slightly, adding 51 delegates under pure proportionality and 41 delegates in an unmixed district system. The real difference came again from the two critical states of New York and Pennsylvania. Their large blocs of delegates brought Ford victory. It is likely—but unprovable—that he would have won these delegates in open primary contests. Their decisive impact, however, must be partially attributed to the strength of the party organizations in these states, and their old-fashioned ability to deliver, rather than to the personal popularity of the incumbent president.

Not only the final results, but the strategic environment would have been different under different rules. An important part of the environment in nominating contests is the temporal sequence of primaries. Early victories can be decisive, as they give the legendary quality of "momentum" to the first bandwagons and eliminate potential rivals. Recall the Republican campaign, which had three distinct pre convention stages: initial Ford victories, a string of stunning Reagan successes in early May, and see saw outcomes in the final weeks. In past years, these early Ford triumphs would have led to an unstoppable surge of party support. New rules, however, limited the effect of these victories, and Reagan was able to hold on, aided by federal financing, until he recouped in later contests.

Let us reconstruct those early results under hypothetically revised rules. Through the time of the Pennsylvania primary, Ford won 252 delegates in the direct elections, compared to Reagan's 80, a ratio of 3.2:1. As seen in table 18.3, a plurality system would have magnified these victories considerably. If New York and Pennsylvania are included as Ford delegations, the Ford margin would have been overwhelming, probably causing Reagan to withdraw from the race. By contrast, a pure proportional system in these early races would have left the candidates at a virtual standoff if the two eastern states are excluded or would have considerably reduced Ford's lead even if they are counted in his column. Ford's weaknesses would have been more obvious under this system, and it might well have provided the small increment needed

TABLE 18.3
Hypothetical Results of Early Republican Primaries[a], 1976

| Electoral System | Ford Delegates | Reagan Delegates | Ford/Reagan Ratio |
|---|---|---|---|
| Actual | 252 | 80 | 3.2 |
| Pure Plurality | 294 | 54 | 5.4 |
| Pure Plurality (with N.Y., Pa.) | 551 | 54 | 10.2 |
| Pure P.R. | 199 | 149 | 1.3 |
| Pure P.R. (with N.Y., Pa.) | 426 | 179 | 2.4 |
| Pure District | 260 | 88 | 3.0 |
| Pure District (with N.Y., Pa.) | 487 | 118 | 4.1 |

[a] Primaries held before May 1, 1976 are included.

to bring Reagan the nomination. In the real world, the rules prevented either a quick decision in the Republican party favoring Ford or an early stunning blow by Reagan.

*Effects of Apportionment*

The apportionment of delegates among the states is the third important rules change. The effect of this change is particularly evident in the Republican party. In general, delegates have been transferred from the older sections of the nation and the historic bases of the party in the Northeast and the Midwest to the newly emerging Sunbelt in the South, Southwest, and Far West. These shifts are partially caused by the movement of the national population. They are accented by the Republican bonus rules which award delegates in relatively equal numbers to states won by Republicans, regardless of the size of the state's population or the number of votes cast for Republicans.

The results can be seen if we undertake another hypothetical reconstruction, this time of the convention roll call for the presidential nomination. In table 18.4, we present both the actual 1976 roll call and the hypothetical distribution of votes under the apportionment of 1952. Delegations are split between Ford and Reagan in the sample proportions as they actually divided in 1976. However, each state's numerical distribution is different because of the lower total number of delegates in 1952 (1,185 compared to 2,190 in 1976), and because of the different allocation in effect in the year of Eisenhower's first nomination. (Since no fractional votes are permitted in Republican con-

**TABLE 18.4**
**The Effects of Republican Reapportionment**
**(in Order of Relative Gain in Delegates)**

| State | 1976 Apportionment | | 1952 Apportionment | | Comparative Ratio |
|---|---|---|---|---|---|
| *Gaining States* | Ford | Reagan | Ford | Reagan | |
| Mississippi | 16 | 14 | 3 | 2 | 3.25 |
| S. C. | 9 | 27 | 1 | 5 | 3.25 |
| Florida | 43 | 23 | 12 | 6 | 1.98 |
| Georgia | | 48 | | 17 | 1.53 |
| Louisiana | 5 | 36 | 2 | 13 | 1.45 |
| Alabama | | 37 | | 14 | 1.43 |
| Texas | | 100 | | 38 | 1.42 |
| Montana | | 20 | | 8 | 1.35 |
| Arkansas | 10 | 17 | 4 | 7 | 1.33 |
| California | | 167 | | 70 | 1.29 |
| R. I. | 19 | | 8 | | 1.28 |
| Oklahoma | | 36 | | 16 | 1.22 |
| Virginia | 16 | 35 | 7 | 16 | 1.20 |
| Tennessee | 21 | 22 | 10 | 10 | 1.16 |
| Arizona | 2 | 27 | 1 | 13 | 1.12 |
| N. C. | 25 | 29 | 12 | 14 | 1.12 |
| Missouri | 18 | 31 | 10 | 16 | 1.02 |
| *Relatively Stable States* | | | | | |
| Kentucky | 19 | 18 | 10 | 10 | 1.00 |
| Michigan | 55 | 29 | 30 | 16 | .99 |
| Maryland | 43 | | 24 | | .97 |
| N. J. | 63 | 4 | 36 | 2 | .95 |
| W. Virginia | 20 | 8 | 11 | 5 | .95 |
| Ohio | 91 | 6 | 53 | 3 | .94 |
| Colorado | 5 | 26 | 3 | 15 | .93 |
| Indiana | 9 | 45 | 5 | 27 | .91 |
| Illinois | 86 | 14 | 51 | 9 | .90 |
| Oregon | 16 | 14 | 10 | 8 | .90 |
| *Losing States* | | | | | |
| New York | 134 | 20 | 83 | 13 | .87 |
| Connecticut | 35 | | 22 | | .86 |
| Washington | 7 | 31 | 4 | 20 | .86 |
| Kansas | 30 | 4 | 19 | 3 | .84 |
| Idaho | 4 | 17 | 3 | 11 | .81 |
| Minnesota | 32 | 10 | 21 | 7 | .81 |
| Nevada | 5 | 13 | 3 | 9 | .81 |
| N. H. | 18 | 3 | 12 | 2 | .81 |
| N. M. | | 21 | | 14 | .81 |
| Vermont | 18 | | 12 | | .81 |
| Wisconsin | 45 | | 30 | | .81 |
| Penna. | 93 | 10 | 63 | 7 | .80 |

(CONTINUED)

| | 1976 Apportionment | | 1952 Apportionment | | Comparative Ratio |
|---|---|---|---|---|---|
| State | Ford | Reagan | Ford | Reagan | |
| Delaware | 15 | 2 | 11 | 1 | .77 |
| S. D. | 9 | 11 | 6 | 8 | .77 |
| Utah | | 20 | | 14 | .77 |
| Wyoming | 7 | 10 | 5 | 7 | .77 |
| Iowa | 19 | 17 | 14 | 12 | .75 |
| Nebraska | 7 | 18 | 5 | 13 | .75 |
| N. D. | 11 | 7 | 9 | 5 | .70 |
| Maine | 15 | 5 | 12 | 4 | .68 |
| Massachusetts | 28 | 15 | 25 | 13 | .61 |
| Totals | 1123 (51.2%) | 1067 (48.8%) | 662 (55.9%) | 523 (44.1%) | |

ventions, delegate votes in 1952 are rounded to the nearest whole number. Alaska, Hawaii, and the District of Columbia and the territories are excluded from these calculations, lowering the total number of delegates below those actually present at the conventions.)

The 1952 convention is an appropriate benchmark for this comparison. Like the contest of 1976, the earlier conclave was essentially a two-man race in which an avowed ideological conservative fought an acolyte of the traditional party establishment. In both years, the decision was not determined until a rules dispute was settled on the convention floor and, in both years, the nomination was not final until the counting of a single dramatic roll call. The 1952 convention also marks the end of the more traditional era of party nominations before television became fully intrusive, before the impact of widespread population movements, and before the onset of party reform efforts.

Comparing the real and hypothetical roll calls shows the vital effect of apportionment. In 1976, Ford won a very narrow victory, gaining only some 51 percent of the delegates from the 48 states which could participate in both elections. If the old apportionment had been in effect, he would have won a considerably more comfortable victory, garnering almost 56 percent of these delegates.[16]

The political character of the shift can be seen further in the ordering of the states. This ranking is based on the last column of the table, which presents a ratio comparing the increases in delegates among the states. All states had more delegates in 1976 than in 1952, since the total size of the convention had increased by a factor of 1.85. To calculate the last column, the proportionate increase in each state is normalized by this overall ratio. Where states gained more than this average figure, they show a ratio above 1.0; where they lost in relative strength, the ratio is below 1.0. (States of equal rank are listed alphabetically.)

There is a striking relationship between gains in apportionment and support for Reagan and, conversely, losses in relative position and support of Ford (Yules Q = .88). Of seventeen states increasing in relative power, all but Florida and Rhode Island voted for Reagan. Of those losing in relative position, two-thirds voted for Ford. Among large states declining in relative convention representation, only Indiana voted for Reagan. Otherwise, the pattern was consistent: the traditional areas of Republican power—such as New York, Pennsylvania, Ohio, and even Kansas and North Dakota, stayed with the nominal head of the party even as these states' grip on the party was loosening. The new fortresses of the G.O.P., such as South Carolina, Texas, and California, were predominately in support of the challenger, Reagan. The rules reflected a geographical transfer of power and almost promoted a personal transfer of power as well.

The effect of these rules is not likely to be changed in the near future. Reapportionment for the 1980 Republican convention will operate under the same bonus system as in 1976. While the effect of the 1976 election will be to take some seats from southern delegations, amid an overall reduction in the size of the convention, these shifts will not in themselves affect the ideological character of the party.[17] In fact, if we recalculate the 1976 votes, while Reagan would lose only 129, the big losers among the states will be such Ford bastions as New York, Pennsylvania, and Ohio. California will actually gain one delegate, and the changes in the South will affect states which supported Ford such as Florida and Kentucky, almost as much as the Reagan areas such as South Carolina and Georgia. Thus the rules will continue to foster conservatism in the Republican party and perhaps will again aid a Reagan candidacy. (This calculation includes all of the units voting in the 1976 convention, including the territories. The allocation of delegates can be expected to change somewhat as a result of the 1978 elections, with states electing Republican governors, senators and congressmen receiving more seats.)

The results are quite different if we make a similar calculation for the Democrats. In this case, we use the 1960 apportionment, since the convention saw a neat confrontation between a liberal northern candidate, John Kennedy, and a diverse field, and the convention roll call was almost evenly divided between Kennedy and his combined rivals. If that apportionment had been in effect in 1976, Carter actually would have done better than he did in reality, as his percentage of the total delegates would have been 2 percent higher.[18]

Carter endured this small disadvantage in the 1976 convention because the new apportionment system of the Democrats gave less weight to the South. Instead of rewarding states for electoral victories as such, it gave premiums to those areas with large populations and large Democratic turnout. The advantaged areas therefore were the traditional key states in presidential elections, the industrial areas of the Northeast and Midwest.

## Implications

The rules changes of the past year appear to have some important effects. The spread of primaries to new states aided the presidential nomination efforts of Carter and Reagan. The particular rules of 1976 worked to the benefit of Carter, who would have lost delegates under a strict system of proportional representation and might have been at a strategic disadvantage as well under a universal system of winner-take-all elections. In the Republican party, proportional representation might have worked to Reagan's advantage in the early campaign, while a plurality system would have benefited President Ford. The reapportionment of delegates has had contrary effects in the two parties. Among Republicans, power has shifted to the South and Southwest, and will continue to benefit relatively conservative candidates. Among Democrats, the new allocation of delegates has increased the relative power of the large industrial states. While this change worked to the advantage of McGovern in 1972, it was mildly disadvantageous to Carter in 1976.

From these data, we can readily imagine different results in the major decision of the 1976 conventions. *If* no new states had enacted primary laws after 1968, and/or *if* the primaries had been conducted under a purer system of proportional representation, and/or *if* Democratic reapportionment had been even more radical, Jimmy Carter might well be back permanently in Georgia. Among Republicans, a spread of primaries to additional states, fuller use of the proportional principle, and larger allocations of bonus votes (unrelated to state population and Republican votes) would probably have made Ronald Reagan the candidate, and perhaps the president.

A full explanation of the nominations of Carter and Ford must also take account of other factors. American politics has been significantly changed by the decline of partisan attachment and the weakening of party organizations. These trends have come close to transforming the nominating conventions into ritualistic institutions, which only ratify decisions reached in other places. The power of state parties had been supplanted by that of candidate centered organizations and by the mass media. New elites and ideological activists have arisen, creating and manipulating new rules. Furthermore, in politics, the individual qualities and skills of participants will always have an influence. It remains true, however, that all political actors must operate within the established set of rules. As the rules change, candidates and organizations will seek to bend them to their purposes, but some will be better able to adapt than others. Rules are neither neutral nor infinitely flexible. In 1976, they do not provide a sufficient explanation of the outcomes, but they are necessary elements in any analysis.

Beyond the fortunes of individual men and even beyond the policy outcomes which follow, the changes in nomination procedures affect the character of our political parties. We are evolving a party system different from the accepted textbook descriptions of decentralized, cadre organizations. The recent burst of party change ("reform" may be inappropriate) is converting our parties to national organizations. The shift of delegates from one state to another is a constituent act of a dominant political body, a manifestation of sovereignty comparable to the Congress' reapportionment of state representatives. The outlawing of winner-take-all primaries and imposition of requirements for proportional representation is an assertion of power by the parties as against the state legislatures, and a destruction of the previous autonomy of state parties. This movement is more advanced in the Democratic party, but the principle of national party supremacy has been at least stated by the Republicans as well.

To speak of sovereign parties suggests the development of strength in these national institutions. The Democratic party indeed seems to be evolving into an organization of considerable scope and power. It has in place functioning bodies with executive, legislative, and judicial powers, a formal party charter, and biennial conferences. Yet this presumptively strong organization is unable to control its most vital decision, the choice of a leader. In 1976, it was a mechanism available to the most aggressive and able mechanic, and was ultimately driven by the aspirant with weak support from the states using more traditional means of delegate selection. Gerald Ford, on the other hand, won his narrow victory by relying on the less modernized means of delegate selection and the less nationalized appeals.

The new nationalization of the parties does not mean, at least not yet, the development of strong national party organizations. There is a different character to the new party system, particularly evident among the Democrats. It has an individualist base and plebiscitarian tone. The extension of the primaries, the emphasis on "making each vote count" through proportional representation, and the allocation of delegates are alike in their focus on the individual voter. The state party as a distinct organization is not accorded a legitimate role. It does not choose the delegates, it cannot operate as a unified delegation on the convention floor and, indeed, it has almost no ability to bargain over the presidential nomination at all. But nominations are no longer seen as the decision of distinct and legitimate factions whose interests must be compromised, or vindicated, or vanquished, but at least acknowledged. Rather they are now reviewed purely as the decisions of a collectivity of individuals, and all barriers which distort their opinion must be removed. Primaries must therefore replace state conventions; proportional representation must replace plurality systems; and delegates must be reapportioned. The same reasoning supports a national presidential primary and direct election of the president. The plebiscite is replacing political organization.

## Notes

1. John P. Roche, "The Founding Fathers: A Reform Caucus in Action," *American Political Science Review* 55 (December 1961): 799–816.
2. See Austin Ranney, *Curing the Mischiefs of Faction* (Berkeley: University of California Press, 1975); and William J. Crotty, *Political Reform and the American Experiment* (New York: Thomas Y. Crowell, 1977), chaps. 7, 8.
3. For previous developments see Paul T. David et al, *The Politics of National Party Conventions* (Washington: Brookings, 1960), esp. chap. 10; and James W. Davis, *Presidential Primaries: Road to the White House* (New York: Thomas Y. Crowell, 1967).
4. Eugene B. McGregor, "The Uncertainty Principle and National Nominating Conventions," (paper delivered at the American Political Science Association Meetings, Chicago, 1976), p. 34.
5. William Keech and Donald Matthews, *The Party's Choice* (Washington: Brookings, 1976), p. 9ff.
6. Democratic National Committee, Commission on Delegate Selection and Party Structure, *Democrats All* (Washington, 1973), Sections 11, 18.
7. See Congressional Quarterly, *Election '76* (Washington, 1976), pp. 52–65 for details on the state systems. A table summarizing the primary rules of 1976 is available from the author.
8. James I. Lengle and Byron Shafer, pp. 25, 29f; "Primary Rules, Political Power and Social Change," *American Political Science Review* 70 (March 1976): 40.
9. If the California results are included, the results are as follows:
   The district results are unavailable and are based on proportional division of the California results. Compare Lengle and Shafer, table 4, p. 29.

**Hypothetical Results of 1972 Democratic Primaries**

| | Actual | Winner-Take-All | Proportional | Districted |
|---|---|---|---|---|
| Humphrey | 284 | 446 | 419 | 429 |
| Wallace | 291 | 379 | 370 | 387 |
| McGovern | 672 | 519 | 437 | 461 |
| Muskie | 56 | 18 | 87 | 51 |
| Others | 59 | 0 | 50 | 29 |

The district results are unavailable and are based on proportional division of the California results. Compare Lengle and Shafer, Tables 4, p. 29.

10. In constructing these figures, the lack of data and the variability of primary laws has required a great many assumptions, but these are not likely to change the basic thrust of the results. The operational rules employed for each state, and detailed tables, are available from the author. Generally, wherever possible, the statewide vote is used for the hypothetical proportional division of the delegates, with the proportions rounded off to the nearest whole number (and whole person). For the district system, all delegates from a district are awarded to the leading candidate, even if separate election is possible. Uncommitted and other candidate choices are combined in the ''other'' category. For this reconstruction, it is assumed that all delegates are elected from congressional or other districts established by state law and that there are equal numbers of delegates from each district. The best pre-convention reports are found in *Congressional Quarterly Weekly Report* 34 (July 10, 1976; August 10, 1976): 1794–1811, 2188–96.
11. William A. Gamson, ''Coalition Formation at Presidential Nominating Conventions,'' *American Journal of Sociology* 68 (September 1962): 157–71.
12. Paul T. David et al, ''Operations and Consequences of Proportional Representation in National Convention Delegate Selection, 1976,'' (paper delivered at the Alternative Program at the American Political Science Association, Chicago, 1976), p. 19.
13. The effect of the rules is given less emphasis in Larry N. Gerston and Stephen J. Cohen, ''Presidential Delegate Selection: Political Structure and Party Reform, 1976,'' (paper delivered at the Western Political Science Association, Phoenix, 1977), and Gerston, Jerome Burstein, and Cohen, ''Presidential Nominations and Coalition Theory,'' (paper delivered at the Western Political Science Association, Los Angeles, 1978). These differences in interpretation stem, in part, from the data bases. The papers by Gerston and associates employ the final convention votes, while this article is an attempted reconstruction of hypothetical results prior to the Carter bandwagon or the Republican convention showdown. Their concern is also basically different, emphasizing the regional concentration of coalitions, while the focus here is on cross-regional influences.
14. *Washington Post*, June 27, 1976, cited by David, p. 24.
15. Gerston and Cohen, p. 22; and Gerston, Burstein, and Cohen, p. 33. Also see David, p. 21, whose conclusions are that Ford would benefit from a plurality system, Reagan from proportionality.
16. Roll calls are found in Richard C. Bain and Judith H. Parris, *Convention Decisions and Voting Records*, 2nd ed. (Washington: Brookings, 1973).
17. *Congressional Quarterly Weekly Report* 35 (July 9, 1977): 1427.
18. Detailed tables reconstructing the Democratic convention vote in 1972 and 1976 are available from the author. The data are less interesting than in the Republican case, showing a relatively small effect, and are based on a less clear factional division. For these reasons, and to conserve space, they are not presented here.

# 19

# "Democracy" in British Political Parties

*Co-Authored by Patricia L. Sykes*

Of all the words in the lexicon of politics, none is more ambiguous or more debatable than "democracy." In the specific study of political parties, this ambiguity is particularly marked. Proponents of organizations as diverse as the U.S. Republican party, the British Liberals, and the Soviet Communist party all invoke the name of democracy on behalf of their cherished body. In this chapter, we will examine some of the different meanings of democracy and their empirical realization in British political parties.

We will deal with four concepts of democracy, and with the ways in which these concepts are paralleled in the organization of political parties. We certainly do not expect to resolve the conceptual problems that are inherent in this term. Rather, we use the four models as characterizations, perhaps caricatures, of four ways in which political parties conduct their business. In each section, we outline one of the four models of democracy and then focus on our principal research material, British party organizations.

These models and their party counterparts are:

1. Democracy as popular selection among competing elites, reflected in the Conservative party of Britain.
2. Democracy as the choice among competing policy programs developed by active party members. The empirical parallels are the practices and objectives of the currently dominant wing of the Labour party.
3. Democracy as participation at the grass roots by active individuals. The Progressives in the U.S. favored this approach, and a (partial) British analogue is found in the Liberal party.
4. Democracy as the competition of diverse factions, resulting in the consensual achievement of the public good. Quintessentially American, this is the Madisonian theory of pluralism. It is exemplified by the new Social Democratic party, a force that may permanently change the character of British politics.

This research is based on a year's residence in the U.K. Much of this time was spent learning about British politics impressionistically—reading, watching, attending the parties' annual conferences, following candidates in critical by-elections. More systematically, we interviewed professional organizers of the parties' central offices, most members of Parliament in the new SDP, and a few prominent national politicians.

To focus our research, we selected two parliamentary constituencies for detailed examination. Using unique criteria[1] we chose Hendon North, a predominantly middle-class suburb in north London, and Bradford, an old industrial city in Yorkshire. Obviously, no two constituencies can be a "representative sample." We do believe they are useful locales for this case study, and vary sufficiently to suggest the diversity of British politics.

We spent considerable time in these two constituencies, attending party and committee meetings, interviewing leaders, observing local election campaigns, collecting documents, and simply drinking with new-found friends in pubs. We rely principally on the information we obtained through this "poaking and soaking." To supplement, not replace, the material we obtained in this semi-anthropological fashion, we mailed a questionnaire to the most active party members in these areas, that is, the members of the executive committees.

The survey gathered data on the members' political experience, attitudes toward party politics, views on public policy issues, and demographic characteristics. Overall, we received returns from some 250 party activists, about two-thirds of those surveyed in each of the eight party organizations.[2] Relevant data from the survey will be introduced where appropriate.

## Democracy as Popular Selection among Competing Elites

Our first model of democracy focuses on political leadership. In this construct, the chief actors are politicians, who use their positions in and out of government to court mass support. The role of the electorate is to approve and disapprove of these actions, so that democracy becomes defined as a system in which "individuals acquire the power to decide by means of a competitive struggle for the people's vote."[3]

For purposes of this model, the leaders themselves can be postulated as being interested only in power, not in public policies. Thus, they "formulate policies in order to win elections, rather than win elections in order to formulate policies." Downs explained the logical consequences of this political axiom. Leaders will not have fixed ideological beliefs, but will vary their policies in order to get or maintain office. A party, united in its search for power, will usually support any policy favored by a majority of the electorate. In some circumstances, however, it will attempt to gain victory by taking the side of a series of passionate minorities that can be cumulated to a total electoral majority.[4]

Like each of our simplified models of democracy, the competitive elites construct implies a particular kind of party organization. We would expect it to be relatively hierarchical in structure, with an extensive central office dedicated to the support of the leadership elite engaged in the critical electoral competition. Programmatic research would be as concerned with the relative popularity of policies as with their substantive merit, and there would be even less emphasis on the ideological purity of these policies.

Principally, this party organization would be concerned with marketing, with the most technically efficient means to sell its products to the consumers, the voters. Marketing might involve, following Downs, finding the appropriate location in an ideological space, but there are considerable limits on the ability of parties to alter their locations.[5] More often, particularly in a two-party "oligopoly," ideology can be subordinated. Then, marketing would include advertising, campaign research to discover the consumer preferences and the best means to appeal to the electorate, an economic distribution of scarce campaign resources, and technical expertise in the use of polls, the mass media, and sloganeering.[6]

Like any organization, the market-oriented party must provide incentives for its members.[7] This need presents a potential problem for the party leadership. Commitment to a fixed policy program might be disadvantageous in an election, if the program does not accord with voter preferences. Therefore, the party leadership would like to deemphasize ideological incentives. Yet, the most obvious purpose of activity in a political party is precisely to achieve public policies, and these goals most clearly differentiate parties from other organizations.

To resolve this problem, the parties of competitive elites will seek other incentives. If available, material rewards are an alternative, such as patronage or paid employment within the party. Alternatively, reliance may be placed on less tangible rewards such as solidary goals—the pleasures of associating with congenial persons—or on status rewards—the intangible benefits of position and honor within the organization.[8]

Providing incentives to the mass membership, however, remains a problem. Individual effort is not critical in a period when most campaigning is done through the mass media, but this emphasis requires much higher financial contributions than in the past. Material incentives can be used to purchase the talent of skilled technicians, but obviously most donors must be offered other rewards. Ideological commitment is the most obvious appeal to direct-mail subscribers to the party. It contains within it, however, possible dangers to the electoral flexibility of the party.

In Britain, the Conservative party most closely fits the model of a party in a system of competitive elites. Since the end of the Second World War, the party has consciously sought to achieve managerial efficiency in politics. There is a large central headquarters, staffed by over three hundred persons, and financed by over five million pounds in individual and corporate contributions.[9] Professional election agents are recruited by the party, given a six-month training course, subjected to a "licensing" examination, and then placed on a meritocratic ladder that offers advancement to area and national levels. As a result, paid agents can be found in about half of Britain's 635 parliamentary constituencies. When an election nears (and one is always possible in a system without fixed terms of office), resources are shifted to maximize electoral effect. Canvassers are recruited from areas in which victory or loss is certain and sent to marginal constituencies.[10] Before the election, all constituencies are arrayed by electoral margins to determine the most useful areas for deployment.

The stress of electoral efficiency is evident on the constituency level as well. The Hendon North Conservatives raised an annual budget of twenty thousand pounds, which is fairly typical of the party's associations, but many times more than the revenue of their local rivals. The stress on efficiency is evident even in small matters, such as keeping records on turnout on polling day. While the Conservatives used typed lists, with carbon copies that could be discarded as the day went on, the other parties needed to rely on single handwritten copies.

The marketing ability and resources of the Conservatives are only high, however, in comparison with those of their competitors. There has been a considerable decrease in party efficiency. There are fewer agents than in the past, and their salaries have declined in inflationary times. Moreover, agents must raise their own salaries from local funds, so much of their energy is diverted from politics to fund raising. On the national level, there are frequent complaints about the deficiencies of the research office, while local parties have yet to make much use of such techniques as telephone canvassing—an obviously attractive alternative to walking through the cold, wet British weather. What distinguishes the Conservative party is not how well it applies techniques to politics, but how much it stresses their importance.

In a party of a competitive elite, the purpose of the mass membership is to support the leadership, but not to intervene in the choice of leaders and policies. As our data show (table 19.1), Tory activists are satisfied with this role, and are uniquely prone to believe that parliamentary members and leaders "should hold the most political power" in the party, rather than local activists. The structure of the party is also based on this principle. The constitu-

**TABLE 19.1**
**Attitudes Toward Political Elites among British Party Activists***

| | Conservatives | | Liberals | | SDP | | Labour | |
|---|---|---|---|---|---|---|---|---|
| | H | B | H | B | H | B | H | B |
| "Who should hold the most power in your political party?" | | | | | | | | |
| Active members | 24 | 31 | 25 | 20 | 16 | 12 | 22 | 31 |
| All party members | 5 | 12 | 33 | 56 | 53 | 45 | 44 | 31 |
| National party office | 3 | 0 | 0 | 0 | 3 | 0 | 0 | 6 |
| Parliamentary members and leaders | 68 | 50 | 29 | 16 | 26 | 31 | 9 | 0 |
| National party conferences | 0 | 0 | 4 | 4 | 0 | 2 | 22 | 25 |
| Elected representatives on national executive bodies | 0 | 6 | 8 | 4 | 3 | 10 | 4 | 6 |
| "Where is an MP's FIRST responsibility?" To: | | | | | | | | |
| Active members | 3 | 6 | 0 | 0 | 0 | 0 | 4 | 7 |
| All paid-up members | 3 | 6 | 0 | 4 | 0 | 0 | 4 | 33 |
| His/her constituency | 72 | 50 | 40 | 69 | 68 | 71 | 29 | 33 |
| Those who voted for him/her | 6 | 6 | 0 | 4 | 0 | 8 | 12 | 0 |
| Parliamentary party and leaders | 8 | 12 | 0 | 0 | 3 | 0 | 4 | 0 |
| His/her best judgment | 8 | 19 | 60 | 23 | 29 | 21 | 29 | 13 |
| National party conferences | 0 | 0 | 0 | 0 | 0 | 0 | 17 | 13 |
| *N* | 37 | 16 | 25 | 25 | 38 | 49 | 24 | 16 |

*Entries are percentages, adding vertically to 100% for each question, except for rounding.

ency associations are organizationally distinct from the governing party or the central office. The leader of the party is chosen only by the Members of the House of Commons, and even this limited electorate constitutes an expansion of democracy from the 1960s, when a leader simply "emerged" from discussions among "the big beasts in the jungle."[11]

Policy making is reserved for the party leadership. The rank and file cheer these decisions; they do not discuss or endorse them. When the leader makes her appearance at the very end of the annual Conservative conference, her purpose is not to persuade the members, but to ignite their enthusiasm for the coming year, to receive their plaudits as "our fair lady," and to share in the fervor expressed by the closing patriotic and religious songs.

An anecdote from the 1981 Conservative conference makes the point in a singular fashion. Talking with a party "representative" (Tories disdain the term "delegate," with its connotations of policy instructions), Sykes had the following conversation:

> *Sykes*: What do you think about the dispute between Thatcher and Heath?
>
> *Tory*: This is neither the time or the place to discuss such matters.

> *Sykes*: But this is your party conference.
>
> *Tory*: This Conservative party conference is intended to demonstrate the party members' support for our leader.
>
> *Sykes*: But do you support Margaret Thatcher and her policies?
>
> *Tory*: That's not the point. She's our leader.

To be sure, loyalty is not based simply on the charm or title of the prime minister. It is also based on a political calculation appropriate to a power seeking party—that a resolute and united party, even if held responsible for unpopular policies, might fare better in the next election than a party fighting itself. As an election nears, "For the sake of party unity, [ministers] will make the supreme sacrifice of holding on to their jobs."[12] The electoral reasoning was expressed well by a journalist:

> Better that Margaret Thatcher should go down with all guns firing, with a faint hope of impressing the voters with her "guts," than that she should get the worst of both worlds by giving up her reputation for tenacity and making no more than a small and temporary reduction in the unemployment figures. One never knows in politics what may happen.[13]

Presciently, this strategy was particularly appropriate when the crisis of the Falklands war enabled the Conservatives to regain popularity.

The prospect of office is sufficient incentive for the party leadership, but it cannot explain the dedication of those who have made the British Conservative party a mass-membership organization, indeed, the party with the largest mass base in the nation. It is common to have 5 percent of the party's voters actually enrolled in the local association—equivalent in the U.S. to a million dues-paying Republicans or Democrats. In Hendon North alone, the party has 4,000 members, paying an average annual subscription of three pounds.

Material incentives certainly do not account for this support. Undoubtedly, some activists do fantasize that they will eventually sit in the Palace of Westminster,[14] but these opportunities are clearly very restricted. Tangible rewards are severely limited in Britain. There is no patronage similar to U.S. appointments to "no-show" jobs, and even elected positions in local and county government are unpaid, and, in purely economic terms, unrewarding. To the extent one can trust responses to such a question, material incentives are rejected in our survey—and not only by Conservatives. None admitted that their political activity was principally stimulated by a search for "useful contacts for my work," and few even chose the more acceptable alternative, "I would like to serve in public office" (see table 19.2).

Ideological incentives are an alternative attraction. We do find ideological commitment by the Tory activists, who have a distinct set of policy prefer-

**TABLE 19.2**
**Principal Reason for British Party Activism***

| | Conservatives | | Liberals | | SDP | | Labour | |
|---|---|---|---|---|---|---|---|---|
| | **H** | **B** | **H** | **B** | **H** | **B** | **H** | **B** |
| Improve my local community | 20 | 19 | 40 | 40 | 34 | 15 | 17 | 19 |
| Can meet interesting people | 0 | 6 | 0 | 0 | 0 | 0 | 0 | 0 |
| Further national policies I favor | 37 | 31 | 36 | 24 | 34 | 38 | 67 | 38 |
| Seek public office | 9 | 0 | 4 | 0 | 8 | 2 | 4 | 0 |
| A position of significance | 0 | 0 | 0 | 0 | 0 | 2 | 0 | 0 |
| Interesting leisure activity | 3 | 0 | 4 | 0 | 3 | 2 | 0 | 6 |
| To learn about politics | 0 | 6 | 0 | 0 | 3 | 2 | 0 | 0 |
| Help to elect people I like and trust | 17 | 12 | 12 | 28 | 11 | 19 | 8 | 12 |
| Useful contacts for my work | 0 | 0 | 0 | 0 | 0 | 0 | 0 | 0 |
| Promote policies for people like myself | 14 | 25 | 4 | 8 | 8 | 21 | 4 | 19 |
| *N* | 35 | 16 | 25 | 25 | 38 | 48 | 24 | 16 |

*Entries are percentages, adding vertically to 100%, except for rounding.

ences (see table 19.3). The Conservatives also support, moderately, such a stance for their party. On a scale of "ideology-pragmatism" developed by Wright,[15] Conservatives, like Liberals, fall between the more highly ideological Labour members and the more pragmatic SDP (see table 19.4). Furthermore, individual Tories will explain their activism as motivated by their de-

**TABLE 19.3**
**"Left" Policy Attitudes of British Party Activists***

| | Conservatives | | Liberals | | SDP | | Labour | |
|---|---|---|---|---|---|---|---|---|
| | **H** | **B** | **H** | **B** | **H** | **B** | **H** | **B** |
| Restrictions on British nuclear weapons | 3 | 0 | 12 | 42 | 8 | 6 | 88 | 100 |
| Reduced British role in European community | 8 | 18 | 16 | 27 | 16 | 14 | 92 | 88 |
| Increased nationalization of industry | 0 | 6 | 4 | 15 | 0 | 6 | 88 | 94 |
| Relief of government restrictions on unions | 0 | 0 | 4 | 8 | 0 | 2 | 48 | 88 |
| Increased role for National Health Service | 3 | 0 | 16 | 42 | 24 | 33 | 84 | 94 |
| Reduced role for independent schools | 0 | 0 | 44 | 58 | 42 | 47 | 96 | 100 |
| Decreased restrictions on immigration | 0 | 0 | 56 | 46 | 39 | 33 | 64 | 81 |
| Liberal abortion laws | 42 | 53 | 80 | 69 | 79 | 61 | 80 | 81 |
| *N* | 38 | 17 | 25 | 26 | 38 | 49 | 25 | 16 |

*Entries are percentages of each constituency party's activists who take the two more "left" positions on a 4- or 5-point scale. Detailed distributions are available from the authors.

**TABLE 19.4**
**Ideological Commitment of British Party Activists***

| | Conservatives | | Liberals | | SDP | | Labour | |
|---|---|---|---|---|---|---|---|---|
| | **H** | **B** | **H** | **B** | **H** | **B** | **H** | **B** |
| "My party should always stand fast to its goals and principles, even if this should lead to a loss of votes." | | | | | | | | |
| Strongly Agree | 58 | 59 | 44 | 46 | 24 | 47 | 76 | 50 |
| Agree | 34 | 35 | 44 | 50 | 53 | 43 | 16 | 44 |
| "My party should attempt to win the votes of as many groups of people as possible and to represent their interests in government." | | | | | | | | |
| Strongly Agree | 5 | 6 | 8 | 4 | 0 | 0 | 16 | 0 |
| Agree | 3 | 6 | 12 | 12 | 11 | 10 | 16 | 25 |
| "Politics is more a matter of getting the best possible out of a given situation than of stubbornly sticking to principles." | | | | | | | | |
| Strongly Disagree | 10 | 12 | 0 | 4 | 0 | 4 | 32 | 19 |
| Disagree | 29 | 29 | 8 | 27 | 11 | 12 | 32 | 38 |
| "My party needs a philosophical basis for its aims and policies." | | | | | | | | |
| Strongly Agree | 18 | 31 | 60 | 54 | 32 | 33 | 64 | 44 |
| Agree | 58 | 56 | 36 | 35 | 55 | 43 | 16 | 44 |
| "Mean ideology-pragmatism score (4 = most ideological); 20 = most pragmatic) | | | | | | | | |
| Strongly Agree | 11.3 | 11.2 | 11.1 | 10.4 | 12.3 | 12.1 | 8.5 | 9.9 |
| *N* | 38 | 17 | 25 | 26 | 38 | 49 | 25 | 16 |

*Entries are percentages of each constituency party's activists who provide the designated response to the given statements.

sire "to maintain a free society" or, in one extreme case, the fear that "the victory of Benn would be the last free election in this country." In response to the questionnaire as well, the proportion of Conservatives stressing policy programs was similar to that of the Liberals and SDP, although less than among Labour (see tables 19.2 and 19.5).

We do not doubt the deep sincerity with which Conservatives hold these policy views. We find, however, that while policy motivations can explain why these individuals *are* Conservatives, they cannot explain members' activism *as* Conservatives. The Tory style of politics is less concerned with the details of issues, and more with a general orientation toward policy. Thus, as one observer at the annual conference commented to Pomper, it seemed that the representatives were as ready to cheer the prime minister for maintaining

**TABLE 19.5**
**Importance of Party Functions to British Activists***

| | Conservatives | | Liberals | | SDP | | Labour | |
|---|---|---|---|---|---|---|---|---|
| | H | B | H | B | H | B | H | B |
| Developing policy on national issues | 55 | 62 | 44 | 42 | 53 | 63 | 84 | 88 |
| Involvement in local problems and issues | 84 | 88 | 84 | 89 | 89 | 92 | 80 | 100 |
| Gaining publicity in local press | 63 | 62 | 40 | 54 | 58 | 37 | 56 | 44 |
| Holding protests and demonstrations | 0 | 0 | 8 | 11 | 0 | 0 | 24 | 31 |
| Canvassing voters | 90 | 69 | 72 | 73 | 68 | 55 | 72 | 75 |
| Organizing political meetings | 31 | 12 | 12 | 27 | 18 | 18 | 56 | 69 |
| Working with other political groups | 0 | 0 | 8 | 15 | 26 | 20 | 16 | 13 |
| Fundraising and social activities | 82 | 50 | 24 | 42 | 34 | 47 | 24 | 31 |
| Offering party candidates to voters | 76 | 81 | 68 | 85 | 53 | 69 | 80 | 62 |
| Recruiting new party members | 89 | 75 | 72 | 85 | 71 | 59 | 92 | 94 |
| *N* | 38 | 16 | 25 | 26 | 38 | 49 | 25 | 16 |

*Entries are percentages of each constituency party's activists who regard the designated activity as "very important." Because multiple answers were permitted, percentages cannot be added.

her policies unaltered as they would be to praise her for a "U-turn" required by a "change in circumstances."

This impression—and we admit it is no more than that—is supported by two incidents. At one point, an activist in Bradford said that he would find it inappropriate to attempt to change party policy. "If I wrote to the national office, I'd probably get a letter back asking, 'Are you sure you're in the right party?'. " The other example of abstention from policy controversies came at a monthly meeting of the Hendon association, which took place as the prime minister was considering major cabinet changes that would signal the future directions of government economic policy. As the minutes dispassionately recorded, "The meeting discussed the impending Cabinet changes and rejected a suggestion that a letter should be sent to the Prime Minister listing the changes the Committee would like to see."

Indeed, it is striking how little emphasis is placed on policy discussions in these meetings, particularly when contrasted with Labour's intensive and arcane disputations. For example, a local Conservative report on the party conference emphasized not the content of policy resolutions adopted or the vote of the associations' representative (as occurred in the Labour meeting), but only the fact that the representative had been given the honor of an opportunity to speak.

Rather than material or ideological incentives, Conservatives emphasize intangible rewards. There is the competitive satisfaction of winning an election, a pleasure that came to members in both Hendon and Bradford in the May local elections. There is the social satisfaction of working with others of similar mind and background. These exist in any organization, but they may be of greater import to the Conservatives, who show somewhat more social homogeneity among their members than the other parties (see table 19.6), and where meetings have an atmosphere more resembling that of a club of associates than a casual and instrumental organization. In contrast to Labour and the smaller parties, it may still be true that "the social life of many Conservatives tends to be closely linked with their political organization."[16]

Possibly the most important of these intangible incentives is honor or status. The Hendon party, for example, has four thousand nominal members, but it can expect only a tenth to engage in an election campaign, and has no more

**TABLE 19.6**
**Selected Personal Characteristics of British Party Activists***

| | Conservatives | | Liberals | | SDP | | Labour | |
|---|---|---|---|---|---|---|---|---|
| | H | B | H | B | H | B | H | B |
| Political Experience | | | | | | | | |
| Previously in another party | 5 | 0 | 28 | 12 | 58 | 35 | 12 | 31 |
| Ever ran for public office | 40 | 65 | 76 | 62 | 47 | 20 | 40 | 6 |
| Parents paid members of a party | 42 | 44 | 24 | 42 | 29 | 22 | 20 | 50 |
| Age, by Political Generation | | | | | | | | |
| 1970s generation (below 26) | 8 | 6 | 0 | 4 | 17 | 8 | 8 | 44 |
| 1960s generation (26–35) | 11 | 12 | 16 | 27 | 33 | 24 | 36 | 38 |
| Postwar generation (36–50) | 39 | 12 | 52 | 38 | 28 | 35 | 20 | 6 |
| Prewar generation (over 50) | 42 | 69 | 32 | 31 | 22 | 33 | 36 | 12 |
| Education | | | | | | | | |
| Left school by 16 | 28 | 40 | 12 | 15 | 6 | 10 | 32 | 6 |
| "O" Levels | 19 | 20 | 20 | 12 | 3 | 14 | 12 | 6 |
| "A" Levels | 17 | 20 | 0 | 4 | 19 | 10 | 4 | 6 |
| Polytechnic, etc. | 19 | 0 | 16 | 12 | 8 | 20 | 16 | 31 |
| University | 17 | 20 | 52 | 58 | 64 | 45 | 36 | 50 |
| Occupation | | | | | | | | |
| Manual, including skilled | 0 | 0 | 0 | 8 | 0 | 4 | 4 | 0 |
| Clerical, small business | 32 | 47 | 20 | 32 | 22 | 16 | 39 | 8 |
| Technical, teacher, student | 24 | 20 | 48 | 60 | 25 | 62 | 39 | 85 |
| Business executive | 24 | 20 | 32 | 0 | 22 | 9 | 0 | 0 |
| Professional | 21 | 13 | 0 | 0 | 31 | 9 | 17 | 8 |
| Union Members | 8 | 6 | 44 | 54 | 21 | 42 | 67 | 88 |
| Sex | | | | | | | | |
| Male | 53 | 81 | 68 | 92 | 78 | 76 | 64 | 88 |
| Female | 47 | 19 | 32 | 8 | 22 | 24 | 36 | 12 |
| *N* | 38 | 17 | 25 | 26 | 38 | 49 | 25 | 16 |

*Entries are percentages of each constituency party's activists.

than about two hundred true activists. Like any voluntary organization, it must find ways to stimulate and reward these workers. Nonpecuniary honors are a typical method. Occasionally, a party activist is knighted, and that official honor enhances the status of every canvassing drudge. At the local level, there are ceremonial but prized recognitions, such as being asked to be present at the official count of the poll or being invited to a party dinner.

More general and more available is social honor, recognition among one's peers. To increase the effect of these solidary motives, Hendon Conservatives are organized not only in the constituency and in its five wards, but in thirteen smaller branches, which may have as few as ten associated friends and neighbors. As a result, almost every activist can have a title and personal recognition. This stimulus may be particularly important in a deferential party within a still-deferential society. A branch party may thus have a president, vice-president, chairman, vice-chairman, secretary, treasurer, and membership secretary. (In one small branch, only one person lacked an office.) Any remaining persons may be designated as committee chairmen or even "road stewards"—a dignified name for persons responsible for distributing party literature on streets where they live.

The significance of solidary rewards is further indicated by the extensive social activity of the branches and constituency party. In meetings, rather little time is devoted to policy discussions, even when the party is preparing for an election. The emphasis is on fund raising, increasing membership, and efficient electioneering. A typical local meeting was largely devoted to the budget and social matters, with the only overtly political note coming in a "pep talk" by the chairman about the forthcoming local elections. Similarly, a monthly diary of events in the constituency listed six social affairs, three ward or branch meetings, a "surgery" or constituents' complaint session with the local councilor, and only one clearly political event, a briefing by the area's MP.

This emphasis is partially caused by national party rules, which require local associations to raise their own funds, including the agent's salary, and to make payments to the national center. It is also in keeping with the members' own inclinations. More than the other parties, Conservatives give major importance to fund raising and social activities (see table 19.5). In this, as in the other aspects we have discussed, their party "fits" the model of democracy as a competition of elites.

If the Tories exemplify this model, however, they also illustrate its logical problems. There are endemic, even ironic, contradictions in the model, stemming from the irrepressible character of ideology. Ideological incentives cannot be entirely eliminated. Even if they are subordinated, a voluntary political association must rely on them to some extent; otherwise, there is no particular reason for people to join a political party rather than the local school association or the British Legion. Without material rewards, and with other outlets for solidary needs, parties must resort to some extent to ideological appeals. To the extent these incentives are used, however, the flexibility of the party in changing its policy positions is limited, and consequently its competitive electoral position may be damaged.

The demands of competitive electoral politics usually induce party leaders to moderate these ideological demands from the membership. In certain circumstances, now apparent in Britain, these constraints may not operate. Perceived failures by the opposition party and perceived economic difficulties allowed the Conservatives to win the 1979 election on an ideological, monetarist platform, demonstrating that "where it was possible, parties and candidates would prefer a non-competitive position, one nearer to their own ideological bent."[17] Extremism in policy is always possible, in response to the preferences of the rank and file. Extremism is also possible—and even more significant—when it represents the preferences of the leadership itself. This is the situation in contemporary Britain. The Thatcher government has committed itself to free-market policies that have raised unemployment to Depression levels. Thus far, it has refused to bend to the electoral wind, and indeed now sees victory likely from the combination of the Falklands victory and limited evidence of economic recovery. Whatever the course of future events, the important point is that the leadership is committed to maintaining an ideology despite possible electoral loss.

The model of democracy as competitive elites requires a strategy of "vote-maximizing by the party only when this is either necessary or advantageous. At other times the parties have a limited freedom to adopt those policies nearer to the hearts of their supporters."[18] Furthermore, party leaders can actually enhance their internal position in the party by promoting more extremist policies, and thereby providing more ideological incentives. In satisfying their own desires and those of their supporters, however, leaders can subvert the long-run viability of the party and its ability to adapt to changing needs and popular wishes. The ironic danger to an elite party is that its leaders may have principles after all. Adherence to principle can cheer the membership and satisfy the leadership. In an organization that seeks to win elections rather than arguments, however, the demands of victory can clash with the appeals of philosophy, creating organizational uneasiness and possible decline. In a democracy of competing elites, leaders are allowed to choose, but in choosing they may dig their party's grave.

## Democracy as the Choice among Competing Policy Programs Developed by Active Party Members

In our second "model" of democracy, the focus changes from leadership to policy. In this construct, parties represent principles and they consist, to quote Burke's famous definition, of "a body of men united for promoting the national interest upon some particular principle in which they are all agreed." Their public purpose is to present the electorate with alternative sets of policies and, following the judgment of the voters, to realize these programs. Such parties are usually committed to the process of democratic elections, although there are some variants of the policy-oriented party that see it as the instrument for revolutionary action, such as the Leninist party or the Militant Tendency within the Labour party.

A party commitment to specific policy objectives and even to a broad ideology does not logically necessitate a particular structure. Certainly, a highly centralized and authoritarian party could pursue these objectives, as demonstrated by the Leninist party. Nevertheless, in current democratic politics, we typically find the stress on an ideological party joined with a commitment to membership participation and internal party democracy. The expectation is that the individual members' ideological concerns lead to broad membership participation. The development of a clear policy stance to put before the electorate requires a process of ideological discussion.[19]

This participatory model has a long heritage in writings on political parties. Ostrogorski champions the single-interest party as a vehicle to achieve policy programs.[20] The arguments for internal party democracy echo Michels's disappointed hopes for an active and controlling grass-roots membership.[21] Finally, the classic advocacy of a "responsible party system" for the United States shows both the features and the contradictions of this model. Those reformers sought an active party membership as well as highly centralized party institutions. Such parties, they argued, would "bring forth programs to which they commit themselves" and would "possess sufficient internal cohesion to carry out these programs."[22]

The implications of this theory for the organization of political parties are unclear. Parties must be disciplined at the center, that is, governmental officials are intended to further a party program, as defined by the party, not by themselves, and to follow the election "mandate" achieved by the party. Yet, this program is to be developed through broad popular participation within the party, a highly decentralized process. This ambiguity, if not contradiction, raises the possibility of conflict between the membership's policy preferences and those of the central party organs.[23] It also raises the possibility that some members may be "more equal" than others, because they have the "right" ideology, and therefore participation may come to be restricted to them.

The incentives to members in this party are principally ideological, although other varieties will not be completely excluded. Members will care deeply about policy questions, particularly those affecting the nation as a whole. They will also be concerned with internal party democracy as the means to implementing these policies. Party meetings will reflect these emphases, and party campaign activity will stress winning minds rather than votes alone. Policy in this party is the goal, not only the means to other goals, such as the victory of an elite group.

The British Labour party has always fit the participatory model of democracy to the extent that its members are primarily concerned with policy. Clause Four of the Labour Party Constitution explicitly states the party's traditional commitment to the "common ownership of the means of production, distribution, and exchange," and its message is printed on every membership card.

The current Labour party fully illustrates the participatory model. Formerly, the party gave less attention to the forms of participation, and to the respective roles of the leadership, the Parliamentary Labour Party, and the national Conference.[24] Since the 1960s, however, ideological purists on the left of the party—always present but previously a minority faction—have become increasingly numerous and increasingly disillusioned with the politics of compromise. In addition, middle-class intellectuals and leftists previously excluded from Labour as members of organizations on the pre-1973 "proscribed list," have recently joined the party. As the Left has gained strength in the unions and constituency parties, it has been able to propose certain reforms, in the name of democracy.[25] These reforms highlight specific features of the participatory model and, at the same time, serve to demonstrate the inherent contradictions in this democratic theory.

The first proposal, as yet not adopted, would transfer effective control over the party manifesto from the leader of the party to the National Executive Committee, in an effort to make the manifesto more binding on elected representatives in Parliament. Presently, both cabinet members and the NEC are involved in drawing up the manifesto, and the PLP does not regard it as compelling observance. Leaders may disregard some Conference decisions as James Callaghan did in 1979 when he deliberately excluded any reference to the proposed abolition of the House of Lords from the manifesto. Reformers argue that the NEC should incorporate Conference decisions into the party manifesto—decisions that are believed to reflect the sentiments of ordinary constituency members. They insist that a detailed and binding manifesto would ensure that Labour party policy, formulated largely by constituency activists, should be implemented as a program in precisely the form presented to voters.

The major problem with the proposal for a binding, NEC-originated manifesto lies in its unclear democratic legitimacy. The major claim on its behalf is that it would provide constituency parties with a greater share in the policy-making process. In reality, it is likely to permit a few large unions, using their block votes at Conference, to control party policy. Moreover, these unions include (and cast Conference votes on behalf of) members who may not even exist (Conference votes are decided on the basis of financial payments, not membership rolls), who may not be Labour supporters at all (some are Communists and many are Conservatives), and who are not consulted, in any case, on specific policy or frequently on leadership (British unions do not hold periodic elections in many cases).

Michels's theory of the oligarchical tendencies of political parties could be cited by activists on the left in defense of their support for restraints on the leadership. Theories of collective action, on the other hand, help to explain why delegates and the General Membership Committees do not represent the interests of Labour voters at large or of all the rank-and-file party members.[26] If a ward has one hundred members, only thirty are likely to attend a meeting; therefore, it is possible for fifteen members (or less, given skill, unity, and education) to control the meeting. As a left-wing councilor explained, "They may be a small proportion of the mass electorate, but they will have a large influence. Especially because the others will follow their leadership in recognition of their hard work. These are the few people who put politics above work, and who would like to make politics their full-time work." In fact, these activists often have no other employment. Our data shows that in both Bradford and in Hendon, active Labour party members are less likely to have full-time employment than other party activists.

Therefore, at best, the manifesto reform would provide small groups of constituency activists with the power to effect policy making. But these constituency activists—particularly those selected as delegates to the national Conference—are far more radical than the average party member, as evident in the 1960s CND campaign and in the Bennite support in the 1981 deputy leadership battle. (It should be noted that a Marplan poll found that 61 percent of the Labour voters supported Dennis Healey for deputy leader while only 21 percent supported Tony Benn.[27] As Beatrice Webb quoted her husband, "Constituency parties were frequently unrepresentative groups of nonentities, dominated by fanatics, cranks, and extremists."[28] Several previous studies of the Labour party[29] provide a more diverse picture, while our own research reveals that Labour activists are quite radical (see table 19.3), but are neither cranks nor nonentities.[30]

The second proposal, now in effect, is another demand for greater accountability. Mandatory reselection of members of Parliament (i.e., renomination of incumbents) could dramatically alter the power relationships within the party. MPs must now submit themselves for reselection at least once during every Parliament, and must therefore pay attention to their local supporters as well as to the parliamentary leadership. Previously, MPs automatically ran for another term, while receiving deference and little criticism from members of their constituency party. Now party activists are able to demand that the MPs vote according to the manifesto and give more attention to local needs. Parliamentary seats are open to challengers when the MPs fail to fulfill the party's promises or to respond to constituent demands.

This reform also raises questions on the meaning of democracy. Mandatory reselection of parliamentary candidates alters, but does not necessarily improve, the "electoral connection" between MPs and those whom they represent. The reform does not make MPs more accountable to constituents, or to Labour voters, or even, as argued, to the constituency parties. Only those on the GMC who attend meetings, usually a small group of political activists, select the parliamentary candidates. In Bradford North, for example, the members of the local GMC (which is dominated by the Militant Tendency, a Trotskyist group within the Labour party) deselected the long-time, center-right MP Ben Ford and voted for Pat Wall, a member of the Militant. When canvassing with activists in Bradford North, Sykes observed repeatedly that some ordinary, card-carrying Labour members were completely unaware of the deselection. The NEC objected to the selection of Pat Wall as a parliamentary candidate chosen by the Bradford North constituency party. After reviewing the procedure at the selection meeting, and investigating Pat Wall's "anti-parliamentary"[31] views, it concluded that the reselection process had been conducted unfairly.

The third reform is the institution of the electoral college, a device to remove selection of the leadership from the PLP alone. Now, under the electoral college system, the constituency parties cast 30 percent of the votes for leader and deputy leader, the trade unions cast 40 percent, and members of Parliament cast only 30 percent. Reformers intended to give constituents a voice in the selection process, and to ensure working-class representation in the form of the trade union vote. Yet this reform is also questionable as a democratic measure. The 30 percent vote cast by the constituencies is actually decided by the GMCs in many cases, not by the total membership. The union votes are even more dissociated from the rank and file. In 1981, relatively few unions directly consulted their members in the contest between Benn and Healey for deputy leader. Some decided their votes through their executive bodies. A few held membership polls, but at least one major union disregarded the result. The largest union, the Transport and General Workers, altered its vote from one week to the next, with no ultimate basis in democratic legitimacy.

In addition to the contradictions inherent in the recent reform proposals, the Labour party suffers from problems endemic to any organization that seeks both a high degree of centralization and a participatory role for its members. The party has always had a peculiar structure that has created conflict over the location of sovereign power. The general doctrine has been that the annual Conference is the supreme body, and that its resolutions express the mandates of the party. Yet this doctrine does not thereby lead to democratic control by the individual membership. The PLP has typically been allowed to act autonomously, to have a major part in the writing of the election manifesto, to decide on the timing and detailed implementation of the party program, and, until 1981, to choose its own leadership. Moreover, the Conference itself has been dominated by trade unions, not the constituency parties, and by the unanimous or bloc votes that the unions cast. Consequently, the unions have been able to cast approximately five-sixths of the total votes at Conference, and six unions alone could carry a majority whenever they were united.[32]

This conflict between centralization and grass-roots participation surfaced at a Bradford West General Management Committee Meeting. The meeting took place a couple of days after Michael Foot's announcement that Peter Tachell, a radical from South London, could not stand as a Labour parliamentary candidate because he was, in Foot's words, an "anti-parliamentarian." One member from the GMC proposed a resolution to oppose Foot's decision and "affirm the right of the constituency party to choose its candidate for MP" Supporting the principle of party democracy, a member said, "We have taken great steps to democratize this party. Foot's action is a step back." Arguing the opposing principle of centralization, a well-known right-winger immediately responded, "You need to be reminded that this party does not allow the constituencies to do whatever they want. The result would be sheer anarchy. . . . This resolution does more than protest Foot's decision. It recommends a fundamental change in the rules of this party." An overwhelming majority of the GMC voted to pass the resolution, but the NEC responded by ruling that the resolution was "out of order."

The principle of mass membership participation also conflicts with the necessity of common agreement in a highly ideological party that emphasizes policy formulation. This fundamental problem leads some Labour party members to hold the notion that there is a right or correct view that should be held by all, and that only the right people should participate in debate.

When asked why the Right in the Labour party has virtually disappeared in Bradford, one left-wing activist explained,

> They don't show up at meetings anymore because they know they'll lose the argument. They always did. They know we're right. The only way they can fight us is by using old machine politics. For a long time, they tried to keep us out of the party by "losing" applications at City Hall. But they've never been able to win an argument with us.[33]

The Militant Tendency's tactics demonstrate the possible effect of this self-righteous attitude about political beliefs. At the Bradford district party meetings, someone selling the Militant newspaper approaches members as they enter the room, and the Militants berate those who do not purchase a copy. At

GMC meetings, the Militants often create distractions when center or right-wing members speak. Emphasizing ideological unity, these "reformers" apparently do not wish to compromise or to reach common ground.

One further anecdote illustrates the willingness, on the part of both the Left and the Right in Bradford, to resort to any tactic in order to "win" an ideological dispute. Several years ago, in Bradford ward X, the Left (not just the Militants) attempted to gain control by packing the ward meetings. They distributed membership cards, registered in false names, to local Pakistani residents who attended meetings in return for certain "favors." The Right retaliated by using the same method to employ Bangladeshi residents to attend the meetings. It was not unusual, at that time, for a ward meeting to have a hundred members present, only ten of whom were white.

Admittedly, the Militant Tendency is only one small faction of the Left. Its greatest strength is in the constituency parties, and the group dominates two of the three Bradford constituencies. In Hendon, where there is a more typical Left-controlled GMC, we did not observe similar tactics of intimidation. Hendon activists varied from the middle-aged worker who said, "We've heard all that Marxist nonsense about the unity of the oppressed," to the young, middle-class bureaucrat who was devoted to creating just such an alliance. Although there were class differences and policy disagreements in Hendon, party members conducted their debates in a fairly amicable fashion.

Consistent with these constitutional disputes within Labour, we found that incentives for activists in the Labour party are largely ideological. In fact, Labour respondents in our survey most frequently cited policy concerns as their primary reason for political participation (see table 19.2) and were most likely to accord major importance to this function (see table 19.5). Previous studies have also observed Labour members' preoccupation with policy, noting that "the Labour party is an ideological movement, and the people who gravitate toward it usually display a keen interest in policy issues."[34] Turner has described the Labour activist as one "who is issue-oriented and who derives pleasure from the discussion of issues that are of intellectual and personal concern.[35]

Illustratively, while observing the local election campaign in Hendon, Pomper took part in Labour canvassing the night before the poll. Before the actual canvass began, he spent a half hour participating in a discussion about the absence of a Socialist movement in the United States. The experience provided a sharp contrast to any campaign in the States, where the pre-election talk normally focuses on the number of leaflets to be distributed on a given street. The Labour discussion should not be dismissed as armchair speculations made by impractical ideologues. The philosophical awareness evident in the discussion provided the stimulus for these canvassers (and another fifty or so like them) to go out on many lonely and rainy nights to spread their message in a generally unsympathetic area.

The atmosphere of a Labour branch meeting demonstrates the party members' concern for policy issues, in contrast to the other political parties' meetings. In the course of a year, almost all local Labour meetings are devoted to policy issues or party rules, with social matters or even election strategy deemphasized. Invitations to send representatives to issue groups, such as the Campaign for Nuclear Disarmament, are considered seriously, and invitations are always accepted. (There may even be an occasional contest for participation.) In the other parties, these communications are more likely to be disregarded or treated as an onerous duty.

The Labour party activists' policy emphasis is clearly distinct from their Tory opponents' preoccupations with electoral success. Another example from Hendon demonstrates Labour's indifference to the electoral consequences of its policies. In an area with the largest Jewish population of any constituency in Britain, the Hendon GMC adopted a pro-PLO position and publicized it in the local press. In response to criticism of this action, the party had a meeting at which an outside speaker was expected to present a more "balanced" or more pro-Israeli position, but instead, this speaker also expounded a pro-Palestinian view. When asked why the GMC did not simply neglect this issue, which could only have harmful electoral implications, one member said, "It just wouldn't be right." In contrast, the Hendon Conservatives were willing to consider the unusual action of protesting to the prime minister if the government were to take a pro-PLO position.

The preference for policy clarity over electoral success is further illustrated by the Labour activist who enthusiastically adopted the motto, "A choice, not an echo," for the Labour party. He was unaware that Barry Goldwater used the slogan in 1964, or that it presaged an electoral disaster. Nevertheless, the Labour activist would probably have held this position, even if he were aware of these facts.

Policy concerns supercede personality, as well-as electoral considerations. At a fringe meeting during the 1981 Brighton conference, MP Dennis Skinner exclaimed, "Policies are important, not personalities. . . . We need to push power away from the moderate elitists and down to the rank-and-file. . . . We can't afford to be mealy-mouthed about how we win our victories." Tony Benn added, "We are fighting a battle that can be won, has been won, and must be won. This party must go on to decide the policy, select the candidates and the leadership that is to implement the basic principles to which it is committed."

Labour party policy is devoted primarily to national (as opposed to local) issues. Our Labour respondents chose national policy as the top priority for their constituency party more often that activists in any other political party. In Hendon, the local election literature of both the Labour party and the Conservatives stressed the importance of preserving the environment, but with different emphases. The Tory brochure stated, "One of our greatest fears is the risk that Barnet could be sucked up into a plan for the extension of Inner London into our pleasant and indeed rural outer London suburb.'' In sharp contrast, Labour stressed a national threat, arguing, ''The greatest danger to our environment is the nuclear one, and the effect on all our lives of the Government decision to spend 10,000 million pounds on Trident is only too apparent.''

Of course, other incentives are important to Labour activists, although less so than the ideological motivation. Several members expressed the desire to be parliamentary candidates, ''if the prevailing ideology of the members is suitable,'' as one activist put it. And, although one doesn't find Labour party activists drinking cocktails before and after the meetings (well, perhaps a pint of bitter during the meeting), there appears to be some social incentive. At a GMC meeting in Bradford, two ''Young Socialists'' were necking in the back of the room. Occasionally, they stopped and voted. After the meeting, when Sykes questioned the chairman about the couple, he joked, ''That goes to show you how bad our economy is these days. Used to be the kids would go to the movies on a Friday night. Can't afford it anymore. So they join the Labour party instead.''

In conclusion, there are several difficulties with the participatory model, and with the Labour party in particular. First, there is a conflict between the degree of centralization required and the demand for mass-member participation. Second, another contradiction exists between broad participation and unity in policy agreement. The emphasis on ideology means that members will always be claiming the right to have their views represented, and many will go so far as to argue that their views are the proper and ''truthful'' ones. This attitude encourages a sense of ''we know what is best for the working class,'' while the trade union leaders fail to consult their members and the GMCs neglect their constituents. This last problem reveals the anomalies of the restrictions on participation in an ideology that champions participation abstractly. It also indicates a certain contempt for the nonideological working class and for ''house-wives who are only interested in making sandwiches.'' Third, each reform measure lacks a clear basis for claiming democratic legitimacy.

Unless Labour is able to resolve some of these problems, internal disputes will continue to weaken the party, both organizationally and publicly. Those with the strongest ideological preferences (e.g., the Left) will fight the hardest, and may ultimately succeed in controlling not only the constituency parties, but the NEC and the PLP as well. In sharp contrast to the Downsian model, the Labour party's future is threatened by the fact that it seeks to win arguments rather than elections. As members from the center-right leave the party to join the new SDP, Labour may at last find itself ideologically pure and consistent in policy. But it is likely to be a minority party, whose democratic concerns are lost in the battle for socialism.

### Democracy as Participation at the Grass Roots by Active Individuals

In a third theory of democracy, emphasis is placed on individual political activity. When carried to its logical conclusion, this theory of liberal individualism provides no defined role for intermediary organizations, such as pressure groups and parties. Rather, politics is to be the concern, and under the control of, atomistic men and women who are motivated by their own consciences and views of the public interest, and who willingly engage in activities such as the discussion of issues and the administration of local governments.

John Stuart Mill, especially in *Considerations on Representative Government*, is probably the best representative of this theory of democracy. Mill has two concerns: a negative desire to avert tyrannical and class-biased government, and a positive wish to promote the moral development of individuals. Both of these goals can be furthered by enhancement of individuals' political capabilities, so that universal suffrage and broad participation are the hallmarks of the best state:

> The ideally best form of government is that in which the sovereignty, or supreme controlling power in the last resort, is vested in the entire aggregate of the community; every citizen not only having a voice in the exercise of that ultimate sovereignty, but being, at least occasionally, called on to take an actual part in the government, by the personal discharge of some public function, local or general. . . . A completely popular government . . . is both more favorable to present good government, and promotes a better and higher form of national character, than any policy whatsoever.[36]

In this individualistic theory of democracy, the emphasis is on the self-sufficient citizen, who does not need structured institutions to mediate between himself and the state. Even if accepted as inevitable, parties must be carefully restrained. Their interests must not be allowed to obscure the more general public good. Mill's concern for individual autonomy implicitly leads to party structures that are highly decentralized and internally democratic, just as it does explicitly to electoral systems, such as that utilizing the single transferable vote, that weaken party discipline.

Incentives in this kind of party, indeed in this kind of a polity, must be largely intangible. Materialistic lures such as jobs and patronage are disdained, while the English are praised by Mill as a people who "care very little for the exercise of power over others." Policy rewards are acceptable, but only as they are pursued as part of the general welfare, and not as class legislation, "the sinister interest of the holders of power." The basic incentives are the psychological satisfactions of being a "good citizen" through service to others, and particularly on the local level. These may be supplemented by personal intangible rewards, such as honorific positions in the party or community that recognizes those model individuals "who act on higher motives and more comprehensive and distant views."[37]

In the United States, the individualist theory has found its fullest expression in the Progressive movement. The Progressives distrusted political parties, both because partisan organizations promote particular interests at the expense of the common good, and because of their typically hierarchical character. The ideal form of government for Progressives would be direct democracy, with the institutions of the modern large state approaching that ideal as closely as possible. The closest embodiment of the Progressive theory in Great Britain is the Liberal party, although it is anomalous to speak of any party exemplifying a philosophy hostile to parties.

One anomaly is the party's stance toward power. Historically, until the 1920s, the Liberals were one of Britain's two alternating ruling parties, led by such revered figures as William Gladstone and Lloyd George. With the rise of Labour, however, the party went into a long decline that led Duverger vitually to predict its elimination.[38] In the 1970s however, the party revived electorally, receiving almost 20 percent of the national vote in the first 1974 poll.[39] Yet, under the plurality system of Parliamentary elections, the party gained only 14 of 635 Commons seats,[40] and the disproportionality continued in the second 1974 and 1979 polls.[41] Debarred from the actual exercise of power, the Liberals could still sense its presence, first under the Lib-Lab pact with Labour Prime Minister Callaghan, then in the prospect of a victorious electoral alliance with the new Social Democrats.

Temperamentally, it is unclear if the Liberals are ready for power, a consequence of the party's Progressive inclinations. In the Progressive theory, participation is always a good, but power has traps as well as trappings. One party activist found four different attitudes toward power in this one small party: "idealists" concerned only with issues; "community activists" doing good works; "local councilors trying to keep their small areas" of influence; and "practical politicians" striving for national power. The last group is certainly represented by the party's dynamic Leader, David Steel, who created the Lib-Lab pact, encouraged the formation of the SDP and the Alliance to "break the mould" of British two-party politics, and challenged the 1981 Liberal Assembly "to return to your constituencies and prepare for government." Yet, Steel does not personify the range of liberal attitudes:

> Most Liberals love drawing up policies on every subject under the sun. For Mr. Steel, polices without power are mere idleness. He does not have policies, he

> has party strategies. . . . He has never been through that political adolescence which most Liberals never leave: the "Wee Free" or Exclusive Brethren phase, when the romance of the party consists in its being limited to a select few.[42]

Steel's position is challenged by those Liberals who are more suspicious of power holders than eager to hold power themselves, and some see the Liberals as "the natural party of opposition"—a position in keeping with Mill's commendation of the English citizenry: "Not having the smallest sympathy with the passion for governing, while they are but too well acquainted with the motives of private interest from which that office is sought, they prefer that it should be performed by those to whom it comes without seeking."[43] An example of this hesitancy toward power was provided by the chairman of the Association of Liberal Councillors, local government officials, who proudly asserted that, "the Liberal Party had never been interested in power for its own sake. One of the party's finest traditions was its disrespect for the trappings and seductions of power." Insisting on the importance of policy commitments, he said, "We simply don't want an Alliance government which is a British version of Jimmy Carter, which is all smile and no substance."[44]

The greatest problem associated with possession of power is the inevitable compromises it brings. Purity of doctrine and integrity of conscience can be maintained by a party that always loses elections; they are difficult to maintain when in office. This inescapable result helps to explain why one Liberal organizer actually expected to lose members if the party became more successful at the polls. It also explains, in part, the difficulties that have emerged in the detailed formulation of an electoral pact with the SDP.

Some of these frictions are readily interpretable simple as division of the spoils: each party would like a clear run in those constituencies most likely to fall to the Alliance. Personal ambitions have also obviously intruded. A likely Liberal or SDP nominee has often not been eager to give the other party's candidate the glory of being a candidate for the House, or the potential power of an actual seat in Westminster.

Yet Liberal reluctance has had another source. There is a resentment in some areas over the SDP's "Johnny-come-latelys," a belief that candidacies should be the reward for participation itself, that Liberals, having toiled long in an unproductive vineyard, should now receive the wine of nomination. This feeling is expressed not only in constituencies where Liberals have greater electoral support, but even in some cases where the SDP would seem to have better prospects of victory.[45] Thus, in one London constituency we observed, some local Liberals were dissatisfied that the seat would be allocated to the SDP, even though demographic and electoral analyses supported this decision. The Liberal claim was not based on electoral effectiveness, but on membership participation, specifically, that the Liberals had advanced a (hopeless) candidate for twenty-five years in the area, and that the women's organization (incidentally, called Women's Libbers) had been active in fund raising in the area.

In most cases, Liberals do not participate in the expectation of reward. If they did hope to gain personally, they long ago would have joined the Conservatives or Labour. To the contrary, tangible rewards are regarded with suspicion, one national party official asserting that "it wouldn't be proper" to pay local agents. For similar reasons, some Liberal constituencies have been reluctant to accept MPs defecting from Labour as the Alliance candidates for Parliament, despite these legislators' proven ability to win an election in their area.

Liberals consciously and conscientiously seek to be the "good citizen" required in the individualist theory of democracy. Despite their previously hopeless chances, they have been more likely to run for public office than the other parties' activists (see table 19.6). Their volunteered comments evidence their concern. One party member reported that his/her interest in politics derived from "a feeling that democratic government was too important to leave all the work to other people," while another remembered that, "Having joined the United Nations Association, I realized political activity was necessary as well." To fulfill their democratic responsibilities, Liberals devote a great deal of effort to policy questions, not to fit them into a single ideology, but in order to deal with each question exhaustively. The result is that Liberal manifestos are generally conceded to be the most thoughtful in each election.

The Liberal concern with policy is different from that of the other parties. At least until the present, a person who wanted to accomplish particular policies would have been better advised to join the Conservatives or Labour. If that person had a radical vision of social reconstruction, a Labour sect such as Militant Tendency would be a more likely outlet. To Liberals, policy is considered more purely for its own sake, and it is important that the policy be correct and complete, even if it is not likely to be realized. National leaders of a more pragmatic bent have recognized this characteristic, with Roy Jenkins asking the party to ally with the SDP and not "fall back on your ancient purity," while former Leader Jo Grimmond asked the party Assembly to be less concerned about "every policy question from dog licenses to the details of world government."

This emphasis on the purity of policy is another reason for the party's reluctance to negotiate with the SDP. Purity can best be maintained in isolation, but may be corrupted by power, or even the prospect of power. To avoid corruption, one Hendon activist argued, "you should only have an alliance if you agree on policy." His insistence on prior agreement was unchallenged by his fellow Liberals, but would have been astonishing in an American party club, and even in many British meetings.

The defining characteristic of Liberal doctrine is classic liberalism itself, the rights of the individual against the state. Where our Liberal respondents differed from their SDP allies, it was on questions affected by this sentiment, such as liberal abortion laws, independent schools, and restrictions on immigration (see table 19.3). This individualism is also revealed in the Liberals' distinctive belief (see table 19.1) that an MP owes "first responsibility" to his own judgment, even more than to his constituency—an echo of Burke's Whig ideal. A further element in the Liberal program is opposition to class politics, a doctrine they share with the SDP. Much as Mill would argue, Liberals believe in the pursuit of the public welfare. "The Liberals charge that both major parties are beholden to limited segments of society, so that neither of them can govern in the general interest. . . . Only a party free from special interests—the Liberals—can break out of this morass and restore good, effective government."[46]

Structurally, the Liberal beliefs in participation and individualism lead to an emphasis on localism. This feature is evident throughout the party organization. Its party handbook has as its keynote, "Liberals believe in representative democracy with genuine self-government, and have consistently opposed concentration of power and autocratic institutions. This belief is reflected in the present party structure which is decentralized, democratically representative and limits the powers of central committees."[47]

The decentralization of the Liberal party is evidenced in the local constituency's control over the nomination of both candidates and agents, and in the election (and potential recall) of the party leader by direct vote of the party membership. Until its recent narrow adoption by the SDP, this system of leadership selection was not employed by any other British party. This localist system is further reinforced by the party's limited financial resources. As a result, the central Liberal party does not have even the theoretical power to enforce agreements with the SDP on individual parliamentary seats. Illustratively, in discussing a national proposal for the share-out in Hendon, the local executive committee could do not more than resolve that it would "do its utmost" to reach a negotiated agreement, while making it clear that only the annual general membership meeting could make the decision. In contrast, the SDP in the same constituency was told by its chairman that the decision on parliamentary candidacies was a national decision that they must accept, because "politics is the art of the possible."

Structural decentralization is paralleled by Liberal members' concern with the local community. More than others, Liberals were likely to cite, as their major reason for party activism, "I am able to improve my local community" (see table 19.2), and were also most likely to cite "involvement in local problems and issues" as the single most important activity of their organizations.

The members' practice conforms to these prescriptions. In Bradford, when discussing unemployment or the economy, members proposed practical, local community efforts to solve these problems. These included "surgeries" by members of the chamber of commerce to counsel persons who might want to start a small business. Similarly in Hendon, issues arising from national trends were dealt with in terms of local schools or rates, not in terms of central government financing for education and municipal services. (A Bradford cynic said such manifestos read as if "they were written for Toyland.") Along the same lines, each Liberal association distributes a monthly bulletin on local affairs. Members believe that "democracy means access to City Hall for community groups" and take particular pride in their concern for "grassroots" problems such as "pavements in one street, rats in a derelict house in another, or fighting the closing of a village school."[48]

In their electioneering, Liberal campaigns are decentralized to the ward level by design, while the other parties either operate more centrally (Conservatives), or decentralize only when required by electoral conditions (SDP) or by intraparty differences (Labour). This practice follows the advice of national Liberal strategists: "National issues and international issues are very important. . . . But they have *nothing to do with local elections*. So go out and campaign on local issues. Base the whole election campaign on these local campaigns."[49] This Liberal belief in the virtues of localism is strongly held, even in the face of evidence that most local voting is determined by national party loyalties and events. For the Liberals, however, it is not only an article of faith, but a rational strategy. Weak nationally, they have been able to achieve some local successes, for example, in Liverpool, by their stress on community politics. It was this local stress, as their SDP allies concede, that enabled the Liberals to resist the Conservative upswing engendered by the Falklands crisis.[50]

As they participate in their individualist, decentralized politics, Liberals are attempting to realize the Mill-Tocqueville ideal of the good citizen or, as one Bradford member put it, "to always look for the good and the noble in political activity." Their rewards are limited in power terms, even with the recent growth of the party. Still, there are incentives, largely those of status and honor. As a national organizer commented, in explaining his colleagues' willingness to wage unsuccessful campaigns, "Many Liberals don't mind losing, for it's an honor just to have been a candidate." For some, in fact, the satisfaction of standing, of fulfilling a duty of citizenship, may be even greater than the more ambiguous position of holding office. There are related status rewards. Liberals are generally too limited in resources to hire professional agents, but they do appoint "Honorary Agents," and the title can mean something to an individual as he or she spends evenings talking to recalcitrant voters. However, status is a finite if intangible reward, and can cause problems similar to the distribution of material patronage. Explaining the reluctance of some Liberal activists to make room for the SDP, a Liberal leader explained, "A bloke likes getting his name in the paper, and he doesn't like another fellow coming in on his patch." In addition, there are policy incentives that stimulate this highly educated and articulate group of activists (see table 19.6). And, as in any group, there are social rewards: "It's fun—why else spend twelve hours a day on politics," one Liberal explained.

The Liberal party evidences both the moral attractiveness and the inherent problems of the individualist theory of democracy. Local community effort does promote the personal development of individuals, but it does not solve problems of national and international origin. Even in electoral terms, years of Liberal effort on community problems had little impact on the May local elections, when support for Mrs. Thatcher's Falklands policy won unusual success for the Conservatives in communities throughout the nation. Still less could grass-roots activity affect decisions on such questions of foreign policy.

More basically, the ideals of the Progressives and Liberals raise fundamental questions of human motivation. Can one build a party and a policy on individualistic efforts and altruistic motives? Optimistic philosophers have often seen their hopes disappointed, while even Mill and Tocqueville—not to mention Madison—have pointed to the importance of self-interest as a political stimulant. The limited success of the Liberals over the past sixty years is not good evidence to support the efficacy of individualist politics.

It is questionable whether the modern large state and the interdependent planet can be democratically controlled in the ways outlined by the tenets of liberal individualism. The historic forces of economics and class conflict emphasized by Marxists and Labour activists are real, despite the Liberals' disdain for class politics. The problems of world disorder and social disorder emphasized by Conservatives are real, despite the Liberals' preference for international and domestic harmony. The other parties may not have valid means to cope with these realities, but it remains unfortunately true that the problems of economic distribution require more than an appeal to the general interest, and that the problems of peace require more than an appeal to the United Nations.

Most generally, the individualist construct is not a theory of power, and therefore in a basic way it may not be a theory of politics at all. It is a philosophy of moral and individual action, but politics involves hard choices between moral objectives, sometimes requires amoral decisions, and often compels individually immoral actions. (War is the obvious example, particularly vivid as we write in the aftermath of the Falklands invasions.) Politics involves compromise when it succeeds, conflict when it fails. The British Liberals, as they take their first steps toward a restoration to power, will need to become a political party again. They may then wonder whether it profits a party to (possibly) gain the whole world but lose its soul.

## Democracy as the Competition of Diverse Factions

Pluralist theories, most notably Madisonian democracy, exemplify our fourth and final concept of democracy. In contrast to our previous models, this construct does not emphasize elites, activists, or individual citizens. Instead, this democratic theory relies on a notion of group politics. According to this theory, politics is the art of compromise, in the attempt to achieve consensus.

In a pluralist society, various interest groups compete with each other for public support. James Madison describes such a system in *The Federalist*, number 10, when he prescribes a remedy for "the diseases most incident to republican government"—instability, injustice, and confusion caused by the violence of factions. Size is the crucial variable in the famous Madisonian model, because a large republic produces a multiplicity of factions. Madison advises, "Extend the sphere and you take in a greater variety of parties and interests." The greater the number of such groups, the less likelihood there is that one will emerge as a tyrannical force.

The second important variable in this theoretical construct is the principle of representation. In a representative democracy, as opposed to the "pure" democracies of ancient Greece, the electoral system acts as a sifting process that serves to "refine and enlarge the public views" by elevating the most virtuous to public office. If a republic is extensive, it is possible to elect a large number of people—sufficient to "guard against the cabals of a few"—and yet this group is still only a small percentage of the population.

In the absence of ideological concerns, personal ambition motivates party activists. The social incentive is minimized by the fact that party members also lack a common tradition (i.e., ethnic, religious, or class ties). The Madisonian model allows for personal ambition by recommending a system of checks and balances to control it. "Ambition must be made to counteract ambition." If an individual's personal ambition is channeled properly and balanced by the aspirations of others, it can prove to be a healthy motivating force in politics.[51]

The parallel between Madisonian democracy and the new Social Democratic movement in Britain is striking. Just as Madison wrote in response to "complaints . . . that our governments are too unstable, that the public good is disregarded in the conflicts of rival parties," so too the Social Democratic party was launched, in part, as a response to the public demand for moderation and consistency in government policy making. (In February 1981, the party's founders read a University of Essex public opinion poll that indicated such a demand.) On 26 March 1981, the SDP published "Twelve Tasks for Social Democrats," the first of which reads as follows:

> Britain needs a reformed and liberated political system without the pointless conflict, the dogma, the violent lurches of policy and class antagonisms that the two old parties have fostered.

The Social Democratic party is founded on the Madisonian belief that democracy functions best when there is consistency and stability in policy making. The Social Democrats blame current economic conditions on the frequent alteration of political parties in power. In a Downsian fashion, Social Democrats reason that the Labour party has moved too far Left, while the Conservative party has moved too far Right. The subsequent twists and turns in government policy have created economic chaos.

Instead, the Social Democrats want a "middle of the road, centrist party," in the words of many party activists and party leaders, "one that is modeled after American political parties." David Marquand, an ex-Labour MP and one of the founding members of the SDP, predicted that "the SDP/Liberal Alliance is going to generate a new consensus in British politics," defining consensus simply as "the broad agreement on the aims of government." According to Marquand,

> We've lost that in British politics. It's gotten to the point where Labour views a Thatcher government as totally unacceptable. And the Conservatives view a Bennite Labour Government as equally unacceptable. The new consensus will include approximately 70 to 75 percent of the population. The remaining 25 percent or so will be ensured representation by PR.

The Social Democrats claim that the ideological disputes in British politics have not only stifled economic progress. Ideology has also perpetuated serious class divisions in British society. Social Democrats would agree with Madison that class is "the most common and durable source of factions"; therefore, the party seeks to be a "broad church, a classless party." As one SDP member of Parliament recalled, "I didn't join the Labour party to win the class struggle. I joined it to end the class struggle. That's why I'm in the SDP now," and he added, "We need to get rid of the ideological battles in this country and get down to serious business." Another MP explained:

> The SDP is a classless party. It will appeal to the common sense of the British people in all classes. . . . The British will leave behind their traditional loyalties and support practical solutions to political problems.
>
> After all, the British are naturally social democrats. They believe in consensus politics, broad economic policies, consistency in government policy.

As a result, the Social Democratic party has emphasized pragmatism and compromise, rather than ideology, in the policy-making process. In our research sample, SDP members proved to be the most pragmatic activists, and the least ideological. At local meetings in both Bradford and Hendon, the word most frequently used in discussion was "pragmatic," followed by "realistic." This has been one of the chief stylistic differences between the SDP and their Liberal partners in the Alliance. The Liberals believed that policy agreement was crucial before the Alliance could be truly cemented. Instead, the SDP suggested to the Liberals, "Show us your policies and we'll tell you if we disagree." For the SDP, electoral strategy preceded policy formulation. SDP members insisted that policy agreements could be made after electoral victory for the Alliance.

The preamble to the party Constitution further reveals the "practicality" and "sensibility" of SDP policies. It states as its first aim, to "foster a healthy public sector and a healthy private sector *without frequent frontier changes*" (our emphasis). In addition, the party hopes to "eliminate poverty and promote greater equality without stifling enterprise." At the same time, the party sees "the strength of a competitive economy" but wishes to ensure "a fair distribution of rewards." The remaining principles are worded in a similar manner.

The following incident, which occurred during a local Steering Committee meeting in Bradford, illustrates the party's eagerness to reach a compromise policy position, as opposed to a rigidly ideological one. The committee meeting focused on the local party manifesto. When the controversial subject of raising the city's rates was discussed, the membership was divided over what position to take. Some members wished to increase rates in order to improve social services, but others seemed to believe that low rates were the priority. In the form of a classic compromise, the manifest read: "The Social Democratic Party aims to keep rate increases in line with inflation without decreasing the level of social services." The Hendon SDP manifesto includes a similar compromise policy, and it should be noted that both statements are consistent with the national recommended statement on rates for local manifestos.

In framing the Hendon local election manifesto, many members personally favored increased public spending. But the membership agreed to eliminate all proposals in this direction from the manifesto, in recognition of voter opposition. In sharp contrast, the Labour party admitted that "the majority [of its manifesto proposals] will involve increased public spending."[52]

As a consequence of the party's emphasis on both electoral appeal and compromise policy making, the SDP is accused of being all things to all people.[53] Its critics joke that the SDP is a "nice party, with nice members and nice policies," and the popular critical phrase is: "Keep politics out of politics.

Join the SDP." Ironically, Alec McGivan, the party's national secretary, told us that he was actually pleased with the slogan. According to McGivan, public disillusionment with current politics makes such a characterization of the SDP attractive to the ordinary voter.

A Conservative MP attributed the SDP appeal to the fact that it is "moderate and lovely and fuzzy." The party, he argues, simply does not need specific policies to win votes. Issues are only "instrumental" to the SDP, whereas they are "expressive" and more vital to Labour or even to Tories. During the by-election in Crosby, campaign workers searched for the "nuclear weapons hack" to write a statement on that issue when it was raised by a voter. This incident provides a sharp contrast to Labour's preoccupation with the same issue.

The party's legitimate claim to moderation is clearly the main reason why the SDP initially attracted so many supporters. In October 1981, "Weekend World Television" polled 290 members of the Social Democratic Party (4% ex-Conservative, 16% ex-Labour, 4% ex-Liberal, 71% no previous political affiliation), and asked members why they joined the SDP. Twenty-four percent said they wished to "break the mould of British politics" (the SDP's own slogan). Nineteen percent wanted a "middle ground party," fourteen percent "disliked extremism and polarization," and twenty-one percent objected to the left-wing dominance of the Labour party. Essentially, all the respondents expressed, in one form or another, the desire for a new, moderate political party. This evidence supports Anthony King's recent claim that the two major parties in Britain are losing their electoral appeal as they tend toward extremes.[54]

The twenty-one percent in the WWT report, who objected to the leftism of the Labour party, referred specifically to the recent takeover by left-wing factions. As explained in our section on the Labour party, the Left succeeded in instituting the electoral college as a leadership selection procedure at the Wembley Conference in the spring of 1981. It was this reform that provided the final impetus for the SDP founders—Shirley Williams, Bill Rodgers, David Owen, and Roy Jenkins—to denounce and leave the Labour party. The "Gang of Four," as they came to be known, feared the power of both the trade unions and the constituency parties under the new selection process. In particular, they were concerned because several constituency parties had become dominated by the radical Trotskyist faction known as the Militant Tendency.

Therefore, the leaders of the Social Democratic party shared a Madisonian fear of factions. In drafting their party constitution, they tried to emulate Madison's remedies for the "disease" of faction. First, they followed his advice to "extend the sphere" by organizing most local parties on the basis of areas rather than constituencies. Second, the National Steering Committee, imitating Madison's design for an electoral sifting process, proposed that MPs (not the general membership) select the party leader. This measure was rejected by party members who resented efforts on the part of the leadership to thwart party "democracy." Rank-and-file members, favoring a more participatory model of democracy, successfully argued that the party started with the concept of "one person—one vote" and should abide by its founding principle. Finally, both the leadership and the members have advocated proportional representation as a means to secure minority representation—to guard against tyranny of the majority.

The party's organizational principles attempt to combine centralization and membership participation. The latter is demonstrated by the members' choice of leader and by the belief that policy discussion should take place at the local level. But membership power is directed to and by a center. Dues are still predominantly national. Furthermore, the party was organized from the center, with two hundred persons contacted and asked to set up groups in their area. Since there is resistance to constituency parties (none exist in Bradford or Hendon), leadership is organized usually on a borough basis. It is likely, however, that the SDP will pay more attention to local problems in the aftermath of its widespread defeat in the May local elections.[55]

One party activist in Bradford expressed concern over the high degree of centralization in the party, noting that there are no real local organizations. "They [the National Steering Committee] are afraid to give us any autonomy," he said, and then added, "They think I'm trying to build my own empire in Yorkshire!" David Marquand explained in more detail:

> There is a primitive feeling among members of the Steering Committee. They are afraid to give up any power. They have gambled their careers on the success of the SDP so they worry about mistakes and are afraid of risks.
>
> SDP members were seen as political virgins at first. . . . Now they are prepared to assume responsibility. . . . Sooner or later power will have to shift to the members. They joined the party because of its democratic principles. They will not settle for less. . . .
>
> There is enough element of truth in the perception of the SDP as a southern, London-dominated party for it to be worrying. The party is far too centralized.

In part because four national leaders founded the party and organized it on a national scale first, there is a high degree of centralization within the Social Democratic party. This is most clearly demonstrated by the relationship between the SDP and its "allies"—the Liberals. The two parties had a great deal of difficulty dividing the parliamentary seats to be fought in the next general election. At the SDP/Liberal negotiations in South Yorkshire, the meeting erupted into an argument over who should be consulted in the decision-making process. The Liberals wished to consult their local party activists before making any final decisions. The Social Democrats, with their national representative present, were prepared to make an agreement. Furthermore, the Liberals were concerned about the strength of their local organizations in the various seats, while the SDP negotiators had only a national perspective. The meeting ended without any agreement. According to the SDP, "That's a lesson in Liberal party 'democracy' for you. Nothing ever gets done. No decisions are ever made. God help us if they ever try to govern!" The Liberal view is that "the SDP doesn't know the meaning of the word 'democracy.' The leadership tells them to jump, so they all jump. They're all ex-Labour and it shows. They're used to being told what to do by the central office."

Ex-Labour members (or "refugees"—the term used by other SDP members) have influenced the nature of the new party. Social Democrats have a distinctly national outlook, similar to Labour's preoccupation with national affairs. SDP members of Parliament frequently talk about foreign relations, nuclear armament, and unemployment as top priorities. This is not surprising since all but one of the twenty-eight MPs are themselves refugees from the Labour party. In contrast to Labour, however, SDP leaders are distinctly bipartisan. Whereas the Labour party challenged and criticized the Thatcher government throughout the recent war in the Falkland Islands, the SDP believed that the crisis called for national unity and bipartisan cooperation. The element of bipartisanship in SDP political thinking is further demonstrated by the Alliance formed with the Liberals and by the discussion of a possible coalition government with the Tories after the next general election.

Not all SDP members are "refugees" from the Labour party. In fact, many members are political "virgins"—people involved in politics for the first time. What has stimulated the interest of these new political activists? First, as suggested earlier, party members believe that they have an opportunity to alter current politics. Party activists in both Hendon and Bradford expressed the overwhelming desire to moderate and stabilize British politics, mainly to achieve economic progress. They explicitly stated on several occasions that they wished to "Americanize" British politics both with regard to policy making and in terms of style.

The SDP has made a concerted effort to commercialize by selling ribbons, banners, tee shirts, pens, coffee mugs, and even baby bottles to advertise its "product." As one activist inquired in Bradford, "Do you ever think we'll be able to copy the razzle dazzle of an American party convention?" After party meetings, members seemed to enjoy going to the local pub and showing off their SDP paraphernalia. In addition to the desire to alter the policy-making process, SDP activists clearly think politics is fun.

Another important incentive for SDP members stems from personal ambition. We derived this impression of SDP activists mostly from conversations rather than survey results, since respondents are always reluctant to admit ambition is a motivation. Clearly the new party provides many opportunities for those who aspire to hold political office, and we spoke with several activists who expressed a desire to be a member of Parliament someday. In particular, the party activist who was accused of wishing to "establish an empire in Yorkshire" stated that he would like to be an MP, and admitted that his chances have improved since he joined the SDP.

Many Labour MPs switched to the SDP in part because the mandatory reselection reform threatened their careers. This is not to suggest that these people lacked conviction or principles. It is simply to state that in most cases, it was in their self-interest to join the new party. When Sykes asked one of the original founders, "What has most disappointed you since the founding of the SDP?" this leader confessed:

> So many people have joined for purely selfish reasons. That's not true of the early members. It took a great deal of courage in the beginning and those who joined were highly committed to social democracy. But once the SDP became successful, many just jumped on the bandwagon.

There are several problems that the Social Democratic party must resolve, many of which are inherent difficulties in the Madisonian theoretical framework. First, there is the internal, philosophical contradiction created by the founding democratic principles (i.e., one person—one vote, devolution) and the organizational checks and balances designed by the national leaders to preserve stability within the party.

Second, there are general problems with the SDP's notion of a democratic polity. For example, what is the "public good" that the party is striving to promote? Madison never really defined that term and neither has the SDP. If the "public good" is achieved by the satisfaction of the multiple interests in society, if majority rule is really "minorities rule," then the Social Democrats need to be reminded of traditional critiques of pluralism. Some groups may dominate in a pluralist society either because they possess more wealth or influence or both, and they may determine the political agenda. Especially in Britain, where specific groups have always been represented by one of the parties, there is the possibility that political activity void of party ideology will fail to protect the interest of the less fortunate groups in society.

Furthermore, if ideological distinctions are removed from political competition, electoral choice may become more restricted. Even when there are major policy differences between candidates, the public may be confused without recourse to traditional party labels and all their ideological baggage.

The party needs to resolve additional problems if it is to succeed as a political organization. SDP support has declined dramatically since its peak in popularity last December. To a great extent, this can be explained by the fact that the SDP has discovered that it cannot continue to be all things to all people.

As the SDP formulates more specific policy proposals, its public support wanes.

In addition, the SDP has had difficulty convincing many Labour members to join the new party. If the SDP is to become the only viable alternative to the Conservative party, it must recruit more working-class members. The distinctive middle-class character of the party has led one *Times* reporter to describe SDP members as "moderate chic."[56] Of course, if David Owen later becomes leader, the party may assume a more radical role. Nevertheless, the trade union affiliation with the Labour party explains why many Labourites will not join the SDP. Another, less obvious, reason is that working-class citizens are either unwilling or unable to pay the eleven-pound membership fee.

Whether the SDP succeeds or fails depends on its ability to deal with both its philosophical contradictions and its organizational difficulties. Clearly, the SDP aims for electoral victory, but there are several ways to measure political success. It is likely that the SDP will not win its struggle to "Americanize" British politics. But it will probably moderate the recent extremist tendencies in the two other major political parties. The new party has already reminded both Tories and Labourites that the British public supports a middle-of-the-road approach to politics. Tony Benn remarked cynically, "Britain has had SDP governments for the past 25 years." If that is true, then the SDP may not break the mold of the British two-party system, but it may mold Britain's political future, by mending the nation's recent break from her past.

## Conclusion

"Democracy," wrote Winston Churchill, "means that an early morning knock on the door is the milkman." The Anglo-American peoples do derive comfort from the knowledge that they live in a liberal, democratic society, and most assume that their rights and liberties will remain secure so long as democracy is preserved.

Political activists are not content simply to derive comfort from the individual security of the status quo. Instead, they join together, willingly and ardently, to pursue the realization of an ideal democratic regime. Although their visions differ—from democratic socialism to social democracy to "pure" free-enterprise democracy—all the activists that we met shared a common energy and commitment to the pursuit of a better society. Even if their political aspirations are never recognized, the vitality of their political activity reveals the essence of democratic citizenship, which in turn breathes life into the body politic.

These activists are concerned with democracy both in the polity and within their own party organization. Most would argue that the two concerns cannot be separated. For Socialists, party democracy is crucial because it is the means by which the working-class masses mobilize to achieve a program of social reconstruction. Liberal democrats seek a democratic party organization for a more basic reason. They believe that the political party is a fundamental vehicle for participation and active citizenship in the modern world.

All four "models of democracy" discussed in this paper have serious flaws. The new Social Democratic party seems unable to decide whether it is radical or moderate (as evidenced by the close election campaign between Jenkins and Owen), while it seeks a coherent philosophical basis for its pragmatic policies, at present aimed toward consensus. Its Liberal allies often disregard the problems of power, insisting instead on the supremacy of moral principles resting on an abstract notion of civic duty. While the Labour party moves toward left-wing purity and the Tories, toward "genuine conservatism" (as one activist put it), both parties are losing their electoral appeal.

Therefore, each of these parties is unable to reconcile its own democratic theory with the necessities of political life. In short, the institutionalization of ideas, in the form of political parties, is not an easy task in contemporary Britain. We conclude with the sentiment of the intellectual progenitor of students of political parties, Robert Michels:

> The democratic currents of history resemble successive waves. They break ever on the same shoal. They are ever renewed. This enduring spectacle is simultaneously encouraging and depressing. . . . It is probable that this cruel game will continue without end.[57]

## Notes

1. Pomper chose Hendon as the principal focus of his research while on a train to the Labour party conference in Brighton. Imitating his affable father-in-law, he struck up a conversation with his seatmate, a friendly party activist from Hendon, who invited him to spend time in the constituency. In recognition of its founder, this method is termed "the Manny Michels Selection Technique." Sykes, for her part, intended to spend time with relatives in Bradford, and found that they had many contacts within the political parties. In recognition of the author of *Roots*, we call this method the "Alex Haley Selection Criterion." Our greatest debt is to the party activists who cheerfully and fully answered our sometimes brash questions. Only promises of anonymity restrain us from listing these respondents and new-found friends.
2. Because of the variations in the parties' organizational structure and strength, the areas from which these data were gathered vary somewhat. In Hendon North, the Conservatives and Labour are sufficiently numerous to provide adequate numbers from this single parliamentary constituency. Among Liberals, however, it was necessary to obtain respondents from all of Barnet borough, in which Hendon is located, to gain an adequate number. The SDP in Hendon is organized basically on a borough basis, so this area was used for the questionnaire. In Bradford, only Labour is meaningfully organized in each of the four constituencies. To make the responses comparable, data were gathered from comparable citywide bodies for

each of the four parties. These differences should not affect our interpretations, since we are interested not in a particular parliamentary constituency, but in the character of party activists, who are not likely to differ much from one part of the city of Bradford, or one part of the borough of Barnet, to another.

3. Joseph Schumpeter, *Capitalism, Socialism, and Democracy* (New York: Harper, 1950), p. 269.
4. Anthony Downs, *An Economic Theory of Democracy* (New York: Harper, 1957).
5. David Robertson, *A Theory of Party Competition* (New York: Wiley, 1976), chap. 2.
6. Alan Ware, *The Logic of Party Democracy* (London: Macmillan, 1979), chap. 3.
7. James Q. Wilson, *Political Organizations* (New York: Basic Books, 1973), chap. 6.
8. James Q. Wilson, "The Economy of Patronage," *Journal of Political Economy* (1961): 369–80.
9. Commission upon the Financing of Political Parties, *Paying for Politics* (London: Hansard Society, 1981), p. 47.
10. Cf. Robert E. Holt and John E. Turner, *Political Parties in Action: The Battle of Baron's Court* (New York: Free Press, 1968), chap. 3.
11. Robert T. McKenzie, *British Political Parties* (London: William Heinemann, 1955), chap. 2.
12. Hugo Young, *Sunday Times*, March 7, 1982, p. 32.
13. David Watt, *Times*, October 16, 1981, p. 14.
14. Holt and Turner, *Political Parties in Action*, p. 264ff., also report this fantasy.
15. William F. Wright, *A Comparative Study of Party Organization* (Columbus, Ohio: Charles E. Merrill, 1971), pp. 312–32.
16. Holt and Turner, *Political Parties in Action*, p. 280.
17. Robertson, *Theory of Party Competition*, p. 133.
18. Ibid., p. 183.
19. Wright, *Study of Party Organization*, pp. 45–53.
20. M. Ostrogorski, *Democracy and the Organization of Political Parties* (London: Macmillan, 1902), vol. 2, pp. 651–57.
21. Robert Michels, *Political Parties* (New York: Collier Books, 1962).
22. American Political Science Association, Committee on Political Parties, "*Toward a More Responsible Two-Party System,*" *American Political Science Review* 44 (September 1950): supp., p. 1.
23. Cf. Herbert McClosky et al., "Issue Conflict and Consensus among Party Leaders and Followers," *American Political Science Review* 54 (June 1960): 406–27: Jeane Kirkpatrick et al., *The New Presidential Elite* (New York: Russell Sage, 1976).
24. McKenzie, *British Political Parties*, chap. 8.
25. David Kogan and Maurice Kogan, *The Battle for the Labour Party* (London: Kegan Paul, 1982).
26. Mancur Olson, *The Logic of Collective Action* (Cambridge: Harvard University Press, 1965).
27. *The Guardian*, September 25, 1981, p. 1.
28. Cited by Edward G. Janosik, *Constituency Labour Parties in Britain* (London: Pall Mall Press, 1968), p. 26.
29. Cf. ibid., Holt and Turner, *Political Parties in Action*, and John E. Turner, *Labour's Doorstep Politics in London* (London: Macmillan, 1978); Bruce Page and Peter Kellner, "Labour Party: The Left versus the Left," *New Statesman* 101 (June 12, 1981): 5–8.

30. We did not rely heavily on the survey data from the Bradford Labour party largely because we received only sixteen responses at the time we wrote this paper. We would like to attribute the low response rate to the Marxist dictum: "The philosophers have only interpreted the world, in various ways; the point, however, is to change it" (Marx, *Theses on Feuerbach*, 11). In other words, the Labour party activists in Bradford are not anxious to participate in academic work because they view scholarly activity as a useless intellectual enterprise.

    Sykes asked her Labour contact (a member of Militant) why the response rate was so low, and he offered three explanations:

    > First you have to remember that you entered a pretty hostile political environment when you came and asked questions about the Bradford Labour party. We have had a pretty rough history of Labour fighting, initiated by both the Left and the Right. Now that the Left has won in the Bradford constituencies, we're faced with the threat of expulsion from the party. Second, we have no time to fill out questionnaires. Your survey treats political activity as a career or a hobby. What you don't understand is that politics, for a socialist, is his whole life. We're politically active one hundred percent of the time. Third, you've got to consider the level of education of these people. The working class doesn't understand research and they don't fill out surveys.

    (It should be noted that none of our respondents were unskilled workers.)
31. This phrase, "anti-parliamentarian," has been used recently to describe members of groups that advocate change by means other than the legislative process. The current controversy over whether or not Trotskyist organizations should be allowed to work within the Labour party involves another dispute over the meaning of "democracy." Is the Labour party committed to parliamentary democratic reform or does it also condone more revolutionary strategies to achieve its socialist aims?

    It should be noted that the Trotskyists are not the only ones who advocate *extra*-parliamentary activities (a more accurate descriptive term). Our data show that ordinary Labour party activists in both Bradford and Hendon support organized protests and demonstrations far more than active members in the three other major political parties. Furthermore, Tony Benn, at the 1981 *Tribune* rally, explicitly stated that proportional representation would make Parliament irrelevant, and suggested that the working class would subsequently need to work outside Parliament (Kogan and Kogan, *Battle for the Labour Party*, p. 105).

    One Labour party activist explained that extra-parliamentary activities are advocated because the MPs are not sufficiently responsive, even without a system of proportional representation. Other forms of political expression, he argued, are more truly democatic means to achieve change. "If by democracy," he added, "you mean rule by the people."
32. Lewis Minkin, *The Labour Party Conference* (London: Allen, Lane, 1978), chap. 1.
33. It is worth mentioning that the Left is adept at machine-style politics, as well as the Right. While canvassing, a left-wing member of the Labour party accidentally knocked a pane through a glass door. When an angry homeowner appeared, the activist quickly explained, "I'm here to campaign for the local Conservative party"—a tactic reminiscent of James Michael Curley's campaign style.
34. Holt and Turner, *Political Parties in Action*, p. 271.
35. Turner, *Labour's Doorstep Politics*, p. 178.

36. John Stuart Mill, *On Liberty* and *Considerations on Representative Government* (Oxford: Basil Blackwell, 1946), p. 141ff.
37. Ibid., pp. 160–88.
38. Maurice Duverger, *Political Parties*, 2nd English ed. (London: Methuen, 1959), pp. 207–28.
39. David Butler and Dennis Kavanagh, *The British General Election of February 1974* (London: Macmillan, 1974).
40. Vernon Bogdanor, *The People and the Party System* (Cambridge: Cambridge University Press, 1981), pp. 146–53.
41. Samuel E. Finer, *The Changing British Party System, 1945–1979* (Washington: American Enterprise Association, 1980), p. 38.
42. John Vincent, *Sunday Times*, October 18, 1981, p. 43.
43. Mill, p. 160.
44. *The Guardian*, September 17, 1981, p. 3.
45. Michael Steed and John Curtice, *From Warrington and Croyden to Downing Street* (Manchester: North West Community Newspapers, 1981).
46. Jorgen Rasmussen, in Howard Penniman, ed., *Britain at the Polls, 1979* (Washington: American Enterprise Institute. 1981), p. 163.
47. *Structure and Organization of the Liberal Party*, p. 1.
48. *Times*, May 17, 1982, p. 3.
49. Association of Liberal Councillors, *How to Fight Local Elections and WIN*, p. 3.
50. *Economist*, May 15, 1982, p. 34.
51. The quotations are from James Madison, *The Federalist*, nos. 10, 51 (New York: Modern Library, 1941), pp. 53–62, 335–41.
52. Labour Party of Barnet, *The Real Alternative*, p. 4.
53. Ian Bradley, *Breaking the Mould?* (Oxford: Martin Robertson, 1981).
54. Anthony King, "Whatever is Happening to the British Party System?" *PS* 15 (Winter 1982): 10–17.
55. *Times*, May 17, 1982, p. 3.
56. *Sunday Times*, December 6, 1981.
57. Michels, *Political Parties*, p. 371.

# 20

# Party Politics in 1984

No citizen can ignore the critical policy issues that will face the United States after the presidential election. All of us, not only the next administration, must meet the threat of nuclear confrontation, repair an uncertain economy, and comprehend emerging new technologies of robotics, bioengineering, and computerized communication. Policy problems can only be resolved within the American political context. My concern—and my theme—is that this political context will make it more difficult for the nation to resolve these policy issues.

Politics is the means by which a free society makes the basic value choices that create policy, the fuel for the engines of government. Politics is the means by which a popular majority decides what it wants and who will act in its name—the mechanism by which presidents and legislators gain legitimacy for creating a welfare state, redistributing the tax burden, or exposing our youth to death and our territory to destruction. By politics, bargains are made, interests are collected, trade-offs are accepted, and the business of the nation goes forward. Most generally, politics is the way we resolve the problem best posed by James Madison in *The Federalist*:

> In framing a government which is to be administered by men over men, the great difficulty lies in this: you must first enable the government to control the governed: and in the next place oblige it to control itself.

Recall Madison's basic solution: "A dependence on the people is, no doubt, the primary control on the government." Madison went on to become the first party leader in the House of Representatives, to organize America's first political party, and to lead that party to victory twice in presidential elections. He was a committed, active, and successful politician.

As Madison's experience suggests, the crucial agent for political action is the political party. Parties promote coherent policy development and coherent government in three ways. On the level of mass political action, parties bring together coalitions of individual citizens. In seeking votes, parties assemble diverse groups into coalitions with a common cause. Through slogans, speeches, and platforms, they combine these voters behind programs—sometimes vague and sometimes specific—of governmental action. As organizations, parties make sense of our complicated electoral system. By registering voters, they turn residents into participants in the democratic system. In nominating candidates, they screen aspirants to office. By reducing choices usually to two candidates and programs, they simplify the electorate's decision. In government, parties provide critical bridges between our separated institutions and across our federal system.

This political context is today less supportive of coherent policymaking. The parties are less capable in all three respects. As mass coalitions, they command less loyalty. As organizations, they are severely challenged. As governmental bridges, they need major repair. There are, fortunately, some opposing trends, but the weakened parties are the most evident feature of our politics. Like a seashore that has been eroded over many years, there is little comfortable space remaining.

Looking at the political party as a mass coalition of voters, through most of our history the two major parties have held the loyalties of the overwhelming proportion of the electorate. Persons were virtually born as Democrats or Republicans, and were true to this "birthright" by voting straight party tickets in individual elections and by voting for the same party from one election to the next. In some areas of the country, the party vote was perfectly predictable from one year to another. In one southern town, the election officials always knew that there would be a single Republican ballot. When there was an unexpected second Republican vote one time, there could be only one explanation. The outraged registrar complained, "The s.o.b. repeated."

In 1952, when the first full academic study of voting was conducted, close to 90 percent of the electorate acknowledged some loyalty to either the Democrats or Republicans. Admittedly, a considerable share of this partisan loyalty was based on tradition and habit, as well as being a commendation of General Eisenhower's leadership ability or Governor Stevenson's economic policies. While voters were not immovable or unchanging, most did approach an individual election with a bias, a "standing decision" subject to change, in favor of one of the two major parties. For politicians, this stability meant that there always was a secure foundation. Their party would not be completely blown away, regardless of shifting winds of opinion. They could, if only sporadically, offer a dissenting view—as Senator Flanders did in opposing Joseph McCarthy. They could, at least occasionally, suggest new policy departures, as Stevenson did in 1956, when he first proposed a ban on nuclear tests.

Today the parties stand on a weakened electoral foundation. In the 1980 election, independents comprised over a third of the electorate. Democratic loyalty, once an absolute majority in the nation, barely reached 41 percent, while Republicans comprised little more than a fifth of the nation. Projecting into the future, on the basis of the attitudes of younger voters, partisanship in the electorate is likely to wane even further. Among the youngest age-group in 1980, fully half were independents. This figure contrasts sharply with the youngest voters in the 1950s, when only a fourth disdained the parties. Even older voters show some loosening of underlying party loyalties. More significantly, all voters are more likely to describe themselves as "weak," rather than "strong," Republicans or Democrats and to behave accordingly. Split-ticket voting is now common, and defection from party loyalty frequent. In presidential elections, only a third of the electorate has always voted for the same party's candidates. In congressional elections, incumbents can often now win a majority from the opposition party's "loyalists."

There is some good news in all of these data—if you are not a party politician. Voters evidence greater concern for public issues and the qualifications of individual candidates. Skepticism about the virtues of political parties, and a willingness to pick and choose, are desirable attitudes in a democracy. Making politicians somewhat insecure about their jobs is likely to foster honesty and responsiveness. Yet, as in life generally, there are trade-offs, and losses in every gain. If voters rely less on party labels to guide their decisions, they must listen to other cues.

Alternative sources of advice are provided by campaign consultants, the media, and incumbent office-holders. Consultants are ready to write the electoral script and provide new cues for the voters. They are no less self-interested than parties but less responsible for the results. A political party that nominates and elects a thief or a charlatan eventually pays the cost by defeat in the next election. A consultant for that candidate simply collects a substantial fee and moves on to the next election. The media dispense a considerable amount of free information. Yet, it would be hard to argue that they raise the level of public discourse above that achieved in purely partisan debate. A major study of media shows that the attention paid to relevant issues and policy problems in elections has decreased substantially with the increased importance of television. Incumbents also provide cues, and voters are increasingly likely to reelect officials—other than presidents—because they know something about those in power while they have far less information about their opponents.

The weakening of the party coalitions has transformed the realities of our electoral system. Politicians do whatever they need to do to succeed in elections. When partisan loyalty was high, politicians won office by working their way up a party ladder, by campaigning together with others on the party team, by defending, necessarily if unhappily, the party's record and promises, and by supporting the party's leaders in office. Voters at least knew who to blame or reward for the ills and good that government caused. Today a politician is on his own to a considerable extent. Able to defy party bosses, he still needs friends. Free of entangling party alliances, he still needs to build an electoral coalition. Independent in office, he still needs guidance on policy issues. As parties provide less help in all of these respects, politicians increasingly m. turn to interest groups. This change is most marked in regard to money, ''the mother's milk of politics.''

Political action committees (PACs) are a major development in American politics. Their growth began in 1974, in the wake of Watergate. In a perverted reaction to that scandal, which originated with illegal election spending outside of the political parties, Congress provided for more extensive but legal spending outside of the political parties. Corporations, trade associations, unions, and ideological groups are now encouraged to collect funds from their stockholders, members, and sympathizers and to contribute or spend these funds to influence elections. PACs are now far more important than the parties in providing election money, outstripping them by margins up to five-to-one. In the 1982 congressional election there were close to 4,000 of these organizations providing about $85 million. Outpacing inflation, PACs have stimulated a major expansion in election spending, so that the total bill is likely to be over $1 billion for this year's campaigns. That will be more than $10 a voter—while allegedly corrupt city machines could buy their votes for $2 or less.

The problem is not the total amount spent. Free elections should be worth a small fraction of the dollars we spend on deodorants. PACs spend money, like everyone else in an open market, to buy goods. They do not bribe legislators, but they do purchase ''access,'' the opportunity to plead their special causes. Their gaining access means that policy decisions are bent toward those able to provide campaign contributions, and away from those who lack financial resources. Not coincidentally, the largest contributions of banking PACs go to ranking members of congressional banking committees. Nor is it coincidental that these committees were quick to listen to the industry's contrived arguments against tax withholding on bank interest payments. The PACs' concerns, unlike those of parties, are inherently narrow. Parties are not always paragons of virtue, but they are more likely to sell out to win votes rather than to gain contributions. Bowing to a majority may not always be courageous, but it is at least democratic.

The second contribution parties make to American government is in their role as organizations, associations of activists who manage the electoral system through their nominations of candidates and their simplification of voting choices. Another aspect of this contribution is the way in which parties promote participation in politics. By registering voters, and stimulating their turnout at the polls, the parties provide a peaceful route to power, an alternative to protest and violence.

Parties do these jobs because they are selfish, because they want to win power, not because they are public-spirited community organizations, but good effects can still follow. When parties were strongly rooted in local communities they fostered local participation. The story is told of how Tammany Hall representatives greeted immigrant ships. The precinct captain would provide three consecutive services for new immigrants: get them jobs, register them to vote, and then help them walk off the ship. Those were the first steps that eventually enabled a descendant of Italian immigrants to become governor of New York and a descendant of Irish immigrants to become president of the United States. Today there is still the need, once met by Tammany Hall and the other urban machines, to bring people into politics. The nation is receiving one of the largest migrations in its history. The names are now Rodriquez, Rusanne, or Diem, rather than Cohen, Kelly, or Kronowski; but they too require the services, the compassion, and the influence that parties have provided. Yet, for most the parties are invisible. The new immigrants must get their own low-paying jobs. Many enter the country illegally, swimming across rivers instead of walking down ramps. They become not citizens, contributors to the democratic community, but hideaways and isolates.

For those born in America, participation in politics has grown considerably in the past two decades, but a major study concludes: "Americans are participating more and enjoying it less." The forms of participation have changed considerably, away from those activities involving the political parties. Fewer people vote—a bare majority of the adult population in 1980, a drop of ten percentage points in twenty years—despite civil rights laws and the easing of registration requirements and other legal barriers. There is no single explanation for this decline. The enfranchisement of eighteen-year-olds, and the coming-of-age of the postwar baby boom is one cause, since young people always have shown less interest in voting. Turnout at the polls has also decreased among older voters. There has been a decline in feelings of political efficacy, a belief that the government does not respond to the electorate. This cynicism is well-grounded in the frustrations of many groups.

The falloff in the vote is related to decline in the parties. According to one analysis, a third of the drop in voter turnout can be attributed simply to the fall in party identification. As local roots are eroded and party loyalties weaken, voters find less reason to express those loyalties at the polls. If they bother to cast a ballot at all, it may be for a Wallace or an Anderson. In a reinforcing cycle, parties have had fewer loyalties to mobilize, making the parties seem even less relevant. The cycle is like that of the Oakland "As": poor performance brings out fewer fans, who get less attention from the management, causing lower attendance at games and even worse play on the field. In politics it is harder to remedy the situation by bidding for bonus players.

As people turn away from the ballot box, they turn toward other forms of participation. Demonstrations and protest were once considered appropriate only for those at the fringes of the political system. The act of protest itself was illegitimate. By now, we are accustomed to tractors being driven around Washington, truckers clogging the highways, and mass rallies occurring almost weekly. For the personal commitment of time and energy involved in party work, others now substitute the impersonal and isolated activity of writing checks. Along with the expansion of the PACs, membership and contributions to special interest groups have grown. At the local level, neighborhood associations have assumed many of the tasks previously undertaken by parties, including registration and community welfare.

The newer forms of participation are all legitimate expressions of democratic opinion. Yet most lack the virtue of political party activity: interchange of opinion, mutual learning and compromise, and the achievement of a community through involvement in a common cause. Worse still are the obstacles they create for policymakers. They operate differently from parties which emphasize accommodation and recognize divergent interests. Protesters emphasize the "nonnegotiable demand," single-interest groups suffer from tunnel vision, and neighborhood groups are inherently parochial.

There are other difficulties for the parties as organizations. Parties are more isolated today from the citizenry, but being more alone does not mean being left alone. The unique function of parties as organizations has been the nomination of candidates. Even in this regard the parties have lost considerable autonomy, and the loss has further complicated coherent policymaking. The point is most apparent in the most important nominations, the selection of candidates for president. Presidential nominations have been transformed from an exercise in diplomacy to a demonstration of conquest. The major participants have changed from the party leaders of semisovereign state organizations to reputed leaders of mass opinion. Critical decisions are no longer made in smoke-filled rooms and private conferences, but in television studios and Grange halls. The result is that the presidential candidate is no longer a person chosen by the party as its leader, but an individual who has thrust himself upon the party. The system of courtship that once led to marriage between leaders and parties has been replaced by a series of fervent but brief seductions.

Through most of our history the choice of the presidential nominee was made through internal processes, chiefly by negotiation among state party leaders before and at the national conventions. The goal was to find a candidate who would satisfy the broadest possible coalition and therefore, given the importance of party loyalty in the vote, the candidate who would be most likely to win the election and the spoils of office. The system had its defects—technically known as the Warren Harding syndrome—but it also had its virtues, demonstrated in the bargained nominations of Lincoln and Franklin Roosevelt. The chief advantage, not obvious at all, was that it provided for peer review. It assured that the skills of the politicians seeking the presidency would be examined by experts in the field, the major politicians of the nation. Aspirants passing muster with these specialists were likely not only to run a good race but, if elected, to have the necessary qualifications to be successful in the White House, where political leadership was most critical.

Whatever its virtues, the system broke down in the 1960s. Mississippi blacks could not accept procedures that violently and fraudulently excluded them from Democratic party caucuses. Young protesters could not accept endorsement of the futile and seemingly endless war in Vietnam. Chicago's Mayor Daley and police could not endure the abuse of heckling. Television could not permit its exclusion from any decision-making site. Soon, party leaders could not resist the call for widespread change in nominating procedures.

The new nominating system is complicated in its details, but the clear underlying principle is egalitarian democracy. One major tenet which follows from this principle is that individual voters should be directly represented and have direct control over the nomination. This philosophy leads to quotas among convention delegates for demographic groups such as women, blacks, and youths, as well as to proportional division of delegates among the presidential hopefuls. A second deduction from the egalitarian principle is that all persons in the party are the same, so that a party official or officeholder has no special claim to be a convention delegate. Third, elections are seen as the appropriate way to make decisions. This view led to the doubling of the number of presidential primaries from 1968 to 1980.

Unfortunately, achieving democracy is more complicated. In a nation as large and diverse as the United States, direct democracy will never exist. There will always, necessarily, be mediating institutions which represent and interpret the popular will. To get a better picture of public opinion, we should not be seeking to invent a faster and more precise Polaroid camera, which immediately produces a single print. What we need are better methods of developing film, so that the eventual product is more refined. The new system has not developed nominations into precise pictures of the nation's democratic opinion: it has only transferred decisive influence over these nominations to new processors.

The screening of candidates is no longer done by a process of peer review. It is done by campaign consultants who decide which candidate looks electable and by mass media commentators who decide which deserve serious consideration. The selection of delegates is not made by party leaders or even by all voters. The critical decisions are made by the minority of voters who participate in primaries, generally in small and unrepresentative states such as Iowa and New Hampshire. These early contests provide candidates such as McGovern and Carter with momentum that becomes almost impossible to resist in an age of instantaneous communication. Bargains are not made by state parties but by interest groups such as the National Education Association, which had more delegates at the 1980 Democratic convention than the state of California.

Once nominated and elected, the successful candidate may lack the ability to govern, which ought to be our basic consideration. We often complain of the ineffectiveness of our recent presidents. The fault may not lie in them but in the means by which they have been selected. Chosen without the aid of other politicians, sometimes over their opposition, a president comes to power without an effective coalition. Representing only some voters, he also lacks a deep popular base. Having relied on the media to display his image, he always faces the risk that they will seek a new face. Beholden to the interest groups he has mobilized, he may find himself immobilized in promoting new policy initiatives.

This year's Democratic nomination, particularly Gary Hart's candidacy, provides a good illustration. The Colorado senator almost succeeded in duplicating the successes of McGovern and Carter. With no base in the essential constituencies or leadership of the party, he still rose to the front rank on the basis of the media's decision, and his own adroit manipulation of the media's need for a "horse race." A miserable 15 percent showing in Iowa won him attention, and an 11,000 margin in the Republican state of New Hampshire won him the front covers of five news weeklies. Fortunately for Walter Mondale, this spurious momentum could be reversed because of new party rules. What if Hart had won only one more primary, and had gone on to become the Democratic nominee and the president? Would he have been able to govern without the backing of the core groups of the party—labor, blacks, Jews? Could another avowed opponent of the Washington establishment work effectively with governors, senators, and congressmen? Recent experience suggests otherwise.

In the development of policy, parties have ameliorated the problems inherent in our constitutional system of checks and balances. Presidents, congressmen, and governors have often cooperated because they shared a party label and a common electoral interest. Today these ties provide few bonds. In all but a handful of states, governors are now elected midway through the president's term, removing any political incentive for them to cooperate with the chief executive. Congressmen are secure in office, with 90 percent of incumbents reelected, protected by the perquisites of office, advised by large staffs, and fortified within the "iron triangle" of executive agencies, legislative committees, and interest groups. Within Congress, the limited centralizing powers of the leadership have been challenged by the proliferation of committees, the individualism of the members, and the spreading influence of interest groups, reinforced by PAC contributions.

What is the result? In the past quarter of a century, there have been only two instances of coherent policymaking by the president and Congress. The first was in 1965, the creation of the Great Society. Even then, party cohesion was not strong, but the extraordinary, two-thirds Democratic majorities permitted action. The second instance was in 1981, the first Reagan year. Republicans voted overwhelmingly, in some roll calls unanimously, for the new president's economic policies, while 90 percent of Democrats voted in opposition. Still, the solidarity of both parties soon cracked under the pressure of national interest groups and local demands.

These circumstances are too uncommon to provide a model for normal government. The more typical inability to deal with basic policy issues is illustrated by recent events. Everyone agrees that the budget deficit must be reduced, but the two houses of Congress and the president are unable even to meet the goals of the 1984 budget resolution, much less to approach a balance. Everyone agrees that illegal immigration must be curbed, but the conflict of interest groups has resulted, after long delays, only in an incoherent and probably unworkable bill. Everyone agrees that the Equal Rights Amendment should be resubmitted to the states, but the House was unable to pass it. Everyone agrees that improvement of public education is now a national priority, but no additional funds have been provided.

Our political institutions now appear so debilitated that policymaking can only go forward by entrusting policy to appointed commissions. In the absence of electorally responsible alternatives, such commissions have recently been entrusted with development of policy on the social security system, nuclear missiles, and foreign policy in Central America. We cannot boast of a functioning democracy when our elected officials must delegate responsibility for resolving such vital issues.

Thus far I have argued that changes in the American political system, most evident in the status of the political parties, make it increasingly difficult to develop coherent public policy. On the electoral level, the parties lack stable and loyal coalitions. Without the support of these coalitions, elected officials must rely on less stable and less accountable sources of support, such as consultants, the mass media, and political action committees. Party decline also means that popular participation is channeled less through the electoral system and more through sporadic protest, narrow interest groups, or failed efforts to establish direct and egalitarian democracy. The problems are particularly illustrated by presidential nominations, in which a system of peer review has been replaced by individualistic competition that detracts from effective coalition building within government. The result is that policymaking tends to be sporadic, fragmented, and even undemocratic. Politics is the fuel of the governmental machine. Deficient parties lower the octane rating of the fuel—the machine knocks, wears, and may even eventually stop until repaired or replaced.

There is hope. On the theoretical level, the importance of the party system has now been recognized by various prestigious groups, including President Carter's Commission on America in the 1980s and the Advisory Commission on Intergovernmental Relations. More practically, there are a number of recent developments which relieve some of the gloom I have felt and tried to convey.

The latest data indicate that the decline in party loyalty has been stabilized and that there may be a slight increase in identification with both the Republican and Democratic parties. There is also little reason to expect that an Independent party, whether headed by John Anderson or anyone else, would have succeeded in 1984. Moreover, party loyalty now is more closely tied to policy concerns than in the past. Among Republican identifiers, a mere 5 percent consider themselves liberals, although the Democratic party is more evenly split between conservatives and liberals. When it comes to the actual vote, even greater consistency of belief and action is evident. Conservatives of both parties vote for Republican candidates, and liberals vote Democratic. There is a mass basis for meaningful party programs.

Also encouraging is the development of the organizational capacity of the parties. A long-term study of state parties shows that they have become better staffed, better funded, and more bureaucratically efficient over the past decade. At the national level, the increased capability of the parties is more dramatically evident. Instead of ephemeral growths, appearing only every four years, the national Republican and Democratic parties are now hardy perennials. They have their own large headquarters in Washington, lengthy direct mail lists, and budgets up to $40 million a year. Amendments to the election finance law in 1978 strengthened their position in relation to PACs, allowing larger contributions to the parties and permitting closer coordination of campaigns for local, state, and federal office. As a result, we find the national parties providing such services as polling, advertising, and even candidate recruitment for their constituent units. Even the Supreme Court has helped a bit, by declaring national party rules dominant over both state party practice and state laws.

We also see evidence of increased participation in the electoral process. The turnout in the 1982 midterm elections increased by five percentage points, particularly among low-income voters and blacks, groups which previously have been least involved. We may be on the verge of a major expansion of the active electorate, which would significantly increase the democratic legitimacy of our politics. Signs in this direction include the heavy growth in black registration in Chicago, Philadelphia, and Boston, as well as the positive response received by Jesse Jackson; the increased political awareness of women, and the two-party competition now under way for Hispanic support.

The political impact of increased turnout could be dramatic. This year, the last of the baby boom comes of political age, adding 10 million potential voters to the rolls. Another 17 million of those post war children have never voted, but may have been aroused by Hart and others. The potential black vote is the most significant. Consider this calculation: if only a tenth of previously unregistered blacks vote Democratic this year, that would switch 105 electoral votes from President Reagan to the Democratic candidate. Black voting is up 20 percent or more.

Finally, the parties are trying to win back some control of vital decisions. At this year's Democratic party convention, over 500 delegate seats will be reserved for officeholders and party officials. Interest groups, such as the AFL-CIO, are trying to exert their influence within the Democratic party, by preprimary endorsements and active campaigning. The number of presidential primaries has been reduced, for the first time in five elections. Congressional Republicans have campaigned on common party themes, "Vote Republican, for a Change" in 1980 and " Stay the Course" in 1982. The Democratic House caucus has developed a consensual party platform and showed some muscle in disciplining one renegade, Representative Phil Gramm of Texas.

Are these the first waves of a new tide bringing party renewal and, with it, greater policy coherence—or are they only eddies in a continuing stream of party decay? It is too early to tell. The 1984 election will provide further evidence. Without being overtly partisan, I welcome a number of developments that indicate further resurgence of the political parties. Walter Mondale, the Democratic candidate, is the most suitable representative of its philosophy and its constituent groups. Appropriately, he will contest the election with President Reagan, the personification of the party record. A large part of the responsibility for the campaign will go to Reagan's closest elected associate, George Bush. The election ideally would be based on the administration's record, with congressional candidates of each party united to defend or attack that record. Turnout at the polls would increase significantly, especially among younger voters. The election results would be a direct answer to that famous question, "Are you better off than you were four years ago?"

I conclude not by predicting but by remembering the warning of Benjamin Franklin. As he left the last session of the Constitutional Convention, a woman met him on the street and asked, "Well, Dr. Franklin, have you given us a monarchy or a republic?" He answered, "A Republic, madam, if you can keep it."

# 21

# Strengthening the Political Parties

The Committee on Party Renewal is a voluntary group of some two hundred political practitioners and researchers. Bipartisan in membership, we share a common concern for the survival of our political parties. We see them as vital instruments of democracy, but as organizations which are threatened in their very existence.

As we declared at our founding at the Jefferson Memorial in 1977, "Without parties there can be no organized and coherent politics. When politics lacks coherence, there can be no accountable democracy." Without parties, we then warned, we are threatened by "a politics of celebrities, of excessive media influence, of political fad-of-the-month clubs, of massive private financing by various 'fatcats' of state and congressional campaigns, of gun-for-hire campaign managers, of heightened interest in 'personalities' and lowered concern for policy, of manipulation and maneuver and management of self-chosen political elites."

As we approach the culmination of the presidential election of 1980, the need for party renewal is even more evident. It has begun to be recognized by respected commentators, by the voting public, and by political leaders of both the Republican and Democratic parties. Discontent with the present arrangements is widespread, as evident in the low degree of trust in our national institutions, in decreased voting turnout, and in the widespread abandonment of party loyalties.

Rebuilding our political parties will require greater involvement by individual citizens, but we are not content to rely on vague urgings of participation. Effective participation requires appropriate institutional structures, which must be deliberately designed by the parties themselves and by formal statutory change. The actions we recommend are directed toward three goals: increasing the membership of the parties and the effectiveness of political participation; providing the parties with necessary resources, particularly money; and re-establishing functions for the political parties in the overall political system.

Toward these goals, we recommend the following specific actions:

1. Less emphasis should be placed on primary elections for the choice of national convention delegates, while more delegates should be chosen

through party caucuses and conventions. Increased representation for party officials is also desirable.

2. If public financing of campaigns is adopted, these funds should be channelled through the parties, with a portion reserved for general party purposes. Direct public financing of the political parties is also widely advocated. Many backers of strengthened parties believe that public funds should be provided for such purposes as party organization, research, publicity, and fund raising, and such support is now provided by a number of states. Other analysts urge increased private support of the parties. While acknowledging these different approaches, we agree that support must be provided to the parties themselves, rather than to individual candidates.
3. The parties should be given more freedom in their financing. Contributions to the parties should be allowed in greater amounts than to individual candidates, and expenditures by parties for research and organization should not be included in campaign expenditure limits. State and local party committees' expenditures on behalf of national slates should not be included in expenditure or contribution limits. In general, party contributions to candidates should be preferred above those of individual or political action committees.
4. State law should provide for party caucuses and conventions, open to all party members, to endorse candidates in the party primary. Such endorsement should be indicated on the primary ballot, with the endorsed candidate normally given the first place on the ballot.
5. Parties should consider holding periodic issue conventions (e.g., in congressional election years), on the state and national levels. These meetings may invigorate the organization, consider policy questions, and hold officials elected under the party label accountable for the actions on party platform positions.
6. State parties should establish rules that facilitate widespread participation. These rules should include adoption of formal charters, broad public notice of nominating procedures and dates, affirmative action to promote participation by all elements of the population, and apportionment of representation in party bodies on the basis of population and/or electoral strength within the party.
7. Local parties should regularly hold open, well-publicized meetings, at which current issues and contemporary problems are discussed. Positions adopted at such meetings should be forwarded to state and national platform committees.
8. Parties should establish a dues-paying membership. For modest fees, the parties should provide these members with such benefits as copies of the national platform and other policy statements, and a regular report of activities. They should regularly determine members' opinions, and provide information on means to influence the choice of convention delegates and party officials.

9. Federal law should be amended to provide regular access to television for the major political parties. In particular, debates for president and other major offices should be under the control of party bodies, such as the national party committees. Access should also be provided for third-party and independent candidates with sizeable followings.
10. The political parties should establish commissions nationally, and in each state, to promote joint efforts to strengthen the parties, particularly through public education programs and statutory change. Training and research programs through academic institutions should be developed.

# Index